Dudu Aiber | **Management Mastery in Life**
Craft, Art or Science?

Dudu Aiber

Management Mastery in Life

Craft, Art or Science?

Senior Editors & Producers: Contento
Editor: Yossie Bloch
Cover Illustration: Maya Shleifer
Book Design: Liliya Lev Ari

Copyright © 2015 by Dudu Aiber and Contento

All rights reserved. No part of this book may be translated, reproduced, stored in a retrieval system or transmitted, in any form or by any means, electronic, photocopying, recording or otherwise, without prior permission in writing from the author and publisher.

ISBN: 978-965-550-509-2

International sole distributor: Contento
22 Isserles Street, 6701457, Tel Aviv, Israel
www.ContentoNow.com
Netanel@contento-publishing.com

To my wife and children
Tsvia, Sarel, Danielle and Moaur!
For serving as my overflowing wellspring of sensitivity,
Teaching me what attentiveness really means,
Helping me to know myself better,
And being there for me as an endless source of inspiration...

D udu Aiber is a retired Captain from the Israeli Navy.

Throughout his service he held a great variety of positions mostly engaged with operational and wide-scale educational assignments. He began by commanding quite a range of different sea fighting crafts, went on leading sundry combat units and finally headed two bases, the last, being the Naval Training Camp.

Aiber holds a BSc in Mechanical Engineering, specializing in Shipbuilding, and has a Diploma in Senior Management, Economics and International Relations studies.

Over the long course of his assorted occupations in the military, in civilian frameworks and in academic societies – he functioned, inter alia, as CEO of evolutionary enterprises, research centers and Israeli and foreign firms. These entities, directed by him, were of diverse character and content, multi-disciplinarian, wealthy – some at the very apex of advanced scientific fields.

During his extensive range of jobs, he led and dealt with many technological processes; built up and steered human-resource mechanisms; outlined financial strategies and delineated business plans; launched and ran marketing arrays; guided and supervised data and information monitoring teams; set up and regulated quality assurance and control systems; and oversaw and handled combined technical-logistical support bodies.

Throughout his career, he adopted and adapted innovative organizational cultures and administrating techniques, while maintaining working relations and reciprocal ties with the state and formal institutions of the highest caliber in Israel, and abroad.

Talble of Contents

Author's Notes 15
Introduction 27

The Keystone
Between Intelligence and Emotional Intelligence . 33

First Treatise
The Equation of Self-Conduct — Controlling or Being Controlled 47

Prologue 48
The Heart of the Matter – How to Achieve Success 51
Setting the Target 57
Acquiring the Demandable 62

    The Essence: Self Satisfaction 62
    The Foundation: Fulfilling the Spiritual Needs 63
    Human Development Stages:
    Essences and Means to Nourish the Soul 64
    Feeding the Spirit – Principles of its Realization 79

        Meditation – Super-Spirituality and Extrasensory Study 81
        Negative Energy as a Matter of Fact 82
        Discharging Tensions – Practical Advice 83
        Restraining and Removing Negative Feelings –
        Pragmatic Counseling 84

Conquering the Desirable 87

    The Essences – Desire, Faith and Passion 87

The Practical Implication: Hard Work with no Respite	89
The Back-Up: Non-Denial of Wishes and Patterns for Achieving the Desirable.	91
The Power of Continually Wishing.	92
Avoiding the Vain Effort of the Tendency to Resist	94
Consenting to all Positive Desires Leading to Achieving the Goals	96
The Portrait of the Emotions and Navigating for their Best – the Ultimate Extraction.	105
Smashing the Inhibitions	111
The Skeleton of the Concept.	111
The Cure	112
The Purpose of this Cogitation — Interim Conclusion	129

Second Treatise

Guiding the Own Life and Leading Others – The Outcome Starts with Thinking First 137

Opening	138
Definitions	141
Organizations – Characteristics, Structures and Processes	145
Planning, Management and Control Theories and Methods – Principles of the Best Ones	155
The Role of the Leader – the "Credo"	160
Building Up Leadership and Operating Policy – the Various Stages	163
Establishment / Integration and Formation – the Opening Steps	164
Setting the Mechanism in Motion – from Theory to Practice	170
The Nature of the Thesis – Clarifications and Emphasis	172
The Ingredient of the Conception – Headlines at a Glance	172

    Constraints – Bottlenecks or Forced Defects 173

    Management by Constraints – a Few Points to Ponder 173

    Non-Constraint Factors – Their Contribution to the System. . . . 175

Operating a Start-Up Company at the Intermediary Phase – the Concept 177

Hints for the One in Charge – A Reminder 188

Philosophy of Leadership 190

    The Root of the Matter: Either One Has it or Not... 190

    Leadership – Noblesse Oblige 196

    Professionalism – the First Step towards Appreciation 202

    Managing from the Heart – the Path to Interpersonal Conduct . . . 208

    Strategy: the Pragmatic-Practical Direction of Any Business 219

    Reality and Vision: Tomorrow, Built Today, Based on Yesterday . . . 231

    Planning and Preparation: Deployment of the Policy's Outline and Getting Ready for its Execution 237

    Decision-Making – Vigorously or Patiently 240

    Verified Truth versus Gut Feelings 251

    Hero or Zero – the Outlook of the Ambitious 255

    Organizational Changes – a Real Necessity for a Constant Development-Renewal. 259

    Flowing with the Reforms – or Disappearing 264

    Everyone Has a Boss – But He Should Also Have a Replacement . . 266

    Persistency – the Secret Navigator and Hidden Factor for Success . . 271

    Management's Effectiveness and the Way to Measure It 274

    Contributors to Correct Leadership – Which Are Indispensable . . . 279

        Order as a Way of Life. 280

        The Time Resource – a Prime Asset when Correctly Used 283

        Monitoring Methods and Means – a First-Rate Tool 287

        Public Relations – as Augmentation of Image 291

        Steadfast Durability – a Must for Success 297

Fortune – as an "Enlightening" Factor,
Bestowing Confidence and Daring 299

The Family – Always Above All 302

Principles of Conduct and Leadership Wisdom:
an Intermediate Abstract 303

Technological Strategy or **"Which"** is the Chosen Product . . 306

Preface 306

Choosing the Portfolio – the Opening Move 309

The Product Strategy – the Second Phase 311

Managing the Technical Implementation Itself – the Third and
Crucial Phase 312

Production Proceedings – Business's Nature by Darwin 318

Quality or Productivity – Which Comes First 319

Managing Events in Projects – the Proven Guidelines 321

Performance Quantifying and Scientific Investigation – Essential
Steps towards Proper Management 322

Knowledge Treasuring – What is Not Written Does Not Count . . . 324

Research and Development – the Real Chance for a Breakthrough . 326

In Summation 328

Human Resources Strategy or **"Who"** Are the People to Work With 329

Preface 329

Creating a Winning Team – as an Appetizer 331

The Art of Interviewing Begins With the Ability to Listen 333

Optimal Absorption of the Chosen –
an Uncompromising Second Phase 334

A Correct Working Atmosphere Augments Loyalty and Productivity . 337

Excellent Employees Need, Generally, Outstanding Managers . . . 339

Organizational Excellence – the General Good is Much More
Important than Personal Gain 346

One Must Always Invest in Good People 350

A Manager Who Does Everything on His Own Defies the Mission . . . 351
Behind Every Employee Lurks the Person in Him 354
From an Ordinary Laborer – to an Enlightened Worker 358
The Hierarchy's Pyramid – the Proper Steepness 360
The Opening Speech – Love (or Hate…) at First Sight 361
Most People "Tend" to be Dragged –
rather than Chart their own Course. 366
Relationship with Subordinates – Axioms worth Adopting 368
He Who Seeks Loyalty Should First be Faithful Himself 371
There are no Teams of Stars – Only Stars within Teams 373
In summation 377

Financial Strategy or "What" are the Rewards versus the Costs 378

Preface 378
Financial Intelligence as the Central Contributor to Economic Success 383
Organizations as Convoluted "Webs" of Economic Elements 386
Building a Budget as the First Realization of the Policy 389
The Power behind Management Strength –
Absolute Domination of the Financial Details 393
Credit by an External Source – or Equity 395
How to Make a Profit – Welcome Priorities and a Practical Choice . . 399
The Price – Fixing Without Erring 402
The Competitive Advantage as a Winning Cause 407
Economic Success – Achievement out of
an Unconventional Orientation 410
The Business Development Division –
"the Right Intelligence Lobe" of the Manager's Virtues Graph 414
The Wisdom of Specialization – being Engaged
only in what is Best Understood 415
The Art of Business – Integration or Seclusion 416
The Business Vision – the Essence and Way of Persuasion 418
Considerations of Organizational Financial Engineering –

    Things to Internalize and Adopt 423

        Headquarters Staff – Thrifty or Wasteful 423

        Stock – as a Financial Cause 425

        Treatments' Planning Ahead as a Profit Multiplier 427

        Purchasing Power – Life with Inflation, Deflation and Stagflation . 428

        Online Training – Efficiency Improving and Employee Control Means . 429

    Financial Accounting: a Standard Presentation of the Company's
Performance (Trusted Measure of Management Quality …) 430

        Accounting to Monitor Activities as the Basis
for General Information. 431

        Reporting Principles as a Basis of Language Comprehension . . . 437

    Financial Reports – Analysis of Management Quality and Monitoring it 440

    Initial Financial Criteria for Instant Economic Analysis 445

        Financial Values – the Organization's "Identity Card" 447

        Financial Ratios – The "Report Card" of the Organization 449

        Additional Indicators – as a Complementary Gauge of Financial
Management Efficiency. 452

    Proper Cash Management as a Cardinal Goal 459

    In summation 462

Marketing Strategy or **"How"** to be the Best Seller 464

    Preface 464

    The Marketing Mix as the Central Being 468

    Market Study: Basis of Advertising and Promotion Technique. . . . 472

    The Organization in Relation to its Operating Environment –
a Coordinated Segmented Strategy 474

    The Customer as the Pivot around which Everything Rotates 477

    The Art of Marketing: Building Emotional and Brand Identity. . . . 483

    Characteristics of Competitive Positioning:
Four Customary Observations 492

    Globalization and Mergers: Creating Next-Generation Business . . 495

    Timing is occasionally a Matter of Luck – but Grasping

and Exploiting the Opportunities it presents is Totally Different . . . 505

Some Other Considerations of Marketing Methodology 508

    The Product Between the Marketer and the Client 508

    "Practical" Modesty – a Virtue that Surely doesn't Harm 510

    Suppliers and Brokers – More about the Middlemen 511

    In Summation 513

Entrepreneurship — or The Bud of Business Development . . 514

    Preface 514

    The Manager as Entrepreneur 516

    Entrepreneurship – a Blessing or a Curse (When Needed to Manage the Daily Routine, of Course…) 519

    Entrepreneurship with Control – Setting Limits for Managers 527

    In summation 530

Knowledge Management (KM) — or The Road to Constant Improvement 532

    Preface 532

    Information Management (IM) – What is it? 534

    Data Work – Building Up and Using an Informative Array 536

    Information Technology (IT) and Competitive Advantage 540

    Knowledge Treasures – the Way to Safeguard Them 541

    Constant Improvement – Utopia or Practice. 543

    In Summation 546

Deming in a Contemporary Cloak — Epitome of the Executive 547

Epilogue

Correct Management – What is it…? 565

Author's Notes

How ironic it is when the price of poor leadership and its injustices is paid precisely by those who are led by it...

The Author, August 1974

Just as the tongue keeps touching a loose and painful tooth, arousing, over and again, with an unexplained persistence, the agonies of the inflicted part, so did my mind return stubbornly to the burning questions which have been gnawing on and tormenting me tremendously in the last few years: which is the way to assemble, give shape and put on paper a collection of ideas ripening in my mind for a long time? How could such thoughts assume form and content worthy of sharing with the public? What is the proper format in order to turn a wide-ranging world view into a doctrine, specific enough on the one hand, and comprehensive on the other, phrased in a measured, clear and easy-to-remember style?

And exactly how – without being carried away too much, but still employing the aforementioned metaphor – can one condense and pull together all the insights, knowledge and first-hand experiences in his life, into a single canon presented in a sole text? Indeed, why do it at all and especially why now?

Why?

Most of my days, I have toiled and been absorbed in a search, reflecting on the right paths on which to tread securely. Whenever I found one of those, choosing to follow it, I dedicated myself with all my heart to its conquest, not only for my own sake, but for my fellow men too. For many years I have been employed in jobs requiring me, one way or another, to make decisions whose outcomes determined, to a large extent, my as well as other peoples' fates. In making these choices, I have weighed, among other considerations, a reciprocity with those surrounding me; I have found that working with people impacted considerably on my attitudes and views concerning my own conduct, since no man is an island: one's deeds and work do not occur in a void, but affect his environment. Moreover, a human being is molded by **his** (or **her**...!) community: he is rooted in it, studies those with whom he socializes and links to; he picks up from their expressions and gestures which he internalizes, mimics, and reacts to; he adapts the norms set by others and sometimes he learns from their mistakes to his own advantage.

Therefore, it is clear that an individual's behavior and conduct are influenced, first and foremost, by those with whom he comes into contact, and by the power of these relationships; this understanding is actually the key to the thesis underlying this book.

The lion's share of my life so far, I have been involved with working with people: attaching myself to and toiling for them, integrating them into teams, managing and leading them to different goals.

It all started in my early childhood. From the moment I became aware of my surroundings, through my youth, I took an active part in my neighborhood's liveliness. Playing team sports in the alleys during my teen years – the summit of our daily routine – it was always clear that the general benefit surpassed any personal gain. In school-life dynamics, including the complexities and problems of growing up, my involvement in all these fields of activity gave rise to natural leadership – to its positive as well as its negative aspects.

Since then, I have been aware of the robustness of human

partnership. I absorbed, subconsciously as it were, concepts such as laying groundwork, taking control, planning and leading. Then I encountered these in their popular guise – in street dialect – but only later did I learn to understand them in a real-life context. I encountered a vulgar language consisting of terms such as: a bunch of guys, a buddy, a fixer, dilettantism, shoddy work, moonlighting, brouhaha, combination, scheming, prevarication, confrontation, cover-up, bad-luck etcetera.

From the secured neighborhood circle – an easy and unbounded environment – I sailed into a rigid military structure, where for decades I commanded women and men: motivating, instructing, directing, leading vigorously, supervising and preserving. The military (especially the Navy...) gave me many opportunities to deal with large and cumbersome organizations as well as small, sophisticated and high-tech rich societies; in and out of uniform. These were in Israel and abroad; some overflowing with resources, others thrifty and constrained; each one was different and unique, in character as well as personnel. I did all of this for a long time and at high intensity.

Through these varied experiences, I learned that the common assumption regarding the Israeli Defense Forces (IDF), that it was founded and built on command and nothing else, is patently groundless. And that is because, in truth, the IDF is the main human and technological melting pot of the State of Israel— frequently reviewed, covered by the press, fluent, logical and analytical; an investigating, analyzing, deducing, and producing milieu, striving constantly to improve professionally, substantively and morally. Such a lineup cannot function without genuine management – and its ability to advance, even a single tiny step, by commands only, is doubtful. In our era, being a leader requires more than being an outstanding general; a true one, supposedly versed in the economy, public relations and marketing; **he** (or **she**...!) has to be a real wizard of human resources, a diplomat and even a psychologist. However, I do agree that a natural-born excellent commander can do without outstandingly positive managerial qualities, and vice versa.

I owe a lot to this chapter of my life, since I had the opportunity to participate in quite a few workshops and studies dealing with leadership and conduct; I had the occasion to examine thousands of soldiers and civilians, and to study at close proximity the human soul and its behavior in times of peace and (for the most part…) under the threats and dangers of war. I was graced, fortunately, with the chance to learn the secrets of the human soul and its intricacy – perhaps better that I might have learnt in any illustrious academic institute, since I was fortunate to adopt and assimilate some of the most advanced cultures and methods of organization in existence. To this Golden Age of my life, I attribute an overwhelming influence on my intellectual development, during it, I extracted insights which left in me – while dictating the nature of my innermost being – significant impressions of all those spiritual and scientific experiences. It was a prolonged test, during which one could hardly dissemble.

Why Precisely Now?

After retiring from the service some twenty years ago, while becoming acquainted with the vicissitudes of civilian life, I was dumbstruck by the administration's malaise and the backwardness of the authorities and government infrastructure. I was left astonished and was forced to adjust to an unfamiliar climate. I needed to fully implement those traits which I had acquired and inculcated in my past training – but exponentially, with ever-growing intensity – though my measures were insufficient.

I found an atmosphere hermetically sealed against innovation, crushing healthy competition and encouraging exclusiveness – a monopolistic, centralized wilderness of intrigues, ruled by egotistic, profit-driven cartels and their yes-men. The key to graft stems from the right connections to decision-makers, who are masters of business and politics as well, protecting themselves from any kind of rivalry. It was a bubbling cauldron of buckets of corruption, abundant in paradoxes and absurdities. Thus, although Israel was apparently galloping proudly to join the enlightened west of the third millennium, taking a place of pride amongst the nations who opted for free, competitive markets – the facts tell a different story about our little country.

I discovered the existence of quite a few anachronistic pockets of power, whose raison d'être is no longer appropriate to the Zeitgeist; they are redolent of self-serving hedonism, representing a destructive attitude to the economy's progress, arresting it from leaping forward. Correspondingly, the market leaders are shackled by a tradition of collective ownership – a remnant of an Orwellian socialism in its worst incarnation. These hives of might swarm with public servants, entrenched in their jobs as an outcome of tribal, factional favoritism – not thanks to qualifications compatible with their responsibilities. This stands contrary to any candidate for the simplest position, who is required to undergo "suitability, adjustment and qualification" tests at some fancy Recruitment and Evaluation companies.

Additionally, our companies are still ruled by a nepotistic organizational culture, of family, friends, neighbors and lobbyists, filling their favored coffers through the guise of social justice. Moreover, our political culture dictates that the country's management is entrusted to the diplomats of the logorrhea temple – the Parliament: elusive quarrel-mongers accompanied by their apprentices, all of them pious hypocrites; the so-called servants of the establishment, their contribution to their workplace and constituents is nil. The floors of their rooms are paved with thousands of unsolved problems, victims of their horrible hard-heartedness. They hold to the splendor of reputation as to the horns of the Altar, surviving thanks to mutual back-scratching and hand-washing – refusing to obey the norm customary in any proper democracy: "He who fails shall not prevail...". Those who grovel and creep up to the media, as to a stage for fraudulent shows, awash with cheap demagoguery, slander, pharisaism, misinformation and lies, in order to gain political capital – toadying to journalists for a sympathetic headline; zigzagging farcically in their stances like clowns on slack ropes. These are individuals whose vision and ideals reach as far as the next news broadcast, and their daily schedule is adapted to TV programming – true exhibitions of cynicism and exploitation, lined with pathetic worthlessness at its worst. Instead of making their mark on the systems with which they are charged, they are stamping their feet in the mud surrounding them.

As an old sage said in acrimonious irony: "For God's sake, even a bordello deserves good management...". "Even anarchy needs some order...".

At the same time I was exposed to the private sector, mainly to its crown jewel: the High-tech arena. It had a wide scope of huge creativity and vision – but was afflicted with outrageous employment terms, wild self-enrichment dreams and a bizarre, even ridiculous, work morality. This field was in desperate need of a revolutionary change of its operating system – which was indefinitely delayed, by the way, so as not to shake the ground under everybody's feet – since it was a far cry from the old, right and good management rules. And the rest of the sector is mostly comprised of private enterprises, run tyrannically by their masters, who on the whole owe their positions to their consanguinity only (in disregard of the fact that it doesn't matter who the parents are – but what kind of people their children are...), with the price of oligarchy being paid by the business and its personnel.

This is where I first encountered a meaning unknown to me of the term "leadership." I saw degenerate organizations, suffering from business gangrene, guided solely by selfish considerations; and no PhD in textile studies was needed to realize that the king is naked...

Only then did I understand the challenges facing a manager in the civil sector, and how he is obliged to navigate under the threat of gales breaking against a calm seashore. If one is successful in repulsing blood-thirsty sharks, cunning sneaks will be lurking in the dark; when entering a jungle, rather than donning nice manners and civility, he should arm himself with a sword – mobilizing all his energy, vigor, moral strength, talent, experience and wisdom, in order to survive, first of all, and to show results at the end of the day. My immediate conclusion was that in order to face these challenges one must prepare thoroughly by aligning his personality meticulously, spiritually as well as corporeally; for it is not necessary to wait for the devastating outcomes of a "managerial-organizational tsunami", in order to finally comprehend that a right and first-rate management style would improve miraculously both plains of our lives – private and certainly public – benefiting us all, since the inconsiderable little citizens are always required to pay for the mistakes of their great leaders...

Charged with a huge accumulation of deep sensations, and after listening to and watching dozens of interviews with political figures and first-rate experts who were exposed to exceptional phenomena, I became determined to try and present a kind of guide to those holding the reins of leadership. I have been blessed with a proper amount of leisure, and beside my regular occupations, I was able to organize my ideas on the subject – some from the past, others which formed and emerged while preparing and writing. For me, it was definitely an inwardly purifying experience, a rare opportunity not to be missed under any circumstances. However, as more and more books, articles, newspaper clippings, and manifestoes piled up on the shelves of my study, so grew my doubts. I discovered that each of these focuses, as it is, on a single aspect of management, with cumbersome wording and verbosity. Each is difficult to read: one emphasizes charisma and authority, another underlines human relationships, a third one deals with corporate structure, a fourth praises marketing and selling, a fifth stresses the importance of finance, and so on and so on...

How?

All I meant was to create a universal document, encompassing most conduct and management disciplines, one dealing with nearly all organizational aspects, relying on most of the ideas taught by the current schools of leadership, guidance and supervision – the harvest of academia. I hoped to mold a selection to be easily approachable, something focused and deep enough, containing practical suggestions in professional, however elementary, terms, understandable to all. This approach is supposed to rise as a command from within – from the innermost core of the self – and spread out like waves on the surface, with no contradictions allowed between one's interior and exterior; and if any such conflict appears, the text should teach a way of reconcile both views in spite of that.

I aspired to arrange my thoughts in a book, unlike any other, that would not gather dust on a shelf after being read, but would be a comprehensive and penetrating composition, drawing anyone with a real interest in the subject to its pages whenever the need arises, and would serve as a devoted tutor, always available. The model I related to was that of a classical composition, to which, after the first hearing, one always craves to return.

As for the writing and wording style: in principle, I wished to present my ideas as a matter of fact so as not to tire or bore the reader; to create a concise text, with punctuated titles and a choice of chapter headings defining what is to be done and what is to be avoided, in a sharp, accurate, polished and clear form; a reservoir of exhaustive messages accompanied by a short and focused background of brief clarifications, remarks and supplements, wherever it seemed necessary; and precisely chosen quotations, detailed and sharp as razors in their meanings, but considerably influential, like bullets departing the barrel of a gun.

I am aware of the rapid changes which are taking place in the global economy, having direct implications on enterprises and companies, and of the fact that new planning and control theories are springing up all the time – only to evaporate and make room for their successors; therefore, I have made an effort to emphasize the constant and steadfast basics, common to all dogmas and theories, that will always stand by the leader of any organization and will stay relevant to its functioning. I strived to make these points conspicuous, so that they might be easily inscribed in the reader's memory and burned in to his consciousness. Some of them I collected and quoted – those I encountered somewhere, read someplace, heard about here and there, which then permeated my cognizance, found their abode within me, until I gave them their voice in this book. Others were born of themselves within me through the stream of my meditation.

Many a cow I milked, but the butter I churned by myself…

It would have been possible to add to this compilation a variety of additional tales and stories and a multiplicity of anecdotal piquant accounts; but this would have produced a thick epic of many tomes, where one cannot see the forest for the trees – missing its target on the whole.

Furthermore, in order not to interfere with the flow of reading – requiring in any case a high level of attention and concentration – I chose to forgo references and footnotes, except for those attributions integrated, and "cruise" within the text (perhaps due to my reading of Darwin's modestly-written introduction to his pioneering book, *The Origin of the Species*: "The facts I furnish aren't always mine by origin – but the consequences from their outcome are the interesting issue in summation…"). Therefore, I believe that the importance of the ideas hereafter presented, their true value and the conclusions deduced from them are the essence, not what caused their composition and production…

On the other hand, I chose to open with a very detailed table of contents; one that can easily direct the reader to any subject of special interest, without having to sift through the book from beginning to end.

This book is designed for anybody intending to lead others at any time; to beginners taking their initial steps in this field; to experienced and senior managers who are supposed to lead other managers in politics, commerce, communal work, education and sports; to officers in the army, police and other such organizations; to statesmen, teachers, commanders, soccer and basketball coaches and revered stars all together; observant as well as atheists, religious and secular too.

It is also dedicated to whoever is driven by a desire for achievement and is restrained by pressure and coercion from below – labor unions and such, or from above – the rulers; and to those seeking to order and organize their domestic lives, since the family is a major contributor to stability and peace of mind, which are preconditions for enduring the daily grind.

The text is also meant for those who are unsatisfied with things as they are, and interested not only in the product, but in understanding the process, its formation and the rationale behind it; for these who believe in emotional intelligence, in a right balance between inner happiness and material success and in an attitude in favor of thinking before doing – those who consider the two a credible and promising blend for daily conduct and performance.

And when one is well-versed in management, the particular field dealt with is of no consequence. So each reader may adopt whatever is in his heart.

While writing I had to make peace with countless words in order to be as concise and precise as humanly possible. For that reason, I felt like someone climbing a very steep mountain; the summit kept its distance from me, again and again, as I was crawling and ascending toward it.

It is customary to rejoice at the completion of something when the fruit is ripe, when all the parts are in their proper places. I had my fill of exertions and changes, of moments of elation and sobriety. Tired of assaults and retreats. I laid eight drafts before me, incarnations and variations (remembering Garcia Marquez's dictum: "Writing is carpentry but reality is harder than any wood…"; and William Styron in a harsher tone said that "Writing is hell…" – striving just to adopt hedonist Hemingway's motto: "Writing is architecture…"). Only now, ten years later, when I consider all the processes of developing and producing to have been completed, have I decided to let free my reflections, publish them and voice them – and not without hesitation. I have the horrible fear of a visit to the dentist to take care of the toothache which I mentioned in the first paragraph of this introduction, but also the "liberating" dream to be there and finally be done with the pain. Even after signing the manuscript and bringing it to light, the inner dialogue is flowing within me like a fountainhead: still I reflect on its topics and struggle with them, and the boundaries of my studies are forever widening.

The present version is completed, but the quest to investigate these issues is surely not done yet…

And in summation

Behind the thousands of lines gathered in the following pages, stands a huge camp of followers, who assisted me in composing myself in advance of the writing mission depicted above, in collecting, formulating and editing. This gigantic crowd functioned as the pillar of fire, leading my camp of whispers, murmurs and inspiration – even without them always being attentive to their part in this "secret mission". Because of the large number of my companions – and due to their being unaware of my endeavor – I am unable to commend those people personally. Since I cannot mention their names, I am obliged to forgo praising and crediting each and every one of them; even if I could, there are not enough words to do it.

Nevertheless, my very deep thanks are given to all of them...

Dudu Aiber
June 31st, 2009

Introduction

He whose inside is unlike his outside is consciously highly self-divided...
The Author, November, 1990

There is no doubt that one's life happens to be his most valuable enterprise. And Its primary layout which requires mastery and control – is the mechanism of self and its existential equation. This responsibility accompanies the human being from birth to his last moments alive. From that fact, as it is, stems the basic tenet presented all throughout this book: management begins neither by leading an organization nor by orchestrating a functioning framework – but by planning ahead, deliberately and rigorously, the entire personal life; this principle expresses itself in an ongoing supervision of a man's day-to-day subsistence, routine, effectiveness, yield and their quality.

Moreover, the aspiration to improve and ameliorate life by assigning and attaining spiritual and material goals is similar to the workings and the output of any productive organization whatsoever. Guiding one's ways of existence in an intelligent and controlled manner truly means an inner management of the heart and soul while preserving the bodily mechanisms, on the one hand; and mastering the activities of the mind and the whispers of cognition, as a response to outside occurrences, on the other hand. This is the art of intelligence, ingenuity and resourcefulness at its peak, engaged in a hard, demanding and constant struggle; an equation equal to the one governing performance in any daily technical-professional practice.

Correspondingly, it is very likely that the individual's nature is reflected in the culture and character of the subject to which one devotes himself – just as his outlook of his own activities and business is a mirror-image of his wishes and identity; since there is a significant correlation between a manager's personal degree of internal happiness and his attitude towards and treatment of his subordinates. For precisely this reason, someone who is mirthless and unsatisfied may undermine – even unconsciously – the very matter he is in charge of and be unable to repair the damage, unless a thorough self-examination and analysis of the reasons for his conduct is meticulously executed.

It becomes clear, therefore, that a very powerful mutual relationship exists between one's personal patterns of behavior and those governing his external performance; and a nearly complete comparability is apparent between the intrinsic and the extrinsic, the private and the business, the emotional and the professional. Thus, almost a full analogy is created between the spiritual and the physical, as these two spheres of activity, seemingly contradictory, are actually made of the same ingredients. And since there is a symmetry between these two spheres, there must also be a correspondence in the way one chooses to live them. Moreover, because of the strong link between them, a prolonged struggle for dominance starts to evolve: which world will rule, dictating the course of life, and which one will be ruled. This is an ongoing fight, accompanied by clashes and inconsistencies, recurring until an ultimate point of balance is achieved – a position which may eventually secure a harmonious integration of personal satisfaction and professional success.

Therefore, these are the three main messages to guide the reader through the length and breadth of this book:

- **First and foremost one must shape and stabilize himself, to develop personally and subjectively. Then, and only then, it becomes appropriate for him to dare holding the reins and** motivating others in particular, trying to steer organizations and enterprises foresightedly, in a meticulous and cautious manner, tempered with a considerable amount of emotional intelligence (the Holy Grail of human management and proceedings...).

- **Once thoroughly familiar with the right way of management, the specific application is of no consequence (nor is the scope, apparently...); doing it properly is simply a generic issue.**
- **An optimal combination of professionalism, art and science is required to run any entity correctly and effectively.**

Thus, the chapter named "The Keystone" was selected to be first. It deals with the parallelism of the forces of wisdom – the rational and the emotional – and their eternal struggle deep within each human being, a kind of never-ending jiu-jitsu competition...

From this point forward, the aim is to present an agenda purporting to deal with the book's subject, and with the main question which arises from its pages: "What is the appropriate form of management for life?". This is a quest with the goal of acquainting the reader with a world-view involving many conflicts regarding its daily application; a kind of journey entangled with countless thoughts and attitudes concerning the manner in which to discuss the best and the most profitable personal conduct and managing styles of day to day self-sufficiency. At the same time, the reader will receive the perception that these can definitely be translated from theory to praxis, convincing him that what he reads is not another impractical dogma, but a very pragmatic essay, lending itself explicitly and easily to realization.

This book, in its entirety, spreads out the vicissitudes of man's daily life, while toiling for himself, but mostly when he is charged with managing others. In which domains should one specialize in order to thrive on routine? What kind of problems and specific environmental threats should he prepare to face with the drabness of convention? Primarily, how should a person act in order to succeed in all endeavors?

It presents an associative succession of basic truths and clear insights, while trying to address the aforementioned questions, speaking manifestly to the intellect as well as to the heart. It is a text invoking ideas, some of which are, probably, known to many readers, who perhaps wait nonetheless for someone to put them in the correct order, in a sort of substantial progression – clarified, in-depth, step by step.

On the other hand, this book also contains fresh systems analysis, assumptions and conjectures coming "straight from the oven". It is a compilation of practical and simple pieces of advice, one layer above the other, intended to teach the reader how to internalize changes and adopt them as a means for advancement, in what way to employ learning and adaptation processes for constant progress and improvement in both the private and public domains of life.

All of the afore-depicted make the following tome a thought-provoking and very practical guide for the reader, from A to Z, through everything worth learning on the subject; a treatise dealing with the "soft elements" of business administration (personnel, qualifications, styles, values, theories, et cetera…), as well as the "hard" ones (hierarchies, strategies, tactics, action modes and so on…). This outlook simplifies the understanding of various processes occurring in organizations, expressing the symbiotic integration of the "what" and the "how" without undermining the logic behind them or their essence; a bundle of thoughts and ideas slowly regulated and very carefully worded, by foresight and due consideration, so as not to miss any human or professional aspect – be it the minutest – necessary to conduct a perfect private and business life.

The basic intention is to offer the reader a path leading to his personal success. In other words: to instruct him, meticulously and systematically, in achieving an optimal self-knowledge capability, by which he will be able to determine his own personal "activity curve". As an outcome of proper conduct and management, he may arrive at the ideal blend of inner happiness and outward ambition and achievement, a kind of most personal "line of work", suitable solely and aimed only for him, a direct and fulfilling path which will lead him at the end of the day to the summit of his wishes.

In summation

This book is introduced, generally, in separate articles, which may create the impression that each of them "stands alone". However, this sense is only superficial.

Firstly, they were written in different periods. That is why it is worthwhile to take note of the dates designated at the end of each piece – mainly in order to estimate and weigh each one's relevancy and acuteness in relation to the time of its writing.

Secondly – and mainly – because the afore-described essays are sequenced in a way designed to simplify their reading and comprehension. On the other hand, the reader should notice that their boundaries are somewhat blurred, as some of the views, subjects and notions reappear in various sections of the overall volume.

It is possible, and even recommended, to read the content as is, since the main concept is best absorbed and completely understood by delving into the following sections in the order in which they are presented. However, it is also allowed to wander back and forth among the book's chapters – and perhaps re-examine one or more of the subjects for better realizing and extra inculcating some of its relevant points in light of what may be learned further on. Most importantly, this is a work of non-fiction; therefore it is suggested to "take it easy", reading these articles at leisure, letting the message permeate slowly and be fully appreciated and comprehended...

January 1997

> **The Keystone**

Between Intelligence and Emotional Intelligence

One sees clearly only with the heart, since anything really essential is invisible to the eyes...

Antoine de Saint-Exupéry, *The Little Prince*

For many years, perhaps too many, the enlightened world has gone too far in emphasizing Man's intellectual capacity, which is measured in the Intelligence Quotient (IQ) tests. Experts, as well as the general public, assume that this quantity alone bestows on a human being the most essential and significant advantages in life. For countless generations, this measure was considered as the ultimate signifier of the cerebral potential granted to each person in the genetic lottery. For a long period it was believed that this hereditary gift, by itself only, indicates each individual's special qualifications, determining the highlights of his fate and path on earth.

True enough, when considering large statistical samples, a strong link may be found between IQ and economic class – and therefore social status. It is most likely that those suffering from a low mental capacity would be occupied in simple, menial jobs and their living standards, as well as their achievements, would be minimized, and thus their socio-economic position too. On the other hand, there is no doubt that the most successful businessmen all enjoy significant intellectual gifts.

Recent research has proven time and again that the aforementioned distinction is based on a narrow-minded observation. It becomes clear that these tests, purporting to distinguish significantly between the intellectually gifted and those less so in the population, are based on a blatant misunderstanding of the qualities of reception, perception, judgment and reasoning; in other words, of the structure and constitution of human intelligence. It has also been found out that high one-dimensional aptitude does not guarantee success. On the contrary: many of those considered prodigies by their fellow men were far from flourishing and triumphant in life. There is plenty of evidence about geniuses who behaved with total madness and lack of control, irresponsibly ruining their own lives – and sometimes those of others too. In contrast, there are prominent cases of unknown people of average brainpower who made it in a major way.

Generally, it seems that in recent decades, in conjunction with the intellectual progress of humanity, there has occurred a significant erosion in the foundations of public safety and the tranquility of the civic domain. Villainy and violence are spreading like a plague – and no cure is in sight.

Therefore, wondered the scholars versed in psychology: what else is needed for the masterpiece of creation to gather all his hidden qualities, to fully employ them in order to lead a happy and comfortable life, fulfilling all his wishes? Thus, they came upon what turned in time to an axiom: wisdom is an innate trait, inseparable from those to whom God has bequeathed it, but insufficient on its own. Another component is necessary to complete the human fabric – a factor imbuing a dimension of wholeness, enabling it to cope successfully with Aristotle's challenge, posed by the Greek philosopher in the *Nicomachean Ethics*, written to his father in 350 BC: "Anybody can become angry – it is very easy; but to get mad with the right person and to the right degree and at the right time and for the right purpose and in the right way – this is not within everybody's power, and it is not that simple...". In other words, there is a logic behind any individual's responses, as well as a compelling reason; however, achieving the ends of such actions and reactions requires a non-negligible amount of sensitivity and tact in their timing and mode of expression. So, the above mind and behavior investigators undoubtedly faced a very solid belief expressing one of the main ideas presented in this book: **intelligence is no longer the sole teacher guiding their daily conduct – certainly not the only guarantor of a successful life.**

The missing piece, which would lay in man's consciousness the foundations of a humane, cultured, moderate, fair, balanced, heart-moving and successful system, remained elusive for a very long period.

That unknown element has been glimpsed for the first time, only after a thorough analysis of the outcomes of the research regarding the conduct, tendencies and impulses of human beings in the multiplicity of their incarnations through tens of thousands of years. These findings gave rise to a glimmer of hope within the mass of scholars, who until then had been groping in the dark, concerning the emergence of that hidden factor. A "strange" phenomenon was observed, recurring time and again all along of mankind's evolutionary changes – from the ancient cavemen's era to our days, rich in technology and science. This laid the groundwork for a diagnosis of a hitherto-unnoticed trait of the crown of creation: whenever affected by rage, fear, love, sadness or similar impulses – Man reacted in a berserk manner, his behavior indicating a clearloss of control and an irrationality which may be described as stupidity in the best case. This pattern of conduct raised the curiosity of the researchers, each of which, through his own method and discipline, tried to reach its sources and understand its mechanism.

The journey of observation into the essence of Man's complex consciousness shed light, leading to these hereunder five new discoveries, explicating only some of the weighty facts mentioned above:

- ▸ Exposure of the **emotive structure of the human brain** (the emotional architecture...) and its functioning, vis-à-vis the alignment in charge of thinking, sensation and guidance – the "computer" structure known and accepted from time immemorial. This discovery led to the understanding of the power games and reciprocity amongst the different functions of the brain and to the identification of the control by the emotional functions over Man's mode of behavior; it also pushed to the development of methods of coping with such tendencies – how and when they are restrainable. Since then, we have witnessed an ongoing process of detection and explanation of the traits of human conduct, as well as the means to mold it each time.

- Evaluation of **neural elements and links** as major vehicles **having power over** personal impulses. On the other hand – developing the knowledge necessary to identify and decipher such impulsivity when other people exhibit it.

- Acknowledgment of the model positing **personal inclinations as a critical and stable** component of human decision-making, and internalization of the fact that a **mental balance** – between the spiritual and corporeal needs – provides major assistance in preserving the health and wellbeing of the soul.

- Insistence on the fact that the innate **cerebral circuits** set a typical starting point for each individual's distinctive characters and only for him – but they are **adaptable and open to forging**. Therefore, one must learn to identify opportunities to mold, change, and shape undesired personal behavioral patterns, to convert them into what is acceptable to most other human beings and even to try and make them useful.

- Realization of the dangers due to inherent inabilities to control **the inner kingdom of boiling and bubbling sentiments** and caused by the difficulties to predict their imminent eruption. In other words: the importance of knowing, sensing and analyzing them in order to build up capabilities to recognize the peril they pose and to prevent the outbreak rather than treat the symptoms.

Tracking the development phases of the human brain and its preservation during the many millennia of its existence, from pre-history to the advent of Homo sapiens, was enough to understand, as it is, what happens within it. This amalgam of cells, fluids and nerves – serving as the ultimate center monitoring and controlling the body – grew, broadened and "became refined". That formation might be understood, actually, by the way nature reconstructs this evolution in the fetus in utero, from conception all along to birth. A chain of discoveries in the subject led to the realization that the brain acts with one of two mechanisms: the first thinks, considers and is composed; the other erupts upon any provocation, i.e. reason or emotion. Although each of them has its own physiological system, and is "responsible" for a unique line of activities prima facie, they are intimately connected. The structure of emotions keeps feeding the rational component and influences, definitely, the decision-making process; however, the later one softens and calms the vibrations of desires and cravings by wielding a right of "absolute veto". Man is not only divided between **two types of mental activities – the rational and the emotional** – but a constant tension exists among this couple. However, the one cannot survive without the other, and both are required to unite their labors in order to produce optimal functioning of the human being.

It has also became clear that one section of what is known today as the entire "brain system" – the one reacting immediately to stimuli, without resorting to consideration (limbic…) – existed ages before the birth of the thinking, prudent, studious and critical section of the system (cortical…). By the pair of the most basic instincts – smell and taste – our earliest ancestors survived, defending themselves from dangers, finding water, food, mates for copulation and reproduction and shelter from the nature's elements — all of which enabled their existence and continuance. The origin of these was the cerebellum, way in the back of the head – just like the one which is found in amphibians – when it was the only part of the brain in existence. An "apparatus" that was in charge of some autonomous impulsive emotional functions of the body, long before the growth of the newer thinking layer that rules, as it is, all the higher intelligent functions – the neocortex. This pair of afore-said senses, alongside the three others with which the prehistoric Man was blessed, guided the course of the ancestors of the crown of creation, until he walked proudly on two and destroyed every good spot in the enchanted Garden of Eden, abandoned to his caprice. Therefore, it is entirely natural that this subconscious and spontaneous mechanism of impulses (responsible for the two cardinal motives of human conduct all through its evolution – survival and reproduction…) had and will have a say in all decision-making concerning the essence of life – especially when parts of the worlds of instincts and physiology are not fully clear to those who investigate them…

That is why, the sentiment, founded mainly on gut feelings and intellectual stimuli from within and without, is very dominant in human behavior, sometimes more than reasoning, and its influence is evident during emergencies – exactly like the "strange" occurrence mentioned in the lead of the present article. During these times, a network of neural links takes control of the lion's share of the brain – including the thinking portion – captivating complete command. The emotions, therefore, enjoy a certain intelligence of their own; a prudence that can nurture views and enlightenment independently of its twin – logical cleverness. The impulsive aspect stirs the thinking process – in an identical measure, if not more than this – just like its mate which rules the thoughts, the one which absorbs, deepens and analyzes.

Moreover, these sentiments – although bubbling inside – find external expression, mostly, by exhibiting vital signs and biological gestures, each enhanced by a shade of its own. These effects seem to be instinctive reactions – but are translated, actually, to physiological reflexes. They are very similar natural phenomena, totally different in their essence, but fully compatible.

Here are a few examples of this kind of response:

Freezing and turning pale as a result of a horrible anxiety: in this case all the blood in the body flows down to the large skeletal muscles, draining suddenly from the whitening face. This sudden cascade is accompanied by a drop in body temperature; therefore, one becomes paralyzed like a stone.

Reddening of the face as a result of sharp, overflowing anger: in this case, while in a terrible rage, the blood flows to the extremities of the body, the legs (making them run...) and the arms (motivating them to hold fists and use them...), the heart rate increases, the face is blushing fiercely (becoming furious...). These reactions requite a direct order from the brain: hormonal secretion is intensified, straightening the back and putting the interior on general alert, ready to act. Nevertheless, all attention is concentrated on the threat which forces one to evaluate the situation quickly, resolve the proper action and improvise immediately an optimal response.

Raising the eyebrows as a sign of surprise: here, actually, the field of view is being broadened by enlarging the aperture, enabling the entrance of more light to the reticules. New enhanced information is being absorbed by the addition of parameters to those already existing. Data-processing becomes complicated by the overflow of information, hindering the execution of a proper plan of action.

Drawing the upper lip aside and turning the nose up – expressions of disgust at a bad smell or a metaphorical representation of total rejection. This is a reaction to a foul odor or awful taste. Blocking the nostrils from the stench and preparing the mouth for spitting are the old-time sources of these classic gestures.

Facial expressions and modes of behaviors of this sort, in fact, prove overwhelmingly the existence of involuntary grimaces for no apparent reason – which means that these are controlled by another brain center, in addition to the "considering", "cooking", "concocting" and "directing" one. That is why one ought to recognize both cause and effect, to adapt himself to and become familiar with them, in order to know how to command and control the two mutually.

It is obvious, therefore, that despite Man's sharpness of mind, sometimes he fails in reading the events of his life. This ignorance is curable; it can be overcome by attentively paying attention to "gut" messages, by an educated use of inner signs and their lucid expression and by a proper response to their demands. Recently, psychologists discovered this and termed it **emotional intelligence**, based on the adoption of self-consciousness, personal control, and the integration of belonging, proximity and devotional relationships. Together with skills such as listening and cooperation, they join together and become an art of conflict resolution.

An intelligence of this kind is necessary for anyone wishing to succeed – no less than a sharp brain and an incomparable rationalism; and if it is not inborn, one can definitely acquire, internalize, assimilate, practise and especially cultivate such a trait.

As a result of the above-said, what is needed is a full fusion of the intelligence skills and the sentimental imperatives, an uncompromising symmetry between ratio and emotions; one should not orient the two as opposing each other. On the contrary, they ought to be treated as nearly identical partners striving for the same goal. And just as the first is a precious and essential asset without which one can hardly cope, so does the second serve as a refining and ameliorating agent for this composition.

This sensitive, conductive layer of human texture, covers for intellectual weaknesses if those exist; moreover, it enhances and doubles thinking even at its peak. In the absence of such an equilibrium, the alternative is a poor intellect: something akin to an unbalanced rudder, sweeping away the craft it directs to one side, since the rational and the emotional ingredients need each other desperately in order to function properly. The great American writer, F. Scott Fitzgerald, made this claim in 1934: "The overall intelligence's examination at its acme is in the power to learn and hold, at the same time, two controversial opinions – and still find the 'golden path' which enables sustaining an emotional balance for quite a long period…". Thus, a new and indispensible factor was found, contributing to both inner happiness and outer achievements, namely "personal success".

But at the end of the day – and despite the equal contributions of both intelligences to proper daily human conduct – King Wisdom, "dweller of the upper floors", is the one guarding the heart's desires, "residents of the middle apartments" – and it is supposed to be the last judge concerning the calibration and regulation of the emotions and gut feelings; since he who lets the rational be manipulated by nothing but the emotional creates the exact opposite, from prince to pauper. The Roman philosopher of the first century AD, Lucius Annaeus Seneca, expressed it well: "One who wants to remain faithful to himself is better not to allow his feelings to sweep him away – only sanity will show him the way…". And Galileo Galilei, son of Pisa, who is considered by many – and was crowned by history – as the father of modern science, argued forcefully in the 16th century against the tyrants of the Catholic Church: "I do not feel obliged to believe that the same God who has endowed us with sense, reason, and intellect has intended us to forgo their use…".

Therefore it is highly recommended – and relevant in most cases in life – to hit the switch from "Robotic" to "Common Sense"…

The following are several dictionaries' definitions for some of the basic terms which are the linchpins of the dogma presented in this book.

- **Intelligence** – the endowment of cognizance, thought, apprehension, conception and judgment:
  The capacities to understand, explain, argue, learn fast and absorb

contexts immediately or readiness of comprehension;
Brain capacity, insight, coping, knowledge;
In other words: **Wisdom** – thinking power, rationalism, and intellect;
Head, brain, grey matter, memory:
Common sense, logicality, wit;
Mental ability, understanding, reason, cleverness, judiciousness;
Resourcefulness, creativity, sense awareness;
Quickness of mind, smartness, sharpness, shrewdness, inspiration; and openness, personal superiority, being gifted, talented, genius.

A few centuries ago, only those excelling in the exact sciences, the arts or music, were considered geniuses. With the progress of research into the essence of talent, humanity understood that actually there is no one dominant intellectual domain in which a person may excel and express the aforementioned terms, but a variety of disciplines. Those investigating deeply Man's intelligence and natural distinction claim that there is no limit to the branches of the individual activities in which it might discern superior, above-average personal talents; the professional literature enumerates at least twenty such fields. Here are seven historical examples of people blessed with outstanding intelligence who were seen by their contemporaries as geniuses who reached the pinnacles of their professions.

- Logical intelligence, incomparable talent in mathematics and physics: Newton, Einstein.
- Musical genius: Mozart, Beethoven.
- The art of spatial vision and its perfect reproduction: Leonardo da Vinci, Michelangelo.
- Verbal superiority, the capacity to edit ideas logically, an exceptional proficiency in wording and expression – rhetorical virtuosity: Aristotle, Demosthenes.

- Interpersonal and leadership aptitude: Moses, David Ben-Gurion.
- Kinesthetic excellence: Michael Baryshnikov, Michael Jordan.
- Philosophy: Confucius, Socrates.

- **Emotional Intelligence** – attaining high consciousness of self, coupled with a brilliant and wise use of emotions, in order to:

  Achieve better control of bad feelings;
  Spread self-confidence and belief in the good – optimism;
  Recruit enthusiasm, zeal and faithfulness in goals – motivation;
  Inculcate persistence and devotion to objectives while facing their difficulties and frustrations; and
  Strengthen the ability to weave a net of personal relationships and mutuality – empathy – cooperation, kinship and social harmony.
  And there are two cardinal spheres of the preceding:

  - **Inward Intelligence** – man's ability to create an ideal, however real, self-model, in order to aspire and stick to it continually and perfectly, while understanding all operating factors directed within. This is the senior of the two intelligences mentioned here, constituting the backbone of this ever-so-complicated intellectual structure; for self-openness and seeing into the soul are crucial for the reading of others…

    That kind of wisdom is the basis of all the ideas interwoven and elaborated upon in the first tractate.

  - **Interpersonal intelligence** – the cognitive faculty of understanding the other: what motivates him, how he behaves and why, and in what manner may one cooperate with him.

    Fostering patience and tolerance;
    And nothing is more important than these in daily life…

This sort of facility of insight constitutes the leitmotif of the second tractate.

The following tractates vigorously blend the mutuality of the two intelligences into one doctrine.

And one cannot do without the other – just like a pair of Siamese twins who are nourished from the same source, without compartmentalization whatsoever. However, in contrast to the weakness of the example here presented, the text sharpens and emphasizes the wisdom inherent in the ability to weave the two into a synergetic force. To put it differently: the outcome of the cooperation between this couple and of their mutual fertilization, is larger than the arithmetic sum of these intelligences – the intellectual and the emotional – operating on their own; the totting up of both halves is larger than one...

March 2001

> *First Treatise*

The Equation of Self-Conduct — Controlling or Being Controlled

To of all those who are striving for the absolute and nothing but it, misunderstanding the unique hues of life's kaleidoscope; and to those ignoring each and every principle while pretending to stick to sublime principles and ideals: let them not be like one that carries water in handfuls. They should rather look bravely, honestly and soberly into their inner selves, become acquainted with this discovery – and give up aspiring to be anything but what they really are; thus they will become honest also with their entire surroundings...

The Author, 1999

Prologue

The real contest in daily life does not find its sole expression in an inexhaustible struggle to achieve tangible, pre-selected and marked targets; since yearning to attain goals and the pleasure of succeeding in reaching them are only partial elements of one's satisfaction with himself and his performance; they are surely not enough. Complete own-contentment requires a love of what has already been accomplished and a willingness to keep on dealing with it. This kind of self-happiness emanates from a complete harmony between the external material performance of the individual and his state of mind, an unconditional peace among these two.

The key question is, therefore, how to combine all personality ingredients in order to withstand successfully the abovementioned challenge while achieving the maximal joy of creation. This is a very complicated issue, dealing with the following: Which is the correct method to define a goal, suitable to one's realistic potentialities and efforts to reach it? How should one enjoy a success – subjective as it may be – after finally reaching it? In what way may one get up joyfully every morning to a day of apparent grayish schedule, dictated by this accomplishment? How can one handle fluctuating moods throughout the period of production – so that they don't overwhelm it on the approach to the desired objective? And in what way should one take full pleasure in life as a consequence of proper management – materially as well as spiritually – with both spheres coordinated, integrated and mutually fertile to a maximum degree? For these are the real difficulties that Man faces in his daily routines.

This tractate aims, therefore, to stimulate and bring to attention the **inner consciousness, thinking and judgment aptitudes**, and to nurture them in order to develop the potential of **insight capabilities**; to assist in the impartation of the understandings deduced thereof, and in developing the capacities to translate them from theory to praxis in an optimal way as answers to the abovementioned questions. All of this is in order to change life's perception and eventually conduct oneself so as to get the best out of it. Since Man by his nature is a tough and demanding lender, his "sacrifice" is his investment, and there is none like him in collecting his share – with compound interest. Therefore he must not and cannot leave his fate to chance, because it is well known that God speaks to those who take time to listen; and "The best way to create the future is to predict it..." as the management expert, author and teacher Peter Ferdinand Drucker preached in his time.

Such a capability consists of a close reading of the human being: a sober contemplation of the inner self; an observation of one's mental skills, first and foremost, and then of those of others; an inspection of his spiritual processes, and then of his fellowmen's. The goal is to discover the formula leading to the optimal **self-conduct equation**.

As for the role of the joie de vivre in the individual's desire for achievement, let it be said here and now: this is indeed the major stratum of personal success. However, on its own, it is insufficient to solve the equation of human texture, since in order to make it in life one must keep growing by using concrete desires and material ambitions for more and more; and the magic formula requires, apparently, a wise, simultaneous and ongoing utilization of both channels. This is a practical way, though, which integrates a willpower to act and a manner of doing – a synthesis of body and soul aimed at fulfilling emotional desires and material wishes – because one thing depends on the other.

The secret of **personal success** depends, foremost, on one's loyalty to his principles and faith; **on sticking to his inborn integrity and to the natural moral compass guiding him**; on his being drawn like that minuscule needle, carried in his heart, pointing to his private North. It relies on his **pragmatic physical and economical wishes**. No less important is the fact that the individual must **control himself** according to his personality – **and not be dominated** by his short-term impulses or those projected upon him by his environment; to manage – and not to become managed; to be a mover of processes – and not to be led by them.

And, above all, the essence lies in never being two-faced...

November 1994

The Heart of the Matter – How to Achieve Success

While discussing the setting of personal aims, the struggle to achieve them and the way to enjoy and still stick to them, people may be divided in principle into three essential groups: the first includes those who know well and exactly how to reach their destination but are never satiated by the "conquest" of their objective. As a result of this nature, they never take a break to enjoy their success; they are forever bothered by something, clouding their happiness and pushing them compulsively to keep on moving. The second party includes the big visionaries who unfortunately lack operative abilities to carry out their dreams. Then there are those who are missing inspiration altogether, afraid to aim high due to their fear of drastic changes in their known reality, either because of a lack of self-confidence or the fear of failure. Only very few accomplish their goals, on the one hand, and enjoy what has been attained, on the other.

Therefore, success in life should be measured by the quality of the answers to the forthcoming challenge: what is the way to reach that which is desired, to enjoy it and be pleased with its value, and still continue sticking to it, to the achievable? The tendency to continue wanting what has already been won is of utmost importance, since he who does not love what occupies him and his place in life is causing damage, to himself first of all, because he is unhappy; and if he is also in charge of an organization or managing others within it, then by the very fact that he is unsatisfied with his job he is causing tremendous harm to the whole framework for which he is responsible, and even to all those surrounding and in touch with him too.

For this reason, each person's ambition should be the conquest of his own summit. Such a goal can only materialize based on the wisdom of experience: founded upon self-confidence, emanating from a knowledge that the capabilities required to reach the chosen destination exist; built on the force of the inner motivation to do everything needed; and flowing from pleasure taken in the results attained so far by the "self". It, actually, means deriving partial satisfaction – as these are only intermediate products – each day anew on the road to the selected target.

Such an elaborate estimate can only flow from the most objective and full knowledge and understanding of the inner self. The fundamental term relating to such an appraisal is for a person to be not only himself, but to accept and love whatever he discovers honestly from this thorough internal search, even in the darkest recesses of his soul, and especially to make peace with his shortcomings – whatever he is not qualified for and which tasks are beyond his power. Since he who abstains from seeking for the truth shall never fail. In other words: this is the basic necessity required of a human being in order to reach his own acme – his personal success – marked by himself: **enhancing self-consciousness – in an educated and sophisticated manner.** For a person's outer existence is, as it is, a mirror of the cosmos buried in his depths.

In practice, one should pass four principal stages in any process leading to personal success:

1. **Setting the Target:** searching for a point of balance between a real and stable inner happiness and the effort invested in the endless chase for material external success.

2. **Attaining the Demandable:** learning the inner spiritual and private corporeal necessities and satisfying them both – while getting closer to the purpose of ensuring maximal self-gratification.

3. **Conquering the Desirable:** recognizing the legitimacy of physical passions and worldly outlook as positive basis points for achieving material success; adoption of appropriate behavior patterns – without giving up loyalty to one's self, beliefs and values.

4. **Smashing the Inhibitions:** developing a consciousness of common obstacles in routine daily life, which may prevent the realization of inner wishes and external yearnings on the way to personal success, and learning how to overcome them.

At the beginning of the quest, by following the aforementioned path, one gains self confidence in his ability to directly confront day-to-day challenges – without fearing to look them squarely in the eye. However, correspondingly, he must internalize, from the very commencement of his study of the matters described hereinafter, **three important messages**, true to any performance – even following the afore-depicted path; for at the end of the day, life is stronger than all; and these are not, as the old cliché goes, a listeners' request radio broadcast. Or as John Lennon once said: "Life is what happens to you while you're busy making other plans…".

The first message: even after equipping oneself with all knowledge and tools necessary to get to ones aims, nobody is totally immune from mistakes, or from being rapped here and there on his knuckles by the cruel ruler of harsh reality; life does not always serve tasteful dishes. However, this certainty should not dishearten those aspiring to initiate and act. It is true that a ship in port is protected from all storms and all kind of other accidents; but, no vessel was constructed for this purpose in the first place. Indeed, only one who does nothing makes no mistakes; however, the main difference between winners and losers does not lie in the number of errors they commit , but **in the know-how and ability to get back on their feet again after each misstep and continue making every effort to reach the goal**. The overcoming of each obstacle strengthens and refines the individual, contributing to his growth. He who has never experienced deep sorrow will probably not know at all true happiness…

Moreover, if the fall is so deep and hurtful, then one should do his best to straighten up – not just to stand on his feet, but to rise, in grandeur. As stated by the great businessman Henry Ford: "Failure is simply the opportunity to begin again, this time more intelligently…". Perhaps the above-depicted slap is no more than faith's sharp and painful elbow directly in the ribs, as a reminder that reality is full of fresh opportunities to be grabbed repeatedly...

The second message: while being on the up-and-up, one should make meticulously sure, all the time, not to let himself be spoiled. God forbid. "Minor" changes in the "self" are legitimate of course; however, the original basis, true and good, should remain the same. And as speeding on life's freeway, one better check ahead once in a while; if all traffic is coming from the opposite direction, he must be on the wrong side of the road. And this is not enough: **having touched success, beware of haughtiness and hubris** (as of lowliness and melancholy before its arrival...), because in the best of times, as one excels in great flourishing, just then really bad stuff may occur – mostly as a result of neglect rooted in complacency. It is forbidden to allow a temporary feeling of contentment – even if it is justified – to overtake clear vision and accurate judgment.

And the best medicine for that is the "Good Fear": not the paralyzing and freezing horror, but the one activating and motivating common sense and healthy instincts, which flows from calculated modesty, always taking care to pull one's sleeve as a reminder of possible failure. This fear is the legal and moral father of cautiousness – serving in fact as a chief ingredient of risk evaluation in any act performed or situation created – thus being perhaps the factor preventing defeat and disaster caused by overconfidence, smugness and contempt for obvious data and signals. "Eyes wide shut" by conceit and haughtiness cannot avoid calamity and catastrophe, replacing arrogance born of unforgivable bragging with deep depression and pessimism, crushing and burying the individual.

Besides; he who is unaware of the fact that happiness and fear are like Siamese twins, old and steadfast buddies (walking together for ages because of the ever-vital fear concerning the loss of either...), and that only very rarely does one exist without the other is a hopeless innocent or an incurable idiot...

Furthermore; one should remember that the higher up the ladder he is, the longer is the fall following a misstep, and the more dreadful is the blood-curdling horror...

The third and last message: one must accept, as the banal cliché goes, that life resembles a marathon – requiring a consistent and determined mixture of experience, knowledge, skills and a strong will – involving several dashes: some, he wins; and a few, he loses. Since **the real achievement is measured, as it is, only at the finish line**, there is no reason to get overexcited about a momentary lead or to sink into deep depression due to a temporary lag. Moreover; a too-fast take-off in any given domain may be very dangerous; hawks may ascend very fast to extremely high altitudes, but squirrels are never sucked into jet engines.

The problem is that drawing conclusions at the finish line alone may be, in many cases, too late, since there is no way to influence the past. Therefore, in order to prevent a total uncertainty concerning the end of the road – a situation fraught with unpleasant surprises – **one must aspire to be able to develop such insights and abilities which will make it possible to forecast the final outcome, more or less, during the afore-said race itself**.

February 1995

Setting the Target

A correct marking of the desired goal is, in fact, the first practical and right step in the path to its achievement. Therefore, it should be clearly decided before taking the opening action in any field. Such a target should be utterly specific to the individual or totally in line with the organization's character. Since it is so unique, its determination starts bobbing up, in most cases, within the inner feelings, and ends by an external act of drawing physically-defined boundaries. For that reason, its ingredients are a mixture of concealed past experiences alongside hidden emotions, on the one hand, and pure reason spiced with cold, practical considerations, on the other – a kind of an inward and sharp intimacy finding expression, finally, in a material declaration.

Hence, defining the target should be, in fact, a sighting and identification of a unique meeting point, balancing material and real conquests with the way one's inner world of feelings accepts them at any given moment and throughout time. **In fact this is a singular interface – true for each and every human being, or to any cooperative entity, individual to the highest degree**; touching it means, therefore, attaining success.

{ It is important to note, that the outlook offered here, talking in general about "balance", is derived, actually, from an analogy to what happens in daily life throughout the infinite cosmos where everything subsists. From the beginning of time nothing has been better at taking care of itself than nature, which experienced many hardships. Any layman recognizes clearly that it is equipped with a network of intercepting, restraining and stabilizing systems, dealing with the irregular powers active within it, in order to reach a general, constant and lasting overall steady symmetry; for each vector, there is an opposite one, in its direction and force. And this is, obviously, the main reason for the world's continued existence since its creation – otherwise it would, probably, "go out of tune" and fall apart totally. This is what happened in the "Big Bang", which created the universe, or in the "Mega Boom" which disconnected the earth from the sun. In fact, each time this equilibrium is violated, the area collapses and is destroyed and rendered unrecognizable. The development of the globe was paved with all kinds of disasters, such as the biblical deluge, the eruption of Mount Vesuvius, hurricanes, typhoons, tornados and tsunamis, and so on. However, by the end of the day, everything calms down anew as a result of the inherent leveling mechanisms of the plant, and a wide-ranging rest returns.

As evidence, considering the reality of the world of fauna and flora, preserved for such a long time despite – perhaps thanks to – being highly heterogeneous, and again thanks to the equilibrium arrangements created to balance nature's systems. That which is a deadly poison for one species is a delicacy to another; she who bestows sweet and incredibly healthy honey, may cause extreme pain, even death, with her sting; the one who strangles and kills, on the one end, gives life, causes flourishing and growth, on the other; host and symbiont, predator and prey, destroyer and destroyed. Finally, the head turns into a tail, and vice versa, and so on and so forth. And everything, in the end, aspires to a state of repose, to be drained to the center and be in a constant, static stability (homeostasis), just as depicted by the classical laws of science.

The same is true amongst human beings. A deviation of the mind from the center to any extreme undermines its poise. A change in the level of the soul causes upheavals, sometimes totally unexpected. Exploiting one side means missing the other facet, so overusing the right is translated to a horrible neglect of the left; an advantage here is actually a shortcoming there; and an inner imbalance within a person causes destructive contradictions; and a lack of mental stability and leveling gives birth, in sum, to the worst. And even genius, being one-directional, is not always helpful, for global wisdom is usually the deciding force.

So, considering that the chains of existence of fauna and flora in the universe are, in fact, endlessly repeating cycles, starting and terminating at the very same point, there is no place for totally exceptional phenomena, endangering the activity of this gigantic system, which is meant to function stably and continuously and be preserved forever. With the outburst of any local irregularities, the inner balancing systems must take over and quell them immediately.

From this stems the assumption that whatever is good and correct for Mother Nature must be suitable for him of her smallest creatures, even the pre-eminent of them...}.

Half of the way to success runs through correct self-management, a fully harmonious activation of the self, which means a perfect combination of four types of desires:

- **Desires of the Soul**: the foundations and texture of the spirit; the will of the vitality and its yearnings; common sense; emotions of the reason.
- **Desires of Consciousness**: the totality of concepts, sensations and thoughts; the experiences of awareness; the life of the soul; spirituality.
- **Desires of the Heart**: the center of excitement and longings.
- **Desires of the Body**: stimulation of the senses.

Such a combination – a response to true inner voices – is far from simple; it is very complicated, amorphous even, since it is emotionally intensified. Hence one must begin by settling, first of all, the above-described current half before continuing the voyage toward material conquests. Therefore, this harmonious move, directed actually at galvanizing a sense of self-satisfaction and enjoyment of life and an exact definition of its qualities, is the main basis – and the mainstay after being achieved – of stepping towards any chosen destination. However, it requires an inculcation of the fact that it is not a once-in-a-lifetime process, but a scenario that must be repeated continuously in order to preserve its total potential to produce the aforementioned desirable results.

Striving for the external-material aspect of the target is a simpler matter. It seems that this section of the struggle is better understood by the very ability to define the aim with as much accuracy as possible. However, it is only apparently so, because firstly, material success as a goal in life may be understood differently by each person; secondly, it tends, generally, to change constantly: one person may understand it as financial riches, the other as a distinguished job, the third one as a magnificent estate, and so on and so forth (unlike identifying and interpreting the term *"real inner happiness"* – once achieved – that might be similar, in essence and sense, for most people, even if it is an outcome of different reasons for each individual…).

Moreover, one must be very careful in pursuing such an external accomplishment, because the temptation to give up the "self" and "betray" it in order to come within reach of success is very strong, as was very sarcastically and cynically phrased by Oscar Wilde: "I can resist anything but temptation…". Every day, one may read in the newspapers, under huge headlines, about the use of lies and crooked ways by the high and mighty as well as the simple folk, just to get a short-lived and dubious triumph, only for the purpose of putting another victorious notch in their belts (and let no one forget: avoiding temptation altogether is much easier than struggling with it later on…).

And this kind of betrayal of trust means in fact a violation of basic human characteristics, virtues such as love, trust, self-confidence, inner control, environmental comprehension, fundamental honesty, gratitude, compassion, kindheartedness, integrity, moderation, generosity, patience, tolerance, courage, humility, simplicity (lack of theatricality…), bravery, joy and basic innocence. Or as was said by a sage who put truth to oneself above all: "Even if the horse is lost, better that go like a stallion, not like a hyena…".

For that reason, although yearning for material success is a healthy and positive trait, worthy of striving to achieve, one must jealously **guard his spiritual sovereignty** while doing so. Thus, satisfying the self is first among others and essential for the balance aforementioned; or as Eastern wisdom would define it: this is the triumph of spirit over matter.

However, while taking such an attitude, one must remember: excessive devotion of a person to loyalty to himself – lacking a real challenge to confront – will lock him within his own confines, leading him, finally, nowhere.

It becomes clear, therefore, that a person can learn to lead his life – and eventually to guide and direct others – in a way enabling him to experience both internal and external success; to enjoy the full self-satisfaction of finding the position in which may influence at any time and very significantly, but only by the **most correct way in his eyes**; to create a **healthy balance** between his business environment and his private universe. And then one is obligated to do his best to stamp his personality on the domain – his private God's Little Acre – of which he is in charge…

March 1995

Acquiring the Demandable

The Essence: Self Satisfaction

Despite the old cliché – that money cannot buy happiness – most people still feel that real economic wellbeing alone may cause maximal satisfaction and enjoyment in life. However, in times of real crisis, reality strikes one's face time and again: plenty of wealth does bestow coziness and daily pleasures and is a major contributor to inner fulfillment – but the notion that it is the key opening all doors to the personal edifice, is wrong concerning one door at least: the door to the soul.

Man's attribute to be himself does not depend on external factors alone, but on the ability to look into his deepest recesses, and the courage to burrow meticulously inside his guts in order to experience his internality in the most intense manner, as feelings, desires and faith, for without these he is not defined at all. And this **wisdom of intra-personal emotional study** – allowing the human being to make peace with his basic characteristics as is, and the liberty to behave like he wants to and live according to his conscience – this insight strengthens him and makes him happy indeed. Material abundance alone can never cause such a loftiness of the soul – although it definitely assists in a considerable way. And in order not to be shackled by over-serious banalities, the next semi-philosophical quotation will clarify the essence of this perception thus far: "Money cannot buy happiness – but it can certainly finance a squadron of first-class experts to find why not…".

Indeed, it is normal for the consciousness, soul and body, to strive for more and more from the material world surrounding them; and few are those blessed with riches who do not enjoy life in general; but external success – huge as it may be – can effect real pleasure only if it comes simultaneously with spiritual self-satisfaction and a realization of the heart's vision. This contentment paves the road to **inner perfection**, because happiness is Man's basic nature, and can only be experienced after reacting with a whole response to all of the soul's needs and by adhering to the self's principles and its faith.

Therefore, each and everyone should start by understanding that for which the spirit yearns so.

The Foundation: Fulfilling the Spiritual Needs

As much as the body needs air, water and food, not only to survive but also to stay healthy as well, so does the soul that requires various **spiritual ingredients**, in order to grow, to immune and to express itself fully via the conscience, the heart and the body.
Since:

- **The Conscience** helps the soul in realizing its goal on earth by setting its sights with positive thinking and with faith;
- **The Heart** fertilizes the soul with emotional factors needed for its growth;
- **And the Body**, assisted by the senses, nourishes the soul with necessary information and a variety of data, coming from the outer world.

These ingredients find constant expression in daily life as **needs for love, support and recognition**; those are the nutrients of the human soul. Psychological literature usually identifies ten basic types of **spiritual necessities**, essential to enriching, strengthening and preserving the "self": kind of essentials that bubble, daily, during all stages of Man's growth, in blooming and in withering, in life management and everything implicit in it.

Human Development Stages: Essences and Means to Nourish the Soul

The needs for love, support and recognition defined above are natural necessities; therefore there is a self-budding order of their formation. Until a few decades ago, the common assumption was that they are derived from the four main periods in human evolution:

- The amorphous **teen and twenty-something** disconnects himself from the physical and spiritual security of home, matures and gains independence.
- The **thirty-something** is endangered by ambushes and minefields due to his disillusionment with youth and the necessity to finally comply with his commitments to others. In these years, one becomes familiar with the limitations of life and makes peace with the forbidden and the impossible.
- The **forty-something** contains full of fears, physical as well as mental. During this decade, the person internalizes the fact that reality is far from ideal and that daily life is usually imperfect.
- The **fifty-something** is oppressed and depressed, in midlife, which means beginning to move down the slope to the second half. He is starting to give up habits unsustainable because of physical limitations, on the one hand; however, due to this maturation, fresh opportunities for expansion are presented in new fields, on the other hand.

Although general and ancient, this division can still serve as a rather good and practical indication of the individual's conduct and modes of behavior at different periods of his life.

However, lately it has been made clear that for a more accurate analysis of human development, it is possible to divide this growth into more than four evolutionarily meaningful stages. First of all, there have been improvements in the investigative methods for the subject; secondly, since the average life expectancy has significantly passed the age of fifty, there is an additional existence chapter, the enjoyment of which necessitates full control. Ten main living periods (eleven for those who are joining the military...) are defined therefore, during which are created all these needs for love, support and recognition according to stations in time. Each period is characterized by its **crisis**, through which Man passes, according to the significant variations in his feelings, body and mind; because growing up is a war from which none emerge unscathed. These wants are answered, spontaneously and according to the changing requirements of evolution, in continuous feedback throughout one's entire being, until the inner potential and its vitality are totally exhausted.

But, in contrast to these needs for love, appearing in parallel to the normal phases of human growth, there are times in life (to be described later...), during which one is required to satisfy some of the afore said necessaries, perhaps even all of them, immediately and simultaneously. Such a realization is expressed in the repeated fulfillment of inner content as described above – a kind of recharging of the soul's batteries.

One may see therefore the spiritual ingredients – the needs aforementioned – as **healing resources containing remedies for the soul**, storehouses of "supportive stuff," **whose contents may be refreshed and replenished whenever exhausted**. And just as Man makes sure of his car's proper functioning by filling up the gasoline tank, it is crucial to renew these **vitality reservoirs** for the proper functioning of the soul. This is vitality, because a daily response to these existential constraints is more than important for the soul: it supplies its vibrancy, wakefulness, freshness, essence, stability and balance.

Indeed, love (alongside support and recognition, which are actually a constant part and parcel of it...), despite being abused by writer's stories and tales all along history, is still what makes the world go round...

Therefore, first and foremost it is imperative to learn how to recognize such necessities; then what is to be done to obtain them; and finally to be ready and open to absorb these: to recite, sharpen, train, and maneuver in replenishing the need, until saturation – paying special attention to the when. In other words, what is the right way to **manage the interior?**

The following is a prosaic description of the main periods of Man's evolution, cataloged according to the their typical crisis, timing, content and "voids" opened by them in the past – and the immediate and continuous spiritual cures required to survive each of them. In parallel, the text hereinafter clarifies the key characteristics of the qualities and means to nourish and cultivate the soul, those serving as responses to present or future demands of growth, whenever any deficiencies arise as an outcome of yesterday's inner damages.

The age delimitations are not dogmatic, but they are common and conventional periods of meaningful seasons in the life of both genders at their blooming. The limits of maturation periods are set, therefore, individually in reality – not just by the theoretical schema described below.

1. **The crisis of pregnancy and birth stress – from conception to childbirth via the instinctive union with the mother.**

    Providing the pregnant woman fully with all her needs – especially those arising from the drastic bodily and hormonal changes she undergoes – calms her, reconciles her with her situation and ensures a relatively peaceful delivery. It contributes later on to the mental health and happiness of babies and children from the very beginning of their lives.

However, reality is not a garden of roses. Shocks and negative experiences during and immediately after pregnancy and delivery may influence the newborn as it emerges into the world, and later – during all his days on earth.

The required spiritual requisites: **a lot of patience and belief in the good, while investigating and internalizing what is happening in one's surrounding.**

Characteristics of the first vitality reservoir: constructing a semi-surreal relationship with the universe while inculcating the fact that Man is not alone in creation and that there is a supreme power guiding and assisting Him. For the believers, this is the worship of God, with full confidence in his love and support, understanding that nothing is impossible while facing the Creator; for the secular, it means the study of the supernatural – meditation, for example, which is considered to be the true adulation of the divine for those involved in the spiritual aspect of matters. This is an investigation of the sources of all systems and living objects under the sun, and the reason for their making, in the hope that nature will take care of things – as long as one is willing to cover himself with the proper restraint and moderation.

2. **The crisis of absorption and being absorbed – from birth to the age of six / seven.**

These years are of extreme importance in laying the foundation of the mental shape of the infant – especially during the first months and years of life, when the mother is, usually, undergoing sharp mood changes. At this age, the child is almost totally dependent on his parents or on other caretakers. Each intellective interaction, including physical contact with any of them, is inscribed in him forever. On the other hand, he lacks the capabilities to satisfy his demands by himself, but desires to fulfill them immediately. Therefore, it happens often that these wishes go unanswered; this fact gives rise to two opposite phenomena:

At the one end – being short of confidence in one's personal potential, which may cause future confusion between what he wants and what he really needs.

At the other end – an effort to do it all by oneself and now. This "independence" at such an early age may result in a reluctance to accept help and cause one to repulse automatically any assistance offered – real and just as it may be.

The required spiritual requisites: **love and support of the parents**. Characteristics of the second vitality reservoir: meetings with counselors or therapists. These are substitutes – a kind of "a parent to hire" – for the first stage. In time, after becoming acquainted with the essence of the deficiency and the ways to deal with it, one develops personal traits accordingly, enabling him to tackle independently the aforementioned problems.

3. **The crisis of wonder and silence – development from six / seven to twelve / thirteen years of age.**

This is the first experience outside of the parents' authority, the initial exposure to the outer world without their protection and support. The child lacks the confidence to voice his feelings, as well as the knowledge and ability to do so; therefore he is mostly silent. There is a need, apparently, for a close adult to ask, directing by his questions the child to describe experiences and express feelings, beliefs and wishes, while wondering naively about life in particular and the universe in general.

Children of this age group are explicitly entitled to make all the possible mistakes and to learn from them.

At this stage of evolution, the child passes from concrete thinking, where everything is what it seem, to an abstract one, when totally non-specific concepts are also real.

The required spiritual requisites: **love, support of family and friends, as well as enjoyment of their company**.

Characteristics of the third vitality reservoir: fostering old friendships and making new ones too occasionally.

4. **Hormonal crisis and its pressure – the most meaningful growth from twelve / thirteen to the age of twenty-one.**

    A totally different and surprisingly powerful experience, attacking stealthily: the body is filled to the brim with hormones, generating physical changes and huge alterations of the brain and the organism.

    Unknown impulses are awakening alongside questions concerning sexual identity, which, without previous preparation. may lead to folly and even destruction. Transgressive childishness may culminate in total defiance, even unrestrained rebelliousness.

    One compares himself to his surroundings, a competition among peers; a phase of development begins taking shape, in which the proximate society contributes its significant part in forming the personality and embellishes the first layer of the "self" created by genetic heredity. At this point, a deep yearning evolves for personal experiences vis-à-vis close acquaintances. From the other side, close adult relatives lose nearly all influence (Bertrand Russell, the famous philosopher and Nobel Prize winner, defined the situation very well in his book, The Conquest of Happiness: "Beggars do not envy millionaires, though of course they will envy other beggars who are more successful...").

    On the other hand, this is when one begins to be attracted by personal domains of interest, a promising ground for excellence: an uncharted sea, a dangerous lake.

    The required spiritual requisites: **love and support of peers, colleagues and others sharing the same language and similar goals**.

Characteristics of the fourth vitality reservoir: club membership or affiliation in some other supportive group; joining a sports team or nurturing an enjoyable hobby, constantly.

4a. The crisis of military service – sudden maturity

This is a very extraordinary experience which has no equal in gravity and influence over the world's view of adolescents, of both sexes, in later life; a very intense period, of immediately growing up and a sudden weaning from youth – aging suddenly and prematurely. These are unprecedented occurrences at this point in life; without proper preparation, one may be shaken, even destroyed. This is an introduction to violent death, the bereavement and void – corporeal as well as mental – created by it. The military existence creates situations of being stripped and exposed at the innermost level in front of commanders, and mainly peers, at the most critical moments of life. Absorption into the surrounding milieu, coupled with the adoption of the exceptional-extrinsic behavior codes, bring about a climax of the development phase when the environment (esoteric as it may be…) becomes the central and final processor and molder of the personality, above and beyond the pre-induction social ingredients acquired at home and amongst close companions. The young man learns to take responsibility over the wellbeing of others, to devote himself unconditionally and unrequitedly – a total "intoxication" with the setting. During this unique period, one gets acquainted for the first time with how to insist on the smallest details in order to protect life itself.

The required spiritual requisites: **Love and support of comrades in arms and commanders**.

Characteristics of this particular vitality reservoir: military reserve service – preferably in the same unit and with the matching buddies; participating in regular meetings with the afore-said friends in order to grow and mature in a company thoroughly familiar with all one's aspects.

5. **The crisis of craving for independence and its adaptation – self-formation during one's early to late twenties.**

   That period entails a confusion regarding the freedom suddenly encountered after leaving home (or being discharged from the military service…), as well as a lack of self-discipline, when being asked, for the first time, to fulfill self-chosen tasks and live without being dictated to by others. This is a time to mature physically.

   This is a phase of longing for social and group activities in order to feel secure and to finish forming the personality – especially in order to exploit unlimited liberty. This is a golden age, apparently, of wallowing, nearly compulsively, in selfish and vulgar debauchery, the hour of tasting the sweet poison of the beauty of physical-mental development. Joining the ambiance of "catch as catch can," and "carpe diem" – storming everywhere because of the "fever of youth." On the other hand – there is a fear of hanging with the wrong companions, whose bad influence may create impressions like "dreams are not worth fulfilling," or "there is no suitable place under the sun." This is the time to choose independently a direction in life and to face for the first time the dilemma of what one really wants as a grownup.

   The required spiritual requisites: **self-love and the inner support of abilities, beliefs and values.**

   Characteristics of the fifth vitality reservoir: a recognition and confirmation that charity begins at home. One should self-search his qualifications, wishes and yearnings, find out what they are, strengthen and fortify them, and try fulfilling those in any way possible.

6. **The crisis of soul-searching and personal-wish positioning – consolidation from twenty-six / eight years of age to thirty-five.**

The lack of a binding framework creates an illusion of unlimited freedom, while not enough time and thought are dedicated to a deep understanding of the "self" and its shaping. Questions concerning self identity, the nature and essence of life goals, are investigated daily.

All of the past's damages and calamities appear to be evident at this time, and there is a tendency to experience multiple and frequent emotional storms. It is imperative to build up a subconscious "protection and softening mechanism" to guard against being injured by breakups of close relationships, by intimacy. There is an urgent need to cure all diseases of the past. This is the moment to inculcate that a main tier of real adulthood is based on a full acknowledgment of the fact that the "self" is not anymore the center of the universe around which everything turn, but a piece of a much wider, complicated and diverse human-social puzzle. A pressure to find a spouse is starting to evolve; the age of self-discovery and the wish to be loyal to one's inner values and beliefs is already at the door and in full force.

The required spiritual requisites: **romantic love and close intimacy with one's spouse.**

Characteristics of the sixth vitality reservoir: a sharing of the daily routine with somebody, for "it is not good that the Man should be alone..."; "better dead than lonely..." Strange as this may sound, a mutual dependence is essential for self-definition. And it is the law of nature: sexual passion and fulfillment is translated into huge amount of vigorous energy, in all spheres of life. For sex is what makes the world go round, and sexually active people are much happier, creative and positive.

7. **The crisis of dependence on dependents – wallowing in the mire between thirty-five and forty years of age.**

There is a subconscious tendency to give unconditionally and limitless love to a dependent – for the most part, one's children, considered perfectly reliant creatures. A wrong, even cruel, message is thus transmitted, namely that the children owe nearly everything to their parents. Such a notion creates unintentional friction, shaking the family's nest. And those who are unable to give, or perhaps feel that they are not generous enough due to their own past torments and agonies, suffer tremendous frustration. Without a dependent, a reaction is triggered, centered on personal needs, selfishness and seclusion, resulting in a continued dissatisfaction with one's dreary existence.

The required spiritual requisites: **the love of a dependant**. Characteristics of the seventh vitality reservoir: a devoted and unconditional attention to children and grandchildren; at least, taking care of pets endlessly, in return for warmth.

8. **Midlife Crisis – fear between the forties and fifties**.

Arithmetically this is, apparently, the midlife decade! However it tastes of dissatisfaction, emptiness, even a lack of fulfillment, since the "tremendous qualitative charge" that still exists, at least from one's own perspective, has not been fully exhausted. There is still a great self-confidence in one's ability to further contribute. A deep disappointment starts to dominates the soul mainly because of the feeling – perhaps the need to believe – that the present circumstances reek of irrelevant considerations. A wish to bestow on everyone and to impart without limits derives up suddenly – deteriorating into obsessive devotion and self-sacrifice for no proper reward – under the compulsion to satisfy personal needs. The futility of trying to recycle past glories is recognized. The result: a somewhat crazy rush after excitements and changes, giving birth to revolutionary, sometimes stupid, ideas; pondering means and ways completely opposite to the conventional habitual behavior; out of despondency, sticking to quickly-vanishing remnants of youth. In order to realize these out-of-the-blue "notions", one creates a mess – Tower of Babel-magnitude chaos –

within the family, mainly hurting loved ones and intimates. There is a tendency to re-evaluate life and to determine a totally new set of priorities – even at the expense of the existing nest with its "serene atmosphere". A desperate hope to identify a refreshing "personal anthem" stems up strongly.

The required spiritual requisites: **close ties with the community.** Characteristics of the eighth vitality reservoir: investing energy and time in voluntary activities for the benefit of the broader public; donating money to charities and other deserving organizations; trying to do something for the locals in order to turn the resources entirely to positive directions. All this comes from a subconscious will to win recognition and empathy from surrounding social circles with which one is in contact.

9. **The crisis of "the nestlings leaving the nest" – sobering up and maturing from fifty to around sixty-five years of age.**

The autumn of life! An empty feeling emanates from the void left by the lack of someone to care for. The nestlings have flown away and the family domicile becomes empty, leaving a scorching aridness. Spouses, due to the many decades spent together and with nobody else, drift into quarrels. For the first time, there is a sharp and concrete feeling of the meaning of mortality, with darkening eyes and dimming eyesight; bodies get fat, cellulite settling for good, never to be got rid of them, while some kinds of food are strangely forbidden.

A lot of effort is put in sticking to the pace – even though the task is becoming more difficult with every day that passes. Livelihood becomes more important than real work – allowing for less exertion, but still being economically able to spend time enjoying some small private pleasures. There is a huge pressure to remain, mainly to look, young – a very healthy enterprise, by the way; however, the ambition to delay as much as possible the encounters with the withering body and failing mind may lead to ridiculous and funny behavior: trying to go back without really checking the nature of the path, to jump not knowing where – and to take instead of giving. One sleeps less in order to do more, while sentimentality flows, bubbling, at nearly any nostalgic sight or sound.

The required spiritual requisites: **ties with the universe at large.** Characteristics of the ninth vitality reservoir: traveling abroad in order to taste as much of the world as possible. Self-study – autodidacticism – is essential to broaden the horizons regarding the infinite far-flung celestial issues, as well as involvement in unique projects such as: total dedication to absorb a specific topic, long-term volunteer work with special populations, writing a book on an exceptional subject, et cetera. Enriching and deepening worldly experiences allow continuing intellectual and spiritual growth. Opening – glasnost – the soul toward a lasting contact with nature, down to the banished edges of the cosmos, craving to fully understand its real greatness, since growing older means being more involved in life, not less.

10. The crisis of retirement – getting old, from the age of sixty five

All dreams to do and enjoy what has been so far delayed are shattered on the rocks of monotonous reality. One feels a taste of horrible boredom and a deep disappointment from actual idleness; a sense of anaphrodisia and a lack of responsibility towards or for others. Man becomes a being without a defined purpose, therefore lethargic; a sense of loneliness – even if not alone – and helplessness reigns.

This is the onset of numbness, dimness of the mind, heaviness of movement and the gloominess of old age; a feeling of shriveling, decaying and gradual evaporation, as of a drying branch. A tendency to drowsiness nearly everywhere keeps on attacking all of a sadden, out of being uninterested and indifferent (as if making time pass faster…) on the one hand; but the fear of sleeping properly lest he miss, God forbid, something, and be late waking up fights back, on the other hand. One is victimized by the appearance of being worn out, swallowed by deep facial wrinkles, by skin blemishes and strange unexplained moles here and there, by the depletion of scalp hair, complemented by growths on other bizarre spots upon the face and other parts of the skin. Even the body and mouth smells are changing for the worse; the teeth are yellowing and the gums recede. Suddenly one feels as if walking through life's wasteland, because real activity is forgotten and is becoming duller and duller. Impatience and irritation are sky-high, and all of a sudden one grasps that aging actually means gradual surrender. And unexpectedly, death arrives.

The required spiritual requisites: **a vitality of feeling and a physical robustness to fully bloom and to enjoy it.**

Characteristics of the tenth vitality reservoir: positive thinking about the essence of life; preparing oneself to enjoy and smile every minute. For believers in God, this means a total acceptance of the will of the Almighty, worship to the end with full love and intention. For the spiritual types, this is the period for an absolute and true blooming of Man, for which he has been investing, bestowing, suffering, believing and devoting all his efforts until now, and therefore sees himself as deserving of. This means directing and dedicating all daily wishes to the complete extraction of the best of earthly existence; choosing hedonism in its total meaning, as well as setting future goals in order to keep growing; succeeding in doing as much as possible, so as to deprive death, when it appears, of its most frightening aspects (since, actually, when the day comes, one is taken to the highest court of law, calmly and contentedly, satisfied with what was achieved in the world up to that day...!).

The onset of death begins when a person ceases growing and developing, feeling unnecessary and unneeded.

The aforementioned definitions are intended, therefore, to delineate the characteristics of Man's ontogenetic dilemmas across his different life periods; to serve as a mirror, reflecting immediately and in real time, his modes of behavior at each stage of his maturation and the reasons behind them. In other words, this is what bothers one at each phase of his growth, as well as the means to overcome the difficulties by proper self-conduct and an effort to totally control one's inner feelings.

And if it is also customary to think that in addition to what was described up-to-now, there is nearly no human being free from at least one (sometimes more…) of the following primary (somewhat primeval…) known fears natural to Man (as hinted and depicted all through this book…), deriving from the reasons described below and expressed in his daily behavior, as detailed in the following parentheses:

▸ **The apprehension of seeming insignificance**: Man craves to be treated seriously and be appreciated, he is expected at any encounter with others to proclaim his greatness, to do his best to attract attention, to be outstanding and to make his mark vigorously, to present himself as exceptionally unique, expressing in defiantly outrageous opinions, under the guise of the hackneyed cliché "thinking differently is allowed, nay advisable…".

▸ **The fright of surprises**: Therefore one develops an obsession for control, accompanied by an intransigent desire to rule, supervise, regulate and criticize constantly – while trembling in anticipation of the unexpected, and shuddering that he might be unable to respond properly in that case. This goes up to violating occasionally the privacy of his subordinates and those surrounding him and harassing them (which is totally different, by the way, from proper and pedantic preparations, concurrent with the conception that one should do his best to forestall life events, as detailed especially in the second tractate of this book; because no matter how one

- **The worry of not being loved**: Due to the notion of not being liked enough, one becomes overly friendly, reaching obsessive, bothersome and even disgusting altruism; he becomes clingy in his overweening desire to give to everyone, oozing with extreme devotion to others, while forcing himself to give up nearly all of his necessary personal duties.

- **The angst of routine changes**: Since one is oppressed by transformations, upheavals, and even the smallest deviations from his daily habits, he becomes an avoider: reducing his activities, refusing to act out of his dictated "box", preventing himself from engaging in anything out of the ordinary (unlike the distracting evasion urge based on the fear of failure – although, perhaps, these two subjects are connected – as will be described later in the *"Conquering the Desirable"* chapter of the present tractate, alongside a discussion of "diverting impulses"...).}

Thus, even an onlooker can understand and predict immediately from the above said, rather exhaustively and precisely, the behavior of each individual and its meaning – just by his age and his primary reactions, manners, attitude, tendencies and attributes. Consequently, it is even possible, by the classifications above depicted, to infer and foresee a person's style and temperament of conduct (and how does he aim to go on and carry out...) his own and other people's affairs;

And – most important! – in what way one may correct and improve irrevocably the way he handles and manages himself...

Feeding the Spirit – Principles of its Realization

The normal formation of the spiritual needs, described so far, is only the first step of the long and complicated road regarding Man's internal processing. Although nature does so on its own – even when relatives and friends are also caring and supportive – no one's evolution is devoid of mental obstacles. While growing up, the person's deficiencies awake and reappear, and they will not disappear until proper treatment is applied. And recovery stems, in fact, from nourishing the soul with the means described earlier, which are proper cure for mankind's development crises, each remedy in its time and place. Thus, when the wounds are healing, the human being's interior life becomes stable and takes shape, and life can go on.

Discerning these sicknesses and learning to take care of them require **full attention** to the demands of the soul, on the one hand, and **first-rate content** to restore the vitality reservoirs, on the other; this is a choice and clever concoction of the "what" and the "how". And it is desirable to do so whenever the need arises, for it is very essential to stay in touch with the "self" on a regular, continuous basis.

It should be remembered that these inner reservoirs are not equal in their incompleteness, and they change frequently and quickly; therefore, the soul must have them **well-watered altogether, constantly and simultaneously**, for its wellbeing, wholeness and joy. The recharging of these human-motivating energizers ought to be punctilious – not more or less than what is required – and at the right time, just like a car battery.

There are a few reasons for this:

Firstly, weakness in one of these supportive "cells" may cause a regression into faulty patterns, the remnants of childhood and youth, arousing dormant feelings, impulses and fears which may disrupt daily life.

Secondly, the overflowing of a given interior reservoir is a waste of energy. Not only is such a surplus unnecessary, it may even undermine the balance of the soul, by detaching attention from those "containers" which are in real need of refueling, leaving them empty.

Thirdly, in the transition from one period of exertion to the next, emptiness may prevail, accompanied by relief at the conclusion of a difficult assignment, resulting from the elimination of an intensive mental pressure; one feels as if a heavy burden has been taken from his shoulders and he deserves some rest. Precisely for this reason, he must make sure that the vitality reservoir specific to the completed phase in life is properly filled, to ensure a good changeover move to the next stage – without any shortage or surplus, which might cause future problems.

In short: an incorrect handling of internal deficiencies and poor distribution of resources or replenishment of the proper reservoirs, may lead, at the end of the day, to exhaustion – or alternatively to a significant restlessness, accompanied by a deep frustration.

The following offers, in addition, the use of two activity types, designed to replenish the aforementioned support "stockpiles". This is a dynamic which became vital, over time, to leading and settling the soul, and without which the renewal process of the vital reservoirs is nearly useless. This is the "how", the necessary practice, before the "what".

The one is aiming at linking the individual positively to the universe, integrating him within it, contemplating its might.

The additional is taking care of the soul itself for the betterment of its relations with all surrounding associates, making them honest and real. This may be compared to the Ten Commandments: half of them are between Man and God, as is commonly understood, and the others amongst human beings themselves. Nevertheless, a deep study of them demonstrates the numerical superiority of those basic tenets dealing with personal and social aspects – and not unintentionally

– as will be made clear further on in this book. However, all of them share the same importance, and nobody can argue otherwise.

The first activity type is **meditation** of a sort – a mental submission practised by even the greatest masters of eastern martial arts in order to concentrate prior to entering competitions, something akin to fully-fledged worship of God in the world of the believers.

The second deals with acquiring proficiencies in **unloading tension and overcoming negative feelings;** a task much more complicated than the previous one, involving, to a great extent, interpersonal behavior, with a focus on intrapersonal matters as well.

In conclusion, it is crucial that all aspects of the replenishment of the vitality reservoirs take place **altogether concurrently and in full cooperation**; without proper symbiosis the process may lose effectiveness. Yet, even partial adoption of the articles to be detailed below, may contribute something to the inner balance, but it will not be the perfect answer to the soul's cravings.

Meditation – Super-Spirituality and Extrasensory Study

Meditation is a powerful asset, supporting all known spiritual systems of principles and sustained by them. It is a way of looking inside, cut off from any outside contact. Actually it is a takeover of the feelings and thoughts by suppressing intellectual consciousness, the cognition that is the actual perceptive process. This is, in fact, redirecting focus towards thoughts, inclinations and tendencies, by way of gentle, pleasant and soothing channels. This semi-surreal activity is analogous to a total release of the soul and draining of the awareness in order to somewhat disengage from reality, to seclude oneself and "hover" while merging into the cosmos, observing its conception and absorbing its greatness. And it involves the intake and internalization of ideas such as: higher authority, force majeure, the might of nature, destiny, higher intelligence, the numinous, inner potential, driving force, surging energy, greatness of spirit and vastness of love – each one as he prefers it. The believers ascribe all these to the Creator.

Meditation is a sort of relaxation and refreshment while thinking constructively, in a focused and calm manner. It is carried out either periodically and regularly, or whenever the need arises, while allowing the individual to rise above and to feel tranquility within his environs. Positive observation by itself is a **process of appointing goals every given minute of the day**, and it is in agreement with the notion permitting Man to do one thing at a time, in order to form his life instead of being led by chance and designing its events according to his inner wishes. This is akin to delving into the labyrinthine secrets of the Jewish Kabbala.

Negative Energy as a Matter of Fact

Man is constantly charged with energy, immediately discernible, physically as well as mentally. When a person comes upon an obstacle an anger arises, an agitation evolves and an inner tension develops accompanied by "negative energy". Phenomena of this kind are unavoidable; one should accept them for what they are, learn to identify them and study the types of channels and attitudes to combat them.

One may take, for example, acupuncture, which was developed in China 4,500 years ago to stabilize, among others, Man's inner energy. It is clear that already then there existed a heightened awareness of the tensions created within the human being by his brain and the nervous system. These are treated by inserting tiny needles under the skin at some sensitive or painful points. This serves to discharge aggregations of locked pressures, concentrated at certain spots and disrupting the normal functioning of the body, or to pave passages through which to deliver vitality and vigor to those physical self-parts lacking them.

Tension and anger such as this, locked within the soul, are powerfully projected outward. Moreover, such feelings blunt the ability to sense authentic aspirations and also stop growth. It is as if the body grows weak, its liveliness is exhausted and the push to do things dwindles.

The following are the typical symptoms of this state:

- **Inhibited love**: a longing for the heat of courting and desire, which feels totally unsatisfied.
- **Insecurity**: a yearning to be and do more, which is arrested by inner misgivings due to confrontations stemming from lack of faith in the self.
- **Delayed happiness**: a sharp craving for complete contentment, which is flattened by the incapacity to experience it.
- **Cordoned-off tranquility**: an inability to forgive, especially the "self," for past mistakes.

Discharging Tensions – Practical Advice

In order to discharge tension, the next three topics should be considered:

- **How is it to be relieved?**

  One way is meditation; another is physical activity, even a short walk. A third option is expressing feelings in writing – openly and sharply, preferably. Some do it by painting, sculpting, etc. The common denominator of all these activities is that they require concentration and effort, diverting the mind from these tensions and burdens.

- **Where?**

  Nowhere is more relaxing than nature, for there is a marvelous symbiosis between Man and the Universe; some phenomena that are obnoxious to the human being are very useful to the environment and vice versa, enabling a perfectly mutual "exploitation". And when there is no possibility to simply enjoy the outside environment, water is a very good, tranquillize alternative: going to the sea, taking a bath or a shower for example.

- **When to relax?**

As regularly as possible, or at any time one feels nervous and distracted or just hyper-alert.

Restraining and Removing Negative Feelings – Pragmatic Counseling

Everyone experiences negative feelings, nearly every day. This is a normal and healthy phenomenon which is for the best. Nowadays it is common to identify some of these emotions, such as: disappointment, terror, shame, worry, pain, anger, confusion, sadness, fear, sorrow, jealousy, frustration etc. All other minute sensations (such as frustrating, bitter rage, crushing weakness from pain, competitive greed of jealousy, subconscious dependence of fear and others…) felt in fact by any human being stem in reality from the above-said primary group; and anyone who denies them is actually only enhancing their potency within himself…

Negative feelings – such as tension – should be recognized, felt and only then rejected. However, unlike the aforementioned suggested methods of discharging pressure, relief from the above-said "harmful" emotions is, in fact, achieved by **using, understanding and processing these sensations.** Ignoring them would amount to a blocking of existing sentiments and drawing away from the "self," while actually they must be seen as trustworthy compensators automatically engaged in order to correct any deviation from the wanted path. Therefore, one must stick continuously to those sentiments and avoid repressing them. Only by keeping a close contact with them, one may enjoy the small pleasures of life. Because faithfulness to personal feelings leads to feelings of faithfulness.

Four optional ways are recommended for the discharging of negative feelings:

- **Changing the sentiment causing depression**: trying to modify the bad mood by coercively choosing a different subject for the mind to focus on; a conscious shifting of attention from constantly thinking about the stressing factor, in order to get free from the suffocating pressure. For example, if one is seriously upset about something, there is a possibility to bring up an alternative matter, having nothing to do with the present anger – such as an embarrassing incident – and occupy the mind with it until the rage disappears.

- **Past analogy as a doorway for optimism**: deliberately recalling past emotional storms and worries that ended well, convincing oneself that the undesirable outcome may not materialize, as happened on those previous occurrences

- **Preparing for the worst**: envisioning a horrible-case scenario, in which the most horrific may occur (one may even write it down…). Building the highest possible thorough and uncompromising inner readiness – in the shadow of fear – to accept what one imagines might happen; doing the outmost in convincing oneself of having the personal traits necessary to overcome all the projected hardships. Then, when the real thing appears, it always seems less bad than what was expected.

- **Externalization in order to internalize that even worse things can happen**: shifting the depressing thoughts arising out of self-pity to a consideration of the misfortunes of others; reading sad books, listening to dark classical music, watching gloomy movies, joining a support group of like-minded people, etcetera.

In short: inculcating the fact that other people's lives and their daily routines are much harder.

And the most important thing is to think positively, to experience accordingly and to take things in proportion. This does not refer only to the well-worn cliché, but to the presentation of a worldview. A good and naive old soul argued once: "Smile at life, and it will smile back at you…". Since such a hopeful and bright attitude says it all: that everybody must dare more, try without fear once and again, because of a deep belief in success.

And even then it is recommended to approach each subject, touch and enter it with an affirmative outlook, while still being circumspect. This requires something like a winning combination of cool planning and facts with a significant grain of optimism; thus, the scent of this viewpoint-conceptualization will spread by itself among those around. The dark musings allow Pygmalion and his band of thugs to stand upright – and materialize. Besides, pessimists, by their very nature, never achieve anything, nor do they get anywhere…

In fact, this idea was very well expressed by A. D. Gordon, a pioneer of the early Zionist settlement in the Land of Israel prior to its independence declaration, describing the war between light and darkness: "The light does not need to actively fight. Suffice it to withstand; and when it grows in might, it conquers – and darkness flees anyway…". In other words: a real intention coupled with great faith is enough for anyone to accomplish his goals brilliantly.

And all the aforementioned comes with one great sober-minded stipulation: **one must nourish a great and honest hope for the best, accompanied by a painstaking and deliberate preparation for the worst…**

April 1997

Conquering the Desirable

The Essences – Desire, Faith and Passion

There is no doubt that success in life requires material achievements too; without these, *personal success* is meaningless. And the will to grow substantially is actually an acknowledgement by Man of his real physical desires and the sharp need to fulfill them. Devotion to matters of the spirit is good only for celibates and ascetics – not for the pragmatic world of the present; this is why so few are those who are content with quenching the thirst of the soul.

Material success is intended to supplement self-contentment and satisfaction, molding the three into a balanced human fabric, on the path to real wellbeing and prosperity. It grows mainly from **the very desire to arrive at it, the confidence demonstrated on the way to attaining it and the sweeping enthusiasm and determination characterizing what is done for it**. However, this ambition is less crucial to the soul than the factor described in the previous chapter: the full happiness, born out of inner reconciliation with outward activity combined with loyalty to one's self, faith and values. The importance of material achievement lies, actually, in its role as a wave that carries along this internal pleasure, which at the end of the day – as an outcome of this synergy – touches the expected goal; obviously, people of affluence find it much easier to fulfill themselves.

And as for the recipe: first of all one has to mark the longed-for objective exactly, then internalize the idea, understand the details of its execution, be convinced of his ability to achieve it – and finally crave the result as if there is no tomorrow. Now, making the dream come true – using consistently all legal means, of course – becomes a matter of hard work and nothing else. To wit: **desire, faith and passion, spiced with plenty of concern**, are the major factual drives behind each material success; these are, definitely, the cardinal forces pushing human beings to do exceptional things. For almost each and every wonderful saga of a soaring substantial achievement is filled with delays, disappointments, betrayals, impediments and failures; but all those fade along the way due to the burning aspiration, the endless ambition, the incredible self-discipline, the determination not to give up and the mighty resolve to withstand all opposition. **And the more sublime the target is, the higher are the hurdles over which one has to climb**; and only patience, perseverance, and steadfastness shall bring the hoped-for reward.

This insight explains why, despite mountainous difficulties, there are more than a few cases of success. The reason is that their heroes learned the hard way how to be happy with a little less – while displaying decisiveness, indefatigability and plenty of ingenuity in striving for more accomplishments. Compared to these, there are countless cases of superficially dignified prosperity, however short-lived, because their owners lose interest in their occupation and in yearning to climb higher as soon as they become smug, petty dictators, satisfied with money flowing by itself into their pockets. **For deeds alone are unimportant; real potency resides primarily in the passion of yearning, in what one feels, prays and hopes for – and in the strength of the trust he puts into it**. One needs to dream and fight, since true vitality bubbles from the inside out, actually changing paradigms and axioms that have previously determined patterns of conduct and management. The nature of the tasks does not alter; it is the ability to execute them which simply improves as long as it grows actually and honestly from within.

The Practical Implication: Hard Work with no Respite

The above-detailed process – starting with a vision accompanied by introspection, deep thinking and the formation of a perception – continues with a very profound planning, a minutely considered management and a long-term, meticulous and controlled application; in short, hard labor. Any idea, magnificent as it may be, sprouts from a utopian dream and ends with an exhaustive, boring mosaic work. Thomas Edison explained his success thusly: "**Genius is one percent inspiration and ninety-nine percent perspiration…**". More than this: early risers get ahead of the game – because all the rest are still asleep… In other words, the only place where "success" precedes "work" is the dictionary.

In order to embark on such an arduous quest, one should, first and foremost, **believe in his vigor and potential**; this is a vital credit, which a person is required as well as entitled to bestow on himself. This sort of acknowledgment inspires the confidence which permits him to trust inner voices and signals – described sometimes as "gut feelings." Leaning of this kind enables one mentally to start acting while taking calculated risks – but guarding him from feeble-minded adventurism. The feeling of being able to face hard work and unexpected difficulties, which may pop up on the way, along with cushioning optimism, is what readies the correct method, leading eventually to the expected result, without rolling to the unknown chasms of perdition when confronting the first obstacle. An awfully strong faith that greatness can be reachable is required in order to become really great.

However, four important conditions should be considered before moving forward with a high readiness to invest and commit to begin truly sweating:

First condition: **the benchmark should not be beyond realistic abilities**. It is permissible to admit – to oneself as well as to others – having exceptionally high expectations. Still, one must be very down-to-earth when positioning the attainable targets; otherwise, setting a point of reference far above what can be achieved – which will probably end in reaching nothing – may lead to the opposite outcome. Despair and depression might arise from failure, culminating in total dispiritedness, the consequence of which is a complete halt.

Second condition: **It is forbidden to focus on one and only one occupation.** An intense concentration without respite on just a single subject, momentarily exhausting, may turn into a grinding and wearing struggle, lacking any benefits. The reason for this is that overexertion can totally crush and bring about a "drying" of the mind, followed by prostration and total emptiness. This is where the risk lies: such a state may flood the self with a taste of defeat and limpness and drag one down to nothingness. Collaterally it should also be clear that not everything ought to be done alone, especially not now and on-the-spot. When one gets tired, disappointed because of not accomplishing everything longed for – despite investing his heart and soul in the project – he should just give up, let go entirely of the issue and simply rest for a while. And then, when Man is done "banging his head against the wall", a surprising notion pops up. For only if he stops for a minute, taking a deep breath, can he relax and calm down; and while the mind flows, in an apparent trance, a solution presents itself. It is proper, sometimes, to deviate from the hard discipline sentenced on the soul, letting it refresh itself in the daily, normal, small things needed by every human being. Then cognition is set free, the muse sings, a mysterious source of brilliant ideas awakens and a new sublime understanding arises. Or, as the believers think, he is touched by the hand of God.

Third condition: **it is definitely recommended not to become enslaved to a single activity, domain or anything in particular, nor turn out to be attached to it in a deep, compulsive and uncompromising manner**, without allocating time to look around and devote free mental energy to other aspects of life. For in case of a failure or disappearance, the price may be so high as to cause a total spiritual collapse, a complete loss of personal happiness (since frequently, one lives for something, a thing which might eventually be taken from him...).

Fourth condition: **One must not whatsoever allow the uncompromising striving for contentment from the immediate satisfaction of sensual yearning to become a cause of pain**; this is to tackle a case in which the gap between the available and the desirable is widening and self-satisfaction might slip away for a while.

And if the proposed path is chosen and one evades meticulously the aforementioned conditions, then occasionally the road towards the goal, the prosperity of action and the enjoyment of creation – and not necessarily achieving the goal completely – fills a person with authentic pleasure and happiness.

The Back-Up: Non-Denial of Wishes and Patterns for Achieving the Desirable

Beyond the actions taken to get to material success, one should not forget the allies supporting them from within: the loyalty to the sincere wishes of the spirit, and the real push to fulfill them. **However, theoretical constructive thinking and positive intentions are not enough by themselves**, unless deployed practically; actually a negative process takes place of suppressing natural urges and a denying the real wants bubbling from within. For this would be similar to searching honesty with an extinguished candle.

Even pretending that everything is okay – despite evidence to the contrary – will not be useful at all. Because by choosing to replace disappointment from failures and absences (and who doesn't face those here and there?...) with being nice and behaving as if it's "business as usual", one really squelches the yearnings for achievements and may kill it altogether. And by faking satisfaction, being swept by the flow, making do with what is, "swallowing" everything with love and forgiving everybody (due to bowing to the will of God or accepting fate or its indifferent and frustrating relative – chance – as it is, or perhaps by expecting Karma to fix everything...), the fervor for action, creation and striving for success will fade away slowly until vanishing at last. Only by burning with the strong wish for "more" and honestly suffering the agonies of longing for something greater without denying it can positive thinking and intentions help tremendously and contribute to accomplishing the desirable.

In order to complete the back-up readiness for outward activity, it is recommended to adopt, in addition, the following three behavioral patterns, and turn them, actually, into a way of life:

- **Keep on striving honestly for the marked targets.**
- **Neutralize the vain effort invested in any kind of resistance.**
- **Submit to all positive desires directed at achieving the goals.**

The Power of Continually Wishing

Each human being should find his own charmed "Aladdin's Lamp," by whose light he continues to strive for the fulfillment of his longings. An enormous thirst for attainments, a faith in the rightness of the path and its execution and a sweeping enthusiasm for the activity it entails are the ingredients of material prosperity and flourishing. The essence is the following: **never give up that which the spirit truly desires.**

For by waiving the cravings of the soul, Man loses confidence in his ability to reach his goal. This sensation is usually accompanied by the fear of failure. This is a negative trait, and by clinging to such heretical ideas, the human being invites a denial of the most internal true wants. This is the stage at which a cognitive dissonance is born: an inner discrepancy between what one wishes and the belief in his capability to accomplish them, reminiscent of Aesop's famous fable: "Driven by hunger, a fox tried to reach some grapes hanging high on the vine but was unable to, although he leaped with all his strength. As he went away, the fox remarked, 'Oh, you aren't even ripe yet! I don't need any sour grapes...'". For many miss-ups in life are visited upon those who do not know to really appreciate how close they were to success and just give up...

Such a surrender means, in fact, an end of hope, and no power in the world can make the dreams come true. Thus, not only Man's destiny is over and done with, but even his present activities are no longer effective, because in the best-case scenario, such a process is often accompanied by becoming a falsely positive type, regularly refusing relaxation and getting to the point where he loses all interest in fighting for any personal success; the entire energy is turned outward, and he is seemingly interested in the public welfare only. Such an exaggerated niceness covers a refusal to admit that there are genuine private wishes and needs. It comes at the expense of the urge for self-satisfaction and is ultimately expressed in a nearly obsessive dedication to others; altruism and nothing else. In the worst cases, the unwillingness to challenge obstacles begets a deep apathy, forbidding one to do anything for the "self".

In order to avoid such situations, it is strongly advised to deeply study the **appropriate methods of how to work on feelings** contributing to failure anxiety, with the aim of overcoming them; to become weaned from perceptions of doubt, hesitation and fear, arising from disappointment, helplessness, stumbling and sometimes even past defeats. The only way to tackle this sentiment is by substituting the bitter taste of impotence with a straight brave gaze at the light shining at the end of the tunnel. Thus, in time, instead of dwelling upon past mistakes, one must concentrate on the approach he chooses and build up optimism.

Instead of feeling stuck, the freedom of movement should be fully appreciated. While waiting, everybody wants to be on the move, just like in slow traffic. Seemingly there are more red lights than green ones; for it takes seconds to cross a green signal, and eternity to wait for the red to change.

Yet, in this context, two very important things deserve attention:

First: it is vital to realistically and studiously discern real impassable obstacles. Good self-conduct entails, among other things, knowing how not to "bang one's head against the wall"; the ability to distinguish between a surmountable difficulty and an unconquerable barrier; the capacity to spot alternative paths, leading to the same target, and the need to pose another similar goal which is, somehow, eventually satisfying.

Second: when there are plenty of "green lights" on the road to the objective, one "red signal" here and there does not hamper and hardly slows advancement. On the contrary, sometimes they are even advantageous, because they strengthen and teach. Nevertheless, it is always good to adopt a constructive train of thought, which will at all times invigorate one to continue and strive for more and more. **It is forbidden to "think red",** despite the obstacles scattered on the way and the hurdles which one has to surmount while moving forward to the target.

Avoiding the Vain Effort of the Tendency to Resist

Resistance – refusing an unwanted something or someone – eventually translates into a **waste of resources**. It concentrates energy on a wrong subject and achieves, actually, the opposite of the original intention. In a mysterious way, what is negated and fought against gathers strength, apparently, because the efforts and attention directed at it are so intense, that it becomes the main and only daily focus of awareness.

This may be compared to a person trapped in stop-and-go traffic while doing his best to advance faster. Naturally one opposes the enervating plodding and changes lanes. However, just now, spitefully, the vehicle's progress seems to slow even more, as if this is the sluggish route. This is but an illusion, composed of two phenomena: the first is a visual error, due to the relative movements of two bodies, where one discerns just the progress of his neighbor, not his own; the other is mental, stemming from the tremendous objection to staying put. The combination of both and the obsessive quest for a quick outlet from the thicket create the feeling that cars on either flank are flowing more easily.

Moreover, acting obsessively against something in other ways of life is analogous to trying to quench a fire with gasoline. Focusing single-mindedly on objection for its own sake is a folly, because it may cause a feeling of helplessness due to homing on something which may not be subdued; it blurs the understanding of one's true abilities and detaches him from his creative traits. Thus, Man feels that he is unable to achieve his true ambition.

Since everything in life starts generally with an idea which is later translated into action, it is proper to adopt as much as possible positive thinking and creativity in what is wanted and stay away from exhausting false intentions, that drive towards resistance, negation and revolt, all of which are to no avail.

In summation: nothing attracts success better than success itself and the belief in the possibility of achieving it.

Consenting to all Positive Desires Leading to Achieving the Goals

Recognizing four categories of basic desires – those described in the chapter "Setting the Target" – including the fabric of feelings stemming from those, enables one to "reach" into the "depth" of the "self" and get to know it; being aware of their existence, keeping in close touch with these emotions, responding totally to and acting to satisfy them clearly show the road to a joyous life. In other words:

- **Responding to the desires of the soul bestows inner happiness.**
- **Satisfying the desires of the conscious mind stimulates a taste for outer success.**
- **Realizing the desires of the heart brings about a contentment of the personal needs.**
- **Fulfilling the desires of the body creates physical wellness, relaxation and vitality.**

On the other hand, it is imperative to remember that listening to one of these categories does not imply immediate compliance, for its influence will be expressed later on in its unity with the others in the light of its potency compared to their contributions at a given moment. But what is really important to understand is that satisfying the above-depicted wishes should be accomplished correspondingly. Surrendering to one desire, only at the expense of the rest may cause friction within oneself, due to the contradiction which may arise out of the will to satisfy two essentially opposed whims; as the saying goes, one finds himself between the devil and the deep blue sea. Only when attention is equally divided among all treatment methods mentioned above and a harmony exists among all feedbacks is a state of **pure longing** created: one whose only aim is doing good to the "self", having no bad feeling toward anybody, and leading to full and honest contentment.

Respectively there are **shifting urges**, the cause of **diverting modes of behavior**, blunting pure sensations; these feelings function as "involuntary muscles," apparently uncontrollable and distract a person from satisfying his true fancies. The professional literature usually presents twelve such modes of behavior and twelve **treatment methods** to counter these with and neutralize them. Only after studying these preventive techniques can one distinguish between a state of assuming erroneously to know what is already wanted, on the one end, and what the spirit really craves, on the other.

The following is a list of the afore-said shifting tendencies or impulses, the definition of their content and a presentation of the means to resist them by circumvention – without ignoring these urges, but rather by understanding, internalizing and responding correctly to their appearance.

▸ **Attachment:** an obsessive holding on to what is no longer achievable – sometimes out of sheer greed.
It is best to dissociate from old attachments, while continuing to forcefully covet new things.
Another incarnation of such a behavior can result from a reaction to the ordeal of losing a dear person or something of a deep emotional value; the yearnings create a desperate dependence on the past and a feeling that life has come to an end with this loss. However, sometimes what is truly missing is not the physical presence of the absent object, but its purpose or aura which is in fact being lacked. Holding on to yesterday means repelling tomorrow. That is why it is very important to let go of this apparent "sickness" and respond to the need for change; for each alternative or upheaval – difficult as it may be – opens doors to new possibilities, perhaps

even better ones. So as someone argued once: "It'll all come out in the wash...".

This negative trait may also be taken as a deceptive state of mind leading to a perception of material success as the only lane to happiness. Such a conjecture is born of an insufficiently-formed personality, or from a misunderstanding and neglect of real internal needs.

Yet, in contrast to everything aforesaid, one should be very careful, while striving to detach himself from former attachments, not to push aside authentic and useful desires.

- **Avoidance:** rebuffing things out of fear of failure.

It is recommended to avoid avoidance; to stick to inner intentions and fulfill them to the end. Giving up deflects efforts to irrelevant directions instead of channeling them to the realizations of wishes. This is dodging taking care of what is demanded, by null and non-obliged activity. Instincts urging one to shun fulfilling his desires are impure, devoid of any positive or constructive aim. Running away from problems does not solve them, since they are lurking wherever one turns. Delaying involves missing the proper timing – hence, a waste of much energy.

Smelling the perfume of future satisfaction from an accomplished mission and enjoying the expected achievement – these are the cure from such a diverting mode of behavior.

- **Intellectualization**: dominance of logic over feelings and emotions.

Recognizing the influence of intellectualization is justified because in the final analysis, the head was not created only to hold a hat. However, one should not give up attentiveness to the directions of emotional intelligence.

Rationalism drives Man often to perpetrate deeds explicitly contradictory to human nature. It conceals, for example, sorrow, regret and pity, which are the foundations of the self-correcting mechanism on the way to improvement. Overly logical behavior is sometimes a sort of self-persuasion, pointing to an alienation of clear natural sensations of the spirit and their repression. This happens mainly due to a lack of belief and trust in what one may achieve. This tendency – albeit creating an illusion of temporary "relief" from inner ambitions – is harmful actually, encouraging him to desert them even though they may get him closer to the goal, and by this, in fact, it distances a person from the "self" and his intentions.

It is suggested, therefore, to use rationalization within limits – mainly to prevent it from canceling the very important function of the soul in daily activities.

- **Justification**: over-defensiveness of personal positions which might end up in having to apologize.

  There is a need to quit expressing regret; instead of being often defensive, it is required to be attentive to other people's opinions, study them with supreme openness and learn to adopt whatever seems necessary to achieve the goal.

  Entrenchment in personal views and attitudes may, just to spite, distance one from the long awaited target. Denial of mistakes obstructs advertentness, openness and concern.

  On the other hand, admitting errors enables the human being to draw conclusions from failures and is the first step towards a proper personal compensation. Quoth John C. Maxwell in his book *The Power of Leadership*: "A man must be big enough to admit his lapses, smart enough to profit from them, and strong enough to correct these slips...".

- **Reaction**: a spontaneous outbreak leading from grumbling to resentment.

  Responding calmly is better than replying angrily; it is preferable to hold back the reaction and think again before pressing the "send" button.

Attacking the other with wrath is actually a desertion of good manners like politeness and generosity. It means letting the other side exacerbate the situation and set the "rules of the game" according to his will and standards – his character, substance and style – and by this to be towed to where he intended to push the reactor in the first place.

Additionally, after breaking into a tantrum, it is nearly impossible to arrest the unavoidable employment and unnecessary escalation, which might culminate in extremism, even violence, especially, since one never succeeds in telling what he truly meant in the beginning.

Answering, on the other hand, is a weighted attitude, intentionally ignoring momentary madness; above all it does not deflect from what and how is honestly meant to be said.

▸ **Rebellion**: uprising and resisting being dominated by somebody else.

It is better to stay away from rebelliousness and to focus on a freely chosen agenda. The tendency to revolt is misleading: it implants a belief in demonstrating freedom of choice, while indirectly it really means enslavement to outer dictates, since in an uprising the main effort is directed against somebody else's will, and not by personal decisions. Namely: by being reactive, such an urge places responsibility for one's actions at other people's doors, just because he is being led by the events and not guiding them. Mutiny and such confrontations are a waste of time and precious mental resources, since by allowing a hated personality to dictate the moves, Man is deterred from the central path.

In such cases, the methodology is to mislead the other side into believing that he is being treated with respect – as if he were an easygoing person – and reacting to him, deliberately, with prodigious good manners, but actually forcing him to listen calmly and attentively to another reasoning; until due to inconvenience

– or perhaps out of conviction eventually – he may accept, even partially, what he actually does not agree with.

- **Rejection**: disregarding natural internal needs.

    It is important to deflect rejection, to understand the necessity of acquiring what is missing and the know-how to get it.

    Refusing to acknowledge natural needs probably follows past deficiencies which founded an ongoing denial of something longed for very much. Getting used to a life of shortage and becoming adapted to it creates a state of mind in which one is unwilling to fulfill the want even when the opportunity presents itself. A constant negation of basic and normal desires gives birth to craving for things which are not really necessary or possible to obtain.

    On the other hand, denying an internal demand may cause jealousy. Even though it is a common feeling – and acceptable in the right dosage – people, usually, tend to camouflage it. For envy – besides depicting in most cases a dissatisfaction (or lack of support…) with the success of others – characterizes as well an over-excitement for something. Therefore, it is appropriate to distinguish proper jealousy from its positive aspect, meaning a well-developed sense of competition; pushing Man to imitate the achievements of his fellows and motivating him to yearn to feel it someday.

    Developing a burning desire for something opposite to the one given up, followed by its conscious rejection, is one among many methods to overcome the present default. It is somewhat like a contradiction in terms.

- **Revenge**: a burning will to cause pain in return for an injury or betrayal, and a way to also discharge incidentally heavy loads of anger.

    It is permissible to express anger instead of taking revenge, to forgive after offloading inside pressure. Holding a grudge towards the object of rage is a total waste of time and energy, dwelling for free in one's brain and filling his entire entity, instead of routing these precious resources to really preferred, desirable and important routes. All-in-all, vengeance reveals its four origins – pettiness, over-righteousness, sadism and arrogant gloating – a momentary relief having no healing value. In addition, it is a digression from life's proper channels, from faith and essential wishes. It is recommended and healthy to verbally "release steam" born out of being hurt, ridding one of inner grievances by external discharge. Concurrently, forgiveness serves to free one from the tendency to blame others for any mishap. Only by letting go of the horrible will for revenge can the human being take control of his life.

- **Seclusion**: distancing from society as a reaction to pain and sorrow of past interpersonal disappointment.

   It is suggested to open emotionally, to guard against repeated hurt – but to avoid seclusion.
   Staying away from emotional attachment in order to shelter against another disappointment delays and blocks other sentiments and energetic channels. The best form to deal with such tendency is to exteriorize and express the feelings – for example: to put them honestly and directly on paper.
   After learning to forgive, it is possible to draw near and love again.

- **Self-Sacrificing**: limitless giving and bestowing, emptying inner resources until nothing is left to try and provide for private wishes.

   It is preferable to avoid personal sacrifice in the name of love; one should take care primarily of his own needs.
   Making another people happy is good and healthy – in the right measure and time. Continuously bestowing to the other makes sense only when the inside of the giver is overflowing and all his vitality reservoirs are full. Endless devotion would impoverish the soul and put an end to relevant capabilities for self-satisfaction.

It is recommended to adopt a degree of selfishness, egocentricity and importunity – for a time only – until a renewed awakening of the awareness to the inner needs, accompanied by self-love, an experience of personal happiness and the resulting yearning for achievement.

- **Skepticism**: disbelief in the possibility of something to occur – even though it is reachable.

Over-skepticism should be eliminated; yet, one should be open to examining again everything from scratch in order to bypass over-indecisiveness and determine the way to deal with it.
Deciding to exchange doubt for a realization of "just not knowing enough," accompanied by the readiness to learn and acceptance, out of hesitation, the partiality of the answers, while wanting to listen and absorb – frees one to resume his belief in alternatives and to sympathetically examine fractional, but good-enough, solutions to reach the destination. The anxiety from lack of information is replaced by a new openness and a consciousness freed from previous conclusions and prejudices, able to engross a variety of new potential options. Understanding that human knowledge is limited encourages Man to keep on investigating again and again, thus widening the borders of his creativity and expression; if in doubt, one should check the subject meticulously from the start, in order to solve all questions.

- **Surrender**: giving up hope due to a disbelief in their realization.

It is allowed to make peace but not to surrender, to keep demanding without letting go.
Such a situation entails a retreat due to a collapse of confidence in the self's abilities and powers, as an outcome of past disappointments and frustrations – a despair leading to total apathy and loss of will to struggle. It resembles the state of being a turkey at the Thanksgiving table (of life...).

Acceptance of things means deserting protest and anger, facing the present circumstances and conceding what is irreparable or not exchangeable — in other words: a forced adaptation. Given a choice between being accustomed or dead, the former is better. Though, such an adjustment testifies to a nourishment of patience, perseverance and intellectual strength.

Complying willingly with things comprehended does not mean an end to desire. For it takes a peace of mind to accept the unchangeable, fortitude to fix the correctable, and wisdom to precisely distinguish between them.

It is evident therefore that knowing how to detach oneself from diverting tendencies or urges – after acknowledging them and accepting their existence – imparts an ability to create a spiritualistic system, self-nourishing and improving with time. Thus real and pure passion is demonstrated, and a mechanism is being built up to enable the petty adaptations which are necessary for the appropriate conduct of life and everything with which they are involved, all this while starting to deeply inculcate the real pattern of how to reach the desirable aim.

And while dealing with the aforementioned shifting orientations and impulses, one should emphasize curing the sickness, not its symptoms.

In summation: the aspirations to succeed and achieve materialistic and actual gains in whatever one is occupied with are not only positive yearnings; they are also essential to the proper conduct of life. Still, along the quest to whatever Man's chosen goal may be, it is imperative to fully adopt the following concept: **the fear of disloyalty to the inner entity and of denying its ambitions – which may cause the loss of self-identity and becoming eventually an unimportant cog in the system – should horrify the human being ten times as much as the apprehension of stumbling occasionally while following the** road he believes in. A person must trust in what he does during its duration.

The Portrait of the Emotions and Navigating for their Best – the Ultimate Extraction

The last two articles dealt with and discussed thoroughly – apart from spiritual needs including their evolvement and way of nourishment – also the main components which navigate Man's continuous dialogue with his internality. These actually contribute to a mortal's modus operandi, whose source lies within his superior analysis, judgment and control system: **common sense**. For the measure of monitoring the sentimental involvement in one's ability to research, infer and plan on the one hand, or to go on doing uncompromisingly, and react timely and correctly to the unexpected, on the other – is what defines the limits of the human capability to make an appropriate and proficient (or a wrong and failing...) use of his innate intellect, and thus set the degree of his success in life.

The following paragraphs deal with a kind of a "Meta-Ability" which determines the degree of **lordship wielded by the sentiments – in certain cases – over the intellect** of Man.

It seems that some chosen mental faculties, may, with proper fostering and precise application, improve the performance of human beings. Such modes of behavior – the majority of these are recommended in detail later on – point out in fact the tight links existing between the emotional and the rational plus their interchanging domination...

- **Suppression of inclinations for betterment:**
  The essence of self-control, being able to deny stimuli up to full detachment for a sublime goal.

- **Avoiding bad moods and their influence:**

    Silencing cognitive noises, which disrupt and divert attention from what is really important and hamper progress and efforts towards the chosen goal; abstaining from troublesome worries, which are self-fulfilling prophesies; and preventing fear from influencing, even undermining, the processes of thinking, discerning and judgment.

- **Thinking positively:**

    Not giving in to oppressive horrors, to defeatism or to depression in the face of difficult challenges. A constant struggle against panic from potential bitter failures.

- **Adopting an optimistic approach as the big catalyst:**

    Defending from indifference and melancholy by enhancing self-confidence, believing in the good – and removing any worry arising from thinking of the unpleasant uncertainty of the future.

In other words: all the above-said describes a cultured use of the soul's dictations, meaning emotional intra-personal intelligence at its best. This is the proficiency of controlling the relationships amongst the heart and the brain, outlining the skills on which are founded all aspects of natural insight. Such knowledge deeply influences all other human potentialities by either advancing or retarding their realization.

Now it remains, therefore, to understand how to yield the maximum from this enlightenment on the way to a specific target. Obviously it means attempting to enlist the full potential of human motivation at the right location and timing in order to achieve a marked aim; such an engagement of all particles of the inner drive is made of two main stages:

First and foremost, inviting all the mental resources, led from inside by the feelings – such as enthusiasm, fanaticism and an unlimited faith in the one's abilities – for no summit was ever conquered without those.

The other, focusing all these elements, attaching and uniting them into one piece; directing most of the attention, as concentrated as possible, towards the said goal, in order to reach and extract the highest peak of self-functioning throughout the execution.

The output of this physical or mental activity is described as **a flow**. A state of bliss, during which one achieves superiority, perfectionism, uniqueness – or any other fitting word – in spontaneous action. As a result of this the performances, whatever they are, turn out to be ideal – the ultimate; and when such a situation is "rolling" – just precisely at the moments of its happening – it keeps stimulating, overpowering and growing, until those involved in it are actually "exploding" while this occurs – and all of these from their personal evidence.

The ability to flow is the optimal employment of human emotional intelligence at its best. Such a scene "amazes the senses and enlightens the intellect" representing, perhaps, the entirety of the latest rage in recruiting the whole fabric of the feelings to the full service of the brainpower, while totally utilizing the synergy created by their combination. As a matter a fact, this is more than channeling of the complete inner motivating forces, but their acme, concentration and envelopment in the finest sensations, intended to spiritually prepare the operators according to the destination they wish to arrive at.

In order to back up the above-depicted argument and prove that it is more than a mere philosophical hyperbole, it suffices for the reader to search his memory for past events supportive of the aforementioned observation, and bring him immediately back to everyday reality. As proof, for example, he may consider **micro-flowing** – a less extravagant phenomenon than the one described in the previous paragraphs – namely a state that many people chance into occasionally and actually anyone can experience on a daily basis. An exceptional incident such as the last one is especially expressed while "streaming" above apparently insurmountable limits. There are plenty of samples of that, for instance: writing a very complicated analysis in amazingly fluent extraordinary language, a remarkably magnificent artistic or musical performance, a historical athletic attainment, perfectly leading a group of people in a life-or-death battle and surviving, etc. And it seems that the ecstasy of indulgence in love is its most perfect incarnation, in which two persons are carried away and sublimely become harmoniously one; therefore, it is no wonder that lovemaking is the epitome of superlative pleasure.

Therefore it is clear that this "flowing" is a wholly positive phenomenon, characterized by delight and uplift. Since it tastes so sweet, those under its spell are rewarded while it actually happens. So it is easily understandable that they are totally and thoroughly submerged up to their heads in what they are currently occupied with; while they are addicted to their doings to such a degree and so withdrawn, they lose any contact with time and space. Those who experience such situations refer to it as an "out-of-body" exercise: as if looking at a complete stranger, an unknown, in whatever takes place. Moreover; according to their testimonies, while being in such a transcendental state, one should avoid analyzing the condition, so as not to interrupt the flow of the perfect execution; he should just enter a sealed "bubble" and go on doing…

The most conspicuous example of the afore-depicted was experienced, perhaps, by Bob Beamon during his record-breaking long jump while participating in the Mexico City Olympic Games of 1968. Within six seconds, on October 18th that year, just nineteen long and furious strides on the acceleration track lifted him up like a bird, one meter and eighty centimeters (5.9 feet…) in the air, and eight meters ninety centimeters (29 feet & 2½ inches…) he landed, **setting a monumental world top score**. In a single eye-blink, during his first attempt (out of six that any contestant is entitled to…), at the right moment (an

Olympic final...) in perfect weather conditions (a spring day and the maximum assisting wind allowed by the rules – 2 meters per second...), at the accurate place (Mexico City is 2,411 meters – 7,350 feet – above sea level, enjoying thin air and low gravity...) and with a mind empty of anything but an ultimate concentration for the physical-mechanical mission ahead (such was his post facto testimony...) – that's all he needed to exchange near-total anonymity for eternal fame and a place in the pantheon of sport's greatest figures. Immediately after his enormous achievement, Beamon nonchalantly put on his tracksuit, left the field and disappeared – less unknown now, of course – into the dressing room, only to reappear and shine again as an unforgettable symbol of unprecedented human ability.

Of all the records set in all Olympic games previously, Beamon's is certainly the most unexpected – special, impressive and remembered – for the achievement embodied more than a conquest of an apparently unreachable summit, but a rare elation due to contact with such a sublime physical height, seeming impossible for any athlete at that time, especially bearing in mind that jumping records are normally broken by a quantum of a few centimeters. Taking into account, moreover, the hardships befalling his personal career prior to this jump: being an inconsistent track and field contestant; over-stepping most of his attempts; nearly missing qualifying for the American team because of the aforementioned; preparing, for the last two months before the games, on his own, having lost his coach due to incessant confrontations over the treatment of blacks in United States. On the eve of his record-breaking jump, he had to contend with losing his grant for the next year, after being involved in a campus brawl over racial issues. All of this, and he still succeeded in smashing his own best ever score by sixty-three centimeters (2 feet & 0.8 inches...) in his first attempt on that glorious day, setting a bar which was not surpassed for twenty-three years. This cannot be explained without taking the above-written about the flow as genuine and real.

The truth is that neither Beamon, nor any other new-age athlete succeeded in reproducing, or even getting close to, the above-described triumph.

In summation: the practical explanation for all this is derived, actually, from the divine excellence of human neurobiology, a kind of contiguity with a rare ultimate reality; while happening, it becomes the top of the tops. It is clear, therefore, that the know-how and the ability to **correlate its occurrence with the right time, exactly when one needs it; to excel at the specific destined moment; to reach inconceivable (almost surreal) heights within a fraction of a second – these are the ingredients of an authentic victory.**

Thus, in order to blossom and prosper, one must at least strive to attain the flow!

Furthermore, whoever wants to experience a vast success must practice reaching these powers of convergence and concentration, for this talent should not be left only for the few, just as most human beings, considering that they may have to confront very special situations, train and try to prepare themselves.

And the taste of a huge achievement is unknowable as long as one is marching toward it – unless he has actually reached the summit. However, one thing is undoubtedly clear: a great accomplishment changes Man's life to its very foundations (and just watching a moving Nobel Prize award ceremony for an exceptional scientific discovery, or looking at an Olympic champion tears flooded – a world-record holder – standing on the podium with a golden medal around his neck, while his country's national anthem is being played and its flag is waved high – suffice to make sense of what is praised above…).

For nothing is more successful then success itself…

January 1995

Smashing the Inhibitions

The Skeleton of the Concept

Although the method of mixing a correct personal blend of inner and outer activities has been meticulously described up to now, many are the cases when a person is still unsatisfied.

The question, therefore, is, why.

It seems that in spite of everything, there are, concurrently, some influential mental brakes, hampering Man from a truly positive thinking; a kind of "spiritual eclipse", so to say, preventing him from achieving the sought for progress. Such stoppages are expressed as **inner inhibitions**.

In contrast to the experience of negative feelings, a natural and healthy phenomenon (as mentioned in the chapter named "Acquiring the Demandable"…) warning a person "quietly" of an imminent undermining of his inside balance, the spiritual hold-ups are a wholly superfluous mechanism; a significant obstacle, "crying out loud" about the beginning of an internal collapse in fact, because they leave the individual strangled, held back, withdrawn and completely uncreative, since they block his access to whatever he plans to do and yearns for sincerely.

It must be said that the distinction between negative feelings and inner inhibitions is extremely important, because it points to the huge divide between the two, and moreover to the treatment methodology of each. These experiences are totally different in their characteristics and do not belong to the same category. Actually, the above-mentioned preventions "ruin the reputation" of the helpful senses. And this restraint is created, in fact, by fearing to express natural, although negatively connoted, sensations. The sole real value attached to the sighting of any restraint, is the knowledge that somewhere within a misstep has happened, the recognition that helps one understand how and where the lapse occurred and ascertains the direction in which a solution may be found.

The Cure

Here too, as in most other cases previously mentioned in this chapter, it is necessary to cite and diagnose the obstacles causing a spiritual obstruction; only subsequently, when their nature is clear, it is imperative to do the utmost to get rid of them totally.

The path towards removing these impediments starts with the awareness that the one "responsible" for their creation is the person afflicted himself. Knowing the formation of the inhibitions and their characteristics lays the groundwork for the process of subduing them.

Three alternatives are offered as solutions for such hindrances:

The first (and the most preferable, of course, as described later in detail related to each specific case...) is the use of sound logic. After grasping the destructive nature of these inhibitions, one understands their total redundancy. Then common sense must shake itself free from the temporary freeze, forced on it by the deep stagnation, serving as the first motivator of the awakening.

The second – supposedly "semi" spontaneous – is just to "let the brain" be led by the associated negative sentiments in their tendency, so to speak, toward the obstruction being dealt with, even if one is as mentally depressed as possible. This is because it is only normal for the victim of such delaying impulses to encounter them accompanied by and intertwined with very potent natural urges, such as: fear, panic, shame, frustration, etc. And there is no doubt that the intensity of these, when flooding a person – each on its own or all together – is so mightily dominant over the current arresting sensation, that it raises a reinforced activity within him, which in turn encourages him to take actions that would eventually cause an upheaval. In such a manner, the inhibition loses its force, weakens and slowly withers. All this is similar to the famous standard technique of the Eastern martial arts – defeating the adversary by actually turning his own energy against himself...

And the third is recommended if the previous two do not occur instinctively: using some artificial means. The basic method offered here is an exploitation of the "problem" so it will act to "eliminate" itself. How does one actually do it? **Self-conduct and discipline**: by simply "forcing the brain" to recall past events during which similar emotions regarding the obstacle encompassed the person; thinking about them while trying again and again to immerse in this state of mind, so that these sentiments increase and dominate the soul by their might, leading to a self-awakening and diverting the center of attention away from any destructive tendency, condemning it to oblivion.

Behavioral scientists normally point out a dozen inhibitions – sometimes mingled partly within each other and their boundaries seemingly blurred – although every one of them is a unique phenomenon; these may hinder achieving a personal success, or at least delay it. However, one thing must be obvious: every human being – and this is only natural – may be from time to time mired in the muddy states of mind hence described. But after blowing off steam and totally collapsing while experiencing them, one must stand up again, overcome the hurdle, look forward and move on.

The following are all the familiar inhibitions, their natures, influences and the ways of uprooting them.

- **Anxiety:** inner unrest as an outcome of deep pessimism and constant skepticism which may even paralyze a person.

  Such a phenomenon stems, usually, from a past horrifying event which was not properly taken care of; therefore, even potentially sleep-depriving nightmares are being experienced. This tendency – a partial result of a total loss of faith in the possibility that everything will finally resolve itself for the best – pushes to give up the readiness to take risks, minimizing the enjoyment of life. Recoiling from daring chances flattens the path of life, represses yearnings and limits creativity; in short, it hampers growth.

  The overall feeling is that of **collapse and sinking**.

  The Cure: it is permissible, even desirable from time to time, to let this freezing terror conquer the thoughts – but only for a short period. On the other hand, it is necessary to summon the kingdom of the common sense in its full might, to demolish anxiety and start planting the first kernels of optimism; and this may be achieved in two ways, as was earlier described in the present chapter:

  One – to recall intentionally past events, similar emotional storms and worries which ended well; then try to forcefully internalize the faith that all will "come out clean in the wash" this time too. The other – to prepare for the worst but to be mentally convinced in the personal abilities to confront the most horrible difficulties. Thus, in time learn to neutralize this depicted restlessness.

  The following are the sentiments which allow one to overcome this situation: **fear** combined with worry, pain, embarrassment and frustration.

- **Apathy:** a total indifference to everything around.

  This means a desertion of the natural motivation and the willpower to change things in order to acquire that which the heart longs for; taking the dictates of destiny as they are. A subconscious surrender to any minor difficulty encountered while striving for the goals, accompanied by an acceptance of the fact not to bother anymore for a higher summit is unreachable. This is actually an extinguishment of the inner fire; one avoids doing and sinks down to the loss of all significance and purpose in life.

The overall feeling is that of **total despair**.

The Cure: a fight to the bitter end for the abandonment of that careless unconcerned air encompassing all; engage in an all-out effort to change that perception by convincing the self that there is so much to lose, unless one pulls himself out from the shallow waters of apathy – and then, just tries to grab, literally, as much from life as possible, even the minutest pleasure. This must be done until a glimmer of hope appears and a rejuvenation of trust in personal faculties starts again. Only a rebuilding of confidence and meticulous nursing of the inner credit can conquer dullness, indifference and a paucity of initiative.

The following are the sentiments which allow one to overcome this situation: **sorrow** combined with disappointment, sadness, fear and frustration.

▶ **Confusion**: The inability to see clearly, to understand and interpret the true and pragmatic reality.

Such a state of mind occurs when instead of being constantly attentive and open minded, on the lookout for answers one after the other in a natural and logical order – one becomes impatient and desperate to find them all now, clearly and absolutely. When concentrating on an uncompromising – even hopeless – quest for the unknown and incomprehensible, there is a sense of an emotional vacuum and a feeling of being a victim of the circumstances and surroundings; then as fear takes control and the worst is expected – it is nearly impossible to act.

The overall feeling is that of **helplessness**.

The Cure: in order to effectively combat confusion it is important to inculcate the fact that life is a long and ongoing process, unfolding gradually in multiple layers and dimensions, accompanied by trial and error processes from which everyone might learn. This development allows for understanding the nature of existence, deciding which are going to be the future goals, and the ways and means to properly accomplish all of that.

However, sometimes one chances upon a cauldron of mysterious happenings which may repulse beyond the boundaries of reason. A bizarre timing of events, tragedies befalling the "Good" or an unexpected failure in an apparently promising situation – are raising inexplicable moral questions concerning the rewards of righteousness, as the subject was portrayed in Psalms 94, 3: "LORD, how long shall the wicked, how long shall the wicked triumph?"; and occasionally grave doubts arise about the principles of creation its purpose and its fundamental order. Except that these matters are beyond alteration, of course, and being troubled by them can only load the mind and soul with a heavy burden of unanswerable enigmas; but they seize huge amounts of energy for no good. Those efforts are better be employed to take care of everyday occurrences, absorbing the lessons to be learned and deploy the right applications as a reply; thus, in order to remain sane and continue doing whatever is necessary for the existence and progress.

And as for the anxieties of the unknown – perhaps it is, on the contrary, all for the best. Since Man, especially in such circumstances, feels the least safe, as if being, because of hardships, thrown like Joseph to the bottom of the pit, then he is willing and ready, normally under compulsion, to absorb any new thing; and in this condition, the aforementioned disadvantage turns into a significant benefit: he is ready now to draw the most difficult lessons and reach the boldest, most daring conclusions from all those negative experiences, which were his lot so far. And from now on he will have to gird his full willpower, to brace his spirit, to get up and rise again; and when one succeeds in conducting himself properly, he learns in fact to discover the full measure of the inner moral strength and his true competence; understanding that the hurdles in life are, actually, the weights to cultivate his mental muscles, that confronting the rough terrain of reality refines him, sowing the seeds of experience and knowledge that stand by him on the morrow and assist him in overcoming any future problems. This was accurately expressed by Rabbi Nahman of Bratslav in the late 18th century: "The whole world is a very narrow bridge, and the most important thing is not to be afraid...". The following are the sentiments which allow one to overcome this situation: **panic** combined with shame, embarrassment, sadness and frustration.

- **Dejection**: losing the ability to enjoy anything naturally, even the smallest things in life.

Women usually suffer from periods of such a state of mind from loneliness; men from loss of vitality and self-esteem – mostly when feeling subjectively still in their prime. The basic symptoms are: inner emptiness, diminished faith, lack of motivation, minimal willpower and a drop in the energy to perform.

The overall feeling is that of **abandonment**.

The Cure: taking into account that the problem here is a bad mood, something that nearly everyone feels and overcomes here and there in his routine existence (not clinical depression...), the way to repulse dejection is by being in the company of other people and finding new interests or activities in life; because in such a case, it becomes clear retroactively, that if a specific goal is totally unattainable, it probably does not befit one's personality and the circumstances or the location he finds himself in initially.

For example, a failure in a relationship should encourage Man to look elsewhere for love; it is forbidden to think limitedly that there is only one suitable match in the world – or, in general, a sole solution – to any daily problems that pop up. To wit, the real challenge lies in constantly making new acquaintances, finding additional potential resources and alternative means, and identifying fresh opportunities, in order to develop and set more appropriate targets; all this is so as not to be stranded in obstinacy or to get satisfaction from one source only.

The following are the sentiments which allow one to overcome this situation: **sadness** combined with panic, anger, sorrow and frustration.

- **Grudge**: latent hatred accompanied by deep anger over a perceived feeling of mistreatment.

This is the evolution of a very deep animosity toward someone who harmed the grudge-bearer severely in the past, until revenge became nearly the sole subject occupying the mind, consuming meanwhile most of his creativity potential. Hence, very little remains for other positive domains of life; the ability to bestow love and attention and to cherish family and friends disappears, while concurrently new opportunities for further development are missed. That is to say: the person remains nearly incapable of any activity besides investing in nourishing the said hostility. Furthermore, most people identify this tendency, which constantly transmits deep negativity all around.

The overall feeling is that of **being checked**.

The Cure: it is preferable to quit bearing a grudge, since this is one of the worst human urges at times, and it leads simply nowhere; and of all inhibitions – most of which are spontaneous and uncontrollable – this is precisely the one which might and should be dominated and kept at a distance from its very beginning, because it consumes vast amounts of essential vigor towards a clear dead end. And since each person is in possession of a limited quantity of inner energy, then allocating, so to say, a part of it to holding something against another is a total waste of fantastic resources diverted from the really important things.

Deliverance from "bitterness", in so many words, becomes straightforward from the moment it is recognized that it is not the cure for an injured spirit: that the mental damage caused by being enslaved to it is much graver then the marginal pleasure yielded by being vindicated upon the one that caused the hurt, because it keeps the grudge-bearer away from patterns intended to achieve self-satisfaction by the very fulfillment of wishes and the satiation of personal yearnings, the acquisition of which demands maximum devotion. Thus, only by the total abandonment of that resentment feeling, a tremendous relief can be accomplished. Or as Alexander Pope, the famous 15th century English poet, put it best in words: "To err – is human; to forgive – is divine; to bear grudge – is devilish…".

The following are the sentiments which allow one to overcome this situation: **jealousy** combined with panic, pain, anger and sorrow.

- **Guilt**: not absolving oneself for past mistakes.

Meaning the failure to forgive represses self-love. This continuous culpability suppresses self-esteem and the possibility to feel the natural innate innocence which mankind was born with. Feeling guilt thrusts many a man to extreme altruism – supererogatory over-doing for others – at the expense of satisfying his own needs, a situation which may be described as "Divine Hell"!

In such cases, it seems that the opinion of others carry more weight than self-appreciation. This phenomenon encourages excessive niceness and discomfort in refusing, actually, hindering one from demanding his due and self-satisfaction.

The overall feeling is that of **unworthiness**.

The Cure: it should be understood that a release from the bonds of guilt can only be achieved via a full grasp of the meaning of innocence. Man enters this world pure and clean in his desires, simply because he does not know otherwise; therefore, he enjoys a primordial credit and is worthy of love even while going astray here and there.

Cognizance of a wrong perpetrated does not require endless self blame or eternal shame. One may and should experience mistakes, then learn and do his best not to repeat them; then it is imperative to forgo this inhibition, move on and continue growing.

The following are the sentiments which allow one to overcome this situation: **shame** combined with worry, pain, anger and sorrow.

- **Hesitancy**: loss of the inner ability to make decisions.

The main reason for such insecurity comes from an accumulation of past painful events, the outcome of being hurt and betrayed, which leaves a heavy load of deep frustration and in particular of disappointment. Confronting the last two – among the most meaningful and influential negative sensations – does not alleviate, of course, the difficulty in decision-making process. The common symptoms are long pre-judgment deliberations, recoiling from responsibility, continuous consultations with others while choosing objectives in life, and the deferment of simple activities and a lack of diligence. Most importantly, instead of developing an inner creative power, hesitancy gives birth to banality and grayness, ensuring that in the best case a person reacts to events but never initiate them.

The overall feeling is that of **helplessness**.

The Cure: in order to fight hesitancy it is a must, first of all, to quit engaging compulsively past failures. Confidence in one's ability ought be rebuilt and strengthened. Self-assurance projects to the outside and creates trust among others.

Any kind of success demands constant decisions requiring moral strength. Not always there is a way to ascertain the correctness of a choice made – but erring is always better than not trying at all, since he who does not reflect makes no mistakes. A commitment to an aim is the first essential step in mobilizing the energy to rise up to the challenge; it is preferable to plan grandiosely and to somewhat retreat later than to do nothing. However, in case of a real confusion, it is healthier to take care, first and foremost, of the obstacles that prevent the ability to decide, and only afterwards to re-confront the essence of the relevant resolution.

The following are the sentiments which allow one to overcome this situation: **disappointment** combined with shame, worry, confusion and fear.

▸ **Judgment**: being hypercritical of defects in others and in the circumstances due to arrogance, over-rigidity or extroversion of personal problems.

Criticizing another person with the sole purpose of exposing his weaknesses and insinuating his ignorance – without contributing anything to better the subject – is pure pettiness and leads nowhere besides confrontation. True, an observant eye, able to detect real defects, may considerably assist in increasing efficiency, but it is useless if those standing behind it cannot mentally elevate themselves and know what's what. They must draw a line between important, principle issues related to the matter under consideration, and ancillary, marginal things, irrelevant to the diagnosis they are supposed to carry out. And if their remarks are essentially unfocused, and their content inappropriate, it is a huge waste of time and energy, either unnecessary or impossible to alter. And investing in a side channel, as is already known, always detracts from the power intended for the main path; besides, over-criticizing is sometimes akin to trying to apply subjective criteria to others, the kind of which nobody should even accommodate, and trying to enforce them is considered bad behavior as well; but they are thrown in the air just to be heard, perhaps as a means of self-aggrandizing while diminishing one's fellow-man. Then it is execrably interpreted and reduces effectiveness instead of augmenting it.

Sometimes, a fixation on an unchangeable topic compensates for a different symptom, which is the real problem. For example: picking on another Man's feebleness may stem from acute high self-displeasure; namely, a dislike of what one sees in the mirror. Hence, it is easier and more comfortable to disapprove someone else (which, by the way, represents what the Babylonian Talmud says: "Whoever calls his fellow-man unfit is unfit himself…").

To sum up, it is clear that insisting on exposing in public the other's defects may ironically obstruct the fulfillment of one's wishes. Those condemning rich people and their money, for instance, are blocking themselves, of course, from wealth. A person must practice what he preaches.

The overall feeling is that of **a lack of self-confidence**.

The Cure: in order to quit being constantly judgmental of someone else, it is strongly suggested to point directly at what really is the personal trouble and treat it. A meticulous, sober, inner examination and a correction of the deficiency – while avoiding the externalization of private faults and sticking them to others – is the solution to the problem.

Two modes of behavior are highly recommended:

First and foremost, it is preferable to stay away as much as possible from trying to educate fellow men by personal standards, for none guaranties their superiority.

Additionally, self-marketing should concentrate on emphasizing one's value – main traits, relevant performance, considerable achievements etc. – not by a disreputable comparison of his own advantages to others' shortcomings.

The following are the sentiments which allow one to overcome this situation: **frustration** combined with disappointment, anger, fear and jealousy.

- **Perfectionism**: striving to be perfect in all aspects of life.

  A behavior leading to such an aspiration is considered, in some way, a sickness. The strong compulsive yearning of various people to be unblemished, to always please themselves (sometimes even the others…) is not only a false inhuman inner dictate, but also gives birth to two unprofitable phenomena:

  The one – a waste of energy on marginal practical results, with minimum contribution to the final outcome, consuming considerable efforts and time.

  The other – which is worse – a delay of any progress, in fact, for fear that surely there is still little more to do before going on.

  This attitude, for example, dictates one-hundred-percent effectiveness at the present stage as a precondition for moving forward. Investing in ultimate excellence may become an "asymptotic" war of attrition, driving eventually to total exhaustion. Concurrently, perfectionism also prevents, for instance, simultaneous progress on several lines and improvising in order to improve processes and gain efficiency as required, on an almost daily basis.

  Moreover, this general outlook ensures the opposite result. Since a person crafts for himself benchmarks too high to be achieved in reality, disappointments follows a lack of accomplishment, even leading to an inferiority complex. Thus it happens that such people – even though very talented and highly successful in the past – are forever frustrated and not good enough in their own eyes, even failures, being de-facto afraid to advance. And as a paraphrase to Augustine's (the Cristian philosopher theologian of the 5th century…) humorous dictum concerning creation: "What did God do after completing the arrangement of heaven and earth? He prepared hell for the perfectionists…".

  The overall feeling is that of **dissatisfaction with the self**.

  The Cure: In order to somehow give up perfectionism, one must fully internalize that nothing in reality is ideal and exemplary. It is absolutely natural and healthy to wish for development and improvement in all aspects, but dangerous to strive for divine and uncompromising perfectness, an unachievable aim, turning those chasing it into possessed and restless persons forever. Understanding that everything in the world is, generally, "fluid" and mistakes now and then are human – as long as their lessons are learnt for the intention to avoid repeating them – brings one halfway to freedom from such a pedant, ascetic and impractical mode of behavior. And then, after making peace internally, one accepts what is and finds out how to turn an error or a malfunction into the first step in self-upgrading, converting a negative occurrence into a positive experience, leading eventually to excellence. Perhaps it is best to adopt the saying: "In life, quietude is better than quintessence…".

The following are the sentiments which allow one to overcome this situation: **confusion** combined with disappointment, panic, worry and jealousy.

▸ **Recrimination**: laying the responsibility for any failure on others.

Sticking to such a stance means giving up the ability to recover from misery. This is actually an expression of an indisposition to commit to what is happening in life and a great hesitation; in parallel, to making any real changes in them. An attitude like this reveals a hidden dependence on another person, abdicating one's control over his destiny to the mercy of someone else and a total cessation of self-initiative.

The overall feeling is that of **being betrayed.**

The Cure: first of all it, must be internalized that everyone is personally responsible for what is happening to him, and it is better to quit ascribing all individual hardships to external factors. Second, it ought to be learned to forgive – especially those who sinned by mistake – because the urge to blame is naturally negative, by warding off love and pressing to punish, while the tendency to excuse and make peace augments positive thinking, strengthens creativity, and mainly assists in maintaining good relationships even with those who occasionally hurt others unintentionally.

And in the case of someone who harms his fellow-man willfully, forgiveness does not necessarily indicate a different attitude towards him, but certainly assists in dulling and removing the pain. Except one should then take great care in avoiding that person, in order to prevent a repetition of the previous "damage".

In general, there is nothing wrong with recriminating – as long as it does not serve solely as a cover for escaping self-responsibility – but as an expression of sincere criticism and a fair representation of the external reasons for failure, pain and disappointment; but as soon as the real argument is made totally clear, and what should be done to overcome the obstacle is understood, one should leave behind the tendency to blame others all the time.

The following are the sentiments which allow one to overcome this situation: **rage** combined with disappointment, pain, sorrow and jealousy.

▶ **Self-Pity**: a feeling of endless wretchedness leading to squalor.

Such a sinking might be derived from two cardinal reasons:

The first – out of an unwillingness to tackle difficult situations, occurring as the outcome of an ascetic propensity to belittle past personal successes, resulting in a very low esteem regarding one's true capabilities.

The second – because of an inclination to attract the attention of relatives, relating to whom a dependency was developed, or that of loved and admired personages who hurt one in the past and are currently ignoring him.

This phenomenon may spring from each or both of these above causes.

In this situation, there is a continuous deterioration, instead of trying to draw encouragement and satisfaction from what was already achieved and develop some optimism vis-à-vis the future. Choosing to go on wallowing in the mire of such a wretched and poor temperament – whether out of insecurity or from piteousness – increases depression and prevents trying to escape from the present condition. So it happens that repeatedly one misses new daily opportunities to observe curiously, to look around, to rise and start moving forward. All this is because of an unwillingness, a lack of interest or even out of an expectation that somebody else will take the entire responsibility upon himself, which ultimately brings one to a total neutralization.

The overall feeling is that of **total misery.**

The Cure: in order to avoid self-pity it is imperative to renew belief in the "self", in its energy and competence. It is allowable to agonize over past failures and misses; however, under no circumstances should a person overrate and over-dramatize them, and then be drawn into deep despair, from which it is nearly impossible to recover. It is also absolutely forbidden to develop a dependency on somebody else or on a sole alternative, in the wrong belief that no other would come to the rescue when needed, and direct all inner activities in accordance with these. It must be remembered that there are many options waiting just around the corner; that it requires only the will to look for those – and then just to stretch out one's hand and pluck them.

And if injury and disregard are behind this inhibition, after being released from this pathetic mood, one ought to pardon all these responsible by transcending and pitying their shameful culture of behavior. Then, the obstacle will totally disappear.

The following are the sentiments which allow one to overcome this situation: **pain** combined with shame, sorrow, fear and jealousy.

- **Tarrying**: delaying or postponement of action, fearing unpreparedness.

This is a clear sign of disbelief in one's capabilities, occurring when there is simply a lack of courage to confront what is being perceived, apparently, as a hindrance, a drift explicitly blocking action.

The overall feeling is that of **stagnation.**

The Cure: knowing that this spirit is forged by facing more and more challenges and by learning to cope with crises – it is absolutely recommended to repel tarrying by deciding to start acting; otherwise nothing will be ever doable. It is possible to draw energy by internalizing the fact that the pain caused by giving up wishes and plans is sevenfold greater than the shame due to failure which one strives to avoid. It is also worthwhile remembering that no matter how thoroughly one prepares, there is always trepidation preceding the actual execution. Moreover, it will start disappearing immediately, with the first small step of the active journey.

And here it is desirable to inculcate that in aggregate, in most cases, latching on to the status quo, sticking to stagnation, and choosing to freeze – actually doing nothing at all – were and are among hope's worst lethal enemies: they kill all desires for a better tomorrow and the willingness to develop and progress, for that matter.

The following are the sentiments which allow one to overcome this situation: **worry** combined with panic, shame, embarrassment and sorrow.

And in summation, it is imperative to remember, that everything one tries obstinately to revolt against will certainly come; it is a lost battle from the beginning, holding in store – a common ingredient of all efforts to renounce totally the existence of inhibitions – a terrible loss of time and energy. Therefore it is recommended, when one feels hampered, to go with the flow of the feelings accompanying these impediments, in order to rid himself of the problem, instead of sweeping it under the carpet. And the main motif of all curing methodologies described above is the **rebuilding of self-confidence**; refreshing of personal credit. What this means, actually, is that the **recollection of past achievements is the cardinal basis for attaining future triumphs.**

Overcoming these obstructions not only allows for the enjoyment of external success – it assists also in attaching to the real inside "I"; thus gaining inner tranquility, love, joy – and most importantly, creative energy and confidence in execution. And after learning to experience all these, it is definitely possible to concentrate on doing what one really loves and accomplish very efficiently the most cherished aspiration – all this **without giving up, even for a moment, one's identity and its essence**.

October 1996

The Purpose of this Cogitation
Interim Conclusion

The ideas presented so far in this treatise are offered as an answer to the main question: **how should Man manage his life in order to yield the best results throughout his entire existence?** Assuming that he wishes to control them as much as possible – while not being dragged by the casual changes of destiny, luck's solemn cousin (for it is harder for him to lose in a game whose rules are set by himself...). Ironically, the biggest freedom given to mankind is the choice not to decide upon their fate, and usually not to initiate too much regarding it. There is no greater comfort than flowing with the tide and being constantly directed by others, without being forced to make tough decisions and clearly determine things ahead; than the simplicity inherent in doing precisely what one is told – neither more nor less. And such liberty is bestowed on everybody from his day of birth, actually offered to him on a silver platter, and many are the fools who are tempted to grab it too quickly; those willing to walk trough their days on earth like in a game of dice – being haphazardly thrown by somebody else – randomly fixing their future; They are happy to be stupidly tugged along; instead of directing – being directed; in lieu of leading their affairs – being led by them.

Hence, the essential message so far is that only he who would do well in navigating the coincidences offered by life and in channeling them at will may achieve longed-for success, finding the way to **design his destiny – rather than blindly obeying its commands**, as in a Greek tragedy. For it is imperative to admit that Man cannot rule fortune, but it is definitely appropriate for him to do the best to control its elusiveness. Even after recognizing the immutability of the facts, it is always possible to change the individual's attitude regarding their very being, the mode of reacting to them and what might be driven by this actuality. Because there is no doubt that any person would greatly improve the control over his life if he would be the one deciding on his own criteria...

In other words: Man should never give up and has to think and act forever in that vein. Even in times of awful fear, on the verge of helplessness – when push really comes to shove – precisely at these moments, he must not bend and capitulate. It is vital to continue trying until a proper solution is found. And just then, at gunpoint, the brain must doubly strive to be sharp and keen — to display resourcefulness: inventiveness, coordination and practical wisdom at its best. For nothing ends until the last moment, and one ought to go on believing with all his heart that he must "never say never..."

The message, derived from everything depicted in this present tractate up to now emphasizes, already here and now, the following three essential conclusions – even though we are only midway through the book:

▸ The human mosaic, being so intricate and complicated, requires much wisdom, rich experience and strong willpower in order to overcome the hurdles of self-management and conduct. Otherwise, it may easily become a very deadly weapon, especially because of its weak spots, as has been known since Noah's time (Gen. 8:21): "The intention of man's heart [in most cases...] is evil from his youth...".

▸ The methodology and techniques of correctly dealing with life and its unexpected occurrences are based on the development of inner and interpersonal emotional intelligence, its nourishment, augmentation and integration in all processes dictated by common sense and intellect.

▸ There is no other way to achieve full personal success than by balancing the inner and outer worlds – despite the essential difference between these two components of life; and the more this equilibrium gains in strength, the greater is the potential for thriving and flourishing.

And in summation

The present text does not pretend to change the outer world, for there is no enemy "outdoors". The truly crucial battlefield is within the hidden inner reaches of Man alone. Awareness of the problem brings Man at least halfway to solving it; **thus consciousness must guide the soul and the brain has to teach the heart and body**. All this is true despite the fact that one needs the other; therefore there should be among them a full cohesion and a mutually beneficial fertilization.

As for the implementation, there is one general rule: even though the entire written content so far is divided into chapters ordered in some logical sequence, it should be remembered that life is a different story; human activity as a whole is based on warp and woof – a little bit of this and some of that – and there is no dictated recipe of detailed quantities and timing, but an interweaving of appropriate dynamics, spiritual and physical actions precisely required in the current situation. And the most important is to deeply internalize the fact that once a road is chosen – there is a difference, quite often, between getting to know it and actually walking its length. This is because the way is straighter and sounder than those pacing its paths...

And there is no better way to wrap up this interim conclusion than by offering ten sort of **key axioms**, able to serve as guideposts or warning signs. They are connected to the kaleidoscope of life and the techniques required for the control and direction necessary to manage it:

The first: It is true that life takes precedence over quality of life; however, if one is destined to struggle down its path, it is always better to squeeze out the best of those opportunities he runs into. Since Man's years on earth are numbered and nobody lives forever – not to mention the fact that according to some beliefs life is a circle, beginning and ending at the same point – it is a must to strive to derive from one's time in this world as much interest, excitement and benefit as possible. While it is limited, it is definitely preferable to exploit it and to be extremely happy, to avoid wasting it complaining and whining. Metaphorically, to try and live each day twice...

The second: It is common to think that he who hits rock bottom is immune from further falling; but it must be remembered that there is always a pit deeper than the present one...

The third: No state is worse than feeling unneeded and inconsequential in daily life. It is analogous to treading the path of existence purposeless and bored, desperately trying to send raindrops back to the cloud from which they fell. Realizing that one is wanted and can contribute to someone or something – especially while advancing in years – is worth the whole universe...

The fourth: Success resembles a football: one chases the thing in the game, untiringly doing his best to grab it. However, contrary to what is happening on the pitch, in life, when achieving a triumph and grasping it, one must be very careful not to kick it away...

The fifth: Self-discovery is the best realization in people's endless daily race (that is why they are, probably, named the Human race...). Some embellish their curriculum vitae with special and distinguished positions in order to gain a more comfortable and rewarding job. However, due to lack of openness or readiness at all – or perhaps just fearing to disrupt their comfortable gray routine – they avoid thinking deeply, researching and making sure that the path on which they are walking is the correct one for them, cheating themselves instead, thinking that this is the only way to pass a peaceful day. But the moment arrives when these lies fail and collapse; one morning those creatures wake up just like that to a reality, in which they find that despite their vast worldwide toil and rich experience – built and bought through many years of blood, sweat and tears – there is no link, whatsoever, between their actual occupation and their desired one…

And without disregarding, even for a little bit, the spectrum of performance and the importance of acquired know-how and skills, it is necessary to halt once in a while the obsessive and depressed march towards the objectives defined by momentum. One must look inside the essence of his actions and find out the measure of satisfaction derived from them – lest it be discovered that this is a race on the wrong track. Even though the conclusion of that investigation may cause a total turnover, it may lead, eventually, to self-contentment and real pleasure in life.

The sixth: Amid the pressure and noise of climbing up the route to the top, some relaxation from the constant focus is due, in order to allow the obvious, simplest human needs to take control of body and soul. That is why it is recommended to consciously deviate occasionally from the rigid and ascetic regime constantly forced on the spirit, according to the old Japanese proverb: "Even fish cannot always live in clear water…". And if actions are dictated by choice – than he who decides stands above the afore-said "rat race", not out of it…

The seventh: Any theory, convincing as it may be, requires personal substantiation and examination. It is always prohibited to accept things at face value, like a written law from Mount Sinai. Or according to the Buddha: "Believe nothing, no matter where you read it or who said it, even if I did; pay no mind if I have said it, unless it agrees with your own reason and personal common sense…". For questioning the truth just buttresses it, in fact. Albert Einstein expressed it bluntly and in a more penetrating way: "Blind faith in authority is the greatest enemy of truth…". Or to quote Socrates' general opinion about the above matter: "The unexamined life is not worth living…". Because "all men by nature desire knowledge…". as Aristotle argued in an even broader context…

The eighth: It is permissible, even highly suggested, to fly as high as possible on the wings of vision, fantasy and inspiration; poetically, "The future belongs to those who believe in the beauty of their dreams…". For the real power, actual changes in patterns of conduct and management stagnated by paradigms and axioms are born and grow from yearnings and wishes of the heart. But, in order to avoid disappointments which might accompany a sense of failing to live up to expectations, one thing should be remembered: the true space of freedom enabling execution is identical, at the end of the day, to the length of the rope stretched out from imagination to reality…

The ninth: It is essential to devote means to the "maintenance of the self", namely to take initiated, disciplined and ordered care of the four dimensions concerning the human machine: the intellectual, emotional, social and physical, like any other technological array or system. The routine might be boring from time to time; it may seem like a real bother producing no immediate benefits, the allocation of time for which requires all of the willpower – but it is indispensable for being in the perfect fitness in all measurements, a precondition for achieving life's goals, for producing the best out of their conduct and enjoying them in the most proper way. Because there is no greater betrayal than the disloyalty of the body to the spirit's dictates, and vice versa, one that expresses in the most woeful way the lament of human mortality. In other words, Man should appreciate his being alive and healthy in all aspects! For all the rest can be bought with money (if there is enough…), and these are indeed just marginal items…

The tenth and last, combining, in a way, all the previous ones is the following: The key to success of any kind lies, to begin with, in Man acting by himself and for himself; applying the maximum of his wisdom, skills and desire to attain his wishes. "If I am not for myself – who is for me?" the Jewish sage Hillel taught generations ago. Or as an old African proverb ironically warns: "Each one should blow his own horn (or Vuvuzela…) – for all the others are busy playing their personal trumpets…".

And perhaps it is most proper to end this present tractate, including the afore-mentioned sayings and advice, with Rabbi Arie Levine's meaningful moral answer to his disciples, who approached their spiritual leader to play a trick on him, trying to test his ancient wisdom. One student held a butterfly in his hand and asked the honorable teacher if the creature was alive or dead. If the rabbi had said alive, he would crush it; if the rabbi had said dead, he would have set it free. The sage outwitted them by reply: **"The thing is in your hands…"**.

September 1998

> *Second Treatise*

Guiding the Own Life and Leading Others – The Outcome Starts with Thinking First

I believe that the most appropriate way to live is by constantly seeking to better ourselves...

Socrates, 5th century B.C.

Opening

Now, when it seems that there are sufficient tools to determine how to run one's private life, and what should be, especially, his daily inner manners – having reached the midpoint of the quest which takes him to an overall personal success – it seems possible to embark, with a shaped soul and a stabilized spirit, on the second part of the mission: outlining the right path to external material achievements. In other words: how should he confront the challenge of guiding other people to set procedures in motion, running businesses and leading various organizations to economic and physical growth and prosperity – while maintaining his own interior reality, pleased with the mode of action and style of accomplishment at all times, and be fully self-satisfied with the road taken to attain the longed-for outcomes.

And if there is, already, a status in which the soul is functioning in a right and desirable form, it would be a pity not to seize this opportunity and fulfill what is by now necessary, in order to achieve the afore-mentioned materialistic success in a practical, calculated and proper approach.

That is why two important issues require the reader's full attention.

First and foremost: the essential management ingredients of any given assignment and its characteristics are mostly a built-in thing; and when these are coupled with qualities of personal leadership, with which Men were graced by nature, it is definitely possible to acquire those elements, to understand how to grow with them and to perceive in which way to implement them optimized. Indeed the observations, ideas, exertions, conclusions and advice described henceforth in this essay are a selection of fundamental principles and tenets pertaining to the guiding policies and doctrines of productive systems and organizations of all types and their pattern of carrying out their missions; an impartation of insight capabilities serving the deployment and execution of management at all levels and activities having to do with the above-described in general and its interpersonal angles specifically. However, these aspects relate purely to the leader and to how they are seen thru his eyes only; those depending on and influenced merely by him – implicitly or explicitly – and demanding the framing of strategies, proper solely from his point of view. Furthermore, a "productive entity", having to do with the afore-depicted may be a government, a corporation, a factory, a non-governmental organization (NGO), an association, an enterprise, a project, et cetera – as long as it is creative and prolific – and definitely life itself, of course.

And the second concern which calls for the reader's full focus is the fact that since the entire above-captioned subject is extremely kaleidoscopic and immensely complicated, it appears to be more like many thousands of islands of knowledge and proficiency in the midst of a vast sea of ignorance. And the concealed is ten times greater than what is known.

Therefore, the text from now on strives to introduce the entire components and secrets comprising all attributes of people's leadership and organizations' management; serving as a guide – a manual, comprehensive as well as concentrated – for any and all intending to immerse themselves in this spoken field. And the following presentation tries to emphasize, as much as possible, everlasting principles – rather than ephemeral theories and transient methods that alternate from time to time (although it is recommended to read and learn those continually too…) – so as to sift the chaff from the ever-so-abundant, overflowing wheat.

And the cardinal message inundating the upcoming treatise is thundering, penetrating, sharp and clear: **thinking of the end is a must before any beginning.**

April 1995

Definitions

The following terms are interwoven in the forthcoming material. Since they are rather complicated and their definitions are not always uniform and sufficiently known to all, they will be presented here and now in their most general senses, in order to establish a common language between the text and its future readers.

Vision: A very general idea, encompassing an ideal description of things intended to change and improve for a better future (the depicted notion can occasionally be "larger than life" – but never out or beyond it…). This is a concrete yearning which one intends and prepares to really achieve (otherwise it becomes another unrealistic dream; an illusion; a farfetched hallucination…).

Policy: The way of conducting, leading and putting certain things into practice.

Strategy: Planning, directing and combining the entire range of actions and performances – either politically, economically or military – in order to achieve a certain declared objective.

Tactics: The principles of preparing, organizing, operating, executing (including trickery / cunning...) and all means – as well as their implementation – used to attain a known end. This is the pragmatic aspect of "Strategy" which deals with its carrying out.

Operation: The execution itself (exercising in fact all three former terms, in any kind of activity...).

Philosophy: The intellectual theoretical ingredients and scientific methods – the methodology – of investigating any specific domain. Figuratively: logic, sophistry, outwitting, quibbling, and hatching.

Goal: (Or **"Purpose"** as it is identified in certain formations...) a specific and clearly defined aim, relating to an explicit plan and set in terms of accurately measured time, extent and location (a marked and stated outcome...).

Mission: A practical assignment, quantifiable and facilitating a calibrated measurement and examination of progress to the goal (a defined, given job...).

And the next idioms were put also under this chapter, since they will appear repeatedly throughout the entire text. However, they might come across too in the various terms – separate or combined – as hereunder:

Organization: An association of individuals linked to an external environment, who share a common purpose (with business, financial, industrious, voluntary, military, et cetera orientations and tendencies...) – united in order to focus all their multifarious talents and bring together the collectively available skills, dexterities and resources to achieve specific, declared and delineated targets. May refer also to: communal productive group / society / entity / body / unit; conglomerate, establishment, institute, association, enterprise, corporation, corporate, concern, company, firm, business.

Management: The function in any organization that coordinates the entire efforts of people to accomplish goals and objectives using available resources, efficiently and effectively.
Can be defined in addition as: directing, administrating, supervision and controlling activities; planning, designing, organizing and executing actions; leadership, direction, guidance, headship, governance, running.

Manager: Someone who is in charge of an organization and runs its total performance in all layers and disciplines.
All other phrases mentioned as: leader, boss, chief, principal, director, executive, man / person at the top, man / person in charge, superior, decision-maker, policy-maker, individual in command.

Domain: All terms such as space, sector, front, dimension, plane, field, sphere, profession, branch, subject or interest.

Product: A deliverable (or set of deliverables…) item that ideally satisfies a market's want or need and contributes to a business solution.
Might be expressed too as: produce, merchandise, commodity, goods, services, yield, harvest, crop.

Production: The outline act of making goods and / or rendering services of any kind of organization: May refer also to: manufacture, fabrication, extraction, construction, creation, assembly line, erection process result.

Organizations – Characteristics, Structures and Processes

Generally it can be said that nearly all organizations described from now on are characterized by one of the two main motives of their establishment:

▸ **Producing Units** – to manufacture clear and well-defined products.

▸ **Service Providing Units** – to supply all services needed inside and outside their framework and supporting its main outcome.

The common denominator of all these systems is that their "harvest", in any case, are meant to benefit their owners, members, customers, society, the environment and even the government, and they continue to be driven in accordance with the income they can yield from functioning compared to the cost consuming needed to go on doing so. However, there is a significant difference of conduct between those two types of organizations: while the one concentrates in crafts, activities or processes vital to **production** – the other coordinates mutual labor **around** created merchandise, services or markets having the same characteristics. In most settings, small as well as large, these two operating schools are combined in order to possess, ultimately, an optimal effect resulting in the highest possible output; and so it happens that the daily routine occupation blurs, sometimes, the borders between the two above-defined types of creative bodies.

From here the organization advances to the next steps of its establishment, direction and conduct.

1. Defining the Purpose: noting the main motivation for all activities based on and dictated by the founders' vision and describing the criteria by which it can be continued.

2. **Detailing the Goals, Intentions and Missions:** broadening the purpose by clarifying the specifics being deriven from it.

3. **Setting the Strategy:** recapitulation of the planning, the direction and the totality of activities – while gearing all methods of execution in order to achieve the set target.

4. **Deployment of the Planning:** presenting a detailed scheme of carrying out the strategy.

While all the stages described above will be widely explained in future chapters, the present article discussing organizational characteristics, structures and processes is meant to present an array enabling a proper response to all of them.

The fifth stage is intended exactly for that purpose: an **organizational structural definition**; explaining the platform by which a cooperated body may materialize the required business processes needed to implement its strategy in order to fulfill its missions. In other words: this is a driven process delineating the collective institute's organogram portraying its different units and hierarchy; describing in detail responsibilities and occupational domains of all individuals and groups in its various mechanisms; presenting all patterns of communication within it; and ensuring daily monitoring and auditing of the plans' execution in accordance with the climate which it operates in, allowing achievement of its designated objectives.

Setting an organizational structure can be based on the firm's:

- ✓ Functionality.
- ✓ Specialization.
- ✓ Processes.
- ✓ Products.

- ✓ Regions.
- ✓ Customers.
- ✓ Autonomous cells.
- ✓ Matrixes.

Some of these perceptions are dated and some very innovative, each having its own advantages and drawbacks, of course. Therefore the recommended array is a combination of all these insites, adapted, ultimately, to the uniqueness of each unit's activity.

Operating organizations are normally founded on a systematic and prearranged **division of labor** among their units. Dividing the responsibilities and sharing the load is intended to maximize the performance of all operations required in big and complicated systems, to the extent of accomplishing the defined aims. Such an arrangement bestows on the collective body an advantage over the activities of standalone operatives or of casual socioeconomic associations.

Work distribution, in its different forms, is the outcome of two processes:

- **Differentiation**: meaning, in the first stage, dismantling each task to its primary sections and consigning them to the right hands; these are attached, according to their roles, to specific teams.

- **Integration**: meaning the attachment of all particular designations and different units, as well as their coordinated and controlled activation by appropriately ranked managers. That is, after separating the various assignments, they are all combined with the right timing into one systematic wholeness.

And the work itself is performed by two principles: **simplification and specialization.**

The first – developing simple methods for executing different tasks, without necessitating previous education and studies; this work can be carried out by laborers, very skilled perhaps, but not categorized as specialists in the specific job.

The second – devising more complicated occupations, requiring training, specializations and unique skills.

Accordingly two types of functions are created.

The Random: required by mere managerial calls – such as appointing ad-hoc persons in charge of temporary assignments, incidental observations attached to the mainline work process dealing with the organization's central aim. Mostly these will be simple tasks, appended to the routine mission of the individual responsible for them, who will acquire the necessary skills through on-the-job training (**OJT**).

The Designated: those guided by the organization's policy, derived from its lasting professional occupation. Therefore, the ones performing them – the mainstays of the company – must be proficiently skilled, for the quality of the product is depended on them. Mainly they are required to continue expanding their knowledge while on the job, up to and including specialization in their functions. Such studies are conducted out of the workplace, mostly in between peaks of activity.

The practical test of the afore-said systematic structural correctness is measured by the accord of their characteristics to the conditions in which they function. There is neither good, nor bad, managerial configuration. Each format is examined, at the end of the day, by two separate parameters, which must exist simultaneously. What they have in common is the range of flexibility which they permit.

The one – to what degree does the organizational structure assist the company in executing its mission with maximum efficiency and purposefulness. What is the correct dosage of each ingredient in the mixture of all different perceptions, which would direct the distribution of total labor into specific assignments and tasks, while insuring later on **their best combination and the easiest union of**

the activities into an augmented common product.

The other – how flexible is the proposed array of **proper and quick reactions** to changes occurring within the environment in which it operates.

The outlook described here perceives, therefore, the said entities as open systems, continually reciprocating with the environment in which they function, and the business climate in which they activate. Accordingly, their operators take inner steps to prepare for changes, pressures, stresses, or any other surprise, caused by transformations that may occur generally in peripheral, exogenous commercial situations. This means readiness for:

- **Absorbing business shocks.**
- **Balancing operational versus surroundings demands.**
- **Forecasting changes of all kinds.**
- **Rationing products' supply.**

These measures – if improperly taken – may disrupt manufacturing and distribution of the product.

Based on this viewpoint, big and well-established companies can take initiatives allowing them to choose a comfortable business environment, to influence its behavior, sometimes even to create it. And if until recently not much consideration was given to an organization's living and operating space, nowadays it is regarded as one of the crucial factors outlining their path of action – exactly as water is to fish.

However, the **true, supreme test** of organizations is in their **continuity**, those who will stay alive as long as there is a demand for their product or service. That is why these entities will do their utmost to ensure their survival for as long as possible. To succeed in carrying on they are required to prove constantly their ability to supply a real need, so the proof actually depends on the goals which the members of the public surrounding them and involved in their performance set and intend to achieve.

There is some variation in the types of targets by which the "success" of an organization may be measured, and it is not always easy to gauge and appreciate how achievement-oriented they are, because the benchmark of each differs greatly from that of the others.

- **The target approach** is based on the idea that each organization has predetermined goals. They are defined, agreed upon and easily identifiable. Therefore, the outcome is expressed by the measure of their attainment and materialization.

- **The resources approach** postulates that corporations may survive only by assuring themselves the necessary resources. Hence, the bottom line is judged by the capability to aggregate most of the assets needed for their functioning.

- **The beneficiary approach** relays on the opinion that companies are arenas of contention over benefits among different interest groups. So the total is assessed by the possibility to respond to the demands of investors – often contradictory – desiring each to be the main beneficiary and to supply them with fair returns relative to their contributions or efforts.

- **The values approach** claims that each business outfit is controlled by a set of accepted human and professional values, reflecting the beliefs, preferences and behavior patterns according to which it operates and exists. Thus its output is rated according to its success in fulfilling the social and ideological aspirations of its managers and operators.

All these conceptions actually share a common enough perception: reaching the declared targets set from the beginning. But it should be always remembered that organizational success depends, first of all, on a hidden factor, not sufficiently emphasized in the above-depicted definitions as they are detailed: the degree of harmony between the system's characteristics and the delineation of the environment in which it exists and operates.

Organizational success may be compared to four linked rings. Within a great circle, marking the perimeter of the **survival** ability, are three smaller orbs, indicating the degrees of **purposefulness, effectiveness** and **institutionalization**, all contributing to, or diminishing the achievements of the productive body. These three are interlinked and partly overlapping, and all are very significant factors of success; the more area they cover the larger is the circle surrounding them. In other words, the well-being and prosperity of the company grows as well.

Thus, the orbs of purposefulness and effectiveness reflect the rational aspect of success, while assimilation and absorption within the community emphasize the company's emotional and symbolic values, expressed in hard-to-measure effects: prestige, reputation, appreciation, justification, et cetera; for the ability of an organization to integrate itself within its surroundings and enjoy its support may sometimes be the one and only reason for its continued existence – even if its financial results are very poor. Darwinists explain such a dynamic, by the principle that survivors are not necessarily the strongest, but those first to adapt to reality. And general settling in within communal life is so important, that it is even recommended to consider donating money to the neighboring society – a gesture symbolizing a "capital recovery" for the funding source, which serves to establish the firm in the first place.

For after all, economy and environmental development are nearly synonymous terms. The greatness of a successful business is sometimes quantified by its ability to thank the public within which it grows and develops, as stated by Professor Lester Thurow, dean of MIT's Sloan

School of Management (1968–1993), a guru of globalization and a senior economic and commercial adviser to many heads of state: "Economy is built in fact by virtue of huge social investments [first and foremost...] and only later by basic research...".

The heart and brain, moving this totality of systems, is **management capacity**, which is the **main asset**, holding, healing, pushing and energizing them. This is in fact the scope of their **natural leadership infrastructure** – the one leading them without compromise to their present and future aims, while supplying daily solutions to as many issues and problems, rising and demanding short or long term attention, in light of the complexity of the businesses and mechanisms which are ever-changing, always growing and continually branching out.

Alongside daily management and striving to realize the company's vision, its executives bestow an **organizational culture**: an abstract of the firm's way of life based on molding and assimilation of a totality of memories, traditions, customs, legends, tales, norms and common well-known habits, accepted by their participants. This is a kind of a humane tissue, binding all inner individual's private elements of the institution by a crisscross of social values and recognized agreements; the right leadership obligation by the supervising board against the commitments of the other personnel to endlessly contribute altogether to the designated destination – each by himself then among themselves – serving to overcome the ire and agitation within the unit. This is, in a way, a **convention** that everybody adopts willingly, understandably and through love of their place of work and livelihood – especially by identifying with it; a coming to terms accompanid by an internalization of dominant, rooted, ideologies based on myths, "heroes", jargon and unique ceremonies, invested with a meaning authentic to the system in which they perform. There is, actually, a living pattern of the corporation, determining how all things are being done, dictating the atmosphere amongst its members in their daily routines. Therefore the organizational culture has a central role in all processes of awakening, transformation, development and progress. (And perhaps a good example of the afore-said is the Mosaic speech to the People of Israel recorded in the Book of Deuteronomy. This is a long and all-encompassing monologue in which just before they are about to enter the Holy Land, he summarizes for them – over the course of five weeks, as the Sages interpret it – their history, the events and deeds which have brought them so far. Moses emphasizes the ancient laws, which they ought to obey even more vigorously from now on, rewriting the "religious-social covenant" with the Almighty whose total acceptance will insure their future peace and progress...).

But Life is stronger. The choices for supervising and guiding private or public organizational formats – of any category – are not derived from calculations of efficiency and purposefulness alone; niether from the wish to adjust them to the climate in which they operate; nor even out of the intention to stand for their social conventions, by which they are bound, so to speak. Usually they exhibit a very strong influence of totally personal interests – practically, but not always – which are as distant from serving the general good as the east is from the west. It is mostly the politics of associations and partnership, a complex of manipulations involving **might, prestige, income, promotion** and so on.

In summation

An organization of any type is analogous, therefore, to an **open-ended Cartesian coordinate system,** with well-defined distribution of authority and functions, directed at an assiduous and persistent desire for a trihedral harmony among its three orthogonal contributors as described below – all in order to execute its policy:

Opportunities, the range of choice between prospects and risks in its operational environment;

Resources possessed in the present and those to be acquired in the future; and

Aspirations of its top-echelon management (and its partners…) depending on its character and ambition.

August 1993

Planning, Management and Control Theories and Methods – Principles of the Best Ones

The two previous decades were prolific in various colorful management philosophies. Most of them, superficial and unproven, vanished and were forgotten. "Management coaches" and "specialists in leadership strategies" appeared almost everyday, presenting "psycho-organization" theories, whose authors mainly enriched themselves by their marketing and teaching. (Such was the fate of the pessimists who warned the world against the destruction that the Y2K bug was supposed to wreak – which turned out to be much ado about nothing...) Nearly every combination of three letters served as a title for disseminators of one of those casual and empty dogmas; however, most of these false prophets blew away like chaff in the wind, leaving no trace.

In contrast, there were those who wove yarns of fundamental ideas, assumptions and conjectures, based on deep learning and comprehensive research, in the first half of the 20s century; and those were found reliable, real, even worthwhile – if correctly implemented. These theories have existed for many years between summits of preaching and distribution to the gulfs of oblivion, have been abandoned and reclaimed, and so on and so forth; until, in the fullness of time, these companies' leadership methods became classic by their being products of very bright and fertile thinking. And the thread binding them all was and still is the following: **open minds and common sense**. Moreover, it is clear as day that in managing organizations, a **constantly educated and enlightened use of emotions** is necessary – to the exclusion of all else. For on the whole it is a mixture, strongly connecting wisdom and heart.

Here is a selection of the most accepted management and conduct theories, which the present tractate is based on. The opening one is derived from the "theory of constraints" and the last leans on the "total quality management" philosophy, just as the books have developed. The reasons for this order is included below. But in conclusion, one should remember that the chosen path to leading life and managing others must mostly be a very private combination of all those hypotheses that suit the chief personally.

- **Management by Constraints (MbC):**

    Concentrates mainly on spotting and identifying "bottlenecks" and restraints in the organization, analyzing and treating them until they are removed. This is a very practical attitude and easy to implement; and because of its popularity is accepted by nearly all as being actually "burnt" in the subconscious. It fits life and business in the present, offering a managerial vision useful in the next one or two decades, perhaps forever. This theory was developed in the early eighties by a physicist of all people, Dr. Eliahu M. Goldart, an Israeli who preached its values around the globe.

- **Management by Objectives (MbO):**

    Deals in setting clear and very accurate targets and intermediate objectives ahead. It was developed by two American management researchers, professors Peter Drucker and Douglas McGregor in the early eighties, when it became very popular. Although not classified anymore as a management theory, it is well-accepted among wide audiences, most of whom view its principles as obvious. For example: stockpiling for reserves is a waste of resources; therefore, managers should order materials when needed for exact and dictated assignments, simply "just on time," usually called the JOT concept.

- **Management by Projects (MbP):**

    Emphasizes managerial involvement in emergencies only – or when the company is required to perform special tasks, different from those executed routinely. The source of the system is the "Management by Exceptions" principle defined in 1911 by the father of scientific management, Frederick Taylor. It preaches concerning seniors in the organization's hierarchy only when their attention is really needed. Thus the executives may concentrate on what is really important, using their time and energy economically and efficiently.

    This leading attitude is somewhat analogous to the MbO theory, for it is impossible to promote projects without implementing this current supervision method for targets, timetables, budgets, special demands and setting other elements.

- **Management by Re-Engineering / Reorganization (MbR):**

    Calls for constant orientation to enter competitive markets by a permanent adjustment of the assignments and the organizational structure. This in order to be able to respond quickly and correctly to the rotations and the upheavals of the world's business characteristics and its building blocks. For example: reducing the number of mid-level employees, cutting costs and improving service by avoiding extra bureaucracy.

- **Management by Outsourcing (MbOs):**

    Directing the organization to employ merely its essential staff and deal with its real faculties only. Constantly pushing to outsource all jobs and services to other specializing companies. This type of management results nearly always in cutting costs, but necessitates the sub-contractors' commitment and guarantee of adequate execution – while being supervised by a small nucleus of the company's competent team.

▸ **Management by Changes (MbCh):**

Stresses the flexibility called for in the organizational structure and activities due to variations in scientific and economic processes in the greater business environment. This requires faster reaction as well as proper and early planning.

For example: constant attention to the right mix of temporary and permanent employees in order to match it to changes in means and technology. In most cases the best solution is arrived at by trial and error – except that the "tuition fees" for learning from experience are luxuries which may be too costly.

▸ **Management by Data Processing (MbDP):**

Copes with the communication and data revolution caused by the evolution of hi-tech. Its main ingredients are: skillfulness in spotting and identifying information, in its absorption and digestion pace, in immediacy and quality analysis, in technology of control and the speed of using it to respond. This is to ensure continuous internal improvement in order to be at least one step ahead of the competitors in the current field being dealt with.

▸ **Total Quality Management (TQM):**

Emphasizes quality as the most central element of the organization. This method claims that any company's right of existence does not solely depend on the satisfaction of its clients with the products and services rendered to them – but also on the contentment of its employees and all other partners to its activities, as well as their interest in their occupation in particular and in their workplace in general. The theory was devised by the American statistician Dr. W. Edwards Deming in the 1940s. Rejected in his own country, it was first inculcated in post-World War II Japan as a part of the United States aid for its rehabilitation. Only 40 years later (!), when the Japanese car-making industry was beating its American counterpart, was this management approach shining in the Far East's developing economic empire adopted in the USA as well.

All these above depicted different organizional philosophies may be summarized thus:

If in the 1980s the world of management focused on quality and in the 1990s on reorganization – the first decade of the Third Millennium would witness an emphasis on "managerial quickness": **the agility and ease with which a productive entity is able to change and the immediacy of its business activities**. Perhaps the best metaphor to demonstrate this notion is presented in the famous *National Geographic* poster, where a horrifying lioness is chasing a frightened gazelle. And although the caption makes it rather humorous (despite the apparent cruelty of the portrayal…) it describes best the reality of the entire concept's core: "Leading businesses is just like surviving in an African jungle. On waking up in the morning it doesn't matter whether you consider yourself a mighty matured lion (knowing it must beat the slowest gazelle or it will starve to death…) or a gentle young deer (strongly inculcating that it oughts to be faster than the quickest lion or it will be preyed…): when the sun comes up, you'd better be running…".

However, it should be hoped that these new theories should not distract from the managerial insights and knowledge bequeathed by the still highly relevant, old but classic, business world with its habitual way of operation.

November 1994

The Role of the Leader – the "Credo"

The manager's task should focus on two main tracks:

1. **Set the operating policy of the organization he heads, monitoring and controlling its full implementation from dictation up to final execution.**
2. **Initiate and bring in new businesses.**

Charting the policy expresses actually the various characteristics of the **business vision**. It means setting and defining long term targets, indicating intermediate objectives along the way, and deciding on modes of execution and allocation of necessary resources in order to reach these goals. Application of the above-said management concept and conduct is effected by determining the following four basic treatment arcs, which are mutually and strongly linked and intertwined:

- **Technological Strategy.**
- **Human Resources Strategy.**
- **Financial Strategy.**
- **Marketing Strategy.**

These outlines of planning must be attentive to voices heard from inner as well as outer feedback loops – and in real time. They should react quickly and be permanently attuned to:

Advice and comments arriving regularly from customers and peripheral partners to the operation, and turning points in the relationships with them;

Vital information circling frequently amongst the entire personnel within all the organization's units and branches;

Changes occurring daily in science and technology; and

Constant daily developments and variations in the economic and financial sectors, anything relevant or at least appearing so.

Adoption of the said strategies is done by:

- **Study, examination and dissemination of essential necessary data**: the array of the framework, the product, manpower, intellectual property, financial resources, capital structure, markets, business environment – and the goals of the owners, including their private aspirations.

- **Brainstorming with major function holders,** recruiting and harnessing them to the general effort and its realization.

- **Turning all employees,** first and foremost, and **customers,** as much as possible – into **"partners"** of the organization.

- **Deducing from personal experience** – nothing is more important.

- **Listening to gut feelings**; to those inner voices emanating from above; the thinking, investigating and contemplating "upper kingdom" – to the intuition.

Initiating and bringing in new business constitutes the lion's share of **business development**. In such a creation, one needs all of the four treatment systems above – separately or jointly – to generate new, profitable growth engines.

And in summation

It should be remembered that the world of commerce is analogous to a battlefield.

One should keep collecting and analyzing intelligence in order to fix and mold a strategy as well as selecting a tactic – and realize both in the best manner. In pursuit of this, he must be immediately and continuously updated with all relevant information and be ready to change things and adjust fast accordingly – but not recklessly; for business, even at the highest levels, means scheming and deceit, but in the most positive sense.

Data management serves this purpose exactly, and it is perhaps the fifth strategy, in addition to all other planning and guiding mechanisms detailed so far; an asset improving efficiency, which may bestow a constant relative advantage over the competitors in the field being dealt with, in order to keep on winning all the time. Nevertheless, this is qualified by the following: **strict observance of common business ethics, commitment to public hygiene and to the physical safety and security of all involved** (contrasting with the above-mentioned combat-zone, God forbid...).

December 1999

Building Up Leadership and Operating Policy – the Various Stages

Although the present tractate gathers different management outlooks, the one chosen to demonstrate the steps towards building up a leadership and operating policy in a productive system is the **Management by Constraints (MbC)** in a model of an **industrial organization**; for only very few people – be they even magnates and tycoons (so much the more so for ordinary folks…) – are privileged to be in full control of their total agenda, not enslaved to routine's reality, its perversions and even its gray mundaneness, along with pressures of the moment or needs of the hour, as these are sometimes described. That attitude is, in fact, the most widespread and authentic in Man's daily race and suitable especially to the current era, to the necessities of the circumstances evolving as a result of its business atmosphere, to the fast reaction required to be a part of it, and to the tempo of decision-making, in order to be rooted in it. Furthermore, this common-sense approach renders it appropriate and convenient for immediate implementation.

Moreover, the vocabulary and indices depicted below are adapted to the general concept deduced from this method of management. Even the term "profit" is expressed mostly in monetary terms, albeit, as already said, it is not necessarily so. In any case, it should be remembered that the stages presented in the following form, are relevant to whichever managerial pattern, having any kind of output (including life itself, for example…).

Establishment / Integration and Formation – the Opening Steps

This is actually the opening move of the management policy and activation strategy-building process; but the essence and operational content of such a phase are depending on a couple of different initial situations:

One – leading from the beginning the establishment of a totally new system.

Two – taking on the management of an existing, functioning entity.

In the first case, the scenario is somewhat amorphous, for it deals with a preliminary plotting of an organization's creation, where the said opening stage is actually intended to feature only the foundations, responding to just the general purpose of its establishment; it continues with an intensive investigation of the basic data and a thorough study of the essential facts, being a necessary background for the whole idea, in order to support its future implementation. It concludes with an initial setting in motion of the system in meticulously measured steps – those needed from the very beginning for a correct activation. This evolution is based on trial and error according to the stations below and its character must flow, changed, be matched and accommodated to the reality in which the entity may function with the accumulation of more and more relevant information about it.

1. **Planning the Establishment of the Organization**
    - Laying the infrastructure for the following:
      The technical domain;
      The personnel plane;
      The financial sector;
      The marketing dimension;
      The information-management front; and

The structure and procedure element.

That is to say, **a cautious calculation of the designated assets** – the totality of intellectual and material property – must be undertaken for a proper organizational deployment.

- Studying the relevant operating environment. In other words, **evaluating the future prospects of the business**; the background factors and economic climate having possible effects; resources needed for its propulsion and the type of yield anticipated from the products; target audience; marketing and service aspects.

- Reading the real wishes of the owners and/or top management, thoroughly understanding them and translating these into **a solid basis for a meticulous business strategy from its inception.**

Said otherwise, this requires generating detailed and encompassing infrastructures, paving thoroughly the road towards the establishment of the intended organization and reinforcing its framework.

The second situation entails a much better defined and usual process; the company already exists, so the initial phase is opened by becoming acquainted with the system; getting absorbed into it, being integrated with its personnel and adapting to its ingredients and the character of its missions. The conclusion is taking the necessary steps and actions for its correct operating and navigating after it is re-molded and modified – deploying a gradual development according to these stages:

1. **Learning the Organization**
   - Plunging in deeply for the purpose to become familiar with all facts and data relevant to the formation which one is supposed to lead, and understanding them in conjunction with:

The structure and procedures domain (first of all...);
The technical expanse;
The personnel plane;
The financial sector;
The marketing dimension; and
The data-management front.
Getting profoundly acquainted with the existing resources – the totality of the intellectual and material property.

- Getting to know the relevant environment in which the entity functions, namely **inculcating thoroughly the essence of the business**: the economic background and climate of its operation; the means needed for its continuation and the nature of its output in the aspects of products and markets or services and clients.

- Feeling the true wishes of the owners or top management, deeply recognizing them and **completely internalizing the business strategy** – while being a full partner to its integration, consolidation, design, editing, styling and implementation.

Said otherwise, this requires a meticulous and comprehensive mapping of the whole entity that is about to be managed, in its length and breadth and in significant detail.

From now on both tracks' steps are quite identical – but the substance one pours into them is significantly different. For example: no doubt there is a dissimilarity between the targets of a newly created array just at its commencement and that which exists and functions already, requiring only an occasional alteration and fine-tuning here and there. Naturally there should be also a variation in the criteria set to measure the success in goal attainment – parallel, of course, with the stage at which the organization finds itself currently.

2. **Defining the target**, meaning: **a very accurate mark of the**

organization's final aim. Obviously, this is amassing the most profits from its activities in its specific field of occupation.

However, in addition to the above it should be understood that:

- The purpose of the organization is the momentum of all the toil and efforts invested in it. It is, on the other hand, also the criterion of its existence's justification. However, there are a few types of goals – official, corporate, administrative and operational – differing one from the other by the measure of their publicity, the nature of the clientele they are aiming at and the ability to quantify them in exact terms of time, place and rate of achievement.

- The earnings of an organization are the benefits derivable from its activities: money, an advantage or any other compensation – defined by its original founders or present owners in accordance with their intentions, character, and wishes.

- The application outline of the organization, that which brings it nearer to its target, is called **productivity**; this is an amalgamation of all the best methods, procedures, proficiencies and technologies existing within the institution at any time, in a unified texture, perfectly functioning to maximize the "output" in comparison with all the "inputs" necessary to execute the production process.

3. **Identifying the relevant quantities within the system** – whose demonstration signify the ongoing trend of the **organization's approach** (or vice versa...) **towards its designated target** (or away from it...) – and using them as **indexes of control**, such as:

    - Stock: all capital spent on purchasing stuff intended for eventual reselling.

    - Production: the rate of monetary income, in fact, obtained from all products sold.

- Operational costs: all the money invested in turning stock into products.

4. Setting **measurable targets** in order to **improve** the organization's **productivity**, actually its profitability. These are the clear and quantifiable tasks of the following type in a commercial business:

- Stock reduction.
- Bringing down operational costs.
- Enlarging the output.

Ameliorating productivity means, actually, the ability to provide a higher product value at a lower cost as a corollary of the creativity and innovation of all active partners; increasing efficiency of management techniques and operational skills; improvement of technical assets and bettering workforce training and qualification; and finally, intelligent application of existing resources and technologies. All of the aforesaid is motivated by the need to lead the organization towards a "competitive state" – and not only for the long-term preservation of its economic robustness – which boosts action for constant all-around upgrading and enhancement in order to position and make it stronger in comparison to its competitors.

5. **Setting the absolute values** by which to gauge in a businesslike, unequivocal manner the organization's success in achieving its goals. For instance: examine the following values trough the eyes of a system that has a materialistic connotation, in order to find out its degree of "economic growth:"

- Cash Flow.
- Yield on Investment.
- Net profit.

And the aspiration is not only to magnify each of these on its own, but all three together; for none of them is enough to indicate indisputably an improvement of the unit's financial performance.

It should be noted here and now that when evaluating the organization's profits in order to derive a true assessment of the achievements due to them, it is imperative to register the costs of the aforementioned steps in the proper "lines / columns" of the company's financial reports. Here are a few confusing items and their proper classifications:

- ✓ Depreciation due to aging and amortization: operation costs.
- ✓ Any salable investment, including equipment of the previous item, aside from amortization: stock.
- ✓ Stock maintenance costs: operations costs.
- ✓ Sale of technological know-how or patents: Stock
- ✓ Know-how for a new stock to production process: operation costs.

In addition, one must keep in mind the two types of operation costs: **direct** – on the "factory floor", literally influencing the volume of production; **indirect** – constantly supplying "various services" in support of the main activities dedicated to an organization's commercial outcome (secretaries, drivers, cleaning staff et cetera…), having nothing to do with its quantity and level.

The quantitative values and goals described above are appropriate for the actions of a productive industrial entity, as already noted. Hence for any other corporate it would be necessary to identify, determine and position parallel terms, due to their character and style of operation. These would probably be quite similar in name, but essentially different in their nature and way of examination and gauging.

On the other hand, two things must be clearly internalized concerning quantifiable goals and metrics.

The one: targets and values for measurement, **if not clearly and accurately defined, may do more harm than benefit** – for they will never present a realistic picture of the firm's state; what's even worse, they may lead to wrong decisions.

The other: posing too pretentious and unrealistic challenges, may lead to a Pygmalion Effect — convincing everybody that they are achievable, perhaps already accomplished, while the actual results are far from that.

Setting the Mechanism in Motion – from Theory to Practice

This is the second stage, putting in to practice the entity's determined policy.

6. **A Productive Organization – Six Basic Principles as Axioms**

   These are the basic assumptions for operating an "cumulative body" using the approach of Management by Constraints (MbC) – a logical disposition of associative principles, immediately penetrating and instantaneously making sense.

   a. Organizations are always established for a certain cause; none is built for the sake of its existence only.

   b. By definition, it is always a multi-personnel entity.

   c. Accomplishing its purpose requires, for that reason, coordinated and cooperated efforts of more than one being.

   d. The individual's contribution to the achievement of the organization's goal depends, to a large extent, on the effective action executed by others.

   e. An organization, therefore, is not simply an amalgamation of separate organs; rather, it should be perceived as a chain whose links are intertwined with the aim of fulfilling a common goal.

f. Since the strength of any chain depends on its weakest link, the first step in its operation must be the sighting of that fragile bond – in other words, identifying that very constraint.

7. **The Methodology of Handling Problematic Junctions in the Organization – the Five Steps Cycle**

   The logic behind this approach is also convincing and comprehensible at once:

   a. It is obligatory to observe and identify all constraints in the system.

   b. The optimal operation venues must be found in order to try and make the best out of these problematic junctions.

   c. All resources of the organization should be subordinated to the aforesaid decision.

   d. Additionally and complimentarily, it is compulsory to attempt to minimize, as much as possible, the discovered constraints, while being cognizant of the correct method to be employed.

   e. After neutralizing a constraint, the process should recommence from step "a" – according to the changes enforced on the system by this elimination.

   As a rule: inertia driven by routine must never be the reason to allow the creation of an unintended or unnoticed constraint.

8. **The Optimal Way of Operating an Organization – Required Skills and Qualifications**

   The following capabilities are essential for the right management of frameworks and are supposed to be ingrained in the top leading echelon – either inborn or acquired.

   a. Immediate observation and identification of **critical problems** in the system (meaning also, of course, in conjunction, the entire functional environment – complicated as it may be…).

b. Internalizing the aforesaid revelations accompanied by their thorough analysis and full understanding.

c. Making the proper decisions:

   What to change;

   What to change to; and

   How to change.

d. Paving the road to the accomplishment of the abovementioned transformation – without generating any new ones.

e. Assimilating the aforesaid **changes** within the unit, not only without raising any objections from underlings or partners to the activity, but by explaining and convincing them of the necessity of these variations, so that the they will permeate, will be completely understood and will even be **consensually accepted**.

The Nature of the Thesis – Clarifications and Emphasis

The Ingredient of the Conception – Headlines at a Glance

Most factors contributing to success in running a company can't be exactly predicted in advance, because they are usually concurrently influenced by two phenomena:

- **Dependable Occurrences:** an event or process, or a succession thereof, preconditions the next incident.
- **Statistical Fluctuations:** unexpected different types of data combinations are also variable from one case to another.

There is no way to run a producing entity without "dependable occurrences" and "statistical fluctuations". The amalgamation of such random happenings **disturbs** the process's movement forward, which causes **constraints** thereof that must be brought into consideration.

Constraints – Bottlenecks or Forced Defects

A mathematical law defines that whenever there is a linear dependence between two or more variables of the same event, further variant oscillations in the group will be concentrated around the **maximum deviation**, created by these first forgoing parameters. This "topmost deflection" of the previous action becomes the starting point of the next step; thus, the entire process is **delayed**.

One reason for such holdups is **bottlenecks** in the organization. Any junction in the array at which its supply of products lags behind the quantity it supposes to deliver turns out to be a limitation slowing down the required outcome. It is a forced defect, not necessarily good or bad – but a reality compulsion, **in the absence of which – other constraints would arise**.

In order to neutralize the obstacle's influence in causing the delay, all efforts should be invested so that the flow through it will equalize at least the market's demand. Circumventing such a junction or its obviation means actually raising production; responding faster to costumers' requirements. The implication thereof is an advantage gained over the competitors.

Management by Constraints – a Few Points to Ponder

The production capacity of an organization is precisely identical to that of the bottleneck in its chain of activity. Therefore, in order to augment the output of the entire factory, it is crucial to enhance the outcome only at this very problematic junction; for an hour's loss there means a sixty-minute drop-off for the whole system.

An organization whose **production potential is balanced** (i.e., each of the "junctions" in the array is optimally activated and generating it best…) is not necessarily an entity where all resources' abilities are fit to accurately supply all market demands (even though this is the "wet dream" of any operative manager…). Even if on the face of it the matter makes perfect sense, ironically this is basically a wrong whim; the closer a firm gets to such equilibrium, the opposite becomes clear: productivity decreases, and the system stand to lose quite heavily.

The explanation is quite simple: in this case – and it can be mathematically proven too – the stock would keep growing, while the system's provision capacity would remain actually the same; for it would go on purchasing raw materials compatible with the manufacturing ability of each intersection in the process – whereas the total production would still depend just on the yield of that specific bottleneck in the fabrication arrangement. Therefore, in time a surplus of unused parts of the final merchandise would pile up on the assembly floor, because the flow would be unaltered. In other words, the cost of stock treatment would keep increasing – even as the sale's income would stay about equal. The result is clear: a swollen financial deficit.

Consequently, it is forbidden to try equating the production capacity of each and every factor in the fabrication line with the market's demands as is. One should **optimally balance the whole flow of product creation** – all along the activity chain with its known constraints and obstacles – with the total clientele requirement.

Trying to raise production in a local and uncontrolled manner may create in the system new weak sections in addition to the existing ones. Therefore, the key to a correct workflow in any organization is **dictated by the tempo of activity at its bottleneck**. For that reason, it is recommended to shift such a constraint to the beginning of any multi-staged operation, so as to ease control of the overall pace of production – for example, to the commencement of the manufacturing process.

The real cost of a bottleneck to the organization is the total cost of the system divided by the hours of the stated constraint – a very costly matter. So, working at **such problematic junctions** should be consigned to the **best employees** of the company.

Non-Constraint Factors – Their Contribution to the System

Efficient use of a non-bottleneck unit – even a perfectly functioning one – has a minute influence on the output potential of the whole array, for the final production of the mechanism is determined by the limitations of the **systematic constraint** within it. However, such effectiveness is the "best service" possible to "bestow" under the present conditions, in order to minimize the damage caused by the above-said problematic junction.

On the other hand, an outfit whose non-constraint parts are perfectly functioning locally is not necessarily the ultimate system. On the contrary: it is a **very ineffective conglomerate**. Since we know of organizations where all employees are constantly doing their best and still they never reach their maximum possible purposefulness because the total output of a unit will always depend on the capacity of the its weakest link, thus a large share of the energy invested in it by others would be inconsequential, which is a horrible waste of resources. Therefore such a local optimum would be considered efficient only if its specific operation would drive, alongside all other components of the production line, to the best possible yield of the whole entity.

It should also be clarified that the maximum utility of a non-constrained production – regardless of all other parts of the complex – is of secondary importance, for it doesn't necessarily serve the organization's target. That is because an hour saved at a non-bottleneck facility is a mirage as far as the whole array goes, being an entity whose production capacity is limited in fact by this problematic junction existing within it.

In aggregate:

What was described in the present chapter is definitely true in other spheres of life. A constraint may be **economic, technological, demographic, social, political, cultural** or any personal whim of the top management or owners of the organization. Moreover, it may appear as a **combination of two or more** of the afore-mentioned domains – a potentially lethal union, not necessarily because of their mutual "problematic impact", but especially out of possible contradictions that might arise amongst them. And in the general mixture, each of these may contribute, without restraint according to the "size of its influence," while their integration would augment the existing problems.

July 1994

Operating a Start-Up Company at the Intermediary Phase – the Concept

Until recently, it seemed that a new economic outlook was in effect.

If in the distant past it was common to judge the achievements of corporations by their performance, since the 1980s certain businesses have been measured seemingly by their value – that is to say, by their intellectual property: the talent of their people and unique discoveries they had accomplished. This was especially true in the hi-tech spheres. While years ago organizations were rated by their real properties, particularly by their bottom-line financial profits. Lately, their estimation has been derived from their inventions and registered patents, which may yield a lot of money – but only in the future.

Thus, various companies' prices went sky-high – on paper mostly – because of no more than ideas, groundless sometimes; even if some of those modern musings were practical, their realization did not occur overnight, as sometimes perceived by laymen. The road from a "genius invention" to a brilliant "final product" was found to be long, winding and filled with technological landmines, managerial obstacles, greedy partners and other calamities. For every firm which grew rich, hundreds, perhaps more, faded, died out and disappeared, their founders still finding it hard to recover from that experience. On the other hand, one must admit, the few who did make it, earned enough money to become awfully wealthy securing themselves for the rest of their lives and leave some for generations to come. Even being a drop in the ocean, this handful of cases became the wet dream of multitudes swept in their wake, hoping to be the next winners, easily acquiring a fortune.

In conjunction, a quite substantial group of well-to-do people arose – some of them nouveau riche who deserted their safe sources of income – seeking to get affluent again, easily and fast this time. Thus all kinds of entities were born, some of them rather dubious, specializing, so to say, in discovering and identifying "gold mines" in the form of "joint individuals with an idea to develop", apparently set to conquer the world. By merit of future generous yields, the latter agreed to tie their fortune with this battalion of inventors, and in exchange for investment and support, these magnets bought full control of their discoveries and patents. In addition, the scene was filled with "matchmakers" who filled their pockets just by bringing together "brides" and "grooms" – a whole industry of disgusting, greedy parasites; and a situation was created wherein the wish to give was stronger than the will to get.

And as the desire for revolutionary ideas became desperate, extravagant wages and utopian working conditions – unjustified, by the way – were granted to those who were carrying out the job itself. And more than once these "magicians", as they were perceived in those days, succeeded in doubling or even tripling their remuneration just by whispering, as if unintentionally, the choice they faced of whether to cross the street and join the competitors around the corner, should they not be showered with all kinds of different benefits and stock options; And in no time, this commercial world grew tipsy on the taste of inexhaustible imaginary wealth.

And while all of the above hovered in Alice's Wonderland, second thoughts were explicitly heard, now and again, of the mirages leading the public astray. The question – how long can this financial fairy tale survive before the carriage turns into a pumpkin again? – kept growing stronger. The capital markets all over the world kept signaling clearly, even screaming, that the rush to El Dorado was probably too rash, and that such an economic theory – being a "merchandizing of the maybe" system – must eventually evaporate and disappear.

Slowly, slowly the enthusiasm for this virtual financial world withered and the public voted with its feet, keeping a distance not only from investing in those companies but from buying their shares too. This was only the opening shot, heralding the coming decline. In addition to mass layoffs of junior workers at first and senior executives later, there were struggles over retirement, entitlements and such occurred, large-scale strikes and even far-reaching unemployment benefits. Shouting became cheap, judiciousness, dear…

And from this moment each potential clique was thoroughly examined with a high view of the risk's type; for in shallow water, it is very easy to discover who swims naked. Suddenly it became evident that the business model of quite a number of companies was not realistic, and somehow they were not making any operational, meaning real, profits. And having no significant income, nobody agreed to infuse any cash into their coffers; hastiness turned out to be expensive, while wisdom was low-cost…

All of a sudden, investors grasped the "strange" phenomenon called the "niche gangs": groups stuffed into a unique sector of activity and nothing else. Organizations able to promote and sell for few million dollars wished, demanded, and expected impudently a market premium of half a billion dollars. True, they might be visionary entities; however, they were unable to penetrate the business environment in accordance with modern consumers' requirements due to a lack of robust strategic orientation and solid commercial positions and attitudes, not to speak of the narrow direction their products had.

Consequently that financial bubble swelled hurriedly until it burst in the faces of the multitudes. And the reason for this was undoubtedly the following: **those who were once satisfied with one bird – as long as they held it – were trying now to catch a whole flock, still perching at the tree top**. And in such a gamble, there is just one small step between flowering and withering; the size of the risk equals that of the dream. The balloon, filled with utopian hot air, enhanced by incurable desire and greedy euphoria, has been propelled by a mere increase in the value of securities based on no economic common sense, vanished and turned into vacuum. The snowball acquireed a mass and velocity of its own, conquering stock exchanges around the world, even though it was wholly virtual, existing only in databases and on monitors; thus, it pushed into oblivion the principles of cold and realistic calculation, until it melted like ice under a burning Saharan sun and disappeared.

Only then did the economic world wake up from the horrors of its nightmares, slowly regaining sanity and a sense of proportion, renouncing the obsession which had taken hold of it. Concurrently, young "brides" were ceaselessly trying to scout for fresh "grooms". But now, sober and experienced, the "courted" ones were very careful, checking the "dowry of the spouse-to-be" intelligently and with infuriating moderation. For suddenly everybody recalled that the primary cause of divorce is marriage itself (since statistically, one hundred percent of the separated had been previously engaged…). And the first to dismantle the partnership, made of the wet dreams of easy enrichment – entered into with awful rashness, as described in the previous paragraphs – were precisely those hoping to salvage even a small portion of their investment. All this started to roll as the atmosphere, encompassing the tumbling NASDAQ indexes, was already fraught with bad news.

However, there is no relation – absolute zero – between the aforementioned and the **continued existence** of the hi-tech world. And the incriminating finger of those lacking a minimum understanding in the subject, trying to point at the factors responsible for the situation, nearly **put an end** to the essence of humanity's wondrous development, only because they were drawing the wrong inferences.

Firstly, because targeting the Internet – or the meritorious cellular e-mail and voice ways of contacting systems at the same time – as the main cause of the collapse of this new economy is a huge mistake. On the contrary! These innovative discoveries, which became the leading edge of the global turning point in superior scientific achievement, have become the sole fountainhead of information and communication in nearly all spheres of life almost, standing on the center stage of international progress. They laid the foundations of electronic commerce, a genius arrangement, functioning today at the speed of light: extremely clever inventions, producing direct and transparent bargaining processes, cutting out parasitic middlemen, lowering the barriers of entrance to any business, and establishing a popular, open and equal market offering opportunities for all.

Secondly, since no other technological dimension or factor, varied as it may be, brought about the destruction of this sphere of exaggerated and false capital.

Therefore, those lamenting the hi-tech hectic activity ground are in for a bitter disappointment; and those dancing on its grave are celebrating for nothing. For not only will the inventions in this supreme scientific environment become realized and alive – but many are still in their diapers, nascent and ready for a brilliant future. And whoever blames them for the collapse of the world's economy, is very much like the person who goes looking for a missing coin under the next street light – instead of trying to find it where it was actually dropped.

Moreover, nothing is clearer and more natural than this unique domain of activity, which conquered a state like Israel in a very short time. Since it is situated on a quiet, arid piece of land, nearly devoid of natural resources – not having much to offer its citizens in the way of subsistence – it offers an exclusive arena for scientific accomplishment of this sort, which does not require large spaces, special minerals or expensive means of production, but uses only what has always been the secret weapon of its inhabitants: Jewish brainpower; the audacity to take risks and the ability to employ it with vision and creativity in order to survive in the land of the Patriarchs, a hostile territory full of enemies, threatening day and night to destroy it. And this constitutes the genetic code of its success. Not only is this sphere of occupation and business a natural choice for Israel, but a true life elixir; so it is obvious that this state is hi-tech's expected habitat.

The blame for the economic tsunami which "reddened" the stock exchanges' screens should then be examined from a totally different perspective. It's probably imbedded in the management style of the nouveau-managers' class; those who were not crafted by the system, advancing all the way from the bottom to top leadership, but rather being dropped there from out of the blue, cocksure in their ability to run global enterprises; individuals whose banner was to deal with clean and elegant developments – easy to assemble, quick to sell. They stove to make an easy buck, fill their pockets and brag in the neighborhood bar. These were folks choosing to enter the ring without thoroughly checking the business ground, mostly devoid of financial backing, motivated by an all-consuming desire and a boundless eagerness to get rich effortlessly, satisfying momentary whims and revel in extravagance as fast as possible. They were some type of managerial village idiot, the business-challenged, nothing more. Thus it is clear that the **source of this economic collapse is definitely not to be sought after in hi-tech applications** – of which a large segment is still in the stone age of its evolution; this is an **art** bound to grow and conquer mighty mountaintops, to continue flourishing, thriving, improving and prolonging its life-expectancy.

Not to mention the fact that we are not talking about a crisis hitting this exclusive sector, but about a gigantic positive and meaningful revolution overtaking it. And an upheaval, by definition, demands victims just as in all other walks of life: in politics it means a total collapse of regimes, and in economics the entire disappearance of financial markets. The first casualties here are, of course, the destroyed firms, mostly as a result of faulty management and misreading of the business environment. And this Darwinian process did and does demolish incompetent organizations in the afore-said domain run by **unprofessional** amateurs, while loyally supporting the choice of the herd.

Now that the fantasies about joining the nobility of the rich have dissipated, one fact is clear and above any doubt: **the innovative latticework of this topmost technology sphere is at its beginning**. It didn't fail, but the assumption about quickly grabbing so many economic opportunities, not to be missed, has stumbled and collapsed; the weak attempt, not based on any sound policy, correct conduct, business integrity and financial backing – seeding false hopes and deceitful illusions about making a quick buck easily and for nothing – has totally vanished. The dot-com dream has grown faint.

Moreover; no one can promise that such a "financial bubble" will never strike again – at another economic sector, probably. It may mightily tempt the suckers with – instead of hi-tech gadgets – promises of growth and huge profits in baskets of premiums, promissory notes and a variety of virtual monetary instruments, or via ingenious frauds such as the Ponzi scheme (created by the Italian immigrant Charles Ponzi, who convinced the American multitudes at the beginning of the 20th century to consign all their money to his hands while he promised vast returns, but actually deceived them by using a pyramid sort of game – paying old investors uncommon interest in comparison to the conventional market earnings at that time, using the money from new "victims" of his...). For such "economic episodes" occur usually as a result of failures, emanating from unverified projections and deliberate misrepresentations driven by private, purely uncomercial, greedy considerations that lead to distorted methods of compensation. It is spawned by the willful disregard of warning signs and the handwriting on the wall, abetted by lack of supervision and control of processes – and most importantly, a wrong assessment of risks. And these are all outcomes, mainly, of many heuristic diversions, mere wild fantasies, overconfidence and destructive sky-high egotism.

In short, no one would dare say that such a colossal failure of a similar system, which may install itself in the current business world, can not hit mercilessly the pockets of an unaware, unknowing and misunderstanding public (an event just like stealing from the wallet of an old lady sitting in the next seat on a moving municipal bus...).

Therefore – and despite the blow to the gamblers' pockets – new start-ups may very well appear in the future, like mushrooms after rain, on every high hill, under every thick tree. Except their days will now be ten times harder. For it will take investors some time before diving into their pockets or signing their checks, and many questions will have to be properly answered. In other words: there is no doubt that this sublime domain – although still a ceaseless mixture of geniuses and charlatans – will continue to exist and flourish magnificently. Yet, they should probably manage humbly their newborn company and moderate their financial aspirations, surely away from fiscal adventurism, which has time and again proven itself idiotic. Meanwhile the above-named groups would somehow have to go on operating in reality and its circumstances.

And the period of searching for a robust sponsor is highly pressing. The process in which a producing entity gets overlaid with skin must be conducted with great punctiliousness, each and every step guided by deep thinking and examination while walking in this minefield. All the more so since only a hairsbreadth stands between failure and success in cases of erroneous preparation, behavior or leadership – even if it seems to be negligible.

Consequently, what comes next delineates the correct, good and effective management and operating principles – in the old customary way – of start-up companies in the intermediary phase. This is essential for the existence of a developing firm, tested by its steadfast durability until a strategic investor is found, or in the best scenario, up to the moment of its acquisition. And even if the introduction deals with technologically advanced enterprises, all of the afore-said is absolutely true also for the foundation **of any new business**. For the essence of ultra-modern state-of-the-art entities is not in the merchandise only but in the production, processing and implementation methods: maximum efficiency, high-quality positive attitudes – whether the product is toilet paper or a sophisticated airliner. And the perception meant to guide the organization's policy is the care for the very subsistence of a real footing, providing it with the power for and the prospect of survival: **economic independence and the means of its implementation.**

And in order to continue a firm's development it must be financially self-governing, but limited by a logic derived from its proper conduct and management. "Selling its soul" for money may summon partners whose interests are not always in accord with the paths of its activities and advancement. If that happens, the stability of the corporate and its social-human structure may be shortly undermined. Its founders and leaders will soon lose the authority and ability to drive it towards its pre-determined goals. Their specific sway and influence will diminish, and finally the organization will disappear.

There are three common solutions to gain such a wishful economic independence:

- **The existence of sufficient equity** for at least the interim period until the arrival of a potential buyer or a strategic sponsor.

- **Recruiting a partner from day one** – a person "crazy" about the idea behind the company, identifying himself with its direction, loyal, patient, and willing to keep a distance from its daily running; in reality – a twin of Snow White, since such persons exist only in the world of fantasy.

- **Sighting, identifying and getting involved in external projects beyond its daily engagement**, which are capable of supporting the firm temporarily in dire straits.

This last option makes sense only when the first two are not valid. For in the presence of equity or an ideal investor as described above, why should one bother looking for trouble in strange partnerships or an extraneous workload?

The company's internal operative nature, adopted by its decision-makers upon taking outside projects, must confront the following principles:

- **Releasing key personnel to think about and promote the main issues occupying the company, while maintaining a serene atmosphere between them and the other employees.**

  It is forbidden to allow these tasks, intended to "make a living," to over-exhaust the top management. By nature, they should be freed to the existing intellectual property of the company. Those jobs should conform to the unique professional practices of the organization, and to its regular commercial rituals which match the usual daily activities. Under no condition should the entity enter a strange field of occupancy, demanding an augmented effort by utilizing the high-level workforce; such an action may detract the firm from its cardinal path and purpose.

- **Harvest projects promising a reasonable livelihood on the one** hand, but leave considerable time to continue developing and improving the company's central subject on the other.

It is appropriate to conduct a strict viability test before stepping into the afore-depicted kind of work. It is strongly recommended to check meticulously whether the domain offered is well-known, what its projected investment in human resources is and the marginal profit remaining in the organization's coffers after dealing with it.

- **Avoiding technological entanglement.**

    It is highly suggested to sell know-how only. This is the least risky service. It is prohibited to get involved with adventurous occupations, due to a lack of appropriate skills; this mistake that might trap the corporate in endless troubles, whose hidden outcomes would hamper its secure and calm progress along the chosen course towards the desired goal.

In parallel, the convincing recipe for success in any raising of capital is a combination of an attractive product or a clever technological-scientific application; a proven business model depicting its clear competitive advantage; a low burn-rate based on a clear presentation dedicated to reducing redundant costs; and a **correct and effective management outlook**, designed to pinpoint and emphasize explicitly the company's unique added value in each of its activities.

In summation

Even the worst storms are survivable – **if one bends against the really noisy and turbulent gusts of wind, knowing how and when to do so**. For it is impossible to change the direction of the wind and its force – but one may turn the sails in such a manner that the vessel will continue seafaring, while its masts will remain intact...

August 2000

Hints for the One in Charge – A Reminder

The following articles, from now on throughout the entire book, are a recipe set out for depicting the right mode of conduct and management, combined with "friendly advice"; a sort-of prescription intended to assist the executive in charge while building the guiding policy of the organization he leads on the one hand, and all along the way to its implementation on the other.

This prescription serves the manager as:

- **A tagging list**, used to remind him of everything he is responsible for.
- **A compendium of ideas and advice**, serving him in the process of designing and formulating the strategies he delineates.
- **A sound database,** supporting him in times of decision-making concerning the practical aspects of implementing the organization's operating policy.
- **An amalgam of pragmatic information,** meant to open a window through which he may clearly see and better understand what he is doing in real time

Additionally, it is a tool constantly presenting a mixture of "what" and "how" to do things, in a sequence that is designed to flow with the text; all this in order to avoid too many professional nuances and particular proficiencies of any kind, for this was not the purpose in the first place.

It is worth noting, here and now, that no attempt has been made at this point to shoot the arrow first and then draw the circle around it (meaning to demonstrate hitting the bull's eye, in accomplishment of the quantitative targets…), but rather to spread and present theories of management in order to deduce practical insights as an outcome of studying organizational processes and their role on the path to goals marked in advance: by analyzing them; arriving at conclusions; learning the lessons; inculcating, internalizing and improving them. All this in order to raise existing benchmarks for future performances.

And perhaps **this is the dogma** in its entirety:
To wit, a condensed selection of proverbs and quotes, some of which would most likely fit in more than one chapter; and actually a few of these do appear, indeed, in several places concurrently. That's because certain matters may serve, probably, more than one aim and can refer to multiple fronts at one and the same time. Maybe it is so since the text's form is: a collection of articles wherein the subjects might be presented in different compositions, each time from a various point of view. On the other hand, it is a compilation of sayings and dicta that may be understood as contradictory – which definitely does not make a manager's life easier; however, there is no doubt that each one of the following maxims can be, on its own, the subject of a very heavy tome.

Except then it would not serve the real purpose of those on whose behalf it has been written…

Philosophy of Leadership

The Root of the Matter: Either One Has it or Not...

Everything actually starts with Man's ability to fully and honestly know himself; to completely recognize his characteristics, their true advantages and downsides. And talking about mastering organizations, one must know in advance: either he has it – **a charismatic personality, a natural leadership ability and the capacity to inspire others** – or he does not. And if he totally lacks these unique traits, he should not take upon himself the responsibilities of guidance communal bodies.

Basically these are internal qualities; but very few unique gifted individuals are so lucky as to be fully blessed with them from birth, later gaining a special place in the pantheon of the great leaders in history. On the other hand, the world is full of countless managers of all types and grades, most of them born rather average. Although possessing the healthy fundamentals of good management in aggregate, they definitely need to gain experience, to develop and improve with a view to becoming, one day in the future, excellent chief executives. This is because it is evident that a substantial part of those necessary virtues mentioned above, can be acquired in time – attributes given to study, acquisition, internalization, assimilation, learning by heart and training; even if not with the purpose of leading others, at least for self-conduct. What follows is intended for all these people, because constant practice is the secret of perfection.

But the afore-said basis – a God-given gift – is first and foremost! These essential qualities should be embedded in a person to such a degree as to serve as an initial, firm foundation, on which his own private edifice will be built, endowing him with the real character needed to lead – and what is more important, to manage. For otherwise the essence of directing organizations and guiding people becomes an empty shell, devoid of real content.

The whole dogma of the business's religion, in all its varieties, is embodied in three words:

- **People:** employers, superiors, colleagues, subordinates, employees, partners, clients, shareholders, bankers, lawyers, politicians, employee committees and union leaders.

- **Processes:** technological, social and economic developments intended to harness all materials, equipment and machines to the highest professional industrial level possible. These are constantly directed towards optimally manufacturing products and rendering services – under continuous variations in science, politics and finances – and marketing them for maximum potential return.

- **Benefit:** obtaining personal or common goals; expressed as an advantage or compensation given to the interested parties in the organization – some of whom may be opposing each other.

And advancing such a Dogma involves, therefore, the establishment of a somewhat bilateral entity: on the one hand guiding and nurturing **human behaviors**, demanding at least two-thirds of a manager's time; and on the other, leading **material scenarios**. Perhaps all this is linked to the operation of a three-dimensional "organism" based on **people, people** and **people**: after all people are in the system, people provide the scientific and socioeconomic impetus, and people set the limits of the utility to be attained.

In any case, the essence of action in any such format is an uncompromising struggle of its executives to balance all contradicting benefits claimed by all its operators and partners – conflicting interests continuously imbedded in it from birth and by its very definition – to finally achieve its defined goals.

For it is multi-faceted, this Dogma of management.
It is a tangled network of activities, combining to deal with all its seemingly "soft" aspects, dealing with theoretical matters and terms – such as individual qualifications and skills, conduct styles, human relationships, intra-personal processes and so on – as well as with the "hard" ones, so to speak, attending to the pragmatic-operational components, for example: organizational structures, strategies, tactics, hierarchies, operating modes, etc.

This is a dynamic, multifarious, many-hued fabric: leading and being led; bequeathing and inheriting; hotly embracing and pushing relentlessly for achievements; supportive as well as oppressive; accepting what there is and striving for more; scientific and empirical; exact and approximate; measured and estimated; professional and amateur; calculated and improvised; factual and abstract; logical and intuitive; practical and theoretical; mechanical and intellectual; sophisticated and straightforward; intelligent and simple; flashy and routine; genius and ordinary; personal and communal; introverted and extroverted; past and present; actual and quixotic; innovative and conservative; daring and considered; conformist and open to change; disbursing and acquisitive; efficient and spendthrift; economic and spiritual; visionary and realistic; crazy and sane; real and imaginary

— mainly, winning and losing. A huge game of chess, which besides being saturated with logical considerations it is packed with a very deep emotional load. And in this king's game, as in battle, the key is not only how to plan and plot well – but, and in particular, to be able to predict the opponent's moves at least three or four steps ahead…

In short, a whole variegated world, **invigorating, stimulating, sweeping**; a puzzle of hierarchal creation, not necessarily specified, settled and prearranged, mostly based on informal connections, teeming with broad ascensions and nonstop slopes, aiming for constant stability here, while enjoying the aroma of variety there. All this is told in the text below: describing the main contributors to study the way in which one may walk this delicate path without stumbling and slipping to any of the chasms on its sides.

And when the knowledge of how to manage is already there, the specific area of activity is of no consequence at all.

Managing systems and people is summed up therefore in the wisdom and abilities of the leader to:

- **Motivate People** — The intelligence and talent to goad and sweep others into action; move them correctly; bring them to realize that their contribution to the organization is for their own good; encourage them to think differently, productively and for the general benefit; making them willing to devote and sacrifice themselves, displaying dedication in their daily missions; discovering any untapped source of human vigor, turning it into positive creativity, advancing the overall marked target; materializing the latent potential of all those involved in the assignment, in order to turn it into a continuous way of life, day after day.

- **Identify Basic Problems (and Solve Them…)** — Spotting and quickly marking weak points in the organization; understanding its constraints emanating from basic deficiencies; locating and removing the extraneous sicknesses; correctly responding to these failures by establishing an organizational structure, aligned with the owners' wishes, the operating environment, the technological and financial resources, while appropriately manning the main functions of the unit.

- **Set the Priorities** — Being visionary, having foresight; clearly declaring short- and long-term targets and assimilating them all around; planning the workflow and allocating resources respectively and in the right measure for the present tasks while taking into account future assignments; making decisions expressed in operational changes due to permutations occurring in the surrounding reality; shifting the essential-business center of gravity, as an outcome of the afore-mentioned variations.

- **Delegate Authority** Leading, coordinating and monitoring; activating the entity from above, as by remote control; setting targets and accurately dictating the tasks derived from these; focusing on the goals – not on the details of the ways to achieve them; a guiding and accompanying involvement only in forming the ties, partnerships and unity in the organization, and in balancing its operational outlines and the use of all the required assets; bestowing a living space on subordinates while spurring them to take initiatives and personal responsibility; authority decentralization depending on the character and quality of those receiving it, while always standing guard, funneling reports, measuring outputs and fixing what is needed to fulfill the pre-ordained policy; and constantly improving its implementation.

And from these alone, one can deduce the four basic managing processes – common to the literary classics of the subject, serving those in charge of the system in their daily toil; and in other words: these gradated disciplines, which over time became obvious and customary for the great majority of the average directors within companies; a variety of prearranged techniques, to be detailed hereafter:

- **Planning and charting**: marking the target and setting the best way to attain it.

- **Establishing and setting up**: constructing the body, its manning according to the determined hierarchy, and a meticulous definition of roles to fully focus on reaching the goals.
- **Directing and controlling**: guiding the employees individually and as a team, pushing them for optimal performance and accompanying them in their efforts to fulfill their assignments.
- **Following up and monitoring**: measuring and comparing continuously the planned path to the one taking place in reality, while repairing deviations and closing gaps.

Leadership – Noblesse Oblige

A leader is he who sees the road, believes in it, guides others along it and walks it himself.

He is a shepherd enjoying a pragmatic and proportional future insight, whose head should dwell in the sky, while his legs must surely be planted firmly on the ground; a visionary but a sober realist; a dreamer living with the limitations of practical compromises; a modern Joseph, who was the ultimate "revealer of secrets" in the ancient world. Settled, sound and responsive to the zeitgeist, he must be far from being a furious prophet preaching at the city's gate; and he is the one to find the balance between the desirable and the available – or, to say it differently, the equilibrium between the ideal and the possible.

And to use some florid metaphorical images, being somewhat poetic (if it is allowed in circumstances like these…), a true visionary is someone able to reminisce from the future; for such a person, yesterday's challenge would be tomorrow's nostalgia.

An individual of this type must be made of very resistant and fine materials, and ought to be able to create a community and a set of values around a prophecy; radiating steadfastness and an iron will to generate trust among people with differing interests, in order to turn this foresight into something real and materialistic, inspiring others to further dream, study extra and do more. In addition, he should be one who fully absorbs the feeling of his flock, ready and knows to walk before the flute – or behind it when it is necessary; and not only being "on top" – but predominantly and prominently "in front" too.

On the other hand, he should be strong enough to stand firm behind his decisions – unpopular as they may be (even amongst his usual supporters…); able to implement them – balanced, stable and unyielding in times of crisis, although alone in his convincing campaign. This pertains as long as he fully believes in the righteousness of his actions and that it definitely serves the goal he was destined to foster; because the right makes the might. For according to John C. Maxell, considered by many to be the number-one expert on leadership in the USA: "Even a good conductor, who wants to lead his orchestra well, must turn, eventually, his back on the crowd – the same one that came to listen and enjoy his performance…"

Leadership means **setting an example**.

The person at the top of the pyramid must be aware of the fact that he is being watched and observed under a microscope at all times and in all his activities and conduct in the organization. Therefore, he should try to evoke the "anthem" of the system under his command, in order to be stamped in everybody's consciousness as the ultimate model for imitation.

This executive should remember, in addition, **that people are ready to suffer a lot if their anguish is shared by others too**, namely mutual sacrifice – a salute to humility and frugality, and never showing off. Thus, if the man at the top decides to cut deeply in the organization, his duty is to apply these painful steps through the length and breadth of it, including the most senior management, and even giving up regretfully his own most cherished habits.

And he must understand that as a modern leader he is not expected to succeed in all his endeavors like a grand wizard, but to be sensitive enough to lend his hand and comfort those who really hurt.

That decision-making individual has also to convince the others that the system he leads resembles a huge chariot, and that he is one of the horses pulling it, leading surely, but not just sitting and lashing the whip; he serves as well as rules. On the other hand, he should never forget, even for a moment, his demanding status. He mustn't behave too humbly, giving up the required distance from his underlings, since his authority may not last for him whenever he may find it necessary...

Sweeping leadership begins, first of all, with **integrity and reliability**.

The leader of an organization has to be more righteous than a chief rabbi or more Catholic than the Pope. He is commanded to be bright and shiny like a newborn baby in terms of his probity, or as an old Indian saying goes: "white as the tooth of a hound dog...". And the many sources of the images above only prove a unanimity and an agreement on this matter among most nations across the globe.

This is because personal reliability is obtained by long and arduous effort; this virtue is created, among other things, by accurate and true accounting, first and foremost, and by standing firmly beyond any word uttered; nothing is more precious! Therefore, due to this status, one should strive to make as few promises as possible; but if given already, they must be absolutely fulfilled. On the other hand, he is likely to lose such a dear asset in seconds by the smallest deviation from the accepted criteria of honesty and individual impeccability. And woe to the "poor guy" caught by even the minutest particles of truth! He is like a leper, whom everyone avoids, especially today in the era of electronic communication, when every piece of such sensitive information may cross continents at the speed of light. For as is written in the book of Ecclesiastes, "A good name is better than fine perfume…".

Correspondingly, the man at the top should avoid being over-righteous; he must keep his distance from outward hypocrisy which defeats the demands of what is right and just, from apologizing for his status. What "may seem" or "may be written in the paper" can surely overcome that which is correct and exigent to be done. For he who forgoes privileges belonging to him by his very function, wishing to be more pious than the Pope, is sinning not only to himself, but to his successors as well.

And on the whole: **true leadership is judged by its open mindedness, generosity, morality and honesty**…

And serving as the **captain** of an enterprise **has many facets**.

Besides acting as a figure at whom all eyes are set all the time, the leader's status requires him to engage in three main domains of activity:

Representative:
- ✓ Symbolic: fulfilling ceremonial, social and legal functions as the elected proxy of the organization.
- ✓ Weaving links: constructing informal public relations frameworks with entities outside the organization – private or communal – for future benefit.
- ✓ Spokesman: publicizing the existence, performance and achievements of the entity, as the first and basic link of its marketing.

Political – as the nerve center:
- ✓ Monitoring: receiving information – compartmentalized occasionally and highly classified. Its internalization analysis

and immediate implementation are part of the general action in order to fulfill the directives coming from above, carrying out superiors' wishes, maintaining peace among the subordinates achieving the designated goals.

- ✓ Distribution: passing intentional messages among those around, sharing and mobilizing them for the promotion of general unity.

Policy setting:

- ✓ Initiating: creating changes and waving new enterprises in response to occasional business opportunities.

- ✓ Crisis solutions: taking care of unforeseen problems which none other than the leader by his personal involvement can solve.

- ✓ Resource distribution: assigning various means to sub-units in accordance with pre-planned design; allocating time as to a correct set of priorities.

- ✓ Negotiating: presence in integral interactions with other entities, where fast decision-making is required.

Three common leadership styles are discernible:

- ▸ **Charismatic or Non-Charismatic**: relying on the halo of personality and character, inspiring others and making them follow unquestionably vs. "quiet" conduct, supported by knowledge, analytical abilities, restraint and the gift to bestow a feeling of security.

- ▸ **Autocratic or Democratic**: forcing decisions with the help of yes-men only, while exploiting status to force subordinates to act according to the policy decided upon vs. persuading and encouraging those who are partners in the action to be involved with the process and the decision-making.

▸ **Visionary and Leading – or Friendly, Introspective and Guiding**: infusing future revelation, fostering a belief in it, and nursing conscientious commitment to the resulting system vs. a pure administrative style immersed in a bureaucratic net of interested persons, aiming at preserving what is in a state of temporary settlement for easing their minds.

The classic captain maneuvers among the three above-depicted styles in accordance with the environment and conditions in which he operates, so his leadership:

✓ Encompasses everything forcefully but quietly – based on a solid foundation of deep thought and meticulous analysis.

✓ Enables the continuation of the organization's motion by complying totally with the general policy, even in the absence of the owner (if it is not himself…) – in a really friendly atmosphere of partnership.

✓ Target-oriented for maximum efficiency, but spiced with spontaneity and flexibility whenever possible.

In general: **managers do things right, while leaders do the right things**. Leaders decide on the really important, actual issue, design the ways to deal with it and lay down the desired targets; managers present the right path to the marked goals and order the schedule of execution according to a detailed set of priorities. And when teamwork is a must, whether the mission is dictated ahead of time or during an unexpected crisis, and the circumstances are critical, demanding the utmost coherency – there would always emerge those born to lead, exhibiting the highest resourcefulness and taking matters into their own hands, without actually being appointed. They fill the others with a huge feeling of security; make them wait for their utterance; electrify their colleagues with their words; and quietly "shoot" their performance instructions. These people react with exemplary equanimity, quickly, but not hastily, and with extreme competence

– without missing even one step of the normal decision-making process – presenting in conclusion the most effective solution for the situation, being able at the same time to finally "pull the trigger" when necessary. And when these dominators do not panic, their underlings never despair or totally collapse; if they are not carried away by vertigo, their subordinates don't get dizzy, losing track entirely; they make things happen, and the rest simply let them occur.

And all of this is by **the force of their personalities and natural leadership** – because of the **x-factor they were graced with** – for everybody seeks their command, instruction and guidance…

Professionalism – the First Step towards Appreciation

The skills of the person at the top of the organization are best described by **the way he manages the totality of the system beneath him.** And his added value is expressed by linking all the minutiae of action – emanating from sole people or teams – into one interlinked, solidified product; by coordinating the activities of all his underlings and creating a fabric of fruitful reciprocity among them; by the ability to sweep his subordinates to elation and bring them as a group of **individuals**, dependent on each other, to the their pinnacle **together** – and most important as a **unit**; not in uniformity but in **unison**. For, to quote the well-worn but sharp cliché once again: "If we do not hang together, we shall surely hang separately…".

The executive's efficiency and dexterity are distinguished by the talent to create centers of excellence at all staff ranks which nourish each other; by the aura of force he inspires around himself, with a minimum of words, by striving forward to the development of the corporate and its growth, while everybody feels the presence of the "responsible adult" in the room, who is able to condense ten years of experience into one work year, when other implement a year's experience repeating itself for a decade: so that hardly anything goes unnoticed by his personal radar.

And in addition, he should be also able to **manage managers**...

The esteem of those under the authority of the senior executive comes from the expertise he demonstrates in all the lacunas they have in their knowledge – and not in areas of their special training. They respect him for his faculty in leading decision-making procedures based on professional-technical knowhow – dealing with differing, even contradicting, opinions amongst his subordinates – although his acquaintance with the affair being discussed is rather shallow. Because of their inability or unwillingness to be involved in management and administration, the employees tend to absolutely accept his authority – but only after discerning his superior qualities and sensible leadership methods, promoting, in their eyes, the interests of the company as a whole. And in their opinion this is a professional manager of the first rank, the mentor of the firm and guarantor of its existence.

To the custodians, on the other hand, a manager's professionalism is normally tested by the outcomes of the organization's operation, which they consign to him, as opposed to those they assume and dictate, by their impression of the control he yields over the system he leads and directs.

Controlling the system means its guidance and routing to the defined goals while extracting the utmost from its resources. This is actually ensuring the performance of the six basic activities necessary to any corporate entity, as detailed below:

- **Technical**: producing, processing and changing form.
- **Commercial:** buying, selling and trading.
- **Financial:** raising and managing capital.
- **Safety:** securing the workforce and the intellectual as well as the material properties.

- **Accounting:** bookkeeping, pricing, stock, data gathering, sorting and funneling.
- **Administration:** forecasting, planning, conducting, coordination, control, drawing conclusions and improving efficiency.

The last one is fundamentally different than the other five, in its requiring accurate mapping of the system under the executive's supervision, again and again in such detail as insuring a very good knowledge of what is happening at all levels – their specifications and activities. Such a procedure should be adopted by all underlings – everybody in his own department – in order to minimize the number of faults in the cumulative entity, whose sources are normally misunderstandings among units not sufficiently familiar with each other.

As for specific leading issues, **the executive's knowledge should find expression where the company does not excel, in order to transform it from good to excellent and a frontrunner in its field**; a sphere of action within which his influence will be the most decisive of the whole institute, and his contribution to its success the most weighty; a space of performance and pushing, aggressive and prone to attack. **Identifying such a territory and becoming proficient in it are two of a manager's skills at their peak**. After all, a first-class boss should elevate his working environment to a higher stage than he found it – even if only by his very presence. Or as was once said by an obliquely smiling wise person: "Turn it from nothing into something…".

There are a lot of stories in the business world about such elected persons who grow up in organizations – or arrive there – to lead and jumpstart them to greatness, just by becoming Chief Executive Operators (CEOs); by their unique personalities, they change a special thing or two in the place's managerial attitude. The best example is perhaps Bill Gates who drove Microsoft to the pinnacle of its league, not by any huge knowledge of computer software – but by one of the principles of his exclusive business-managing grasp, for instance, which flashed like a lightning bolt in his mind at the beginning of the road and was rooted by him later on in the company: charging repeatedly over time for the use of his inventions, instead of billing customers once for their sale.

And on the scientific front: a manager should surround himself with the best advisers he can recruit, in order to assist him in performing the six basic activities of the system he runs, as described above – so that he may beat any opponent exactly in his field of expertise, if required. Now, it is impossible for the man on top to be thoroughly acquainted with all the elements of activities in his organization and be involved with every detail of them; otherwise he would not lead his unit, but be just another employee. David Ben Gurion, Israel's first prime minister, found a very exceptional way to express this concept when asked about his deep knowledge of all governmental business by saying: "I do not really understand all of it – but I am a **specialist on specialists**…". This is a very profound management attitude indeed. However, it is a mixed blessing: as much as the domain is rich in hi-tech, and the employees are more gifted, the leadership should be more **transparent** – meaning as in "not felt"; in other words, initiating, pushing and directing to clearly specified targets, but without the subordinates feeling its foursquare determination to constantly move forward towards the dictated goal. This is because it is very easy to create within people of such an Intelligence, nonconformists mostly, the sense that their talents are being challenged; this may lead to irrelevant struggles about "who is more clever and knowledgeable…" – conflicts which may prevent the company from accomplishing that which is good for it.

One of the proven ways to lead such a group is by feigning **humility** – especially in a very cruel competitive world in which people are constantly evaluated by the results of their actions. One should not consider himself the best by forcing a conceptual dictatorship, but display moral strength by adopting a right measure of modesty and being open to learning from everybody; a kind of a **human benchmarking**: limiting the pollution of an ego swollen with self-confidence, by proving that real lessons are learnt from each occurrence, by listening to all, and by taking on successful and tested manners of activities. Concerning the mannerisms of the self, one should better stay away from them (and here it is very important to internalize that any solution for a problem coming from a senior executive is a kind of coercion by itself; for his juniors depend on it immediately in order to placate the boss and stop thinking independently – even if adopting the superior's idea is quite wrong. Therefore it is essential for him to listen before speaking…).

In other words; such transparency is supposed to be compensated by "professional cognitive leadership". One must be **authoritative** at a rate that should enable leading even the most professional people by a **logic that is their own as well**, without forcing them to give up their assertiveness: intelligence, decisiveness and resolve. For, according to John C. Maxwell, people tend to support whatever they feel is partly their creation…

On the one hand, the executive ought to know each sphere well enough to be able to make critical decisions, which will be trustingly and straightforwardly accepted by the employees, by tactfully transmitting the following message: the fact that it was not them who laid the egg does not forbid them from expressing their opinion of its taste…

Alternatively, he must also project enough statecraft and managerial distance, in order to convince the others to accept his decisions without objections – even enthusiastically – and devoid of scrutinizing pedantically the minute details; for anyway the likelihood of standing up to the technical authorities, in their niches of expertise, is minimal. Moreover, such an endeavor may give rise to clashes, in which the senior executive is bound to lose. Since a clever man avoids troubles from which a wise one can extricate himself, it is always better to respect each employee's professional dignity in order to gain his future support for the general conduct of the organization.

In this case, therefore, the secret means to leading others, even inspiring them, is to dictate a sort of "intended managerial obliqueness" in the organizational structure, less predatory and more relaxed; by this, one creates a full identification of all employees with their workplace – without giving up even the smallest measure of proficient perfectionism or conceding any of the demands to accomplish the predetermined goals. The difference is, consequently, in the way to ensure the full dedication of all working hands. Hence it is possible – even desirable – to devise a leading policy of the most general and encompassing type: a total one, which in addition to rigidly preaching to uncompromising professionalism, gives one a feeling that he works for a family business; where the man at the top treats all in a warm, fatherly manner; the compensation is generous, sometimes even higher than what was agreed; and each problem – even if it is private – is handled personally and on the spot. All of this is meant to guarantee that such a cooperative atmosphere will create a conscientious personal obligation and complete commitment to the common good and turn each individual into a part of an oiled and well-functioning machine: blurring totally the "self" and fully enslaving the individual to the collective – in a constant readiness to enlist for battle, on short notice and with no questions – to fulfill the communal needs. For the boss is not there only to give orders and rebuke the fuck-ups – he is there, first and foremost, to draw the best from his underlings...

And in aggregate, **an organization's professionalism** is expressed in an ambiance permeating all that are a part in the group's action – from the first to the last of the employees – including all internal elements as well as external, interested parties. A spirit flows, guided by management, showing an exceptional moral and behavioral code in all its daily dealings – together with the attitude of its employees to their assignments and tasks. For in the atmosphere inspired by the institute outwards, the image of each one of its members is definitely reflected.

Managing from the Heart – the Path to Interpersonal Conduct

The proper way of managing people depends on the **level of ability to communicate with them**. For leadership does not mean control per-se, but **the art of convincing people to act in unison for a communal goal**; the talent to play to the specific motivational factor of each and every one personally, the precise trigger that stimulates him such as: the desire for compensation, achievement, power, independence, security, esteem, fair treatment, belonging or self-fulfillment. Identification with the essence of the occupation, teamwork, open lines of human interactive contacts and talks, bonding, reciprocation, attentiveness and being able to freely express opinions are, after all, the glue, binding different people in joint action for one collective purpose.

Until the last decades of the 20th century the legendary leader-warrior, sophisticated and cunning, was perceived as the ultimate manager, carrying a "black belt" in corporate politics and organizational survival. Nowadays, due to the evolutionary changes in the nature of the public involved in all kind of businesses (being based mainly on the front of technical progress, free global communications and open commercial data for all…), a reduction has occurred in the image of the "fighting", tough and scheming boss – even though it was perceived positively – and he has lost his attraction and popularity. The best example is perhaps David Ben Gurion, Israel's first prime minister, considered the greatest leader in the nation's history: it is certainly possible that even his message would not go through today, and he would not have been elected to his post due to his somewhat stiff personality. On the other hand there is a tendency lately requiring managers, in addition to the previously mentioned qualities, to be "human resources champions", since **it is very nice to be important, but much more important to be nice**. And there is no doubt that skills bubbling from the soul – the emotional ones – play a substantial and central role in any sort of activity; at the end of the day, when discussing people, it is impossible to analyze them and judge their activities dryly by "fact," "conclusion," and "action" solely, as there is a need for something much higher. Said lyrically: "The eyes are the window to the spirit, but true vision comes from the heart…".

Four traits of interpersonal emotional intelligence – correctly implemented – make the real difference:

- ✓ The capability to immerse oneself easily and efficiently in the social environment and professional atmosphere.

- ✓ The ability to create a feeling of a capacity to, first of all, listen to others and be open — not only to accept different opinions, but to appreciate them explicitly.

- ✓ The knowledge to express interest in the personal lives of each employee, even the most junior, and empathy for his struggles, occupied by his problems and his failures due to those.

- ✓ The skill to comment or criticize in a friendly, helping and constructive manner – and not in a judgmental, patronizing and harmful way

Feedback in general serves all partners in maintaining the organization – the manager as well as his underlings. Constitutionally, it refers to information about the performance of all various divisions in the corporate, and assists in distributing educating messages from the top to each sector of the firm, while demonstrating how it is being perceived by other people in the system. Such response and comments influence significantly the rest of the units in the mechanism, of course.

The subject also has personal implications; the feedback is used by the senior executive as a tool with which to bestow on his juniors his opinion of their functioning – letting them know if it is good or whether improvement is due. Without this advice, people are in the dark: having no idea about their status with the boss or their colleagues, what is expected of them, and what has gone amiss in their work so far — faults that may get worse in time unless regularly discussed in an open and creative manner.

However, many managers generously disperse invective – but are very sparing with praise (in a kind of "emotional autism," a type of incorrigible and surely incurable disability; or perhaps less clinically — a lack of human warmth that may unite the individuals underneath around them...) Therefore, this is one of the more important and delicate missions of the superior. Obviously there is a correlation between the manner of criticism and its acceptance. Improper admonitions of subordinates are the main reason for destructive confrontations at the workplace and the worst means to create motivation. On the other hand, **satisfied people, feeling that their efforts are appreciated** (literally pleased with themselves, but not resting on their laurels; secure in the knowledge that improvement is a must at all times...) **always achieve the best results**. Everybody likes compliments.

Therefore, **the technique of criticism is certainly woven into the art of praise**. Thus, it is recommended to convey these censures with a sort of "positive cunning," sounding like clarifications, from which one may deduce what is in need of melioration to progress, focusing on what the employee has done and is capable of accomplishing instead of pointing out one random poorly performed task as evidence of his characteristics and abilities, in **all his activities – not in his personality**. And positive criticism, delivered in a constant, concise, privately and wise manner requires:

- **Being Specific**: describing the problem accurately and defining it explicitly; what is wrong, how one feels about it and and which is the way to overcome the difficulty.
- **Offer a Pragmatic Solution**: presenting realistic possibilities or alternatives as a very reasonable response, ones that the employee may have not even thought of.
- **Show a Presence**: expressing criticism face-to-face with a very personal touch – but not a personal strain; a dialogue intended to pass on cordiality and intimacy. Any other attitude – such as e-mail, memo, even a handwritten note – is too formal and alien.
- **Exhibit over Sensitivity**: demonstrating awareness of the powerful influence of the substance and manner of what is being said to the listener.
- **Allow Reaction**: inspiring a tolerant atmosphere by paying attention honestly and patiently to what the other person has to say in his defense, letting him feel that he is really being seriously heard – and immediately relating to his words frankly and in context.

And it should be noted and emphasized, here and now: in each meeting such as this only the truth must be said – even if sometimes unpleasant. But it is recommended to be practical and raise only points relevant to the subject discussed – not everything that the heart thinks must be blurted out right away, but only the absolutely necessary and related. It is very important to remember that in life generally – scenes like this included – words are like drugs: first used, later addictive. And one can never predict the reaction of the other side to what he has heard – for being overly honest may sometimes cause more harm than good.

Eschewing prejudice is a necessity.
Stigmas may arise in every organization. The most common are those created within it by ethnic, racial or social biases – or by the gossip of outer agents; a taint associated with somebody by colleagues or by his boss, or a "bad label" attached to the entire firm by outsiders who hardly know anything about it. Such prejudices are very dangerous, since a fixation with them means missing opportunities which may come up from openness to innovation; according to Maimonides, "They are the greatest threat to Man's intellectual development...".

A wrong adoption of an ethnic, racial, sexual or religious stigma means giving up on the advantages inherent in having employees of various backgrounds, experiences, outlooks and opinions. In a consolidated, harmonious and coordinated effort of a variety of people it is possible to achieve much better results than with a horribly monolithic singular population, from a human fabric of similar demography and with a nearly identical world view. It must be understood that a homogenous society is a very sick body, because pluralism is a very efficient mechanism, wonderfully protecting it from inside, while a uniform public gives free rein to mistakes, corruption and evil, for there is no one to protest or wave the flag of resistance. A polity with no diversity creates, actually, an obedient community (like the Nazi regime, God forbid...), where the affliction of monotony puts an end to any independent thinking, inflicting the group with a dullness and fixation to the brink of destruction.

Adhering to a slander attached to somebody privately is a disadvantage too, because it may lead to missing the real potential of a person or a system. For the true motives of the "legacy" left by the previous management are not always really known. It is possible that some assessments may have been born out of personal grudges, totally disconnected from authentic and relevant traits.

On the other hand, each member of staff is entitled to a fresh start –

especially if it was decided to keep him in the company despite the shift in management. Were his functioning that horrible, his employment should have been stopped immediately – without delaying the verdict until the arrival of a new executive. Such is an organization; it is deserving of credit – initially at least – until its essence and character is fully recognized and understood, before slandering it in public. Therefore, it is only fair to ignore all subjective "opinions" until proven otherwise. And in general it should be remembered: rumors, defined as baseless or unverified reports, may ruin reputations, destroy a career, and even totally "wipe out" a person. This is a sickness that should be immediately and vigorously uprooted; the source must be identified, exposed, condemned and strongly got rid of.

In short: using prejudices supports "petty politicians" only – or as was jokingly said once: "Darwin was probably wrong: Man originates not from ape – but from the chicken; for people enjoy pecking and clucking all the time, as if it were a national sport..." And even if it is difficult to ignore stigmas, the figure at the top must hold forth in order to prevent distorted discrimination and ensure a fair and equal chance to all. In such cases, it is recommended to:

✓ Change the **atmosphere** in the organization by distributing an open manifesto among subordinates with their full cooperation.

✓ Shape a notion of **when** to come out forcefully against prejudices.

✓ Decide **if and how** to act in cases of intended stigmatization.

Speaking in public does not mean speaking impersonally.
Meetings of employees and managers in the same room are the main interpersonal activities of any organization; actually, they are the nerve center of management. And even if the adherents of contact by internet mail regard this notion as old-fashioned, it is important to inculcate that electronic means of communication or conference calls cannot be a suitable substitute for these gatherings, the physical face-

to-face assembly of partners in the same system, each with his fellow man. Such direct get-togethers – not necessarily being considered as formal conventions – are inalienable assets of any setting that listens to its people and champions two-way conversations. Otherwise, how would directors know what their subordinates are truly thinking? Therefore these should take place in a planned and regular manner.

It is permitted for this sort of forum to contain friendly small talk – even touching on very personal matters – for the sake of enhancing openness and friendship among employees. But when dealing with professional matters, they should be recorded and concluded in detailed summaries, to be distributed amongst all participants. Such a document should state very clearly the intentions of the senior executives, the decision accepted and explicit performance directions. Those directives should specify who is responsible for their implementation and the relevant deadline.

While participating in this kind of meeting, all must be aware of the fact that some of the attendees may be too anxious to take control of the discussion; these ones turn out to be a burden upon the entire group by their desire to stand out and their aggressive attitude, due to lack of the basic ability to understand what is and is not appropriate for collective discussion and thinking. By this, they undermine the correct conduct of the conference and attainment of practical understandings and conclusions. Therefore the chairman should insist on **allowing everybody in the room to express themselves equally.**

One should "acquire" a sound social-managerial acceptability from subordinates and colleagues, which will enable the establishment of ad hoc teams for **unexpected challenges**. The formal structure of the organization supposes to answer easily and currently most usual problems, since these are expected beforehand. But unforeseen difficulties requires irregular actions, made possible by activating networks based on friendly relationships, designed to bypass obstacles

– differing from the dictated customary procedures and hierarchies; and this only happens by all cooperators understanding the importance of the issue and by their commitment to cut bureaucracies and offer unusual help and extraordinary solutions, when the need really arises; by then, it really does not matter what one knows but whom he is acquainted with. The ability of such persons to sign treaties of the abovementioned type, without deviating from personal and social hygiene (which may not only, heaven forbid, ignite the lobes of the imagination but give rise also to the glands of law and morality...) and establish in fact temporarily designated workgroups for special assignments, randomly born, is among the crucial factors of their successful functioning.

Therefore the real "stars" of the organization are those having close connections with employees of all strata: ties of trust, of professionalism and of solid social communication. They are these who are smart enough (especially...) to avoid creating "enemies" without cause just by neglect or things said inadvertently, for those hurt would surely find the opportunity to cause harm at their leisure. Ironically-sarcastically, it has been said: "even the youngest kitten may spoil the prey of the biggest lions and tigers...". And this contrasts with "petit-dictators" full of themselves, or "corporate nerds" afraid of themselves, sitting all day long behind their desks, disconnected from the people and the occurrences in the company's field; these will be forever cut off from the informal political arena, which moves the entire cycle to a large degree. And even being the greatest wizards in the firm's business domain, they are unable to manage, as long as they receive minimal support from their subordinates and colleagues. Or in the jargon: they do not go with the flow, avoiding "under the table dealing" in the most positive sense of the word.

It is imperative to develop and crystalize organizational wisdom. In other words: it is necessary to burn the forthcoming social-professional processes into the consciousness of the entire personnel, so that they may be partners in the work that is being executed:

- **Establishing Groups:** coordinating team efforts; synthesizing the various activities, apparently, done by a collection of people sometimes totally different in kind or character, and setting them in motion as one unit, attaining synergy.
- **Solution Processing**: mediation in preventing quarrels; settling disputes at their very beginning.
- **Encouraging Interpersonal Relationships**: assimilating empathy and socialization; inspiring tolerance; the ability to see things from the other's point of view; readiness to accept different opinions – especially those of friends, clients, subordinates... who may be influenced.
- **Analyzing the Other**: being sensitive to moods, incentives and worries of one's fellow-man – and understanding them.
- **Unite Fronts**: emphasizing the need for cooperation while averting clashes; convincingly arguing for unity of minds – a consensus.

In order to lead such activities and control them, the personal involvement of the man at the top is necessary, his wisdom and experience. And it is important to internalize that guiding such processes is worthless unless backed by his personal example – sticking to the notion of living up to one's principles:

- **Taking the Initiative**: adhering to responsibility beyond the formal definition of the job – especially in helping employees in all fields of their lives, taking a good and unique care of them.
- **Self-Management**: correct time planning scheduled for commitments; sticking to deadlines and avoiding cancellation of appointments, at the last minute, without due reason.

One of the most important indicators of an individual's ability to communicate with others are **his negotiating skills** – the measure of his patience and tolerance – within his private world and his family nest, or any different activity he performs. This virtue is revealed here at its best.

Since one of the main ingredients of discussing and bargaining, in life generally and in business particularly, is emotional, so the key to success in wheeling and dealing is the ability to **predict the personal inner aspirations of each side**, to lower them by persuasion, and finally – to competently **bridge any gaps** between them. And one should always remember: even the bitterest disputes are normally not about cardinal principles – sort of "better die than waver" – but about the limits of **compromise**; thus it is sometimes better to "sacrifice" one set in order to win the whole match. This is if one wishes to see negotiation as a means to overcome obstacles, a kind of a tolerant dialogue in the true sense of the word, advancing things with the intention of reaching a common denominator good for all, hinting rather explicitly at the existence of a win-win situation – and not a process of deteriorating huckstering with a pre-existing record of reasons and a predicted chronicle of its failure (due to a "blame game," so to say...) For if one side would figure himself the sole loser, he would never carry out the agreement – even if it is backed up by a thousand-page very detailed contract. Nobody likes (nor can allow himself, mentally or emotionally...) to be defeated.

And one more thing worthy of internalizing: **he who negotiates toughly intends, apparently, to fulfill the agreement achieved to the letter.** In other words, in such bargaining one needs to be rigid, as well as totally honest and reliable. And then, contrary to the famous dictum by the Hollywood producer, Sam Goldwyn, that "an oral agreement isn't worth the paper it's written on," a handshake is enough to validate a contract, if both sides are truly willing to accept it. And in order to understand how far it is possible to stretch the limits there is a need to deeply be aware of – in addition to the nature of the opponent – his ideological and political motives; namely "get in his shoes" and be emphatic to him, to think in terms of his commercial interests and come well prepared to the meeting. Since in such cases it is not only the matter of knowing what one sells, but it is also the issue of trying and learn well what the other side is anticipating to buy...

And when the process is stuck, unable to move on further, even a bit, it is recommended to "produce" a different and fresh contributor, who may have nothing to do with the intercourse up to now, and throw him into the boiling saucepan. A step like this – not precisely a compromise, but a proposition which might bring both sides to attain their full cravings – can definitely pull the wagon out of the mud. For if the situation is being dragged into "over-argumentation" and no outlet is in sight, it must be ended with an exceptional and unexpected tactical step, one that has to be deeply weighted before actuality offered, since it can be used only once at that kind of event.

However, such controversies should never be interpreted personally and serve to end the game totally. Because on the other hand, one of the most important contributions a manager may bring to the unit he heads **is a fertile relationship with those agents who are not under his direct control**: colleagues, superiors or external factors such as: government ministers, politicians, tycoons, bankers, lawyers, union leaders, et cetera – those real and regular negotiating partners without whose cooperation and generous help the company's future success and thriving may be put in jeopardy. And a great importance is attached to friendship in business – devotion to informal communication relations within (but mostly outside...) the organization in times and circumstances beyond normal working hours that would be profitable, nearly always, in the long run. Yet, it is forbidden to ever forget the moral standards or compromise oneself ethically, even in times of very keen conflict of interests between the welfare of the organization and the wish to maintain good supra-business amity.

At the end of the day, the best of management wisdom in the interpersonal domain lies in a maximal exploitation of the activity climate to breaking down barriers, building up bridges and finding a constant balance between the colliding interests of all involved parties around the ability to convince each of them separately that he is the only child and sole heir of the system.

This is the talent of walking a tightrope while preserving a delicate balance among stock owners interested in a quick yield for their investment, employees frequently pushing for the betterment of their economic situation and working conditions, and clients interested in excellent products or services for the lowest price possible. It is the ability to safeguard against over-deviating to one side, by knowing how to really stretch the barriers of specific professionalism up to the limit – but without even crossing once the law's restrictions. It is the aptitude to hold a healthy tension amongst all the above-depicted factors, allowing everyone to feel that his importance to the organization – and only this – guides the system's activities from beginning to end; in other words, to come out okay with one and all.

After all the **issue is no more the potential of leading people only, but also and in essence, the style of their management and the way of conduct towards them**, since trying to contain all human traits in a single and simple mathematical formula is analogous to wishing and force Cinderella's ugly stepsister's foot into the glass shoe...

Strategy: the Pragmatic-Practical Direction of Any Business

In the classical business world, strategy is conceived as a web of lessons, conclusions, decisions, planning and operative direction relating to the reciprocal activities of the organization, its character and inner management on the one hand, and the environment of its functioning on the other – and the strong interdependence of it all. And one of the most important roles that the top leadership of a company has is the **formation, formulation and assimilation** of these policies and approaches, and their **implementation** afterwards along the way (while continuing their design and broadening, if the need arises...).

This is, in fact, the most comprehensive presentation of the firm's image, its destinations, activities, and domains in the present and future, its expected place in these areas compared to its competitors, and all avenues of execution and asset allocation required for attaining its objectives. That is why, the planned policy must be based on a fully integrated and harmonious assembly of fundamental goals, universal to all partners and understood by them; they must be long-term, encompassing the solutions for the enterprise's survival over time; like the short-term ones, they ought to safeguard its routine operation by teaching the organization how to act on a daily basis.

This kind of **business outlook** is bound to respond for the major ingredients influencing strategy-building: **environment, resources, competencies and values**. It should be built up on opportunities and external constraints, on today's strengths and weaknesses of the company and its potential tomorrow; and on the preferences of the top management and the characteristics of its personnel.

The essence of modern business strategy lies in **singularity**: how to focus on inventing new rules of engagement in an ever-changing market, since being different and exceptional means being **competitive to win**. This is to say: creating an outstanding commercial status for the company, bestowing on it a high level of value and quality, far above its competitors in the same operative sphere. For what is the doctrine of winning "offhand" in any field of occupation? It is simply coupling the strengths of one side to the weak spots of its rivals, something obvious – even instinctive – that should be implemented at the outset, as a first step, and throughout the conduct and existence of the firm. However, the best way to leave all opponents really faraway behind (and in bitter struggles – to defeat them completely…) is by turning, in the second phase, what is conceived to be their greatest advantage into a shortcoming, a deficiency. That is: let them concentrate on what they perceive as their main power and virtue – therefore continuously digging in their heels – and while absorbed in their notions of "inner performance", skirt their positions by creating original vocation stages and unique benchmarks (or in real battles – attack them by surprise wherever they are least prepared…).

Such ambition is only achievable if one understands that excellence in the market should sprout from creative thinking or innovative modes of activity – not from imitating and improving on the competitors. This was best formulated by the known British mathematician G. H. Hardy: "It is not worth an intelligent man's time to be in the majority, since by definition, there are already enough people to do that…". Thus the following principles should be applied at all times concurrently:

▸ **Outlining a unique set of activities in comparison to the others.**

  Positioning of strategic concepts based on original, above-average performance. These planning notions do not contradict each other, sometimes they even partly overlap, finding expression in policy outlines such as:

  - Satisfying the demands of certain sectors only: servicing most (or the entire) clientele, but of a selected segment of customers; not trying to fulfill the needs of the whole market.

  - Dealing with a variety of products or unique services (for the afore-said public…), instead of sticking to one and only commercial line.

  - Adopting a customer-oriented attitude that supposes to engage the consumers in the best and most personal way. Finding very particular and inimitable paths to reach the clients in a super-specific manner.

To wit, this is not solely a matter of identifying irregular business niches and reaching those spots, but of a tailor-made proper response on any basis; and perhaps it is some combination of any two or all of the above-mentioned.

- **Making concessions in some domains of completion.**

    Occasionally compromises are called for in a few fronts, in order to achieve a lasting strategic stability for the following reasons:

    - The worry of presenting inconsistency in image or reputation; the fear of diminishing reliability or losing it altogether due to the introduction of new products from a different line than the leading one.
    - The multiplicity and variety of the activities' character and style. Trying to please everyone at the same time may harm the quality of performance and ultimately the value of what is offered.
    - The limitations inherent in the inner coordination and control of a multicolored vocation – something like "grasp all – lose all", which would definitely hurt the firm's name.

    Meaning: deciding what **not to do**!

- **Striving for full internal coordination of the entire operational methodology and all executing units in the organization.**

    The combination and harmony of all the different active directions of the communal entity – in which no one abolishes the others – are necessary for the strength of its policy and the long term prospect of its existence. The need to harmonize such actions within the company stems normally from:

    - A simple consistency that is supposed to be derived from the general strategy, subordinated to its essence, parallel and joined to it. An attitude that assists in explaining the company's policy to clients, employees and shareholders, while helping to facilitate easily its implementation.

- The synthesis principle itself, mutually enforcing cooperation in various assignments serving the same single goal.
- The optimization of the effort in order to minimize exertion or for increasing efficiency, so to say.

And a policy presenting originality, creativity and healthy, crystallized and harmonized operating systems on the one hand, but a philosophy of concession and compromise when and where necessary on the other, bestows upon clients and stockholders the required confidence; and hence it becomes strong, immune and even long-lasting. Therefore it is very easy to lead the character of the organization by its strategy – and not vice-versa.

The totality of activities described above creates the **accumulative competitive advantage** of the corporate; this is because it is based on a calculated and robust strategy and not only on performance efficiency (which is, actually, prone to fairly good imitation, leading to the blurring of differences among companies and the cancelation of any significant superiority of one over any other...). That sort of policy, rooted in dynamism, uniqueness, cooperation and coordination of production activities, promises a clear priority above all competitors, and only keeps on growing as time goes by; for the synchronization off all units and factors in the firm that executes the said guidelines, consolidates all actions into an harmonic, general and encompassing main processes, perfectly functioning and bestowing it with the solidity needed to create dominance in its sector; one that is not only unshakable, but unduplicable as well.

The explanation is quite simple: as discussed previously, operational effectiveness is easily imitable; because, first of all, work mythologies, management approaches, technologies, improvements of revenues and ways of satisfying customers are spreading fast and subjected to fairly accurate duplication. Secondly, since opponents' points of reference or exit levels are becoming, slowly but surely, so similar until they turn out to be actually identical – technical qualities, distribution techniques, operational time coefficients and partnerships schemes are almost fully replicable.

However, as far as **strategic positioning** goes, it is not straightforward at all. When activities are complementary, strengthening each other and irreparably intertwined, business rivals would not reap any benefits from copying each one separately except by imitating the whole activity fabric. But without having full knowledge of the necessary mutuality of its many working channels among its sectors, sections, cells and individuals, without completely understanding the elements of the glue and its formula holding them together, there is no chance of achieving the operating level of the original company. Namely, the advantage over the foes grows from a total array of interpersonal and systemic movements and doings – not from only one facet of creativity, but an extremely comprehensive dynamic mesh, in which the whole is always much more important and stronger than each of the parts by itself.

The argument above can easily be proved arithmetically: as aforedescribed, the quality of the chosen policy performance dictated is improved with the amelioration of any component that contributes to a higher inter-personal interaction among all partners of its activation, and the upgrading of all its operative ingredients. Since the likelihood of perfectly duplicating each and every mentioned parameter is normally less the one hundred percent (100%), the final result of such an experiment would be an ever-diminishing number, for it would always be an outcome of multiplying fractures. So it is impossible to copy completely to the point the **unique array** of activities, which is actually the infrastructure that establishes the specific strategy of organization in the market in which it is functioning.

Building a strategy entails two main phases: **design and implementation**.
   The design aspect means trying to optimally balance the following three elements:
- ✓ Business opportunities alongside risks in the activities, domains and the functioning environment.
- ✓ The property and total resources – intellectual as well as material – of the establishment in the present and those projected in the future.
- ✓ Values, state of mind and personal wishes of the top management.

The cardinal aim of this intended phase is charting the way of confronting the competition in the sector. The next one is forming the tactics, preparing an operational plan including:
- ✓ Strategic **positioning** to **defend** against business adversaries.
- ✓ Setting a methodology of **influencing** the power balance in the action's surroundings in order to **improve** postures.
- ✓ Preparing a **prognosis**, the best one possible, of all future changes, and a proper **response** to each of them.

The following is the formulation of the strategy. Its basic parameters can be arrayed in some forms:
- ▶ **By Targets**: a concise and fundamental presentation of assignments derived from the general purpose, whose combined fulfillment would lead to the accomplishment of the company's final destination.
- ▶ **By Levels**: clarifying, dismantling and delimiting the organization's structure into different work groups in line with their size and focus of occupation.

- **By Scope**: spreading principles or detailed programs in terms of times and quantities, prone to measured allocation and accurate monitoring.
- **By Functioning**: a clear determination of tendencies and interim intentions according to the fields in work, assignments and the methods of the various departments' activities.

The best form of defining the strategy is the one covering everything mentioned above: it starts by marking the overall target while pointing at more specific goals, encompassing first of all the entire institution; thereafter, it is divided and descends to the level of sub-units according to their sizes and areas of performance (but only those having independent business considerations, which contribute to the entire framework...); and finally describing in detail all the functional abilities of the communal body.

In drafting the strategy, it is crucial to distinguish the "targets" dictated within it – being wide-ranging declarations of the organization's desires – out of the "goals" derived from them, which are plain definitions of obtainable tendencies, disposed to the exact measurement of achievement. And this view may perhaps present the answer to the lasting argument between the two most common methodologies concerning the best way of processing, formulating and adopting strategy: whether to openly, specifically and explicitly present the accurate final aims, or to suffice with their indication as titles, generally insinuating the means of their attainment. It is evident that for the full characterization of the policy and its accurate fixing, its designated ultimate objectives must be undoubtedly clarified, including precise quantification: first and foremost, to **force the management and the decision-makers** to focus on a clear description of the company's trends, while deciding among themselves on what and how they intend to act; second, in order to pass it to the performing craft in a brief, understandable and unequivocal manner. Since the **target is the raison d'être of the organization's active fabric and the**

true criteria of the need for its continued existence.

The other aspect of strategy is the execution, meaning the management and operation of all systems in order to achieve an optimal integration of all partners to the creation, social scenarios, technological developments and the assets allocated to accomplish the policy decided upon. In other words, securing the continued being of all the following dimensions supports the leading job being done in the right way.

✓ Organizational structures and processes.

✓ Proper procedures and rules.

✓ Coordinated workforce motivational mechanisms.

✓ Follow-up, monitoring and reporting systems.

✓ Assigning performance tasks.

✓ Means of rigorously supervising the achievement of goals.

And among all these, steady and continuous interaction is coming about, including a full cooperation between each of the above and all the others and vice-versa, and their harmonic, hopefully synergistic, working evolvement. These allow the improvement and upgrading of the initial strategy, and as a result, the organizational structure as well.

However, for a practical setting in motion of the framework, it is imperative to make sure, beforehand, that the dictated policy is **realistic** and may be **completely realized, inside and outside.** Therefore, a proficient, purposeful and effective enterprise – is the one that succeeds in fully coordinating its established and determined strategy with the implementation of its operative derivatives, well-expressed in a proper organizational hierarchy; in control and analysis management systems attached, with which it weaves its plans to join the environment in which it functions; and in a strict and uncompromising insistence on a continued **uniqueness of concept and handling.**

Concerning all the above, it is worth remembering that:
- ✓ A plan conceived of a sound and correctly built-up strategy is smoothly implementable.
- ✓ In business – as in war, in one aspect at least – if the strategy's notion is right, then the overall view, despite tactical mistakes along the way, will finally prove itself successful, and victory will come.
- ✓ Even a good strategy may sometimes fall victim to incorrect forecasts of competition, performance failures, narrow-mindedness of partners, or an attempt of expanding and growing too fast, devoid of economic calculation and proper planning.

A strategic observation must be wide-scoped and long-sighted to a range of at least **half a decade**. In other words, it has to fit a "planning cycle" suitable to the character of the organization. On the one hand, it must be for a period long enough for its basic principles to be assimilated among the people and enable a proper development of the unique qualitative activity skills derived from it for the attainment of the goal; and on the other hand, for a time span allowing the cumulative entity's control system to check the utility of the present policy while adapting it to the personal, social, technological and environmental changes occurring meanwhile, but without having the people around feel that essential revolutions are taking place too often.

It should be remembered that continuity of management and operational notions and methods within the organization serve to broadcast consistency and definitely strengthen its exclusive identity and reputation. Frequent variations of programs, on the contrary, are very expensive. Daily alterations and an inability to choose a bright stance are causes for strident tones in the firm with a resultant desertion by clients and investors. Therefore the key for growth, even survival, is **a stable and well-positioned strategic posture**, invulnerable nearly to "frontal attacks" of challengers in the market and not easily given to exhaustion (which may be derived, usually, from clients, shareholders or suppliers' reactions, or the appearance of alternative products…).

However, a strategy keeps taking shape and evolving in a **continuous iterative process**. It must be constantly controlled, harmonized, fine-tuned and adapted to its path whenever necessary – even if its main theme remains the same. There are a few clear criteria with which to analyze a strategy, in an orderly and regular manner – especially before deciding on any changes in policy. These yardsticks are supposed to answer the following questions concerning it:

- ✓ Is it clearly defined, understood and implementable (securing its support by all the personnel in the unit…)?
- ✓ Does it make a full use of all opportunities latent in the local and international markets (identifying the correct segments and possibilities, present and future within the limits of the allocated resources…)?
- ✓ Is it realistic and in accord with the company's skills and means to be assimilated (compare the wanted against what is really on the ground, creating symmetry between capabilities and requirements…)?
- ✓ Are its principles internally consistent (a close examination of the measure of its relevancy and similarity with the various sectors of the organization as an entire and unified array, as well as its connection to the character of their occupation…)?
- ✓ Does the level of risk in it make economic sense and work well with the dictations of the policy-makers (an essential distinction between calculated daring that fits well with influential factors within the business and a stupid gamble which might lead it into the abyss…)?
- ✓ Does it comport with the values and wishes of the top management (softening the contrasts between the personal desires of the superiors and the chosen outline in order to prevent a foreordained total failure…)?

- ✓ Does it unite with the required degree of contribution to the public and the economy (going with the current social values' needs in the vicinity so as to give something back; strict compliance with the local and governmental laws; increasing efficiency and thriftiness...)?
- ✓ Does it create an obvious incentive for the communal effort (turning the collective body into an attractive partnership for each individual within it, so that each one's contribution is selfishly maximized...)?
- ✓ Are there early indications of the market's response to it (success in real life, there is nothing like it...)?

A sensitivity test of this kind will motivate strategy changes, when necessary, for its improvement and betterment.

The first two strategic resolutions a company should take are:

1. Choosing its activity's **portfolio**; or as defined in the new age, delineating its **diversification** policy.
2. Adapting and adopting a **competitive position** for any situation.

When considering these issues – which are resulting decrees concerning the technological edifice, the human resources domain, the financial aspect and the marketing field – two serious matters must be considered:

The first: while defining the diversification policy, an attitude must be taken as if the company intends to compete in only one sector.

Even if some concurrent fronts are on the agenda, each one should be treated as if standing alone; but at the organizational level the connotation is totally different: such a multi-purpose commercial array should be approached as something like a split competition in several exclusive and separate branches, requiring therefore a division of awareness and means in the measure demanded peculiar to each domain – management and conduct, which are not self-evident at all.

The second: how to internalize an aspect of competitive edge in an area that is about to fade. One must think of businesses, even shrinking ones, in a strategically positive way – otherwise the disaster is unavoidable, since downturns in certain sectors due to the appearances of alternative or better products are a common thing. In every economy, some industries sink while others flourish, for this is the way of the Darwinian world in general and especially in the commercial sphere. Attention must be totally focused on the diminishing occupation, in order to constantly predict and evaluate which direction has been taken in order to overcome the crisis and make money, and whether it is desirable to remain involved in that field...

In sum, consolidating an overall strategy or its reestablishment is, first and foremost, a systemic challenge, driven and dictated by a **dominant leadership** of the higher echelons. Not always will it be set and defined by the field manager – as is easily understood in light of the preceding; however, he may be one of those laying its foundations, or at least a partner in its positioning, processing and editing.

On the other hand, the **manager must be the one to outline, de facto, the operational rules of the organization for the full implementation of the strategy**; for these instructions are the guidelines for the total activities of the company, and they will eventually lead to the accomplishment of its goals, and later on to the ultimate longed-for purpose.

Reality and Vision: Tomorrow, Built Today, Based on Yesterday

No strategy is able to contribute and assist to the success of an organization, if it is not based on a correct attitude towards the three epochs of its existence: **past, present and future**.

The first – drawing lessons from history and learning from experience (as is done all along in this book…), the commitment to look back in order to know how and where to move forwards.

The second – implementing inferences today according to information thus far accumulated, assisted by quantitative testing techniques and operational research to analyze and process the results of activity in real time, in order to adopt and inculcate further conclusions.

The third – making plans for the betterment of tomorrow's production, trying to boost whatever requires improvement.

And dealing only with one is worthless without considering the other two.

And the best way to do so, according to the book of *the game theory* written by Avinash Dixit and Barry Nalebuff, is trough :

- ✓ Looking forward while thinking backward, for anyone worried by the next, immediate move – to wit: predicting the results of any initial decision and trying beforehand to choose the best alternative among them all.
- ✓ Thinking ahead and looking backwards, regarding everyone who is concerned about the final stage in the process he initiates – namely: to foresee already the last step based on present occurrences, while trying to react correctly, in a timely manner, one step ahead of any advancement.

It seems that there are, more or less, three types of managers in the world.

The first batch are the ones achieving great success nowadays, while obstinately digging their nails into the terra firma of yesterday – having no idea about where to lead the company starting tomorrow. This because there is no doubt that obsession with the past may effect failure in the future (and in this case they must inculcate again and again what that ninety-year-old fellow said ironically while he was trying enthusiastically to court the beautiful seventy-year-old: "Now, under the circumstances, the past doesn't matter – the future is what counts...").

Next in line are those having great plans for the coming decade, while their present business is about to go bankrupt within a few months (while that group should fully adopt the advice one homeless man in Manhattan gave to his unfortunate neighbor on a bitterly cold January morning: "Your plans for the penthouse are great, but they won't help us much if we can't fix the leak in our cardboard tent!...")

And the real good ones – those enjoying **an outstanding connection of a talent for managing routine with a future-bound visionary strategy, which is normally implementable** – are the managers who become ideal winners. Those who, despite their rich experience and many successes are not fixated and fossilized in their notions, but are always open to scrutinize, listen, absorb and apply new data properly in order to combine short-term impressive results with a powerful sweep of imagination and wise foresight for things to show up in the long term. These are individuals who are endowed with a very sensitive and exceptionally sharp personal radar, who does not miss any opportunity that comes their way, who are able to appreciate correctly the commercial potential hidden in the possibilities of every deal (especially the very complicated ones...). All of this is assisted by the ability to estimate quantitatively and rather realistically the probability of certain events connected to the above-said affair and influencing it – the chances of its eventual realization and its economic implications.

These are the traits that make the difference between giants and midgets...

Therefore the real test that the leader of the communal body is facing lies in the ability to create a **proper balance between continuity and**

innovation – and safeguard it; however, naturally the attention is focused, mostly, on the hourly hardships, standing on the verge and demanding attention at the present moment. Hence, it is totally forbidden to give in to today's pressures, abandoning the development of tomorrow and the realization of the dream, considering that sometimes the present is probably already ancient history. For that reason, the manager must have a very strong commitment to the future, even far away and less acute than the daily troubles. For this he should construct tools for the next generation, since only he who is really interested in the days to come prepares all means to face them, as was said around 550 BC by the Chinese philosopher Confucius: "If a man takes no thought about what is distant, he will find sorrow near at hand…".

There is no doubt that tomorrow's market leaders are those constantly differentiating themselves today, in order to bypass their competitors next week – the sooner the better. That is why the senior executives of any system should rather look at the business world through a bifocal lens: one half committed to observing the present path, the other scanning the days to come and the opportunities embedded in them. All this ought to be while relying on their own experiences and all the events and incidents which have happened to their organization before (because he who ignores his past and its occurrences not only cannot restore his successes but may definitely reenact the same mistakes; because though history may not always repeat itself, it does serve as an excellent warning sign…).

Since giving an answer to the current needs while preparing for the unseen at the same time is a very complicated task, it is wise to **trace the functions and set the correct course which may successfully navigate the combined performance of both**. And the question that fully arises is the following: what is the most effective way to take care of the two levels in order to implement the best in every one of them? Who is in charge of which front? How should one deal with each, and when?

As for the functionaries responsible for the abovementioned fields of operation, most authorities dealing with the subject share the same opinion. In the past, with its tempo of events, the great manager could be occupied with common instant bits and pieces as well as with the planning of stuff behind the horizon; but nowadays, when the frequency of changes is determined by data flowing at the speed of light – dictating on the other side the urgency of response – the right solution for the current executive members coordinating the daily routine and future plans stems from a division of tasks between the **leader and his deputy**; flanked by numbers one and two in the organization. Occasionally such a bifurcated mission may be entrusted to designated teams, specifically built-up for this mission and totally devoted to the supervision and development of these fronts: the first deals with the theoretical readying and preparation of the morrow, and the other is in charge of the real current action, proclaiming operative aims for immediate performance. And both have the same importance, for he who fails to decently direct his weekly activities and overcome extant frequent problems – his chances of making it properly to the end of the year are close to nil...

Another reason for separating the two domains of occupation is that he who seeks a vision to determine the nature of future movements should not be bothered by performance limitations witnessed in the present. He cannot allow himself to be committed to both in tandem, for in this manner he may often deprive himself of any pre-planning due to the effort of its execution; because tomorrow is built with utopian dreams and imaginary aspirations, while the daily occupation is a detailed, boring, sometimes Sisyphean toil, whose end is not always clear (which is analogous to what is said with a very bitter smile about the harpist who spend half of his life tuning his instrument and the other half playing it when it is out of tune…).

As for the realization and scheduling method, of utmost importance is the moment in which the senior of the two decides when and how to intervene in order to enable necessary corrections on the route, while he may still materially influence the show.

The path characterizing all natural processes and developments as well as the life-cycle relationships of individuals, groups or corporations is similar in principle to an **S**-curve. It begins, usually, with a slow climb; continues with a hesitant movement and trial-and-error stumbling; followed by improvement, growth, achieving and peaking; ending with a slow creep towards fading.

Such is the route of business! Starting with a cautious motion, accumulating confidence until finally acquiring mastery; however, at a certain stage exhaustion takes control, followed by boredom, deteriorating performance and decline. The real wisdom of managers is measured, among others, by their ability to identify, quickly and accurately, the position of their organization on that curve, trying to envision the commencement of the change downwards; for the life of any ordinary firm may get stuck at some point – if attention is not being carefully paid – while waiting for the launch of sliding down the hill, and later by desperately trying to turn in the totally opposite direction.

The notion is to foresee the twisting junction where it transitions from soaring to landing and to be well-prepared for it. And the secret of continuous growth is in starting and ameliorating a new **S**-curve before its predecessor is emptied and extinguished; for thinking of a fresh challenge charges the one facing it with energy which pushes him further and further onward. And the art at its best is to internalize that it is forbidden to sit on one's laurels, to be intoxicated by success and immersed in a state of nirvana. It is imperative to assign and paint a new target right away when the present one is drained, and what is more important is to know where to place the observation post on the path leading to the first, so as to discern from it immediately and exactly when to begin acting on behalf of the next aim.

Moreover, even in a successfully-run business, one should be ready to sometimes destroy an old entity – even if it still quite fruitful – if there is a wish to build something new and much better.

In other words: building a company's operational policy with an eye to the past, applying it in the present, while continuously drawing lessons to be learned so as to plan a better future is the right way. Therefore a good manager must be very well-versed in the history of his organization, to be always on the lookout and to plan frequently beyond the horizon with an aspiration for constant upgrading.

Planning and Preparation: Deployment of the Policy's Outline and Getting Ready for its Execution

Companies striving to be developed in an orderly manner and to keep succeeding are required to prepare beforehand long-range and broad-minded operative arrangements, something like a "five-year plan;" for the better one knows where he is heading, the greater are the chances of getting there. If he does not know his designated port, no wind in the world can take his vessel there.

But these firms must be ready to change – or at least to adapt – the aforesaid arrangements from time to time, but only if the circumstances justify it beyond a shadow of a doubt. For this is the only way to survive: to lay down a very detailed map that will point out activity patterns, production prescriptions, economic models and competitors' postures; and will keep updating them as new information enters the system. And then as Napoleon once said: "To understand the strategic situation, one needs only to look at the map...". This is the way to prepare: with well calculated and wide-ranging organized methods for future business struggles.

Each strategic plan is divided into three main parts in the same sequence as described henceforth, and each one requires the full involvement of the manager:

1. **Decision-Making.**
2. **Setting the Targets.**
3. **Preparing the Execution Outline.**

However before finally deciding and summarizing the first part above, a thorough and sound examination of the four following aspects is required:

- **The competitive stance**: evaluating opportunities versus constraints and chances against risks. This takes into account two aspects: the potencies and limitations of the organization in the case of joining a chosen business field; and thereafter, its position compared to relevant competitors in the sector – in other words, using a **SWOT** test to analyze four factors: Strengths, Weaknesses, Opportunities and Threats.

- **The first outline**: spreading out a very general course of action and modus operandi in order to make sure, here and now, that these may serve as fair responses to the targets dictated by the owner and top management.

- **The realization capabilities:** presenting the feasibility of the execution manner, depending on inner and outer changing parameters, while pointing out their alternatives.

- **The control methods:** outlining the feedback channels from all layers and units of the company, and the tracking and control tools, in order to enable immediate correction on the road to upgrading.

These examination pathways are intertwined and interlocking, feeding and being fed simultaneously; and only after a meticulous verification that these findings are clear and inculcated does it become possible to continue with a detailed definition of goals and the preparation of specific operational outlays.

But one matter should be always remembered: sometimes, when the situation is high-stress and it is impracticable to painstakingly plan down to the minutest particulars and nuances, then one must immediately decide "on the move" – even only by the current, existing "picture" he has…

The right configuration, which supposes consequently to determine the character of an appropriate executable plan to carry out the strategy exhaustively, should encompass the following steps: **studying the business atmosphere; laying the foundations of an operative base; planting the means of conducting a continuous follow-up of crisscrossing feedback in the framework and out of it; field implementation in accordance with variations occurring in the various fronts; and taking corrective steps if and when necessary**. And a correct course of action – which has also the chances to eventually succeed – must be:

- **Suitable**: accurately and fully responding to the designated goals.
- **Complete**: encompassing all possibilities, means and ways necessary to achieve the target.
- **Practical**: not exceeding the sensible realistic aptitude of its accomplishment.
- **Applicable**: achievable, traceable and with supervisory enforcement.

And here, perhaps, is the proper place to praise preparation. In general, preparedness is the crux of the matter, and there is no limit to making arrangements. It ought to be emphasized that this may concern tomorrow's business meeting as well as long-term setups. Thinking ahead allows one to be cool in any situation, calculated and ready to deal with any subject which might emerge. Moreover; nothing should be taken for granted and one must be very careful all the time and double-check everything; for even the great Andrew Grove, Intel's CEO in the USA, insisted time and again, that the paranoids are the only survivors. He who is well-set for any eventuality will not be surprised by that facet or the other, and leads instead of being led (for even apes in the jungle prefer being a gorilla to being a chimpanzee – a leader, not a subordinate…). And in this context it is recommended to adopt the following rule: a diminishing stock of "plans in the drawer" for days to come means that one is resting on his laurels, losing his sharpness…

But, when matters are not progressing as expected, **improvising is sometimes required; and there is no need to be afraid of it**. The ability to "draw and react instinctively" from time to time, is precisely what makes the essential difference between a mediocre and an excellent organization. A thoughtful deployment is a most crucial element that should not be waived under any circumstances – but sporadic improvisation, when necessity arises, is the spice which makes any plan much tastier.

Decision-Making – Vigorously or Patiently

Making strategic business decisions is far from a simple process – especially if they involve the future of the entire organization up to its last employee. Normally these resolutions are based on a complex net of pieces of information, always fluctuating and sweeping, crisscrossing the data centers of the system. Reservoirs of records, facts and figures are being created in the company, whose total meaning is very delicately balanced – requiring, as aforesaid, a comprehensive constant and controlled examination – so that the most appropriate conclusion can be deduced from them. That is why the above-depicted choices to be made must allow for a full accord among a few cardinal commercial elements – the most diverse mix of totally different parameters – which in some cases may not only be incompatible, but contradictory, for example: the benefits of the performance environment versus its drawbacks; the present resources of the firm compared to future ones; wishes of ownership and management aspirations as opposed to the real objective benefit of the corporate. And this is what makes the procedure described here so difficult.

This is the reason why **business patience** is justified, even rewarding, in most cases; an attribute that is born from deep and thorough reasoning. For this is the name of the game; reality hardly allows for shortcuts in processes that need full maturation. But on the other hand, if and when a resolution has been reached to go ahead, decisions must **determinedly and eagerly** be carried out, especially since surprises might appear during execution, not everything would be realized as expected and immediate improvisations and reactions can be strongly required. As even patience – which is considered a virtue and the weapon of the wise – is constrained by time (for time, being mostly a friend, may turn out to be sometimes also an enemy...).

There are four central questions that a manager should ask himself before concluding on the operating policy which he wishes to impose on the organization he leads in order to attain its goals:

1. **Which** is the chosen product that is about to be manufactured?
2. **Who** are the people available for the prosecution of the mission?
3. **What** is the present and future cost-return ratio necessary to fulfill the dictated goals?
4. **How** to sell the most?

And in addition to the afore-mentioned issues, there is a very serious aspect to which the man at the top must give his full attention. This matter concentrates a lot of thoughts and devotes maximum care to the tools assisting in performing a real-time and fluid status evaluation, in order to be one step ahead of the competitors at any time and place: the ultimate dimension of **knowledge management** – a domain intended to augment intellectual property and create a continuous process of improvement, upgrading and establishing advantage over the others.

And in order to respond intelligently to the above questions, a manager must be blessed with two somewhat contrasting traits, oxymoronic peculiarities in a way: restless imagination and patient determination. Plotting and implementing an operative strategy for an organization is based on **Vision, Imagination and Creativity**, on the one hand, and an **uncompromising faith in the righteousness of the way** on the other. In this lies the pre-eminence of the leader over his subordinates…

In general, each daily activity, to its minutest details as well, **must derive from the ultimate goal**. Therefore one has to act deductively, using logic and a reasoned conclusion, from the broad rule to its particulars. Just as it is necessary to see and appreciate the whole picture, so it is imperative to review in a very meticulous manner all its parts – even those seemingly minor and insignificant. No grandiose systematic puzzle or brilliant operative plan – be it as weighty and serious as possible – is worth the gigantic effort invested in its integration, if it may collapse completely because the tiniest of small pegs is wrongly inserted; and even the best creative and far-reaching vision cannot replace an essential approach to the most delicate nuances. For some say that "God is in the details…" – or as was once argued by an old sage: "Take care of the minutes and the hours will take care of themselves". Consider Operation Eagle Claw of April

1980 (intended to rescue the American hostages from the embassy in Tehran...) that ended in a bitter failure before even starting, just because nobody took into account the minuscule sand granules of the desert rising into the air with the start of the aircrafts' engines, creating an impermeable cloud. It is like the seemingly negligible inattention of a junior loading inspector – all apparently worthless matters, involved in this business.

Actually, the smallest cogs turn to be, sometimes, the ones to carry the substantial weight; and the greatness of the manager is expressed in knowing to choose meticulously those ostensibly secondary elements requiring a thorough examination – on which, in fact, the whole structure is built (and their supervision can be carried out by his subordinates without subtracting anything from his global observation talent...). These minor components suddenly become the heart of the matter, while the main issue is really pushed aside. Therefore, **notwithstanding the obligation to behold first and foremost the whole map in all its multiplicity of dimensions, it is totally forbidden to ignore any detail, be it the minutest, of its parts, to which it is strongly tied and is always based on.**

And truly the most difficult decisions are nearly always made by the leader in horrible **loneliness**, moments in which he discovers himself to be alone, even though others are in the system too. For by his side are indeed partners in the process of decision-making, except he is the only one to carry the responsibility, since no one "volunteers" to share it with him. The infernal conflict falls upon the shoulders of the leader alone, and the higher one climbs, the lonelier he feels. Because in the end the man will be applauded only if he succeeds – and someone will always be lying in wait to gloat over his failure. To quote Lee Iacocca, Chrysler's chairperson between 1979 and 1988: "My father always used to say that when you die, if you've got five real friends attending the funeral, then you've had a great life".

There are two reasons for this situation:

The first is the nature of the status: a ship can have one and only one captain; otherwise its sailors would lose their way. Or in irony defined: "If more than one decision maker is present in the room, the number of people claiming this right because of the position conferred upon them is, surely, the main part of the problem which they were gathered to solve, since one crown cannot be shared by two kings...". The second is because of the character of the senior executives in the organization, or those pretending to be, surrounding the one at the top: their egos are pushing them to struggle to take part in the decision-making process, craving to feel, because of their standing, the power of authority. But if these resolutions present the least danger to their "reputation," they would surely hurry to desert the manager to face the results on his own. "For success has many fathers, while failure is an orphan...". Or as was once said with a sarcastic irony mixed with touching sadness: "At the ribbon-cutting ceremony, they are first in line, their text put in the mouth of their favorite presenter. But when expected to take responsibility for a rotten fuckup, they evaporate as if swallowed by the earth...".

And of this loneliness one may learn from the yearly Passover *Seder*, the presentation of the Exodus of the people of Israel from slavery to freedom, relived for the benefit of all (especially the young...) around the table. All of this narrative without once bringing up, by even the slightest allusion as well, the greatest leader in mankind's ancient history, the sole operator actually behind this founding event of, in so many words, the Chosen Nation; Moses is not mentioned even one time in the *Haggada's* songs, praises and exegesis! Lonesome throughout his life (leading an ignorant multitude in the desert for forty years...) and in death (disappearing upon Mount Nebo, his burial place to remain unknown for all eternity...)!

Responsibility is indivisible.

Nevertheless, he who is in charge must **enjoy authority: the might and the right to decide and act** for the organization and its people, **coercing obedience and discipline** accordingly; and one cannot exist, or even survive, without the other, for both are equally essential to enable the fulfillment of the mission as the guiding force and motivator of all activities in the company. But it must be understood: authority is inborn or acquired later with time; it does not come through the mandate bestowed on the manager by the powers influencing and determining action in the firm (the well-to-do, voters, appointment committees, et cetera…), but first of all from his hegemonic personality. So it must be remembered: if the others surrounding him do not feel it, then it probably does not exist. And one important thing must be internalized: the man at the top is not always to be blamed for the failure of his flock, yet he is always responsible; therefore he is called to pay the price – especially if the fault occurred during his shift…

However, in many cases, men of power abuse the domination granted to them – the right, legally permitting one person or a group to demand, even coerce, others to do something. It happens that these authoritarians exceed public ethics and personal morality without being punished for indulging in hubris. On the contrary, some of the other functionaries in the entity are wont to take responsibility, unbecoming their office in fact. Such phenomena must be uprooted and destroyed in every way and at any price.

Occasionally the most difficult conclusions concern what to avoid doing, for such ostensibly emits a smell of cowardice and indecision. It is not popular and lacks the flavor of heroism. Stretching out the borders of the organization's activities is, without a doubt, one of the least pleasant tasks of its leadership. As was already said: "Sometimes restraint and reserve are the real power; since making up one's mind to avoid doing is as wise, at least, as choosing to do…".

This is especially true when **expanding the business** is on the agenda, for the motives for such a move do not always stem from organizational profitability or financial-economic sense, but sometimes spring from personal-emotional impulses, as follows:

The first and the immediate is driven by a natural commerce urge, normally pushing to grow as fast as possible in anything one does without too much checking…

The second comes from the uninhibited enthusiasm following the entrance of the first coins into the coffers, seeming like sure profits; an intoxicating taste of success at arm's length; something like, "we did it, and nothing can stop us from further advance…". This is a fervor which may bestow an unfounded confidence…

The third is usually caused by the sharp temptation, burning like fire in each manager's bones, to present instantly successful results, mainly from the desire to please the owners and superiors right from the start. A haste which might be from the devil…

The fourth happens, perhaps, due to the feeling that the market is saturated so to speak, and something must be done to achieve a breakthrough. Such an instinct may produce a disregard of all the vital criteria which ought to be double-checked before making any changes, or from the necessity to compromise and give up in certain domains. This kind of a business outlook can sometimes be mistaken, and it is born out of the endless yearning gnawing inside to be equal to the competitors in the shortest possible time. Such a strong desire generates the very dangerous illusion that overtaking the adversaries in the race is a very easy matter…

Therefore there is no doubt that the above impetuses may lead to wrong decision-making.

Moreover, sometimes the main issue should not be how to make more money, but rather concentrating on what is the way not to end up with less. For at a certain stage of growth, achieving more and doubling success is not as important as reinforcing control, strengthening stability and fortifying robustness; this is in order to maintain the business's existence in the sector and its industry for many more years to come...

It would seem therefore that broadening the operational perimeter of the corporate is the nearly immediate decision, taken mostly too close to its establishment; and since it is sometimes implemented instinctively without due deep and ordered thinking, it may be employed without an exhaustive accounting concerning the real potential of the company and the future resources needed to withstand these developments. In such cases it also mostly has no clear stop signs; and steps like these, if incorrectly executed, are well-lit warning signals which appear pretty soon in the following forms:

- ✓ Gloomy results in the periodic financial audits.
- ✓ Decline in the number of customers.
- ✓ Increase in complaints regarding bad service.
- ✓ Dissatisfaction of clients because of inferior product quality.
- ✓ A sense of a lack vis-à-vis a "guiding hand" among partners sharing the communal activities.
- ✓ A feeling of insecurity and disaffection among employees.

Ignoring such evidence may lead to disastrous phenomena, constituting irreversible damage later on. Hence it is strongly recommended not to tumble into temptation, which might drag one into a rash resolution of commerce expansion due to the following factors.

First of all, it is forbidden to fall prey to dreams of aggrandizement at the very first indication of growth, which may herald the spring seemingly, since sometimes it is but a mirage. A growth not proportional with the skills and capacity existing in the company can surely harm its delicate and healthy operational equilibrium and joy of creation. It is impossible to spread out without cost, or appropriate cushioning of means, and **without matching the control expanse to the perimeter of activity: whether by properly recruiting more worthy employees** (not just anyone picked up from the street...) **to man important junctions, or by defining suitable procedures** – for otherwise the system's activity would resemble a curve that tries to straighten into a line but never reaches there, a kind of asymptotic process. The invested efforts' graph would keep climbing, never yielding better returns. Expenses would keep on swelling, returning no due reward – not to speak of the heavy loads, increasing toil and lack of proper production, whose outcome would find expression in bad temper and a decline in the most precious attribute – health.

Second, violating business stability may quickly push to losing control of performance: reduced product value and client service quality, leading to customer desertion. It is worth remembering that good reputation and image amongst consumers are acquired by huge and long-term efforts – but may be destroyed and evaporate within a minute.

Third, adding products, attributes and services foreign to the firm's specialization harms its strategic positioning. Compromises and inconsistency caused by the intention of broadening the business are certain to wear out the corporate's competitive advantage built up from its original line of manufactured goods even among its most fanatic loyalists. Trying to confront several unknown fronts almost at the same time creates confusion among junior employees and the senior ones as well, undermining motivation and organizational focus – both of which are very high managerial virtues. **And when a company loses its uniqueness, its reputation weakens, becoming meager and shriveled.** From here starts the sleeper slope and instead of enlarging gains, compensation is diminished.

Finally, **the aspiration to grow** is perhaps the **most influential** decision, among all other weighty factors, in the process of deploying and fine-tuning the system's **strategy**. In any case this choice is none too simple, since it may generate a destructive boomerang, returning from the field hitting hard, straight in the faces of the policy makers. On the other hand it is certainly possible that compromising, which actually means waiving, might be interpreted as unwillingness to develop – a fact which may itself point to halting growth, that will definitely pit the employees against their management – although sometimes this is the right and preferred course of action to adopt.

Moreover; it should be perfectly clear that business growth is a desirable and blessed process, and mostly vital to any communal framework; but the timing and the way should be selected meticulously and after a thorough check of all surrounding aspects. And if it is decided to go for it, then the execution should be gradual, measured, patient and in a proper manner taking breaks on the path in order to examine the performance, its products and their essence every time anew. And it is totally forbidden to seek augmentation for its sake out of pure scheming for self-aggrandizing or other private beneficial considerations – it must be for the right reasons, which are the good of the organization and increase of pure profits. In general, it is suggested to avoid trying to embrace the whole world with only one pair of arms, to eschew the yearning to act with a couple of bare hands as a "business octopus" right from square one...

In summation
There is no one single management theory, explicitly dictating, teaching and advising on how to make decisions. Half of the dogmas serving the leader are normative, the other part descriptive. One offers a method for improving thought patterns and rules leading towards those formats, and the second explains actually the essence of resolutions in the organization. While the first assumes a rational and honest behavior of individuals, all of them doing their best to

achieve the common goals, the next emphasizes the reasons for companies consolidating different opinions – sometimes ones totally contrary to those expected according to the regular ideational doctrine. Therefore the process by which a person makes up his mind about issues confronting him, is his own business, better done after due consideration and a thorough judgment of all the available information currently revealed to him at that point in time.

And if in addition to the above-said, one takes into account the two following observations:

The first is that the most exhaustive statistical definition of a "dilemma" is the situation when a person has to choose out of two possible options, where the supporting data known to him at the moment points to the fact that the difference in the correctness of preferring one over the other is between 50.1% and 49.9%; and if the gap between those two supporting parameters is larger, even by one-tenth of a percent, then the dilemma evaporates, for the answer is self-evident.

And the second is that reality, on the other hand, is much crueler; decision-making processes are almost never laid out in an utmost clear and sharp manner, quantifiable in such accurate numeric fractions.

Thus, it is definitely possible to understand the huge difficulty ever so often expressed in implementing the above written...

Notwithstanding and regardless of what has been said on the subject, it is heartily recommended that choices of the kind previously mentioned should be taken **far from a deep emotional involvement** with the company. Even if the decision-makers are its parents and attached to its growth wholeheartedly, entirely invested in it, and their skins and prestige are also on the line – still they are required to behave as if things are different. And if they can't take it, they should prefers others free from such sensitivity **to reach a conclusion in their stead**. For he who considers only personal outcomes and their implications cannot be brave; and the one that allows his common sense to be manipulated by nothing but his feelings epitomizes the difference between a king and a feckless man, since it is usually a "make or break" thing. Or as was said by Hans Stern, owner of the famous jewelry shop chain: "The secret in correctly and successfully running a family business is to hire first-rate outside professionals. The family, on the other hand, should be the stockholders, abstaining from daily management of the business...". And even then it is imperative to be aware of the fine difference between necessary bravery and flamboyant stupidity.

And from time to time, when decisions are very urgently required, especially when the man at the top needs to weigh more than one option, an outcome of various points of view or conflicts of interest, it is strongly recommended to be wise rather than right. Better to forgo "heavy fights" over principles – even when the pleader is one-hundred-percent sure of his moral judgment and the high integrity of his goal – and to conduct instead "pinpointed, silent but effective operations"; so that the higher interest for the one in charge will be served; for in such cases **bravery is a noble trait, but clear consideration and logical thinking are much more important.**

Verified Truth versus Gut Feelings

Proper management is **in most cases governed by facts**. The man in charge may certainly act by intuition, but only if it is backed-up by real stuff; since knowledge, based on proven parameters, is the answer in time to any future question. As the 2nd American President John Adams said already in 1770 (and his latter-day successor, the 40th president Ronald Reagan, was wont to quote and misquote): "Facts are stubborn things...". In other words, gut feelings are mainly intended to start processes, while execution should rely on verified data; inner senses help and guide whenever necessary to decide quickly or under pressure – while affirmative information and solid scenarios serve for full implementation.

Spontaneity too is a wonderful trait, having its place in life generally and particularly in business – as long as it isn't used exaggeratedly.

For this reason optimal data-processing is vital to the organization; to wit, the task of sighting, identifying, following, gathering, sorting and analyzing the various news from the field should be carried out patiently, thoroughly and in a sophisticated manner in the first phase. These should be investigated and evaluated in order to draw out most of the conclusions and their best, involving all performing partners, in the second stage. According to the late Michael Leonidas Dertouzos of MIT, information-processing is the ultimate human mental activity, using relevant parameters to solve acute problems, so in fact this is a fundamental change of management and conduct culture, meaning: a transit from wrong perception – that data is a main asset for weaving nets of personal interests and intrigues – to recognition and understanding that it is actually the best if not the only analysis, development and production tool, for ameliorating all aspects and planes of the entire framework's performance.

Knowledge is power, but its potency emanates from its being shared – not from its being stockpiled. Intelligent, fast and skilled use of information neutralizes the advantage gained from its gathering for personal benefit and manipulative use – for example: exploiting it to lead a policy of "divide and rule"; especially nowadays, when nearly all of the relevant facts and numbers are shared by everybody. Therefore, effort and sophistication should be directed at channels capable of producing new levels of organizational insights; those that would facilitate efficient and quick focus on forecasting processes and preparing for them – instead of being dragged (because of the faulty utilization of data for secondary goals…) to reactive situations. The purpose of this activity – including its scientific applications – is of course maximizing the company's profits. And on the other hand, the values and compensation mechanisms of the firm should substantially and materially express the worldview mentioned above – while settling rewarding accounts with employees loyal to its principles.

A pragmatic and realistic manager prefers listening to what went wrong before hearing what goes well. First of all, because in reality there are no perfect systems; so whenever trees are chopped, the chips will fly. Second – and most important – as was said before, only paranoids survive in business. Ignoring bad reports is a sure recipe for fading away, since these are not necessarily negative factors. On the contrary! Sometimes they serve as alarm bells and evidence of the immediate need for change. Moreover, employees should be encouraged to share bad news as well as good, while the organization should be prodded to react and even cherish this kind of information, instead of condemning those who reveal it.

And the finest and most cautious managers would establish in the system in their charge an independent "contrarian entity". Such a body would always oppose the majority opinion, providing the decision-makers with totally different and contrasting points of view. This is all in order to systematically challenge the dominant thesis, by constantly examining the strength and firmness of the general, accepted and chosen position; **igniting revolutionary ideas and creating an alternative logic, thereby sharpening the mind and developing imaginative thinking** (whose task is trying to "prophesy" the evolution of ostensibly irregular scenarios…), **so as to avoid mental fixation and rigid linkage to old beliefs** (or to what is called with exaggerated respect the "common wisdom" to hide behind…) only because the boss favors them. They invest all their energy, acumen, understanding, experience and temper in discovering a "black swan" (the psychological term for an unpredicted, very surprising event, heavily influencing outcomes, which out of lack of knowledge cannot be predicted but may be, however, explained in retrospect…) instead of continually embracing the normative assumption that all swans in the world are white. For the true frightening paradox is that the very unexpectedness of a non-habitual incident makes it more likely; by preparing for something, one learns how to avoid it or at least how to confront it in the best manner (and above all, how to be cured of the human malady known as justifying things ex post facto…). And here, definitely, the leader may be examined in another domain: in his self-confidence to be really open enough – as he actually proclaims by the very establishment of the "contrarian entity" above-depicted – to accept opinions different or diverging from his own.

But on the other hand, it's better to be aware of chronic pessimists prophets, whose single wish is to stand out as the only ones who in truth care for the good of the organization; such employees "volunteer" to deliver unpleasant information to cover, in fact, their own failure.

And one more bit of advice concerning incertitude (the domain which encompasses the unexpected future…): it is recommended to adopt and internalize two very pragmatic attitudes encountering it and taking care of it:

Firstly, in the process of decision-making while preparing for surprises (and the risks they carry…) it is necessary to find the way of **preparing for the ramifications** caused by these events whenever they may occur (while it is possible to get organized ahead of those effects, even relying on past experiences…) **instead of trying to prophesy-guess-evaluate the probability** of the "if" and "when" these destructive incidents might happen (a very difficult, perhaps unattainable matter to foresee…). And this is true mainly (maybe even only…) with reference to the phenomena considered to have substantial influence on the core activity in life (or on the existence itself…) and those that have in fact a good chance to materialize. After all, it is impossible (actually forbidden…) to invest effort in getting ready for everything, especially if its impact on the daily continued survival of the business is marginal. Otherwise, organizing for the unknown would never end and one could lose his mind thinking about what might happen, never having the time to do anything to confront the significant consequences in practice...

Secondly, in a complex environment, characterized by many unique details, the twenty-eighty rule – **the Pareto principle** – should be deployed: twenty percent of the variables make for eighty percent of the result. It is only required to observe and identify these twenty, which is one of the imperative management skills.

But it should be emphasized anew: in addition to what was already said about considerations of reason, the man at the top must be attentive also to inner signals; to the voice of intuition; to whatever enables him to look forward, not out of consideration, but by implementing, not necessarily consciously, past experiences in all of life's domains and healthy hunches. This was very well expressed by the 19th century French mathematician and philosopher of science, Jules Henri Poincaré: "Science is built up with facts, as a house is with stones; but a collection of facts alone is no science at all, just as a heap of stones only is in no way a house...".

Hero or Zero – the Outlook of the Ambitious

He who is not ready to take any chances in life will never prevail. In order to make it big, one should also dare making up his mind now and then get involved in some none-too-small hazards – calculated risks, not stupid adventurism which will cause an inevitable decline into hell. *Jean-Jacques Rousseau*, the French philosopher of the 18th century, wrote that like the human body, any political system starts dying on the day of its birth, because it actually carries the roots of its destruction within itself. Such it is with any productive organization.

Thus, constant good care of its "Stamina" and "Health" is required for the sake of its longevity. But, the experience of the largest and oldest companies in the world teaches us that in order to survive – not to mention "thrive" – keeping in "business shape" and observing "financial stability" are not enough; sometimes it is necessary to excel and **bravely take real risks**. For acting in the fields of uncertainty is the bread and butter of the commercial and professional universe and the name of the game as well; it is impossible to constantly avoid making chancy choices, if the desire is to eventually reap the blossoming fruits. This is the only way for really strong organizations to keep their leading status for so many years, or as put once by an uncompromising fatalist: "He who takes no risks in life is risking death…".

And the first peril is the resolution to continue the business's activities just when it is economically downtrodden, especially during financially hard interludes, whose endpoint is unknown; to wit, the intrepidity not to abandon and to do the best to keep "floating on the water – even amidst heavy gales". while trying to earn as much as possible for survival (and the means to it are described at the summation of the article "operating a start-up company at the intermediary phase – the concept," as previously introduced…).

However, most chances taken in the above-mentioned cases should be premeditated; and even if it might sound a bit theoretical, it is definitely possible to quantify self-endangerment before coming to difficult conclusions. First and foremost an assumption should be undertaken, internalizing that notwithstanding the comprehensive research conducted prior to making any decision, not all information is always available, and some facts may not be completely known. Second, it is imperative to evaluate the significance of that missing data, particularly its effect on the final result.

And then it is time to find the way to overcome these obstacles, minimizing the uncertainty factor of the revealed data – consequently augmenting the rate of reliance on known parameters – and trying to conduct simulations as close to reality as possible. Since this is the only approach, sometimes it is necessary to choose the least damaging alternative.

But it should always be remembered, in cases where a sword is at one's throat, a true expression of "to be or not to be", there is not enough time to calculate the risk; then it is imperative to act fast and as best as possible under the pressure and given circumstances – otherwise his entire existence is jeopardized.

Most people are familiar with only two sides of the coin ; but the special ones – those who wish to think and behave differently – know, apparently, of a "third" facet as well. Unconventional thinking – "outside the box" according to professor Mitchell Koza, Dean of Rutgers Business School in New Jersey – is the one creating the value innovation which turns a small "David" neighborhood grocery into a giant "Goliath" city shopping mall. Those obstinate boneheads who are able to adopt unique contemplation manners while believing that the rules of the games are certainly prone to change – within the limits of traditional decency of course – are the first to make the conceptual switch and lead competitiveness from the deep gray reality to new very high summits. Since most of the human beings were educated not to expect to hold both ends of the rope at the same time, they know no better; but those who truly desire to succeed in business beyond their rivals would do anything to try and prove the opposite.

For in the end, everything is determined by the outcomes.

Nothing is more efficacious than manifest success; no one would dispute that fact. This means achieving desired, satisfying and nourishing results, for the organization, its leadership, employees, customers, and other partners in its activities. Reaping fruits is in any case self-sufficient in most of the justification for the existence of the system and every characteristic of its operations and methods. And on touching the blooming and smelling its perfume, it encourages, forms, strengthens and sweeps to further climbing; and there is nothing like it in leading to more and more new peaks. Seemingly, the success of the manager in the eyes of whoever appoints him is a binary test: "one" or "nil"; make or break. But in full honesty – and especially for the mental sanity of the one at the top – it should not be considered just a dichotomous check, for there are intermediate levels of accomplishments as well: reaching the goals, even partially and not fully, so to say. It is worthwhile therefore to know in what way to measure different grades of achievements, and then to learn how to truly appreciate them; for it is possible to be committed one-hundred-percent to an effort which is unfeasible; thus it is totally forbidden to promise ahead of time a hundred-percent success.

But the real painstaking question is: what is the formula bringing the most desirable results? Which are the parameters of the equation culminating in genuine achievements – compared to the appropriate elements that display a solution addressing the exact essential performance only? It seems that being just talented is not enough; similarly, achieving defined explicit goals is not sufficient. Apparently, a special combination is required to give birth to something far above, a mixture connecting the personal attributes of the leader to the nature of the targets designated by the company he is running; a blend that expresses the operative facet of the necessary management qualities: **"goals directed," potential and daring, meaningful and rational to the organization.**

It seems that the best answer to this issue is the aptitude to guide but in a target-oriented manner; a synergy of (correct management…) **qualities** and (systematically purposeful…) **goals**, leading to ambition and having the power to justify what exists on the one hand, and all the action towards it on the other (exactly what this book has been trying to teach up to now and beyond...) – and in an easy-to-learn and - remember format: **QO** (Quality x Objectives).

Organizational Changes – a Real Necessity for a Constant Development-Renewal

In principle, there is no reason to fear slaughtering "holy cows" – as long as it makes sense. Revolutionary ideas should be welcomed, examined and perhaps even tried in any organization that wishes to go on and stay alive. This can be done only by breaking petrified thought patterns whose time has passed – even if no one around dares voicing it out loud to his superiors. **Only dead fish go with the flow.**

Quite a strong personality is needed to stop, examine, analyze and choose a change of direction in the middle of the way, once it is understood that the path is wrong – although everyone around is sure it is the very truest road. Even if it requires a complete revision, it should not be feared. And if it seems that such a step is a privilege granted to the very few and rarely – the courage and ability to make a complete turn (only if necessary...) amid the operation and start nearly afresh – maybe then the real value of a step like this may be understood. For such a process points to a healthy organization, built correctly, mentally, physically and financially, and prone to give much pleasure, satisfaction and security to its head and owners.

And it is very important to note the above, because it is well known that most people do not usually like to make changes in their lives – even the smallest ones. Former 42nd United States president Bill Clinton would quote Tolstoy, "Everyone thinks of changing the world, but no one thinks of changing himself...". At the sametime, especially for those who are afraid of variations, it must be inculcated:

a curve on the road doesn't mean the end of the way – unless one fails to take it…

However, a very significant reservation must be posited here: **it is forbidden to see change as an objective,** definitely not to cling to the dank smelling cliché according to which "change is the only constant…" (to declare for example publicly for reasons of the ego: "I arrived here to save the situation, so let's start generating revolutions immediately…") in order to create variations for the sake of showing explicitly that something is being done; it is necessary to do amendments only – and merely if – they are really essential and indispensable, beyond any doubt.

The cardinal ingredients of leading organizational reforms may be economic, scientific, social, demographic, political or cultural, while **necessity is the mother of invention.** Consequently any business deals with an array's conditions specific to itself uniquely generates its own changes. The turn is usually initiated and driven by the highest **senior in the system, the one that is "suffering"** more than all from the current situation – or the person who may **gain the most** from the new status. On the other hand it is impossible to plan scenarios of modifications in the company without the supervision of someone high-ranking enough to bridge the technological activities with the financial implications. For this reason, only he who is in charge of one of the two above-said domains may ensure that the variation is fondly accepted, more or less, and successfully implemented too.

These transformations and the changes due to them are similar to the selection and regeneration processes in the universe's nature; the variety of firms as a whole gradually alternates over time; thus it happens that, once in a period of time, certain organizations disappear to be totally replaced by others, better fitted to the shifting and developing environment. Hence it is imperative to consider carefully every step before a decision is taken to shake the corporate considerably, so a situation is not created wherein the original idea is awesome, but rather when the final results are awful.

When embarking on the reorganization of the entire business and its characteristics, modus operandi, human resources and functional hierarchy, it is recommended to adopt at the least the following three principles to assist in its smooth absorption among those supposed to live on a daily basis within its confines:

- ✓ Once in a while there is a need to stand back, even a single step, and examine meticulously the new status quo: is the change solving the real problems that engendered it? If so, how would it be possible to simplify similar future reforms?

- ✓ The variation task should not be broken into a large number of minor assignments distributed among too many people, for then no official would be able to view the entire picture, and everything would get more and more complicated.

- ✓ The new structure should avoid causing a great number of transforms of responsibilities amongst the employees in operative junctions, because these would create great friction which may give birth to a systemic colossal failure.

Any kind of awkwardness – certainly a technological mix up – is a death blow for a reorganization enterprise. Setting a new and fresh excutive, logistic and administrative agenda concerns everybody, and it should be carried out following a very thorough examination in partnership with employers, bosses, colleagues and subordinates as one, and be tactfully presented to them; it is important that such a change be acceptable to all and sundry, each in his own language.

There are two ways to originate reforms in a cumulative entity: the one – by slight but determined and controlled turnings of the steering wheel; the other – by major sweeps of the helm, shaking the system as a whole. Each one enjoys its own benefits and weaknesses. The mode of variation should be selected in accordance with the given situation and the measure of urgency needed in its implementation.

The first policy is preferable, since it avoids disorienting the organization, while advancing to the goal at a slow pace enabling the examination of the obligation of every step at the same time as it is taken, since real significant revolutions are normally established and created gradually. Suffice it to say what happened to those thinking that extreme transformations could be executed overnight – mainly in many startup high-tech companies in the world – to understand the meaning of haste in carrying dramatic variations. However, in some circumstance when time is really of the essence – and as long as it is clear that without an immediate modification a real "socio-economic-commercial tsunami" may occur – there is no option but to cling to the second method by necessity; an attitude requiring tremendous composure and courage. Except that then it is imperative to remember that the next changes following the sharp transformation should be directed again by precise and well-monitored increments of the angle of turn, in order to well assimilate the pressure forced on the unit. What's more important: an overcorrection does not solve the problem of turning too far in one direction (just as two wrongs do not make a right…).

Practically almost every large business entity shifts every five or ten years from a **centralized to a decentralized** leading culture and **vice-versa**. It happens normally with a change of regime in the company. Yet such transforms should not disrupt the system if the control principle described hereunder is adopted; a very simple one which may fit any managing doctrine: a good organizational structure is definable as an optimal blend of modes according to which it directs its total labor distribution to separate missions and tasks on one end, and on the other assures their mutual coordination and unification of their activities for the best product afterwards – to wit: **differentiation and integration**. The concept is very simple – although its execution may, sometimes, be a bit more complicated. And all the rest is merely styles of conduct and no more.

Despite the cycle presented above, it is not always safe to assimilate methods from the past, because environmental conditions and business atmosphere often vary. And in cases wherein alterations are made by following yesterday's lessons, it is imperative to check the same turns regularly to make sure they are relevant and to find out their usefulness; for it is forbidden to use experience as a barrier against new ideas. And beyond this, it must be understood that sometimes in order to keep a static state, modifications must be carried out, ironically...

And in summation: **the really good managers are revolutionaries-separatists** – although only a few of them would present themselves as such. They must be endowed with a **natural "adaptive change" leadership style**, one that assists them to adjust very quickly to acute functional fluctuations and pragmatic organizational rotations, which motivate them with a permanent determination to **uniqueness accompanied by a drive for constant reinvention**. This defies the axiom (which urges that at the end of the day organizations outgrow their founders and leaders...) the option to realize itself.

And perhaps the most important thing here to internalize is: a person who never changes his mind adores himself more than he loves the truth...

Flowing with the Reforms – or Disappearing

He who does not move dies! Or to put it more subtly, as was said by the cowboys leading their herds over the endless prairies of the Wild West in the 19th century: "If you don't raise dust (while riding at the head of the group…) you eat it (plodding at the end of the line…)". For this reason **the manager should be permanently alert to his environment, absorb information, analyze data, draw conclusions, adapt to outcomes and act accordingly – all of these together, all of the time** – so as not to find it hard to breathe due to the "dust clouds" raised by those galloping ahead of him. He should not linger, even for one second, when all these relevant parameters are passing before him, but prepare himself for all these fluctuations occurring just in front of his eyes – always armed with the scalpel of sharp logic and attentive to his intuitions. And the speed required to implement these variations is mostly an outcome of the business sector dealt with – especially the pace of the related data transmission concerning them. For woe to him who rocks on his heels, since he may soon be trampled…

At the end of the day, everything may be summed up really as managing **changes**: in trying to guide chaotic events in a calm manner and an orderly form – as oxymoronic as this may sound – since the number of variables per unit of time is sometimes huge. So he who wishes to run organizations and lead others should be a person capable of absorbing all the above-said current parameters as quickly as possible, integrating them, and finally giving an appropriate answer, in most cases, to problems arising due to these alternating attributes.

And the recommended approach to do all that in the best, most correct way is to watch, listen, internalize, investigate and execute in a very unusual mode. For the majority of the ordinary people see and think in a two-dimensional fashion; the better ones may do it while imagining in a three-dimensional manner; and those considered excellent are endowed with a **multi-dimensional** absorption, analysis and conceptualization faculty. Therefore it should be remembered that if one fails in observing and discovering something in his immediate operating environment, it does not mean that the thing does not exist; it happens because of **the inability to observe properly.**

Moreover; in daily life everything is motivated, frequently, by objectives – a crazy chase after achievements. As was already said before, it is suggested to halt once in a while and examine, like an outsider, the general state of procedures and revolutions flowing around ever faster. Discovering, deciphering and understanding these – and especially deeply studying and wisely drawing conclusions from them – may give one a substantial advantage over the competitors. A profound revision of what's happening in the activity's domains, those things grasped while following and researching thoroughly, reward one with a gigantic personal insight, previously hidden and imperceptible. That is why this intermission for thought is so crucial. The outcome may not be quantified and measured, but it is definitely of great qualitatively and subjectively, considerably weighty if success is sought. For true talent – intelligence at its height – stems from the ability to **associate things seemingly unrelated, as not the slightest connection between them is apparent.**

And in general the whole doctrine of changes and adapting to it at a glance is expressed in the following principles.
- ✓ They happen all the time.
- ✓ It is imperative to anticipate them and be prepared well for any surprise.
- ✓ It is a duty to frequently check their relevancy, contribution and real need.

- ✓ It is required to internalize and adopt these attributes quickly in order to realize them, if and when necessary.
- ✓ One must learn to enjoy them.

And he who tries to catch up with those variations and adopt them belatedly is like attempting to lock the stable doors after the horse had already run away…

And one more issue: any new affair, if repeated enough is eventually understood quite well. So it is totally and absolutely forbidden to be fearful of novelties, for in principle these are the future business opportunities presented, perhaps, once in a lifetime…

Everyone Has a Boss – But He Should Also Have a Replacement

In a sound observation of life's conduct **it would seem that everyone is subordinate to somebody higher up in the hierarchy**; even the highest in the world! A popular council may rule above a sole head of state, a congress on top of a president, a house of commons over a prime minister, a board of directors might govern a chairperson, stock holders control a CEO, or a superintendent stands higher than a subsidiary, et cetera; not to mention religion, in which God towers above all. Sometimes it is a close acquaintance or the keeper of dark secret which may betray an awful weakness, who is given all powers to dictate. Such a situation is valid in the democratic-capitalist world as well as in semi-totalitarian or dictatorial regimes. Since even tyrants are bound, normally, to stand trial eventually in front of the court of nations, or even the people who may revolt against them (and history is full of examples such as Mussolini, Ceaușescu, Saddam Hussein and their like…).

Even when it seems that in certain places or at given times the leader is bound to be the ultimate arbiter in what concerns the populace, technology, different public procedures and financial processes in the system led by him (and woe to him who defies this!...) – at the end of the day he is accountable to somebody.

But the man on top of the cumulative entity is not always a perfect example, regarded by all as a role model and a paragon. On the contrary, some basic truths circulate in our world, regarding the "boss" as mediocre or less than that:

- ✓ A celebrity is someone whose reputation is based on saucy gossip about him rather than on his unique performance and virtues.
- ✓ Imitating the subordinate is the greatest flattery a manager can bestow on an employee of his – even if not said explicitly – particularly when trying to do so is motivated by self-disparaging (adopting that junior's characteristics, those liked by everyone around, in order to conceal the fact that his ideas are no better or even totally worthless…) and not out of competition (taking on these underling's merits for the sake of improving the performance of the entire team, dragging by that all participating in the mission to the highest degree of workmanship, so that the system and its workforce gain, multiplying by the end of the day…).
- ✓ The technique to survive the longest at the top is by taking full credit for the organization's accomplishments, those produced by people underneath, and by being the first to point a blaming finger at them (and deserting those beneath…) during catastrophes.
- ✓ Large and successful enterprises know how to maneuver in a way which "creates glory even in failure". Thus even an average manager, shirking real involvement, may succeed; the question is for how long?

Moreover; it seems that **"Bosses" usually do not like too-strong leaders in their vicinity amongst their subordinates, since they**

pose a threat to their authority. Therefore it is very importatnt to find the "golden path" enabling one to keep presenting an **honest and solid personal status** to colleagues, partners and - employees on the one hand – and on the other, to prevent the "owner" (or the direct superior…) from feeling that his position is being undermined. And the most excellent style to do this is by "managing" him in the good sense of the word: to find out his expectations, loves and whims; how to best expose things to him: in the company of other people or alone; when and in what circumstances; and which are his preferable operative methods. This should be done with a lot of flexibility and self-assurance, not giving up easily, while being awfully careful not to enter into confrontations. It is imperative to show respect and give him the feeling that all good ideas and solutions emanate from him. One must let his manager be sure that he can always expect support and backing, mainly when he is disappointed with himself thinking that he messed up and is in tremendously bad shape, so to speak. Or as was summed up cynically by a certain vice president of the United States: "My job is, actually, to keep the president from stepping in dogshit – and help him clean his shoes if he already has…". No harm would ensue from being politically correct and avoid reminding him of this muddle all the time. And the most important thing is to know how to accept the verdict, even when he makes wrong decisions, for in the final analysis he definitely carries all the responsibility. All of this is for the benefit of the system, which may suffer otherwise from all kinds of unnecessary frictions, due to which its common goals and targets may be considerably damaged.

Furthermore, when the senior executive is no more certain of his situation, the last thing he would like to see under him is somebody who radiates so much confidence in his abilities. And when the superior feels somehow weak, he might use a huge and illogical measure of force, only to secure himself from that successful subordinate. So it is better to avoid naiveté: even excellent performance at work combined with a hope for the final victory of the "good" (or as is said by the bleeding hearts in their righteous innocence: "justice is like water – it always finds a way...") do not guarantee the eternity of the job. (Suffice to say: who are the first to be deposed on any TV reality show? This is not so bad a reflection of the realism portrayed in the present article: it is the dominant, the strongest and the most active persons, just because they threaten the weaker ones who vote determinedly for their removal but cry with crocodile tears when they leave...)

Sometimes the boss "appears" in the guise of a board of directors, whose declared job is to set the company's policy and targets, to guide the CEO concerning its performance and to confirm the methods of its execution, to appoint the key functionaries of the organization (people able to confront all these fronts...) and to supervise the system as a whole and its activities in all dimensions. In addition this body of electors may occasionally discharge the management from some jurisdiction or operation, taking the responsibility upon itself. Thus it is no wonder that such invasion to the inside of a firm is a fertile ground for friction (mainly when the said bunch of executives are a fossilized, numb, even hostile council of "elders"...). For this reason, the manager should exercise extra wisdom and sensitivity in his relations with this forum , similar to his conduct vis-a-vis the owners.

And on the other hand – as possibly the oldest and most well-worn cliché regarding this subject goes – the graveyards are full of people who believed they had no replacement. Very few are the managers – especially the most senior and eccentric – who are willing to live with the fact that they may have a substitute. Most are sure they were appointed forever and in order to guarantee that concept would do anything it takes to prove that nobody is suitable or able to step into their office (thus they will be able to stick to their elevated jobs until the "fullness of time" in a kind of an outstandingly stubborn "Eternally Ruling Syndrome"...). Even if they are finally forced to relinquish their position they would not bother (perhaps intentionally...) to deliver it to their successors after a proper overlapping period, in order to verify their assumption that no proper inheritor was found to "fill their shoes"; and with the purpose of supplementing their own reputation would engender a company's decline after they are gone, presenting this deliberate state of regression.

And maybe it stems from fear that by declaring the next in line for the throne the latter would undermine the "kingmaker" while he is still "alive".

But the opposite is true. First of all, it's the manager's responsibility to constantly control leadership structures in the organization he runs – a duty he must implement by enhancing, directly and indirectly, the "**managing capacity**" of his subordinates, at the system's level and especially at the individuals' standards, among all seniors officers serving under him. Second, the mental capacity enabling him to train the next generation is a sure sign of greatness, of personal integrity, of a brave business outlook conferred on the company and certainly points out that the intentions of the one at the top indeed lie beyond private interests; it is done in order to prepare consciously, so that when the day comes – when it's time to quit and move on – it will be absolutely clear **how to pass the "baton"** to the appropriate figure, and **who is this man**. Such a process should be carried with no misgivings concerning a possible diminishing of the achievements and reputation of the departed on the one hand; on the other, it ought to be done as smoothly as possible so as not to shake the foundations of the cumulative entity, since it must be understood that the unit's future success is **credited to the inheritor as well**. And the best historical example, perhaps, is when Moses is ordering Joshua to assume leadership of the desert flock – an event to be distinguished above all for the power and authority transferred fully to the heir in front of the whole congregation, while the current chief is still alive but he is already doomed.

And all of that is true despite the uncomfortable feeling (literally true sometimes…), that the person soon to be executed is selling the rope to his hangman.

Persistency – the Secret Navigator and Hidden Factor for Success

Loyalty to the path, outlined in order to achieve the target, and **sticking to fixed goals** are major ingredients for appropriate management. And those are the opposite of unnecessary changes, carried on daily in unbearable haste and irresponsibility, as soon as some new piece of data or any obstacle appears, even the smallest.

To these should be added **adherence to the mission** – total devotion, causing one to fully concentrate on the purpose that motivated the entire "quest". An uncompromising focus on the aim, when disseminated to the subordinates, strengthens and molds the system as a whole, proving the possibility of standing religiously behind beliefs out of a strong will; It bestows as well the moral power and the physical might that is driven out of the successors to continue obstinately and show powerful resourcefulness, even facing the unexpected and as the conditions become problematic and onerous. This results from understanding that there will always be difficulties – destined to be surmounted or surrendered to – therefore it is certainly better to eliminate them.

And to use a sporting metaphor – it means **being a winner**: the unbending will to always **be triumphant**; the never-exhausted **striving**

to conquer more and more new summit, the inner molecular structure creating a **huge craving for success** in everything one touches – as long as there is a belief in the goals, a trust in the righteousness of the course towards their achievement and a confidence in the judgment which engendered it.

This tendency contributes significantly to the attainment of a leadership position in anything a person does. As was once said jokingly: "There is a unique rule which must be adopted by anyone motivated to be at the top: if one cannot be the first in what he does – then he must make every effort to be the best...". That is to say, it is forbidden to be satisfied with less than a place at the acme, since history never remembers the second-in-command. Or as was well said by John Nance Garner, vice president of Franklin Delano Roosevelt, 32nd president of the USA, even being deputy to the strongest man in the western world, is "not worth a bucket of warm spit". For excellence is not one more thing resulting from hard training; it is a way of life, a kind of cult. And after deciding what to do and how to carry it out, the intention must be either "going for it" with love and seriousness, full speed ahead, or forgetting about it, for there is no middle way of executing things.

However it is highly recommended to fulfill such a strong aspiration without being **overly conspicuous,** avoiding declaring it daily to all and sundry (with a kind of typically annoying arrogance or something like it...) and trying not to be constantly on the edge – but by positioning oneself there just very near to the deciding moment. Just as that experienced long-distance runner, whose tactic is to keep a short distance from the one who is galloping ahead at the first place resembling a horse with blinders all along the track; such a runner strives not to attract the attention of the other opponents (perhaps preventing most of them from blocking his way to victory...), only to burst forth in the last lap, taking the lead and winning simply at the finish line. And this is purely in order not to create jealousy on the way to the top – and because of it: a deep antagonism – among some of the others who may really obstruct the realization of his plans. For it is well-known that most people do not normally like (certainly do not encourage...) the winners – to say the least. The air at the summit is very thin...

On the other hand, it is totally forbidden that such a fatal submission will drive the manager to enslave his people ("to the death" as they say...) by chasing the completion of the assignment out of personal principle – just to show everybody that he is capable of overcoming the challenges presented to him; especially if significant technological or economic changes occurred compared to the initial situation when the targets were set – and he is aware of it; it may be contrary to the opinions and perceptions of those surrounding him, or when the entire matter may cost dearly the organization under his command – a kind of an unrelenting, megalomaniacal push – in order to prove who is the boss and who is always right, using discredited Machiavellian methods.

True, it is legitimate to constantly aspire for success; however, the leader ought to be pragmatic and take into account that under certain circumstances, reality permits only partial achievement of the goals, including such a situation in which a decision would be taken to give up the dictated aims – in other words "failing to reach the finish line" (for example: unexpected occurrences which may indicate that "saving the performers" has become a priority – even to the exclusion of the fulfillment of the original mission...). Thus it is necessary to learn in what way to prepare for such conditions and how to accept them. All this is because life sometimes resembles a boat sailing: when the weather changes and the sea gets rough, one should internalize the fact that the course must be modified accordingly...

And all in all, persistence (together with readiness for an absolute sacrifice in order to accomplish the task...) is perhaps the single most influential factor in inspiring people to follow the leader. Therefore it is necessary – in addition to nourishing the fire inside – to talk about it openly and inculcate it within all partners in execution, emphasizing that giving up to them means actually giving them up. And when it is projected to everybody below, and they feel its truthfulness, it drives them to stand as one behind the meaning of the dictated activities and to consolidate and stimulate their actions in unison for it; and then it is within its power to turn even the sharpest objectors in the system to its most ardent supporters. For it makes sense that there would not always be a unanimity among all those toiling and carrying the burden. But that very manager, being keen in his belief and totally devoted to the assignments serving the good of the company, without waiving anything, will always succeed in uniting the others around him and will enjoy their full support of his leadership; the very human axiom states that the natural tendency of people is normally to follow the one enthusing them with an idea, for their own good, setting an example by his commitment. Or in the words of Theodor Herzl, the visionary of the Jewish State: "Show them a flag – and they will follow it…" And in this manner, the man at the top will probably find it easier to control his subordinates.

Management's Effectiveness and the Way to Measure It

No leader is free of control and self-criticism. Each manager's duty is to draw conclusions concerning his general operation for the good of the organization which he heads on the one hand, and on the other to learn the essential lessons as to his own conduct. Thus he checks the effectiveness of his personal functioning as well as the effectiveness of the company he runs. This he must do constantly, and the zealots even hire outside, independent expertise (since it is important that justice may also be seen; and it is all the more forbidden to allow those who need to be investigated to interrogate themselves…). Most people are convinced, as already mentioned before, that they should change the environment before even observing whether an amendment is actually due in their individuality.

The effectiveness of a manager is supposed to be generally appreciated by the real "output" which he presents at the end of the day, compared to what he could have made theoretically, according to the academically calculated ratio between his "actual" production and the "potential" one. However, the term "production" is sometimes very difficult to quantify, for the means and methods of its exact measurement are not always in existence – especially when the starting point, which must be kept forever in mind while evaluating the said ambition, is not so clear all the time. Moreover: if the examination of what is being "generated" is done by comparing to overhead expenses which are not exactly of the same "family" – it is not only meaningless, but may even be misleading.

And one of the commonest examples of the above-said is the criterion of financial profits. It should not always be the sole decisive factor of success. Such a key, when on its own, is certainly not enough.

First: it entails emphasizing the bottom line, instead of what is achievable in the case of better efficiency.

Second: the result can be obtained without any of the involved partners in the activities having to lift a finger – resulting only from economic processes which don't relate at all to the performance or its yield, such as those which occur in the world that improve things, a matter of luck per se.

Third: by mere accounting exercises – for example: emphasizing deliberate economizing and cuts in the present – it is possible to show immediate gains looking good today, but compromising tomorrow's returns – a blow to be discovered only in the far future.

Forth: the turnover might be sucked currently into the firm's past deficits, but the situation actually improves compared to the starting point of the test.

And fifth: the organization has other targets – while striving for financial gains turns out to be, actually, a system's constraint (although as a general rule, this is the main objective to be constantly longed for…).

In short: the "bottom line" is often just one item chosen categorically, maybe a mere illusion; even though impressive, it may conceal precious information, as meaningful as what is exposed by its publication. Therefore, perhaps, it should be presented as an index for "improved performance" all around – not, as generally perceived, a criterion for the growth of financial profitability only.

Therefore a set of criteria, **as objective as possible**, should be constructed to examine and evaluate the effectiveness of management from one side, and on the other – as **unique analysis parameters for the controlled entity**, adapted to the essence of its occupation and the form of its operations.

As the first step, prior to the establishing of the above-said points of reference, it is necessary to define most clearly the function to be tested, its expected achievements and the methods of their examination – otherwise there is no data to compare performance against, serving as an evaluation benchmark. Since the role of management entails many personal styles, very difficult to assess in detail, such an interpretation should be normally carried out by him who serves in it. Because no one knows better the organization he heads: the elementary lines of the work required for such a position, the state of the unit as he found it, and its future designated objectives.

However, for this efficiency assessment, it is important to use accepted and customary indexes, derived from the variety of theories describing the management function from its organizational aspect:

sociologists view society as an assemblage of individuals, in which the correct treatment is the one to ensure the desired results; data analysts define it as factors and information-analysis mechanisms and as a main network of decision-making processes, and if it is properly implemented, success is assured; economists and financiers claim stubbornly that it is a body of cash flow, and the quality of its performance is expressed by its balance sheets; and the experts in general management doctrines have no doubt that it is a combination of all three above. Ultimately, the person at the top is the one to combine, in addition, the external influential factors (customers, suppliers, competitors, government officials and so on…) with the internal contributors (owners, bosses, employees, resources and the like…) so as to do the best for the corporate entity.

Thus the testing criteria of management's effectiveness in the framework must be, probably, a solid blend of private parameters, created by the top guy himself on the one hand, with objective estimation parameters on the other; these must be based on all the above-mentioned, in their totality. And on the whole, such efficiency is expressed in the **added value** bestowed by the manager on the body he rules, coming from his abilities to **optimally realize each** of the following activities – separately and bound as one piece – to the accurate mesh, insuring the best effects for the company:

- **Translating goals to operational instructions:** the ability to refine the most complicated processes into one simple fundamental chart, understood by all.

- **Focusing people on assignments:** the skill to join employees to all other existing and allocated resources: organizing, adjusting and motivating them in the maximal intentional mode.

- **Observing, identifying and overcoming obstacles on the path to the targets:** the capability to stress the real problems of the system – especially contentious issues – and clearly emphasize their knotty characteristics, so as to allow for a pinpointed and exhaustive solution to each and every one of them.

- **Nourishing diagnosis, analysis and common sense aptitudes**: the gift in taking the right decisions on time, in view of the unceasing flow of information and changing data, coupled with a realistic anticipation of the future.

- **Distinguishing between primary and secondary**: the knowledge how to fully exploit one's working hours, determining the focus of one's personal contribution; the openness to listen to gut feelings, absorbing the fine points dictating when to avoid involvement and where to delegate authority to the subordinates.

- **Resisting pressures**: the energy and perseverance to carry on during periods of real stress. And in addition – the mental courage not to be dragged into totally irrelevant maelstroms, following the demands of interested parties – coalitions of devastating political intrigue – within the staff.

- **Uniting fronts**: the virtue of making the business into everybody's concern by sweeping all employees in the communal entity and assuring their personal involvement.

- **Raising the company's status**: the proficiency of creating such relationships with external entities including other non-dependent bodies, and recruiting them as contributors to the benefit and the whims of the entire firm.

- **Profit realization**: the wisdom to guarantee the continued existence of the organization.

This is just like playing again and again with the controls of the home entertainment system until attaining the desired, perfectly attuned sound, only then to sit comfortably in the armchair and immensely enjoy its output…

The effectiveness of the manager is measured, therefore, by applying all these **criteria from theory to practice**: quickly, simple and hopefully by a method most accepted by all those taking part in the organization's actions, external as well as internal ones; and all in all – in his ability to achieve any of the goals set in advance; in his potential for change and self-adaptation from time to time; and in the quality of the company run by him.

But it should be remembered: these parameters lend themselves sometimes to rough estimates only. Not in all operating domains are they numerically quantifiable, expressed in immediate arithmetic values of an input / output ratio. And perhaps the following is the best description: if the targets are the main motivating force of all work done in the organization, then the total practical benefit to the company resulting from all related activities by the end of the day is the best indicator of its management and conduct.

Contributors to Correct Leadership – Which Are Indispensable

Like everything in life, done correctly and for long enough, is true for **management** too: it keeps **getting better with time** using those tools, methods and traditions adopted by the one standing at the top, especially those resulting from his **own experience**, out of past occurrences and impressions, from their lessons and conclusions. And in order not to regard errors done out of ignorance as "tuition fees" which must be paid, and to cut expenses due to fines for mistakes made – and if one really wishes to become more efficient and take shortcuts on the path to the target – it is very important to rely upon **other people's experiences too**. For according to our sages of blessed memory: a wise man learns from his own past occurrences and the knowledge drawn of it, but the wiser man absorbs from others' historical happenings as well. Because everything lends itself to teaching and learning, except experience, which must be acquired (and later conveyed, actually, to followers...). And in this context it is important to avoid situations in which it is ready for use, when already unnecessary.

And the following functional elements are not management fundamentals that must be done under any circumstances, or that are unavoidable. On the contrary, there are plenty of senior executives who do not necessarily devote enough attention to some of these conduct modes, though they no doubt find executing their jobs more difficult. Therefore, it is intended here to impart to anyone who runs an organization and guides people **some practical rules**, friendly advice, which may come to be very useful in supervising – especially since they do not exclude other leading principles, but actually add to and even improve them.

Order as a Way of Life

Order is not only a vital tool in life, but a **force multiplier**, administrative leverage. The more the communal body is branching and complex, the more it is needed. Adherence to it is essential – especially regarding the huge flow of information into the system, forcing fast reaction, change and adaptation.

So by a small investment – a simple matter of obtaining operatively efficient habits and a strong inner discipline to carry them out – a huge return is bestowed on him who takes advantage of the usefulness derived from such a regime. It means saving time, which undoubtedly stands for, in most of the circumstances, much more than money; its real value is expressed in the currency of peace of mind and a strong self-confidence – even while operating under stress and very heavy pressures.

"Organization" and "Order" may be synonyms, but not identical in their meaning. One can be ordered, but not organized; **however, the opposite is impossible**. "Organizing" means a total deployment for performance on the way to the finish line, according to logic derived from the global perception of how to achieve the final target; and this is founded on "Order" – which is a methodical mode of preparation dealing with mustering, cataloguing, editing and recording the totality of the most detailed ingredients necessary for daily conduct and routine existence, in the most welcome and comfortable style and at the highest availability. Moreover; they constitute those single "Cents" whose employment perfects the term "Organization" into a full "Dollar." Therefore it is considered a force multiplier: the single pennies yield, in fact, a full hundred.

For illustration, one may imagine three document files dealing with a certain subject, each one perfectly ordered. Assume that for the purpose of handling a matter concerning their content, all are needed simultaneously, but they are situated in three different locations. The first step in "organizing" the work would then be placing them all in the special spot where they are most needed, so as to conveniently make use of all of these papers whenever necessary.

However, **using** these documents for the afore-mentioned function would not have been possible – even if all three were available in one location – were each of the files disordered and mixed up.

What's more, keeping the above-said records in order makes it possible to **trace** rather easily any additional information from each of them when needed urgently (regardless of the original reason for their being gathered in the first place…), and it is even very simple to **fully remember** their content when they are properly written, compiled and well edited.

And one additional, very important rule: when casual new clients find the offices of a company clean and aesthetically pleasing (even polished…), the firm gains quite a few "positive points" as an advance for future business; this is the first and crucial step, actually, in creating its marketing array, because everybody is aware of the correlation between outward appearance and the character of internal management and conduct: if it is organized as well as it seems, the chances are that its services are good as well – which is clearly impossible for a business that gives a messy first impression.

Furthermore, it must be remembered: strict order and carefully arranged things do not stand in contrast to **improvising occasionally**. Sometimes there are situations in which reacting "on the move" or "under fire" is a must, especially when there is not the fraction of a second needed for quiet thinking and orderly premeditating. Then, he whose "quick-draw" instincts are the best would pull out the right response to the unexpected circumstances he encounters (innate inclinations which, by the way, can be developed by training…). And a properly organized array facilitates better unplanned activities, because even improvisation – an act or a set of actions done naturally or mechanically and without preparations – should not be done chaotically. And it really might be better if such ad-hoc operations like this were to be based on a practical collection of minimal "pre-arranged procedures", assimilated into the systems in which it may take place…

Moreover: a company whose first priority is "order" will suffocate creativity. The needed attribute of being well-preparedness in advance should be such that it does not curb productivity and innovation among its employees. And as much as "mess" is not a method, "perfect order" cannot serve as an ideology; it is just a means, not an end. And an optimal dosage should be found – like everything in life – between the administrative asset on one end and the liberty to imagine and exceed dry conventions on the other, without compromising the advantages of systemic organization or giving up the blessed sparks outside the normal gray activity patterns.

To wit: improvisation, timely and measured, is a virtue; as was already said, it is the secret spice turning a pleasant, familiar dish served on the table into a real delicacy...

The Time Resource – a Prime Asset when Correctly Used

An optimal exploitation of time is among the most important management skills which must be adapted by the leader; analogous to distinguishing the essence from the incidental. And if the man at the top wishes to utilize effectively every single minute of the day, and fully extract its potential, it is imperative to learn first of all to differentiate between optional chosen events and uncontrolled duties and commitments. Then he has to update the priorities of what he really prefers to do, decide on the most significant subject at the moment, and dedicate to it the majority of attention as well as systemic and personal abilities. This is true in light of the fact that the capabilities to respond in an opportune manner, to perform swiftly and to easily acclimatize to quite a lot of changes and transformations are so meaningful in the era of cross-border electronic business.

No less important – and perhaps even more so – is inculcating that an optimal usage of the resource of time means devoting a considerable part of it purposely and elaborately to fostering non-urgent staff in daily life; in other words, to dealing with cardinal issues intended to supply essential and encompassing answers concerning the future at work in particular and for the existence in general: vision, goals, long-term planning, preparation methods and such. And just because those subjects are amorphous, not "knocking" alarmingly on the door, they are absent every now and then from the agenda – solely due to a lack of sober business perception. These matters are, to say the least, in domains disliked by most people and perceived as unnecessary burdens; they are accepted as ones that can be skipped in the day-to-day schedule. Not many people are willing to invest routinely in "marginal" things such as: creating social circles not necessarily linked to on-going customary duties but assisting in diversified mental enrichment "only"; scheduling rotational preventive maintenance rounds for all technological apparatuses in order to ensure their proper functioning so that life can go on comfortably; organizing a regular sporting activity guaranteeing the health of body and sanity of the mind; enforcing order strictly preparedness for hard and high-pressure reality-junctions; nourishing oneself continuous with uncommon topics so as to stimulate the development of novel thinking channels. In short, to all the above-said fronts that neither require immediate reaction nor bestow materialistic gains on the spot.

However, it immediately becomes clear that these treatment spheres are very central to the personal-inner development and growth of the leader, and to the material-external evolution of the firm on the path – promising the success of both; therefore, they require allocation of real time. This is out of a deep consideration that a wise deployment and a disciplined way of living – and some may say a routine one (perhaps even a bit "boring"...) – guide the individual, finally bringing him, whenever appropriate or needed, to a physical and mental competence and a maximum readiness to reap that for which he has toiled so much for all his life. **For what truly promises tomorrow's achievements is looking out over the horizon and prearranging in advance and detail, starting already today**.

But here, caution is vital so as not to allow dear Mr. C. Northcote Parkinson, an experienced historian and British official, the satisfaction of proving the half-humorous thesis presented by him to the business world in the late fifties in his book, *Parkinson's Law*: "Work expands as the time for its completion becomes longer...". For people usually prefer delaying performance of that which is not urgent in their opinion. Turned on its head, his dictum argues that with a shorter and limited timetable, much more can be done.

It is advised as well to take note of the fact that junior and middle managers are constantly striving to increase the number of their subordinates; this necessity is not the result of their growing real responsibilities, but of the desire to make a name for themselves in the organization and prove their importance to the system. In order to justify the demand for more manpower they invent additional tasks, whose contributions to their main assignments are negligible, but allow them to convince their superiors of the pressure they are under and of their need for more employees.

In short: it is true that sometimes it is important to dedicate time to non-essential subjects as noted above, but it is forbidden to lose, even for a second, the focus and effectiveness directed at achieving the real, dictated goals, if it is desired to fully exploit every vacant minute and promote with maximum value the organization in one's charge.

Controlling the timing and tempo of events – in addition to indicating the quality of management – allows, inter alia, for:

- ✓ Arriving at each critical activity phase in life – while faced with difficult confrontations calling for tough decisions – relaxed, cool and, mentally as well as physically, fully prepared instead of near-total collapse resulting from being completely squeezed, due to being dragged after events dictated by a badly organized timetable set by others.

- ✓ Arresting and reexamining "from above" what has already been done, taking a pause for extra rethinking and re-analyzing by drawing preliminary conclusions before continuing.

- ✓ Optimal planning of the junctures at which one exposes himself, personally and professionally, to the world outside, beyond the day-to-day grinding routine; taking the best advantages of such designated periods to absorb proficient novelties and inventions and to learn from others.

- ✓ Choosing the most appropriate times for body and mind to rest, recharging personal "motivation engines"; **relaxation**, designed to improve operational capability, being in essence a "**sabbatical for the brain**", refreshing and revitalizing the gray matter.

(This is true especially for type-A personalities – ambitious, competitive, impatient and aggressive in certain situations; those believing themselves an immortal dynamo, charged constantly by movement – a kind of human "Perpetuum Mobile" – thereby pulled against their will into their jobs as if to treacherous quicksand. This kind of people must realize that there is no such thing as a free meal anymore – for the last one occurred amidst the Big Bang generating the Universe, as Einstein was once jokingly quoted, when asked why God had chosen to create the world at that very certain moment, as is believed by scientists investigating the subject. These "Eternity Machines" take a very high toll: physical, mental and social. And to those asserting that the rhythm of their work does not allow them any free time, it must be said: vanity of vanities, sheer nonsense! For how come one may undertake responsibility for leading a hundred million-dollar projects but not be able, on the other side, to prepare his subordinates and himself for taking a two-week vacation each year, enjoying some quality time with the family?!...)

In addition, it's appropriate to leave some designated intermissions free between events, especially for unexpected incidents lurking behind corners (for how does the average daily agenda of a typical manager looks like? No more than a few minutes rest between meetings, each one casting them against problems totally different than the previous ones...). Even more so, one must remember Murphy's Law concerning the entanglement of simple staff due to unanticipated disturbances not accounted for, causing quite a few moments to slip frequently between the fingers, and other unforeseen disruptions tend to inevitably materialize at the most inconvenient moments. Surprises are normally the greatest time-guzzlers, **since it is rather easy to plan for the expected, but very difficult to envisage the unplanned.**

And the first essential step in optimally utilizing such a precious resource should be compliance with timetables. For what is the use of such strict and detailed organization of the daily schedule if no one bothers to stand by it?!

Monitoring Methods and Means – a First-Rate Tool

No declared strategy, dictated tactic, advanced management approach or innovative operational plan, good and detailed as possible, is worth the words describing it or the paper it is printed on unless **efficient supervision processes** to ensure their full implementation and **effective control mechanisms** to guarantee their proper applicability are available.

The best monitoring assets are natural alertness and a sharp eye. There is no substitute for a manager who lives and feels in all honesty – one-hundred-percent – what is happening within the organization under his control. Such a reality requires him, first and foremost, to stay at the factory more than enough and as requested, and in addition, to acquire a virtue of "seeing all before anybody else;" and in no way should he be the last to know what is going on in his company. The famous soccer referee, *Pierluigi Collina* put it this way in one of his interviews: "I am not worried about a single case of me not seeing something happening on the pitch – in which later on five commentators sitting in a quiet air conditioned room, assisted by six television cameras replaying everything in slow motion from half a dozen different angles, would prove me wrong. I am shaking and terrified, on the other hand, by the thought of a situation in which I would miss something occurring just under my nose – seen clearly by a hundred thousand spectators in the stadium as one. Since then, I would no doubt have to retire from refereeing...".

Nevertheless, it is a must to construct additional examination and verification systems to assist personal observation and control, good as they may be. Such tools and assistance networks ought to be:

- ✓ Personal – built by the user and according to his needs.
- ✓ Able to introduce an overall as well as a detailed picture – simple to absorb by its operator (something that indicates the use of prime data management and flowing from it...).
- ✓ Presentable to third parties in a convincing and incontrovertible format, showing them that they are properly fulfilling their functions and the outcome of their analysis is accurate and realistic.
- ✓ Based on random field examinations regarding the specific domain to be checked arbitrarily.
- ✓ Friendly, so as not to lay a heavy burden on the community being analyzed – even if the execution is above its head – and with its full awareness.
- ✓ Easy to perform and understand, not requiring too much time to decipher, so as not to turn into a disquieting nuisance.

Most importantly, they should be custom-made for the controlled ingredient – in other words, depending on the level of trust ascribed to his mastery and professionalism, on the measure of credibility attributed to his standard reports, and for the length of duration he is known in the system.

Dictating activities and assigning tasks without a clear-cut mechanism for real-time, high-frequency, close surveillance of their exact implementation and enforcement is as useless as milling water.

Occasionally, the control and supervision tools depicted above take the nature of **standards** – an array of languages, conventions, scales and symbols. This is, in fact, civilization's **DNA**, without which it would be impossible to communicate and compare in order to follow and estimate the status of the universe from the evolutionary aspect. Those codes serves to publish scientific discoveries and the common methodology of associating all human beings with them for the creation of a uniquely fertile and better-functioning society. These are networks of communication and contact between computers, regardless of their actual location on earth, which allows for breakthroughs, the newest and most promising technologies in databases. And whoever is the fastest at making his standards universal, in addition to learning their use as prime motivators and inner criteria for his own activities would probably acquire a competitive advantage compared to other contenders in any field. Thus, it is no wonder that everybody is rushing to be ISO (International Organization for Standardization…)-certified for example – monitoring procedures and ordinary review instruments – that are indeed being built up by those who are considered, in so many words, to be the experts in the field…

And sometimes **the follow-up and review sensors, as well as the corrective for the man at the top and the framework, are picked up from outside the unit**, professionals away from the primary pool of the organization's employees. This includes psychologists specializing in the following fields:

- **Managerial** – treating the eternal triangle: the manager's personality; the tasks he is entrusted with as well as their derivatives; the people surrounding him at work.

- **Organization** – dealing with strategy and hierarchy framing, dictating tactics and formulating the modus operandi.
- **Human Resources** – sorting, nominating and placing the personnel.

These service-rendering specialists are totally neutral, since their promotions and paychecks are not dependent on any boss, and this is their advantage. Their power lies in the ability to turn into "testers of heart and guts" – exposing the revealed and hidden honest motives of all partners in the system, including the most senior person and his close surroundings, and translating the real accurate feelings within the "intestines" of the company. Their importance derives from the capacity to disclose up-to-date facts felt among employees – even the most junior ones – and not only from word of mouth. And their might stems from their being, regardless of the subjects, a kind of "preacher": talking straightforwardly and saying things that none of the original staff dare voicing, due to the political implications. Thus, they are not only improving the situation of the leader during his loneliest moments in his ivory tower, but also treating him as **his personal aides**.

And in summation: it is imperative to remember that the above-detailed mechanisms, procedures and tools are no more than **a means** – highly important, though – **but in no way the goal**. And setting them in motion does not indicate that the management has become more rigid or intrusive in the personal domains of its workforce, or alternatively submissive and dependent on outer elements – but simply implementing an array of highly effective filters to ascertain the organization's function and direction. But these methods of control and support are totally superfluous if intended to void the freedom of action, creativity and responsibility of workers within the cumulative unit; for an organized and ordered entity definitely requires its people **to obey the rules, but not necessarily to think by them**.

And the application of those follow-up and control instruments on the framework's total activity goes both ways: firstly, everything – but really anything – should be frequently examined; secondly, that all employees of the firm may be coerced to express their inventions and uniqueness at every moment by standard tools and language. For otherwise a situation may evolve within the company resembling the biblical "Tower of Babel," which may wrongly be interpreted as the over-delegation of authority or too much autonomy allowed – either of which may degrade the value of any institution and bring it to the verge of an abyss.

It is evident, therefore, that monitoring apparatuses such as described here alone enable **full control of what happens in the company**. Correspondingly and additionally, they serve **as an integrative test of the leader himself**: an examination of the targets he sets to be his own benchmarks as derivatives of the owners' intentions, their de-facto execution, and his personal contribution to that accomplishment – and whether there is any harmony amongst all of those.

Public Relations – as Augmentation of Image

Public relations are an important and powerful managing tool, serving generally to create a very deliberate image, in the eyes of the general public or a particular segment thereof – or to form a system of close human ties which would be for sure helpful in the future. Such an instrument is meant to perform as a mouthpiece for **desired messages** intended for certain people in order to best **assimilate them** in their ears. This medium may be exploited for the benefit of the entire organization, a definite product, or for personal purposes – so as to advance the success of each or all; it is a totality of ways and methods destined to be directed outwards, inwards, or specifically towards other unique entities – everyone by its own measure.

But the effort invested in producing a pleasant facade and in weaving strong and supportive connections – for the purpose of preserving their authenticity for as long a period as possible – should not, and cannot, compensate for de-facto **reliability and credibility in operation** or for **real achievements**; it can only foster **in addition** to these.

In order to effectively exercise public relations for the organization as a whole or for one of its products (thus enabling to quantify its cost / yield parameter…), it is strongly suggested to adopt the following rules – nearly axioms, actually:

First: they should assist in formatting a present and future declaration of activities' intent. And in order to bestow on them a shade of honesty and a solid qualitative content, everyone around should be convinced that in case of talking regarding a detail or a product that things are really uttered from the heart; and while speaking on behalf of the corporate, they do represent its managerial higher echelons.

Second: their planning and operation should be a well-prepared journey, full of good aims, gestures – and especially a permanent campaign, not a onetime passing wave.

Third: even exceptionally varied and fertile public relations can neither heal a moribund conglomerate, nor revive a bad product already "dead", since their purpose, generally, is to augment a positive picture, to promote a more or less agreed-upon model, or to generate a process of future damage control, if ever. In other words: **first and foremost comes doing – and only afterwards talking**…

Fourth: framing them into bi-directional, simultaneous, close and supportive relationships (which is true for any such mutuality…). On the one end outside, as this is the best means to be exposed, to pass selected and decisive messages and to penetrate the minds of those whose attention is asked for, by efficiently using the written and electronic media as avenues daily refreshed; and the path to the heart of a more exclusive, targeted audience is gained by driving and soliciting satisfied customers to express flattering information and opinions on new clients (especially justified if one succeeds in keeping those older purchasers pleased at all times, so that after a while they become "captive consumers" and "fanatic advocates" later, bravely defending the company or the product…). And on the other end inside, being important because the man at the top of a cumulative body or a product line is in need, normally, of the warm touch of those surrounding him to support his activity all the way, and not only from the outside, but precisely from his own people. Therefore it is sometimes required during the daily routine to give up formalities, to sign "random pacts" with certain "employee strata" and organize ad-hoc teams for occasional purposes. In other words: to built-up a sort of commitment toward himself which would guarantee the loyalties of colleagues and underlings, leading them soon to follow him through thick and thin when he indeed longs for it.

Fifth: when really and correctly interwoven in order to be properly attached to their aimed clientage, they turn out, in fact, to be much more than close relationships or even friendships; they actually become deep moral imperatives. And as for a firm, after their development, this finds expression in the construction of strategies, tactics and operative plans, in cooperation with this dedicated populace and based on feedback it supplies, so as to:

- ✓ Draw more of the public's attention towards the company.
- ✓ Improve the living and working conditions of the operational environment.
- ✓ Become an extraordinary exclusive place to attract quality personnel.
- ✓ Enhance the abilities to preserve good people in the system.
- ✓ Plan and continue deploying effective message-spreading arrays.

Concurrently using public relations for private-organizational benefits is not wrong; on the contrary, it is welcome and even advisable.

Firstly, a manager publicizing himself as the senior representative of the company he runs, is actually performing a good service by being recognized as one. And then all axioms detailed so far, concerning the techniques and the means of utilizing such relationships and mutuality, are valid.

Secondly, there is no reason for a person not to take care of his own interests also.

However, he must well remember that the rules of this game are somewhat different. To begin with, one ought to avoid being too much of a civil servant – whose activities are meant to service the public on behalf of the framework he represents – and confined to his specific skills, those getting him the job in the first place. Moreover, he must be very careful not to appear as a mere "statesman" – a "dry" public activist constantly busy with leading the system under his command, and with conducting its formal foreign affairs. He would be advised to playact the "politician" too: a tactician and a plotter – in the good sense of these words – exerting himself in the name of the corporate he guides cleverly and cunningly, but also for his own individuality. In the real world he is tested too by the ability to interact properly with decision-makers of any entity who would assist the company he heads – as well as his image itself. And because his personal future may be influenced by that, he is cautioned to make his steps diplomatic, even politically correct, when necessary. And his credit may swell as a result of the friendly and blossoming relationship he would succeed in publicly establishing with the firm's stockholders (an achievement that surely may benefit in addition, by the way, the entity he is running…).

As long as the personal aspect is the subject, an impressive appearance, playacting (a strong handshake, a sociable shoulder tap, displaying confidence, straight answers and such…) combined with a sharp sense of humor may be very helpful. Or as the afore-mentioned Ronald Wilson Reagan, 40th president of the USA, put it: "How can a president not be an actor?..." when asked by a reporter "How can an actor run for President?..." during the presidential campaign in 1980.

Still, a manager should not allow himself to be viewed as a "third-degree politician" – a querulous and inciting opportunist – who employs all his deeds and any occasional situation only for his own good and private intentions.

And if the tool called "Public Relations" is used to enhance the reputation of an organization, a product or an individual, and to promote their purposes, it should be entrusted to inner or outer excellent and experienced professionals, whose expertise in this specific field is eminent – those knowing how to do It correctly, making sure that the designated audience receives the messages in the right spirit. Namely: to take good care of the association's texture with all its branches and through all the types of the media by giving interviews, refuting bad rumors and even using any random spin as a legitimate implement – as long as it is not a disservice to the others and while it benefits the publicity of the firm's or the individual's interests and images. For everybody knows that a squirrel is nothing but a rat enjoying good public relations...

Here is perhaps the place to emphasize that any fight with the media is nearly always doomed to fail, because it is much stronger than its opponents (in the Arab literary proverb: "A stone dropped on an egg will break the egg; and an egg dropped on a stone will also break the egg..."). Therefore it is strongly recommended to recruit it for the advantage of the corporate, using it as a tailwind to improve the company's image and promote its business, focusing on utilizing the afore-mentioned powerful and well spread all-over communication entity, and not on trying to direct it; simply to be wise – and not just righteous.

And in summation: it is possible to keep on going even without intensive public relations, but doing business would be more difficult. On the other hand, a clever usage of it will significantly better the reputation and widen the circle of sympathizers who may be of help in times of need; for an organizational or private image is indispensable and can be the crucial factor on "the day of judgment."

However, two very important conditions must be observed.

The one: it is imperative to stick to a **judicious media dosage**: a fair exposure, on the one hand – without over-prominence, pretentions or unnecessary declarations which may just aggravate people, on the other hand. To quote the 11th Israeli prime minister, Ariel Sharon: "Why is the fish being served for dinner? For opening its mouth one time too many…". Since it is well-known that media people tend to mix their own opinion with the news, always interpreting instead of reporting accurately as is expected from them, creating reality in place of reflecting it, while hysterically blowing up, too often, minor issues into major national problems, waving all the while the virtuous, hollow and scorched mantra of "the public's right to know". This they do even while lacking a full understanding of the sense of things or being short of seeing the whole real picture in its details, but only drawing given data out of various contaminated personal megalomaniac complexes. And because provocative "Yellowness" is for them a profession, a living, a hobby and a recreation altogether – a kind of obsessive worldwide sport – they allow themselves, in addition, to become on matters they are writing or broadcasting like the infamous Inquisition, God forbid: being the prosecutors, the judges, the hangmen and the undertakers at the same time, and mostly unjustly. Indeed, occasionally the outcome of what they say is a wretched reporting fiasco, a mixed journalistic farce of instigating cacophonic spins – seducing, stimulating and tendentious, full of irrelevant facts. All this they do in order to assure an audience for lucrative, but quickly forgotten, advertisements. As was once argued in sarcasm mixed with a shuddering sadness: "the media resembles a fire – when far enough away, it warms; when it is too close, it burns...". And here it is perhaps important to internalize an ancient rule, accompanying the people of the book since its foundation, even in its holy writings: "Tales are more dangerous than arms; canons, guns, pistols and swords can harm only those facing them, but slander and evil stories can bring disaster to future generations too...".

The other: one needs to be always on the **alert and ready to react in time to whatever is happening.** This means to know in advance what is going to be published in tomorrow's newspapers before they are distributed to their subscribers early in the morning – so as not to be surprised by what may be found in them when they are already being used to wrap fish in the market...

Steadfast Durability – a Must for Success

No person, aspiring for a top-notch job, would fully admit while busy convincing others to grant him his wish, that he lacks the physical or mental capabilities to face the stress inherent in the yearned-for position. For when marketing his characteristics, he presents himself as the most fitting in the world to carry the load – and all implied by it.

But history might present many examples of high-ranking leaders collapsing under the heavy pressure required by their missions. Therefore when someone prepares to fight for such a tenure, he must first of all examine himself in the most honest and penetrating manner, in order to verify whether he really has the **strength of body and soul and the personal and public courage** necessary for its proper fulfillment. What is needed is a character qualified to withstand the inner tempests and the spirit's vicissitudes, and to stop the moods from swaying too often between peaks of euphoria and depths of depression. These traits underline indeed the **continuous durability** of the individual beyond his activity, fully believing in its importance, even as its popularity is waning. Because nothing is more dangerous than a captain-shepherd who, while all ears are attentive to his utterance, at the very moment when he is called to make the hard decisions, falters just then, leaving his flock devoid of guidance. This is a betrayal, actually, in their tendency to follow him and in everything he symbolizes for them.

It is clear therefore that the above-said energies are compulsory to carry out this kind of hard task. They bestow the enormous power to stand upright in spite of occasional tough times; to face forthrightly passing failures; to bear bravely the temporary fiascos – even these resulting from wrong decisions taken innocently and by impaired judgment based on the data existing at that time in the system; to stand firm and rock-solid facing the entire crowd, even when it turns accusingly against the one who made the resolutions, daily shooting poisoned arrows for what it considers a misstep. This must be done without shaking off responsibility on the one hand or totally collapsing on the other. Knowing how to be lonesome, single against the multitude, holding nontraditional opinions and not being liked because of different views – but nevertheless certain of the relevant judgment and current perception – recalls probably the aforementioned John C. Maxwell's orchestra conductor, who by the nature of his vocation must perform with his back to the same audience that came to listen to the concert being led by him…

Such forged durability derives from a blessedly cool temper and an inner peace to direct long term crises, while displaying moral and mental strength, decisively, vigorously and with much patience – vis-a-vis very heavy pressures – even when things are not moving in the right direction. This is the internal force negating giving up, despair and desertion due to stick-to-it-iveness and the faith in the final cause and a readiness to sacrifice all for its achievement. Most importantly, this is the ability to rise, straighten and steady oneself each time anew after a total decline and encounter with the bottom of the abyss; the might to start again from scratch with tremendous, uncompromising willpower to reach the marked goals. As the old sailors, used to hurricanes, say: "When the waves get strongest, the strongest are exposed...".

This kind of power, as above, guarantees the potential to stay at the top, lacking complacency, arrogance and the smugness of pure opportunism – all while fully understanding that the position at the summit may be sometimes only temporary. And its meaning is not summed up just in enjoying respect, authority, high salary and bonuses and dealing with choice subjects – but in constantly taking also care of the gray, tiresome, sweaty and bothersome toil. In addition, one must be mentally prepared with meticulous planning and in pre-deployment for managing the worst of all at the time of its appearance and manifestation. Because when the going gets tough, the tough get going...

On the other hand, it should always be remembered: the afore-depicted qualities are God-given. But it is possible to **develop, improve and augment** these traits in time and to learn how to use them when necessary. However, if a person is not imbued with those or cannot acquire them, he would better be kept at a safe distance from managing other people and be advised to avoid taking risks in his private life as well. For sitting a long time at the acme is bad for the respiration, since the oxygen there is very thin...

Fortune – as an "Enlightening" Factor, Bestowing Confidence and Daring

Alongside what was said so far, it must always be remembered that the results of the occurrences depend sometimes on the conditions and circumstances (the situation...) and on an uncontrollable set of coincidences (the constellation...). In addition – as Napoleon argued over two hundred years ago when choosing his generals to accompany him in in battle – there is **Luck** (faith's more victorious cousin and talent's best friend...), "that something" whose probability to materialize is very low from the beginning. While the first two may be somehow directed and ingeniously maneuvered in order to turn their drawbacks into advantages – and it is also possible and desirable to leave some personal touch in them – concerning the third, one must do the best, even more than that, so as to try influencing its "windings and twists" and recruit it as a colleague in the struggle for a better life. John C. Maxwell said: "Luck comes to those who are prepared..."; or as stated by Louis Pasteur: "Chance favors the prepared mind...". In contrast, Professor Lester Thurow claimed forcefully in his famous economic dogma that: "Fortune is a necessity; talent, stamina and tenacity per se are not enough to amass wealth...". Which may make one think that "realistic optimism" is bound to leave but a small space for the belief and hope that "miracles may really happen". After all, as was already cited, pessimism leads nowhere (not to mention the fact that "permanent skeptics" on the one hand and "incurable optimists" on the other, all leave the world in the same way – thus it is obvious that life is better experienced from a total positive and bright point of view...).

Three of the less famous people in this community treated humorously – but rather wisely – the subject of taking risks in business:

One of them claimed, whether jokingly or very seriously, that his impressive success was due to ninety percent luck and only ten percent hard, demanding and uncompromising work; but emphasized quickly that he is vigorously pursuing the formula to turn those remaining ten percent into fortune as well...

The second related a story about his secretary asking him what to do with a few hundred CV's received in response to a "wanted" ad. He ordered her to randomly pick up from the large pile ten letters and to invite their senders for a final interview. When she wondered aloud whether better candidates may not be found among the rest, he replied: "Anyhow, I did not intend to recruit the luckless ones...".

And the third insisted that: "No one ever died of a surplus of luck – but many are agonizing over a severe lack thereof...".

The logical explanation for such a worldview is perhaps this: whoever sees himself as fortunate tries and dares creating more and more for himself, and the odds of his success simply grow; and accordingly each problem is actually a chance for development and enlargement via its solution.

Therefore while considering and constructing work teams for any mission, it is always preferable to choose the fluky ones, searching for those enjoying the golden "Midas Touch". Those around whose finger the Gods installed a ring of good auspicious, so that everything would happen exactly according to their will. For it is well known that luck follows, mostly, the good ones – while haplessness tends to perpetuate itself. This was expressed by intellectuals of the ancient world and the Renaissance: "Chance fights ever on the side of the prudent" (Euripides, a Greek playwright from the 5th century BC...), "Stands at the side of the brave" (Erasmus of Rotterdam, a Dutch scholar from the 15th century AD...) and "Sets itself to the right of the daring" (Virgil, a Roman poet from the 1st century BC...).

And from the Jewish point of view one may add a sentence once uttered by a sage: "When someone is providential – nothing matters anymore: he has, most likely, everything he needs in life...". And this, maybe, explains the entire concept.

And since there are so many sayings and proverbs on the above-detailed subject, originating from many peoples and cultures, then it is just possible that they are true and real; so it is strongly advised to start believing in it...

The Family – Always Above All

And one last word:

Many people are completely dazzled by success; and the higher their position is on the ladder, the more they tend to forget where they are coming from and what their final destination is. It happens for three key reasons, usually:

The one, their remoteness from home – mentally if not physically – for long periods occasionally; what gives them the liberty, in their minds, doing everything to compensate for their apparent suffering without accounting for their moral obligations.

The other, dedicating their "souls" and time entirely to their jobs (which naturally seems like the most important issue in the world to them…) whether because of the limitless devotion, or as a result of the tremendous pleasure bestowed on them by their work; and that is the reason why they do not even try to find time for recreation.

The last – and worst – is haughtiness; a spell of hubris; the inebriation of success, gives rise to a feeling of near-invincibility, and therefore being allowed all. So they feel it is safe and even right to abandon all other imperative subjects in life. Thus, without being aware of the fact, they begin neglecting their own family too. Well, regardless of the aforesaid, such an "aloofness" is totally forbidden, for "There is no sanctuary of virtue like home…", as Edward Everett said (American secretary of state, 1852-1853…) – as high and respected as a person's occupation may be; and "Home is the place where when you have to go there, they have to take you in…", to quote Robert Frost (a 20th-century American poet…).

And all these afore-depicted people should better remember: lots of power is intoxicating – and that is why it is definitely misleading as well…

And all this is true for the following reasons:

First: unrest at home makes it very difficult to function outside.

To quote the poet, playwright and author Goethe, writing at the beginning of the 19th century: "Happy is the king or peasant who finds peace in his home...".

Second: disloyalty to the ancestral tribe is a proof of an inability to remain honestly devoted to anyone. As was alleged in the previous chapters, there is a full correlation between one's personal conduct and his business behavior; sometimes it is the best indication. To paraphrase Samuel Coleridge (an English poet and philosopher of the 19th century...) and Joseph Cook (an American contemporary...) respectively: only those who truly love their homes really love their occupations... and only a good home may give birth to a good organization...

And the third and most important: **a person's family is his single real and sure fortress**. No one is infallible; in times of crisis, when everybody seems to desert and turn their backs, only kin will be there to help and support. As Jane Austen wrote in *Persuasion*: "After all she had gone through, nothing was so likely to do her good as a little quiet cheerfulness at home...". George Moore (a British philosopher of the 19th century...) insisted: "A man travels the world over in search of what he needs and returns home to find it...".

The abundance of quotes of so many thinkers, politicians and scholars all from the modern age, dealing with the family and home afore-described, is a sure proof of their importance for all human achievement and success. Man, it seems, is not only the image of his homeland, to quote the poet Saul Tchernichovsky (a 20th century Israeli doctor who also wrote poetry...), but that of his family too...

Principles of Conduct and Leadership Wisdom: an Intermediate Abstract

The more one thinks and occupies himself with the matters above, the more it becomes clear that there is no actual need to develop new management techniques, but only to decide which of the existing ones, previously or subsequently set forth – is worth adopting; which are the elements to use in any given situation in accordance with the real demand. Moreover: these are not just technical methods, **but very deep and considerable thought processes**, firstly flowing from the genetic lottery but certainly have also built-in modes lending themselves to acquirement and improvement in time. Concurrently they are the outcome of **personal experience and that of other** invaluable contributors. And those, each on its own and altogether, bestow the following major capabilities:

To observe – not only to see.
To listen – instead of just hearing.
To feel – in lieu of merely touching.

And as an easily remembered format – the concept can be expressed by this formula:

Management = C^3I = Command, Communicate & Control Intelligently (emotionally & rationally).

What does each term stand for?

Command: in the sense of applying leadership, guiding and taking responsibility; however not to rule by dictating and "shooting" orders only.

Communicate: be constantly in touch with all involved in the operation's activities, as they crisscross.

Control: supervising the cardinal issues, meaning the outcomes; but in addition monitoring from above, and in general, the methods and means.

Intelligently: with emotional prudence and a lot of brainpower.

And in one comprehensive sentence it is possible to end by summing that management – which is, in total, the wisdom and knowledge to deal with self-conducting and guiding-piloting others – is mostly made of **charisma, natural leadership and the ability to inspire others, all spiced up with common sense, constantly attentive to inner signs coming from the heart and supported by continuous and unshakable mental strength**.

And on the whole: whoever is honest with himself and runs his life properly is for sure well-versed in leading the organization under his command in an exemplary manner – and vice-versa.

January 1995

Technological Strategy

or **"Which"** is the Chosen Product

Preface

The term *technology*, in the most general definition, means the application of scientific knowledge, experience and personal skills in suggesting solutions to practical daily problems and industrial issues, in order to continually make life more comfortable and easy for the purpose of improving its routine; and thereafter – the ability to preserve, as much as possible, that which has been achieved. This, in fact, is the functional activity to ameliorate the manners of human existence, due to the investigation of Mother Nature and the unrelenting efforts to understand her. The pragmatic translation of the above-said in any organization is simple: it is the totality of materials, methods, machines, apparatuses, tools, activities and processes, serving it in order to assist – directly or otherwise – in generating the products and services for which this communal body was established in the first place.

The technological factor is, therefore, the basic, cause, underlying the path to attain the goal for which any productive entity is founded. Thus, it has always been considered, since ancient times, to be the cardinal contributor (although never the sole…) to shape and ascertain the character of the administrative skeleton and operative patterns of the organization, the first to influence its color of behavior and work approaches. In light of that point, there is no doubt that there is a strong link between the complexity of the scientific-industrial element – being the source of the company's activity – and the branching pathways of the conductive mechanisms existing within it. This affinity, expressed in the number and types of units being the "technical core" of the firm (those directly responsible for production...) and in their place in its hierarchy, is the backbone around which first of all (and justly...) are created the nature and form of its framework.

But it is forbidden to forget that with the development of new managerial theories during the last four decades, that view was somewhat mitigated; giving precedence to a different perception, insisting that albeit the superior importance of the technical aspect – when all is said and done, it is only one of many factors contributing to the design of the corporate's doings and structure.

It seems therefore that the correct manner to weigh the influence of the **technological dimension** on the totality of the organizational behavior and its characteristics in all its operations, is to say that it is one of the main ingredients dictating the identity of the framework, but compared to the rest it is always "**primus inter pares**". And the connection above is clear and easy to understand; for the designated product definitely delineates which kind of company is supposed to materialize it and how will the firm be erected in all its other aspects. It starts with the business plan, from which are derived the technical work outline and all services supporting it in carrying out the production: passing through defining the operative and administrative functions – who is supposed to carry the load in practice, while detailing the range and type of their assignments; continuing by weaving the institute's structural arrangement and hierarchy; going on developing in setting the marketing, sales and client-relations strategies and final product-manufacturing patterns; and it ends by dictating follow-up and control mechanisms of all systems and applications.

In short: there is no domain free from being influenced by the above-mentioned scientific-industrial facet.

In addition, it seems that the technological dimension has constantly had and still has – albeit not always directly – a profound mass in fixing the degree of identification (or alienation...) which people associate with their toil. This is true because the more unique the occupation, the more it entails a stronger sense of professional pride, such as that which emanates from a belief of belonging to a very specific, perhaps elitist, group (of artisans probably...). This kind of feeling has quite an influence, of course, on the employee's motivation: his attitude to his vocation and workplace, his aspirations to develop personally and to progress, the effort he is willing to invest for the organization's success and his contribution to the quality of the final product. Consequently, it is quite obvious that the afore-mentioned scientific-industrial facet also shapes the scope and prominence of personal communication among the workforce's individuals, the degree of the group's coherency, the fabric of superior-subordinate relations and vice-versa – and especially the informal ways of management which evolve in the firm's matrix. These components leave their stamp, without any doubt, on the company's special character.

Now, after elaborating upon the "Gordian Knot" depicted above and its crucial importance in shaping the process of instituting a cumulative productive entity, its leading scenarios and daily conduct, it is easier to understand the significance of beginning the analysis of the four strategies (mentioned in the "Credo" article and which dictates, indeed, the organization's general operating policy...) precisely with the technological aspect's influence, and why is it drastically vital to be so meticulous during the course of deciding on the corporate's occupation domain and its nature.

Therefore, what follows presents some very remarkable points, which must be taken into account while concluding on the technological strategy and announcing it – including anticipating future variations which may occur in it along the planned path, a subject spread out in separate articles and compositions downstream, apparently not connected, but actually constituting a unified, full and logical mosaic after being read and inculcated.

Choosing the Portfolio – the Opening Move

While choosing the various occupations of an organization – a veteran body functioning for a while or one still lacking such a representative technical selection – it is strongly recommended to prefer, in general, domains which are growing and developing convincingly de-facto and can also be sensed and recognized as such; these having a prosperity horizon, expected to come into fruition and be commercially attractive in a reasonable time: those able to contribute significantly to raising the profits of the company. To wit: one should go for branches whose products are estimated to definitely be in request in the future (if possible in the present as well…), so they will have an economic justification to exist; **for without consumers' demand even the most revolutionary technology, remarkably innovative and choice as it may be, would stay on the shelf as science fiction**. But it must be remembered: there is no easy way to enumerate and accurately analyze terms such as "commercial attractiveness", "promising prosperity horizon" and the like – and gauge a measured and definite indication of clear financial ambition. This is an especially difficult objective when starting to deal with a field, merchandise or invention in its infancy. All this has already been discussed in the "Startup Companies" section and will be described again in the "Marketing" and "Entrepreneurship" chapters.

Since deciding the contents of the organization's business portfolio is such a critical and momentous move, laying the "very basic" foundations of its identity, structure and leading direction, one must be exceptionally careful throughout the process. Because such resolutions cannot be changed each month or even year, it is imperative to turn every stone in the most pedantic manner, intelligently and composedly, while plowing the preferred technological furrow. And before taking the final verdict on the product, it must be assured that a meticulous investigation has been conducted concerning what has been already done in this specific domain by others, near and far. And all of these activities are designed to insure for the firm the most solid infrastructure possible, for if the roots are well planted the tree will survive any storm...

Moreover, even after having chosen the desired occupation, it is necessary to keep on checking repeatedly and correcting accordingly the continuous operation pattern, until the optimal niche for the company is found, adjusted and finalized. A smart organization, striving to function properly, efficiently and profitably, must focus only on its **essential proficiencies, fitting its specific capabilities and unique character,** while outsourcing any assignment may also link to the main path of its activities, but not in the very area of its exclusive professionalism.

Nevertheless, the following business alternatives must be taken into consideration too:

First and foremost, there is no need to disqualify success opportunities in "traditional and mature" economic branches, those running for a long time in the arena and enjoying "continuous popularity". But then it is vital to apply a very thorough and deliberate scheme of global operative policy, combined with daily efforts and infinite patience during the practical implementation.

Second, occasionally really splitting one communal entity into two or more exclusive specializations under several separate sub-organizations (but beneath one unified business umbrella...) is preferable. Such a partition is much better than a situation in which all remain within the same framework, acting under a multifaceted strategy which is vague and entirely unclear. This kind of a business structure requires an ineffective investment in decentralizing energy instead of an efficient effort at its centralization, not to mention the tactic of risk allocation. Mark Twain, the author and humorist, explained this concept well in his book *Pudd'nhead Wilson,* published in 1893: "Behold, the fool saith, 'Put not all thine eggs in the one basket' – which is but a manner of saying, 'Scatter your money and your attention' [a doctrine adopted by many strategists...]; but the wise man saith, 'Put all your eggs in the one basket and watch that basket!' [for sometimes there is no other alternative and this is the very right thing to do...]".

The Product Strategy – the Second Phase

After fixing the occupation domain of the organization, the next step is supposed to relate to the micro: setting the product strategy itself. This, in fact, is the move that expresses openly for the first time **the company's core business stance,** its present value and ethics and future aspirations and intentions. The meaning of such a particular measure is a full elaboration of planning and directing the ways of all activities on the road to the production, marketing and sales processes. In other words, a very comprehensive formatting of the system's conduct modes on all the administrative and operative fronts on which it functions. And this scene enjoys a special connotation, because it is a kind of pact obliging the firm toward its employees, partners and clientele with regards to its forthcoming doings.

Since instituting this policy influences all other decisions taken concerning the whole managerial behavior plateaus of the organization, down to the individual level – then while integrating, adopting and formulating in detail the operative concept of the **product extraction,** it is necessary to clearly define, in everything relating to it, the following guidelines:

▸ **Tangible character**: the nature of the materials, quality of execution, structure, dimensions, designing style, general aesthetics and distribution quantity – in order to turn the fruits of the toil into something attractive and desired.

- **Variety on the production line**: the number of different prototypes, producible on the same technical procession path, so as to minimize the costs and augment the financial effectiveness.
- **The harvest's selection**: the article's variant number, in order to enlarge sales by supplying a personal response to as many clients as possible.
- **The designated life cycle**: computing and finding out the existence period of the outcome from its enterprise stage until going out of proper functioning (according to the four famous stages: introduction, growth, adulthood and decline…) in order to delineate the expected time – in fact, to begin preparing for the birth and employment of the next generation…

Managing the Technical Implementation Itself – the Third and Crucial Phase

The cardinal stage of an organization's activity is the performance itself – and all that can be deduced from it. Setting the chosen strategy, a detailed planning of its implementation and execution – even being the best in the world – are only the beginning of the quest; since they may not even be the slightest surrogate for a defective product or service due to flawed production, extraction and faulty systemic functioning. Because the quality of the final merchandise and its exact timely supply determine the scope of satisfied customers, and the sales volume is what brings, at the end of the day, money to the purse.

The production process and everything surrounding it starts with delineating the **operating management policy** of the whole organization, and is expressed by:

✓ General planning.

- ✓ Resource allocation and exploitation.
- ✓ Thrifty purchasing without harming quality.
- ✓ Delivering materials and equipment on time, and in parallel setting proper stock levels.
- ✓ Continuity of production scenarios, as well as striving to avoid bottlenecks.
- ✓ Spreading a high standard scale of preventive maintenance.
- ✓ Quality control and assurance.
- ✓ A fluent follow-up and monitoring of the operations' totality in all the above spheres, while immediately correcting along the way every defect that is exposed and needs to be treated.

First and foremost, operational management deals with **production engineering**. This is the area taking very meticulous care of all subjects regarding **all managerial-administrative procedures and practical manufacturing processes** divided into the main domains as follows:

▶ **Production planning**; a front meant to handle the standardization of all product extraction methods and routes according to the terms of quantity and time of supply as agreed with the customers – or due to the desired sales pace dictated ahead as a result of a financial profitability analysis from the preparation, training, content and management aspects.

This field is supposed to solve the following issues:

- The necessary resources:
  - Professional personnel.
  - Technical facilities.
  - Machines.
  - Designated equipment.
  - Raw materials.

- Performance approaches:
  - The conventional – taking off the old and familiar "design boards" directly to the real "production floor".
  - Computer Aided Design – CAD.
  - Computer Aided Manufacturing – CAM.
  - Robotics – applying artificial intelligence techniques in designing and manufacturing proceedings.
  - Combination of all or part of the above-depicted methods.
- Coordinating the production capacity within time constraints:
  - The immediate – as a reply to present requirements existing already at the lowest possible cost.
  - The medium – as a response during a period of up to three years with the same turnout capacity based on a "projected demand curve".
  - The long – as a reaction to possible changes in personnel and engineering resources, in order to realize the sales strategy of the company; taking into account technology, markets, competitors, products, scope of work and other alterations and developments.
- An educated sharing of labor tasks' load; a calculated dispersal of all extraction assignments, in accordance with the totality of the relevant resources required for the production processes, to ensure their optimal operation, namely:
  - The best exploitation of professional personnel, technical complexes, machines, designated equipment, etc.
  - A precise setting of output goals to be achieved on specific time tables.
  - Avoiding uneconomical over-manufacturing or stocking.
  - Follow-up, control and analysis of performance so as to prevent the creation of bottlenecks.

- Intelligent physical arrangement of the technical-operative resources array at the production areas, while still possible and worthwhile, of course, with increased efficiency in mind (such as minimizing time and cost of movement; best equipment, space and volume utilization; amplifying safety, accessibility and security procedures; insuring flexibility and easy material flow during the practical process, etc...) due to:
  - The process – when the said array is directed by a necessary proceeding order, pre-dictated in line to facilitate the ongoing operation of the same extraction scenario for a variety of articles.
  - The product – when the said array is organized according to the activity flow of a work line, used to produce a large volume of merchandise with little variety.
  - The technology – when the said array is located by the same scientific application's character, supplying a similar technical standard process.
  - A combination of all the above methods or part thereof, as a response to the type of the main manufacturing output.
- Selecting the character of the action chain necessary for an economically viable production:
  - Single – a unique job "till the end" of one product requiring a very large amount of work.
  - Batch – completing a certain act for a great number of items before moving to the next step.
  - Flow – a continuous, gradual and nearly automatic process of fabricating each article separately.
  - Combined – a sophisticated exploitation of the advantages in each of the above by utilizing a mixed operation.
- Effective timing of the leading performance assignments: accurate coordination of all doings required for the job vis-a-

vis the beginning and ending dates (a Gantt Chart); whether by looking "forward" (from beginning to end…) or by "walking backwards" (from future delivery date to present events…) in order to achieve a smooth and rolling production process:

- Direct interdependent tasks.
- Purchasing points of time.
- Supply dates.
- Inner conveyance to the site.
- Using dedicated resources.
- Indirect activities.
- Concentrating the products prior to distribution.

▸ **Deploying processes**: a domain designing the implementation of the best techniques and their respective channeling so as to extract the product in the most efficient and profitable way, in accordance with:

- A correctly calculated order of actions.
- A smart choice of personnel, facilities, machines, dedicated equipment, work tools and all the other means required.

▸ **Performance monitoring and control**: a field intended to assure a wise employment of technical methods at the right time, so that everything planned administratively and operationally will be correctly realized by:

- The most up-to-date techniques and means.
- The best relevant checkup junctures.
- Setting up a realistic timetable.
- An efficient and effective results-analysis array.
- Delineating truly pragmatic, achievable goals.

In addition to that, the company's operation management sphere deals as well with the following scientific-industrial subjects:

- **Methods engineering** – an accurate, systematic and logical analysis of all performance in the organization contributing to the production processes de-facto.
  - Work measurement – setting standards for actual execution; calculating the right period of time required to fulfill a certain activity in order to define a "work package" as a quantitative unit for any current job to be carried out.
  - Methods research – examining all existing techniques in order to find or develop better attitudes to the improvement of the cost / benefit ratio and extraction periods, presenting the optimal form of their implementation.
  - Productivity enhancement – dissecting the creativity and innovation measures of all the active partners, in all that concerns the utility ratio of the totality of management practices, operational skills and resource exploitation (from raw material purchasing to the final manufactured outcome…) so as to get a higher product value at a lower cost.
- **Supply** – ensuring purchase of materials, equipment, parts and all that is needed for production, thriftily and efficiently so that they are available whenever needed.
- **Adequate stock levels** – defining "optimum quotas", on the one hand and "minimum rations" on the other, according to historical data and standards accumulated in the organization's information mechanisms, combined with relevant parameters provided by updated forecasts already existing in the system in accordance with each product's demand and supply dates; characterizing these with a view towards keeping a sufficient inventory of raw materials, expandable equipment, spare parts and whatever is needed for a continuous extraction of the merchandise from one side, while accurately purchasing only that which is really necessary and cost-effective from the other. Stock levels should be planned so

that with the reduction in quantity due to consumption during the manufacturing phase, touching the above "red lines," it will still be possible to go on smoothly with what there is without harming the work flow – even slightly – until those allocations are refreshed (a supposedly automatic process at that stage...).

- **Maintenance** – scheduling a preventive treatment array for all of the organization's equipment and other technical resources, in order to avoid, as much as possible for a known period, any breakdown accident which may arrest the continuous flow of production.
- **Quality assurance (QA)** – setting the technical policy (norms, timing, junctures...) of conducting grade-level control of the raw materials, extracted products and customer service.
- **Quality control** – dictating the sampling techniques and analysis methods in order to assure that all along the process (viz. planning, purchase, storage, production, and service-rendering...) the materials and work are compatible with accepted reliability and high-class standards.

Production Proceedings – Business's Nature by Darwin

A good production process which generates new outputs, in a proper, well-managed organization, is one in which **"Darwinian Competition" exists**; meaning that there are different enterprises in a constant hard struggle over the inner resources of the company while this course is being followed. The more successful survives in the first place, developing later on to become the firm's crown jewels; the others, being unworthy, die out and totally disappear. This is a very healthy scenario, whose utility rests in the very fact that it directs the system to concentrate on the essential, while the superfluous shrivels and evaporates on its own. Therefore if such a phenomenon does not exist naturally it is necessary to acutely create it: only the choicest among the products, promising the good of the framework and its economic success, should be encouraged to continue "living" – and all those constituting a heavy financial burden, hurting the cumulative entity's prosperity and financial gains, must be stopped immediately.

On the contrary, **a bad extraction process** is evident by the fact that all activity stages around it or linked to it are taking **much more time than the real work done on the product itself.** For that reason, improving operational supervision and consistent optimization of the manufacturing steps reduce redundant and wasted expenditures, while ameliorating profitability and effectiveness.

Quality or Productivity – Which Comes First

Quality of the output and productivity are two sides of the same coin, for both are pushing for the same result: augmenting the yield. Apparently it does seem that improving productivity is the main and immediate engine amplifying the income due to increasing of the turnout, but quality is (and that is the way it should be…) the first and foremost priority. A high-level class of goods – and nowadays the speed of keeping up with customers' request for it, is important as well – is the initial and vital condition for survival and must never be compromised. An intensive advertising array, attractively-designed package and large quantities, opportunely supplied as agreed, normally provide the opening promotion and selling drive – while excellent commodity virtues, accompanied by a first rate technical-specific value, are the factors promising its long term demand. For **a fantastic product is self-marketing, obviously, much better than a thousand salesmen altogether.**

The key to excellent merchandise's value is the easiness of the extraction on the one hand, combined with the simplicity of its pleasing use on the other. To wit, the output of the work should naturally and straightforwardly integrate with the costumer's "comfort zone", rendering him the utmost expected benefit, which gives an immediate feeling that **human engineering** was considered foremost in its designing and production phases, a kind of an ideal compromise between purposefulness and sensitivity. Consequently, it is possible to deduce the desired qualities hereinafter making any commodity of whichever kind – even not being just a technical tool – in great demand:

- **Friendliness**: engaging the heart and eye with operational effortlessness, while promising instant and continuous ideal results.
- **Controllability:** having a minimum number of key data, evidencing regularity by a quick test.
- **Accessibility:** the ease of penetrating into parts or areas, which need repeated care and treatment by the user.
- **Maintainability:** creating a logical status of "if it ain't broke, don't fix it…" – bestowing an actual feeling that periodic maintenance intended to avoid failures (generally caused by neglect and lack of attention…) is a most uncomplicated matter.
- **Interchangeability:** assuring an almost continuous proper functioning by creating a cache of ready replacement parts (existing regularly in the market, easily and cheaply obtained as well as assembled…) in case of stoppage or breakdown.
- **Loyalty to Expectations:** answers to the full range of the purposes for which it was bought in the first place, waiving none of what was promised in the initial-value presentation.

In addition, the product should be accompanied by a **user's guide**, easily understood and straightforward. In short: amiable instruments, allowing for the **consummate integration of the article into the customer's life; a full linkage to the sentiments and hidden wishes of the client, and complete incorporation within his daily existence.**

On the other hand, it must be remembered that even maximizing quality has its limits, meaning it is forbidden to chance upon a situation where a miscalculated investment in an innovative and advanced technology (not yet proven to be economically beneficial...) would cause an increase in the cost for the average designated customer disproportionate with the rise in his income. Because this is a sure recipe for losing a large segment of the potential consumers, and therefore undoubtedly for a reduction in sales.

Managing Events in Projects – the Proven Guidelines

Normally project events are running – especially dealing with, but not exclusively, technical products – by two main planning charts created by their leading team:

A Gantt or Network Chart – thorough outline, spreading and minutely detailing the collection and length of all assignments until the completion of the entire job, each depending on the others and logically synchronized with a pre-arranged order as against the time axis.

PERT – Program Evaluation & Review Technique – the minimal chain of actions required to finish a project, delineating the shortest and sole critical path to its termination according to a schedule conditioned on tasks which are not prone to change because of technical or managerial constraints.

And all of this because apart from the convenience of running, afforded by the abovementioned measures, there is also an authentic need for certain means to execute a follow-up and control process for each and every step taken while progressing. In addition, it is required to analyze and dissect current events, compared to the original plan, for immediate corrections whenever necessary and for the prediction of future scenarios. The time span of each of these operations, included in the above-depicted charts, must be deduced from a well examined **batch of standards** brought together and created in accordance with courses of actions that were tried, thoroughly investigated and derived in the past after a full conclusion-drawing procedure. And those entirely are done in order to know how to organize the activities of the firm in the most correct, accurate and effective manner, thus being able to commit to clients for a timetable and truly be able to stand by it.

Performance Quantifying and Scientific Investigation – Essential Steps towards Proper Management

For the purpose of being able to properly plan, optimally pilot and accurately control the work, it is necessary to define each of its most elementary components in a quantifiable manner prone to measurement. In other words: it is compulsory to divide the general assignment into detailed "work packages", to group them by a common denominator bunching those under one "performance umbrella" and express their duration in terms of hours. These segments should not be excessively large, but capable of containing a sole specific task; and not too small either so as not to turn the matter of classification and separation into an unrepresentative and difficult-to-monitor issue. The outcome is the sum of weighing similar operations linked together, describing all types of occupations in the system relating to the project and all which accompanies them (such as: scheduled leaves, required rest periods, lunch breaks etc....) – while allowing a meticulous follow-up regarding their rates of progress by final and clear countable units. Such a dispersal is supposed to take into consideration the performance of an average but skilled employee, criteria reflecting a realistic status of individual abilities, not essentially a constant hundred-percent output. Rather, it must be authentic and reasonable, a result of continuous experience in the relevant domain. These standard benchmarks – which can be set for any job in any framework – allow the hierarchy's medium levels and the top management the usage of the following tools:

- ✓ Assistance in logically distributing time-dependent activities.
- ✓ Help in budget preparation.
- ✓ Setting the workforce's level necessary for each action.
- ✓ Personnel-requirement prognosis for future reinforcement.
- ✓ Bestowing bonuses according to very accurate achievement measurements and not just estimations.
- ✓ Accurate follow-up and control of the progress in comparison with pre-dictated milestones, in order to straightaway correct whatever needs improving along the way.

The following metrics for analysis and evaluation should be added too:

- ▶ **Working Methods Research**: a deep study of the different existing tasks' performance approaches and procedures in order to draw lessons, come out with conclusions and develop alternative processes and attitudes for their implementation, so as to improve efficiency.
- ▶ **Operations Study**: a scientific analysis of decisions, outcomes and the measures they operate, taken in association with the chosen technology, the kinds of business, systems management and the preference of their execution methods.

- **Model Construction**: a methodical semi-artificial experiment of describing real-world work situations as pragmatically as possible; displaying them in mathematical terms, thus simplifying their understanding and facilitating quantitative weighting of possible results that might come out due to the decision-making processes.
- **Simulation**: maneuvering the above-said models, while trying to imitate in the most matter-of-fact way the dynamics of the framework within which they function.
- **Sensitivity Analysis**: avoiding drastic fluctuations of predicted outcomes following a specific decision-making process by widening key assumption; introducing, if possible, unexpected situations; and testing probable consequential alternatives coming out of the above.

Applying these means turns the operative issue into a first-class scientific matter, neutralizing quite a great number of mistakes because of heuristic deflections, various fantasies and whims of the ego, thus minimizing all uncertainties and risks on the road to reach the desired finish line.

Knowledge Treasuring – What is Not Written Does Not Count

Every idea – even one seeming very simple to implement right from the beginning – **must be, first and foremost,l put on paper**. And if it is not amenable to a clear description and a straightforward illumination, then the thinking phase is not totally "squeezed", the notion is immature and its proper execution is still impossible; for the world is full of "great discoveries" bubbling within any active person, each morning anew. Putting the proposed issue in writing is the initial necessary step for its implementation. Translating the thousands of theories and assumptions squabbling in the inventor's mind into an explicit document, forces him to edit his thoughts logically and in details, while not allowing him to cut corners, deceiving himself and others.

However it is desirable that even the preliminary draft and sketch fully express the spirit of the whole concept down to the last component and detail, without bestowing on them the glory of a an accomplished feat with the standard of a final submittal. It is easy for the creator to fall in love with his own "stew" he himself "cooked" to be proud of, up to the stage of failing to objectively fill its "actual taste" later on; to continue investigating his invention for points requiring improvement or change; and what's more important – to listen to other people's remarks and clarifications concerning its content and execution.

Correspondingly and assisted by the data management array previously mentioned, it is obligatory to create a **solid database**, being also a "binder full of ideas" offering the best solutions to most of the technical problems in the current domain. This should be constructed leaning on past experience – especially previous mistakes – in addition to the science of operations research and other quantitative measurement techniques implemented in the final output itself. **There is no need to always reinvent the wheel.** This is the only way to shorten the trial-and-error scenarios and the production process length. To wit, minimizing the product's "time to market" duration and consequently cutting costs considerably, of course.

And in addition to the last it is required, and even worthwhile, to initiate and introduce the "double use" model – namely, an efficient exploitation of the same database and technological background for military needs on the one hand, and civilian applications on the other. For the systems designated to defend the country everywhere constantly call for the best; and concerning such an important issue, decision-makers tend frequently to disregard the costs, therefore succeeding in being the first to quickly obtain the choicest of the choice. And these advanced scientific developments are definitely prone to being utilized to cheaply build products (as there are no more research and experimentation expenses...) benefiting other fields of activity too, not necessarily classified due to their sensitive nature. Except this mutual "bank of information and parameters" depicted above, must be built and divided so as to allow for similar, maybe entirely, identical processes independent of each other **in every individual sector of the two fields,** separately and totally unattached to each other.

Research and Development – the Real Chance for a Breakthrough

Following the last paragraph's recommendations, this seems, perhaps, to be the most appropriate place to emphasize in bold letters the huge importance of the **Research and Development (R&D)** role for the entire organization. This entity is supposed to be independent and assertive – in what concerns ideas and directions of thought – for the purpose of digging deep and bestowing upon the company the scientific-industrial dimension so crucial for its continuous existence presently and in the future; and the amount invested in this domain is directly dependent on the character of its business. This is actually a unique and original "volcano," intended to bubble and simmer constantly – but it is also able, by one great eruption, to launch the firm in a quantum leap up to the sky. It is not solely by technology, as is commonly though erroneous believed, but in any one of its cardinal activity paths. For the lifespan of any communal creative group depends, among other things, on nonstop learning, tracing, observing – and especially on **advancing its main specialties** whatever they may be; and without any prearranged, structured and consistent development and perfection of its natural choice basics, any company would wither and disappear. Therefore it is imperative to keep striving, emphasizing time and again a strategic-scientific "over the horizon" perception, in order to nourish those things forming the backbone of the firm's main operational field suitable to the technological, economic and social variations occurring in its surroundings, so as to go on maintaining the authenticity of being a meaningful and competitive factor in the market.

This refers as well to organizations in their twilight periods, when everything looks blurred and the coffers are nearly empty (although it is very popular and worthwhile to invest in fronts where success might appear immediately, and maximum glory may be already credited to the one in charge during his present tenure…). Only the really brave individuals, those endowed with personal (and public…) integrity, having persistently and honestly the good of the system which they lead as their first priority, would be ready to be engaged with subjects that promote it – such as R&D, for example – while the chances are that the results would probably not be seen during their watch. And despite the fact that it is reasonable to assume that the reapers of their current toil would be their replacements, or maybe even the next generation, what is more important is that the company to which they are committed today, will be the great winner from those ongoing contemporaneous efforts.

And the main conclusion which must be adopted from the above clause is the following: it is possible and appropriate, actually, to implement the perception discussed here in any other plateau, even in personal life, in order to try continuously bettering oneself. To quote Socrates: "The unexamined life is not worth living…".

In Summation

Beyond what was already described up to now, it is extremely important to bear in mind one more significant issue: **all enterprises' successes are due to their being owned by rich people**. Therefore, even if the technological idea is "perfectly genius", its execution is impossible as long as its economic feasibility and the final cost of its implementation are not clear enough. Only after totally proving its business logic – and so as not to deal with it in a manner similar to Mother Nature's climate conditions (of which Mark Twain remarked ironically in 1892: "Everybody talks about the weather, but nobody does anything about it...") – it is possible, even imperative, to harness to it a sponsor from the business world, in order to fully realize it and harvest the fruits of its creation.

And all in all: even if technology is the primary and main support, apparently, of the construction, design and leadership of the entire organization, it should not be allowed to become a **machine rising against its maker**. On the contrary; it must be like clay in the hands of the potter...

March 2000

Human Resources Strategy

or **"Who"** Are the People to Work With

Preface

From an absolutely clear and pragmatic organizational point of view, human resources are the highest significant spiritual and physical reserve of any cooperative incorporated framework; meant to accompany it all through its existence, in its general daily conduct and its unique professional continuous activity. The march towards exceptional achievements and glorious pedestals, and the processes which one is required to pass from end to end on the way to their accomplishment, **begin and end with people**, whether senior managers or junior employees. Therefore the most important contribution of a leader to the system he is in charge of **is the choice of the right individuals for his team and their optimal absorption in it** (which ought to be planned with the utmost sensitivity and diligence…); and this is, in fact, his essential valued input to the present strategy. He ought to do virtually anything to attract the truly finest from those involved in the relevant métier and weave a net with sophistication and incentivization to watch over them constantly in order to retain them. This is because people are the first priority of any creative communal entity; the time devoted to them by their superior is his greatest remunerative investment. Without an excellent corps, success is simply impossible.

But this is not enough. A wise leader should be able to pinpoint and identify the special virtues and talents of each member of his crew in a special sphere of occupation. And beyond taking full advantage of these individual high-caliber aptitudes, he must also know how to connect them all as an integrated group for global yield and turn it into the super-synergetic genius of the organization as a whole; he ought to be keen on a concretion of greater value than the sum of its parts, due to an intelligent unification of all particular abilities of each and every employee, dedicated to a common product; because the supreme Eagles do not fly in a squadron, but on their own. And the way to do it is by giving free reign to the creativity of every brilliant brain in its unique direction, while focusing them all on the marked collective target. For in the really good managers' world the employees are the actors, players and stars, while they are only coaching the group, being the conductor of the orchestra and acting as the band's agent at the most. Or according to Theodore Roosevelt, the 26th president of the United States of America: "The best executive is the one who has sense enough to pick good men to do what he wants done, and self-restraint to keep from meddling with them while they do it...".

Additionally, he must be very sharp-sighted, able to immediately spot impersonators – all kinds of chimps in tuxedoes actually – as well as lazy and evasive persons, holders of a certified degree in idleness who present themselves in the guise of diligent ants. And then he should be honest enough to admit his own mistakes, committed to his great sorrow, while picking the wrong people, and draw as quickly as possible the rotten apples from the "box" before their putrefaction infects the choice ones at their side.

Hence, it is very crucial to internalize that leading a creative communal enterprise never was and cannot be a one-man show. Its success is a shared accomplishment effected by all those who toiled so hard for it and contributed endlessly towards its final goals with a deep and honest intention. One who desires to personally take for himself the entire glory of achievements must be prepared to get directly in his face all the heat of failure's disgrace.

For that very reason the lines spread ahead in this chapter emphasize the crux of the matters, a keynote in everything concerning the occupation with the general Human Resources (HR) strategy, in seemingly separate articles and paragraphs, but after a thorough and comprehensive assessment of them, the puzzle becomes entirely clear.

Creating a Winning Team – as an Appetizer

Choosing the right team is therefore **one of the critical management dexterities**. And the secret of establishing and integrating a qualitative and effective working corps lies, to begin with, in creating a compatible human mixture of the individuals comprising it. This should be a selective and very pragmatic bunch of people – each of whom an expert in his field – displaying complete loyalty one to another and to their superior. For he who strives to be a first-class coach must, before anything else, guide and train exceptional players…

In such "esotericism" nothing is wrong with "positions of trust." It is permissible to man key posts in the organization with familiar people, proven reliable and dedicated, with whose company one is comfortable due to having a common language, even if they are not one-hundred-percent distinguished, but not a hopeless failure either. As mentioned above, life isn't so sterile, but the old well-worn saying ("Better the devil you know than the devil you don't…") helps somehow to justify the option. However, preferring incompetent candidates just because they are relatives – nepotism in full – is totally forbidden. One must not choose at the expense of knowledgeability, expertise, proficiency, skill and appropriate character, all of which are necessary conditions for a very proper fulfillment of any job (those appreciated not for their wisdom but for their survival expedience…). In addition, it is very important to nominate to the afore-said posts those who have enough courage to express beliefs dissimilar to what others think and fight for them, but are also ready to accept diktats contrary to their personal perceptions and then carry them out in the best possible form, avoiding foot-dragging (understanding that there is only one senior executive who is responsible for making decisions – and absolutely accountable for their outcomes…). So there is nothing wrong in defining this sort of appointments, if the individuals designated for these offices enjoy the **optimal balance of the afore-detailed variety of traits.**

Still it must be remembered that on many occasions, loyalty alone may automatically create a system of yes-men, a framework of those toeing or identifying with the line, whose opinion mainly represent their desire to stick to their positions at all costs. They would shut mouths and prevent a liberal atmosphere where a true and honest exchange of ideas can take place in a straightforward and cultured manner – even if these subjective observations are not always pleasant; becoming individuals pushing to a situation that blocks beneficial processes of open brainstorming which contributes to mutual fertilization and enables a continuous feedback course, helpful in the immediate correction of defects and following that – supporting a constant willingness to improve and to upgrade.

And the smaller the body is – the more should the selection of employees be fastidious. For if two people are doing the same thing there, then for reasons of peace and efficiency, one of them is redundant. On the other hand, in order to create an effective system able to operate continuously and perfectly, there should always be someone that can perform, occasionally, part of the other persons' job, so that a temporary absence of a functionary would not halt, God forbid, the running train of the general operation. And just for this kind of emergency, when the unexpected is taking place, it is obligatory to teach and tutor in advance for each personal duty in the system – from the manager to the lowliest junior – a number two who will fill his shoes whenever necessary without any problem.

The Art of Interviewing Begins With the Ability to Listen

The lion's share of picking first-class teammates lies in the art of interviewing. However it must be kept in mind that it is merely a preliminary filter meant to walk the applicant through his entrance examination; so even if the conclusion is positive, it cannot be considered a hundred-percent guarantee that the chosen candidate will answer further expectations and join the special ones of the organization. In order not to err and cause an excessive fluctuation of personnel in the company, it is forbidden to hurry and judge the interviewee by his appearance, rhetoric skills and his presentation; rather, one must try delving much deeper. It is imperative to avoid the common habit by which the initial impression received at the first seconds of the meeting is the decisive one (and all the rest of the time left in the dialogue intends, actually, to justify only a primarily decision already taken...). Hence one should not rush in, wrapping up all about the suitability of a person for the offered post. And most important is to avoid predetermined perceptions.

To conduct an effective interview, it is vital to inspire a relaxed atmosphere all through the meeting, so as not to put the applicant through excessive pressure; for after all this conversation may be, quite often, very critical for his future. In addition, it is strongly recommended to allocate some extra time – besides becoming familiar with the interviewee and discussing the characteristics of the job – for an informal chat intended to get acquainted with the person's real nature; and throughout the process itself it is better to keep silent and let him pull in whatever direction he feels comfortable with, thus "surrendering" his true character and abilities. It is necessary to be very attentive to the minute details, while trying to elicit more signs of his behavior and preferences and especially to **know what to listen for**.

On the other hand, it is imperative to avoid being misled by a certain positive trait he prefers to emphasize again and again – such that might be later discovered as an artificial "halo" with which he crowns himself – and may impair the judgment about him, distort the perception regarding his personality and present him in an unrealistic light.

And one more small bit of advice: it is recommended to become aware of the family ties of the candidate, trying, in addition to conversing with him, to have a word with his children (if there are any…) but mostly with his wife; those who would have quite a substantial influence on his functioning within the organization over time. For taking a new employee into the framework is, actually in a way, starting a kind of relationship with his spouse (of whatever gender…) and offspring…

Optimal Absorption of the Chosen – an Uncompromising Second Phase

No effort – even the most enormous – invested in selecting employees is worth it, unless everything is being done to absorb them into the bosom of the system in the most proper manner, just like adopting a newborn. The merging of "fresh" workers in the framework should be sprinkled with human warmth, based on sympathetic and supportive attitudes enabling a soft landing. All this must not diminish the effectiveness of the impartation of the background and tools that will assist in further integrating them within the workplace in a successful and fertile way. In the process, it is imperative to dismiss tensions, confusion, doubts, apprehensions, grudges and pessimism which normally accompany new beginnings; alongside the professional incorporation, it is required to create within the newcomer as high an identification as possible with his fresh employment.

Such a move is supposed to take care of two fronts simultaneously: the one dealing with getting acquainted with the organization as a whole and with the specific unit which the "just arrived" employee joins; the other clarifying the nature of the profession in general and the essence of the task he is designated for in particular.

In getting to know the establishment the following subjects should be emphasized:

- ✓ The history of the firm.
- ✓ Essentials of the unit's occupation.
- ✓ The organization's organogram.
- ✓ The cooperation's philosophy: targets, assignments and the ways to achieve them.
- ✓ Reciprocity between the firm and the employee and vice versa; mutual responsibilities and obligations.
- ✓ Policy and procedures.
- ✓ Main sites.
- ✓ Key personnel.

Concerning the specific occupation and task, the subsequent issues should be especially noted:

- ✓ The objectives of the department derived from the entire company's goals.
- ✓ The hierarchic structure.
- ✓ Job description.
- ✓ Immediate means assisting in the completion of the job.

Correct absorption of new people in the organization is profitable at the end of the day, as it stabilizes the system immediately from the beginning of the process. An input like this minimizes the number of those wishing to quit after a short stay in their workplace because of dissatisfaction regarding their treatment since their arrival as they see it; this is a crucial step in the feeling of each "fresh" recruit to the framework to which he is totally unaccustomed, and in his psychological readiness to be immersed within it in view of the fact that it is completely strange to him actually. An accelerated effort in the admission route reins in the personnel instability resulting from a frequent moving of individuals in and out the institution; it lays the infrastructure of industrial peace, enabling, in fact, the corporation to concentrate on augmenting the productivity and achievements of the business even during personnel changes (sometimes necessary…). It creates a stratum of employees dedicated to the firm's goals and loyal to its values. Thus it is even worthwhile to attach to each beginner a tutor – a kind of "adopted friend" that would assist him in adapting, and whose help would be expressed:

- ✓ By presenting all small things – even those seemingly worthless.
- ✓ By directly responding to any problem – even these ones which people are ashamed to ask about.
- ✓ By bestowing on the new person a secure sentiment and making him feel at home.
- ✓ By spraying a taste of companionship and belonging.
- ✓ By giving him a sense of openness and freedom.
- ✓ By being hospitable and sociable while having small talk.
- ✓ By getting in order all real physical arrangements.

And most important is to select only these who are most fitting to serve as "absorbing guides"; those who are really willing to give of themselves and are ready to jump with the object of their guiding and educating into the cold water, helping him to swim while saving him from drowning.

In addition it is highly recommended – especially for the senior executives of the institution – to keep following constantly the absorption stages of the new recruit; to show interest and to ask them occasionally about their progress; to meet them personally with reasonable frequency, thus letting them feel definitely unforgotten.

A Correct Working Atmosphere Augments Loyalty and Productivity

In order to demonstrate that a relaxing ambiance during the admission interviews and the wish to moderate the "shock" of absorption are not a passing episode, serving as a performance intended to impress candidates and new staff members – it is suggested to further adopt a style of management and direction which inspires:

- ✓ A target-oriented working atmosphere – however in an efficient, considered and mostly pleasant flow.
- ✓ A meticulously regulated stay environment – whose rules and procedures are normally applied quietly and calmly.
- ✓ A strong feeling of the existence regarding **a healthy balance between work habits and private life**.

And all this is far – absolutely distant – from dangerous complacency. This kind of management achieves complete identification and full loyalty of all employees with the entity for which they are working; it bestows the power not only to prevent the best people from gazing outside, but moreover, to make them the most fanatical advocates of the company. There is no doubt that such a state of mind raises people's productivity tenfold, since it is definitely possible to achieve considerable results even when running everything smoothly without undue histrionics. For that there are four salient characteristics shown hereunder as to how to lead undauntedly and decisively – but very sanely – the daily routine within the organization:

- **Simplicity:** constructing an easy and comfortable format for evaluating and furnishing an opinion on employees, which enables concentrating on the essential: what to say, when and how.

- **Frequency:** maintaining regular contacts between executives and subordinates in order to ensure a trust-building, ongoing continuous link.

- **Focusing on the Future:** emphasizing tomorrow's aims, being well-defined and fully understood by all, after giving a short, very exhaustive, non-tedious or tiring review of the past.

- **Self-Control:** establishing a procedure by which each person in the system monitors himself and criticizes his own functioning and private behavior; a routine that even asks him to put on paper the characteristics of his specific activities as he sets them – as long as they are in perfect harmony with the organization's ways and needs he serves. Formulating such individual feedback requires deep and detailed thinking encompassing, inter alia, a kind of recorded commitment of the worker's general operation.

Such a chief measure is consistent with the policies of fine leaders, radiating a serene atmosphere of full openness and honesty which lays a solid basis for the core activities of the manager as a "catalyst".

Excellent Employees Need, Generally, Outstanding Managers

In most cases, talented workers need the very best managers. Even if the finest hireling in the world would join a company due to its exceptionally inspiring bosses' echelon, his efficiency, production and especially the tenure of his employment will depend unequivocally on his relationships with his direct superior; because people who are happy at their workplace contribute to a tranquil ambience, improve their effectiveness on their own and yield a better crop. To wit, this issue is not dealing only with recruiting intelligent and professional staff, but also the real way of how to grow and nourish them, so that they will never consider quitting for another job.

In addition, brilliant leadership is judged by the technique through which it succeeds in turning the blessed skills of its subordinates into daily, actual and continuously productive fact. Thus, the head of the company must penetrate into the minds and guts of his people, so as to set afloat the specific abilities of each one and bring him to his true personal summit – without their feeling, for a slightest moment even – that their private views and traits have been "raided," God forbid. Thus, it is totally prohibited to try changing or honing these beings; on the contrary, one must be assisted and reinforced by the uniqueness of every individual. This may guide then to an acceleration of the reciprocal activity between the virtues of each worker and the goals of the company. And consequently, of course, the needs of the customer as the end-user are better addressed: something like a chemical catalyst, expediting the association of two substances into a finished product. For as was already said: an outstanding manager is supposed to cause everyone working around him to be much better. Hence the core actions of the man in charge as a **human stimulus in the organization** are four:

- **Choosing the right person for the job, based on his personal virtues – not only the experience he presents or the decisiveness he emits.**

  The meaning of the above is identifying the special traits of the candidate; recognizing, in fact, thought and behavior patterns, applicable to his intended job, creatively and productively. In addition it is necessary to evaluate his ability to detach himself from his outer life when required and his potential to totally focus on the work he must accomplish.

  And here a manager must distinguish clearly between dexterity and knowledge, on the one hand, and real talent, on the other. Since skillfulness – how to do the job and knowledge – is what one is conscious of (and there is factual knowledge – things he knows, and experimental knowledge – understandings acquired with time and activity...) are virtues prone to acquiring and passing on. However, talent (being the sum of three main domains: effort, explaining why it is exciting; thought, describing the way it is expressed; and attitude, portraying who is endowed with it...) – is, from the other end, an innate phenomenon by which a person is simply blessed: it is either there or not. And this birth gift might be refined or even upgraded, but it is impossible to be learnt or taught.

  And the capability to differentiate among the above terms, so very fundamental, is a must for a manager in order to know to what extent the nominee is able to change and what cannot be altered. So he has to fit the aptitudes to a task and not vice versa, creating a suitable environment enabling them to be expressed and to fully bloom. Since a correct preparation by a great coach means "going" from the players to the game and not the other way. Not for nothing one of the unwritten confidential laws of a successful management is not to try "fixing" people, but placing them according to their gifts and skills and exploiting them to the end – definitely not due to the needs of the system.

- **Defining expectation from the candidate by setting clearly the required results – not the process and stages of their achievement.**
  The emphasis should be placed on the characterization and definition of the desired effect in a clearly understood and uniform manner – not on the performance style. Because uniting and simplifying targets absolve the executive from worrying about setting aside means and methods for attaining the outcomes (this is to say: prescribing communal goals frees the man at the head from minor occupations, plundering much of his time to specify resources to each sector, domain and phase on the road to the destination – mainly dictating how to do it...). This must be left to the care of the executers.

  Moreover it makes sense that the best path to reach from one point to another, in business especially and in nature generally (contrary to what is taught as the first axiom of the Euclidian Elements of Geometrics...) is only rarely a straight line. It is the trail which has the fewest obstacles. That is why the choicest way to turn an employee's talent into daily, continuously fertile work is by presenting him with the final purpose, and spreading out the various methods to help him find the correct path to it – not in directing him down its turns; but all this is only after ensuring that he has all the knowledge and tools to succeed in his assignment. A regular coach may become a genius, not just like that, but if mentally he is able to bestow on his players the most freedom to express their wondrous personal abilities on the pitch – without trying to teach them how actually to handle the ball – as long as his tactical orders are clearly given and correctly understood, and the conditions for their fulfillment are present. In exchange for this, they, in the utmost self-sacrifice, will serve him finally with the victory. (For this reason precisely, Johan Cruyff – Holland's most senior football player and one of its magnificent stars who shone in the 1970s, and as a great admirable coach too during the 1990s

– argued strongly how difficult it is for an excellent performer to become a superlative trainer; because he does not know when and where to draw the line between his will to demonstrate exactly to his boys what he has done so well in front of crowded stadiums – and the stage at which he is supposed to let them "fly" on their own, to blossom and excel in managing the ball – knowing on the other hand to select and position the ultimate team, to assimilate in it the playing tactics most suitable for its members, to create the finest chemistry within the squad and in his professional advisers' group, to prepare them psychologically and physically in an extraordinary convincing manner to face collective goals in the best, most successful way – and to win the jackpot…)

And when the purpose is the essence, exceptions are expected, welcome and sometimes even preferred, in a search for the optimal channel of accomplishment. For it is necessary to frequently encourage creativity, innovation and originality and never to accept duplicates…

▸ **Motivating the person by focusing on his strengths – not by constantly criticizing his weaknesses.**

Employees must be given the feeling they are more than what they are in reality, by stressing their positive traits. In a way, a manager must resemble a novelist: each character he builds must be livelier and different from his fellows in strong individuality (without disregarding weaknesses, of course…) and is intended to play its unique role in the story; so in life. But in actuality, one should augment subordinates' merits by skirting their weak spots and making those vulnerabilities irrelevant regarding a specific job which the workers are supposed to complete; and this – as long as there is a conviction that their virtues may truly contribute, at the end of the day, to the success of the organization. The solution lies with an educated creation of supportive mechanisms, for example: preparing a backup system for a person who has difficulties; searching for and picking up a partner complementing his technical qualities and compensating for his missing temperamental components; transferring the staff member to a different task more suitable than the one bringing him to the firm in the first place; and so on. In other words, this means using any available means to "squeeze" the good from the man while neutralizing his shortcomings as much as possible.

- **According the employees paths for advancement – promotion in the hierarchy**

    It is imperative that every personnel associate feel he has a "promotion horizon", but sometimes it is impossible due to the needs and constrains of the system and its structure. Moreover, not always he who excels in his current occupation is suited for the next step in the hierarchical ladder. It is enough to remember the "Peter Principle", defined in 1969 by the American sociologist Laurence Peter, "In an organizational hierarchy, every employee will rise or get promoted to his or her level of incompetence..." to understand this perception. It means a person should be advanced up to a tenure exactly fitting his level and own qualifications to carry the job honorably – for not all were born to manage and lead. However, they can be of tremendous value to the corporate due to their "specific professional gravity" and the activities within their domain of expertise, in and for the firm. Therefore, it is obligatory to find the right way to compensate those individuals and guard them most seriously – especially, since it is well known that not every talented violinist can develop and become an excellent conductor, in the same manner that not any exceptional football or basketball player grows up to be an elite coach (just as it is obvious that not every trainer who is head and shoulders above the competition has a background of being a star on the pitch...). One is bound to juggle, and the other's job is to unite the troops and lead them as a group in the best format towards a common goal.

However, everyone aspires usually to ameliorate his position in all aspects. That is why it is unfair to leave a person at his place just because he does extremely well in his existing post. Since this is a frustrating contradiction in terms, as if an employee is punished for his excellence. And exactly here is the spot where the management's wisdom should be expressed, convincing with high sophistication and first-rate tact that staying at the same level in the "pyramid" is preferable in some cases as against climbing up to apparent new summits of status. And the questions are: how does one make the worker feel that he is growing anyway? And in what way are his superiors to be really good to him, "rewarding" the man for not being actually promoted?

The following are a few ideas:

First: inculcating in all people below that one step higher on the "hierarchy ladder" does not necessarily lead to the next rung; sometimes a move forward may bring more harm than good when the next status is, in fact, kind of a "individual regression" – a "too small and inappropriate" post for the one to be advanced – by not taking advantage of his full, real, extraordinary potential.

Second: creating "heroes" in each position. Making sure that every job excellently done receives its due recognition, considerable prestige – not below those accorded to the direct seniors above. One of the efficient ways to do it is by publicizing the facts concerning the specific activity to all around, in addition to materialistic stimuli.

Third: generating promotion channels within the unique profession's domain itself by honorable titles (accompanied, every now and then, by definite training...) and ad-hoc ameliorations. Thus a secretary becomes 'an assistant director-general for administration' and a star engineer is from now on 'a head of a development division' – all without any immediate and real addition of people underneath them or any grant. Furthermore, and as a sign of esteem, they are invited to the senior management's health club, or to dine at the table with the president and his deputies. Very rarely, this may be done by even offering them some kind of partnership in the office that involves augmenting their post, additional content and the liberty to express themselves in a more meaningful manner.

Fourth: establishing a proper reward array for workers in whose continued present activity the organization is interested. Such a mechanism widens the "compensation band", and thus the upper echelon of lower management would be remunerated a bit more than – or at least similar to – the lower stratum of job-holders just above them. In this kind of approach, when the star local salesman aspires to run a larger expanse as the regional manager, he knows that the new position would entail waiving a certain amount of his wages at the end of each month, until proving himself in the new upgraded function.

Fifth: using the "musical chair principle". This is a rotation of jobs in the system: appointing an employee to another "tempting" assignment, or transferring him to a different "intriguing" department – without a degree change. This serves in order to alternate his routine and renew his challenges, thus maintaining his motivation and interest.

And finally: appealing to the employee's common sense and heart. Hinting that the direct and close manager's influence over his career is not a guarantee for a continued livelihood – something that no one in the world can ever vouch for – but the best way to spread a "security net" underneath his feet. Such a shield is expressed by presenting pragmatic opportunities to acquire a profession and build status, enabling and ensuring him a lifelong occupation by proper guidance, via putting a mirror in front of his face, revealing to him honestly from top to bottom the whole truth concerning his dexterities and abilities, as the old Indian maxim goes: "Instead of promising a man a steady supply of fish to eat, it is actually better to teach him fishing...". For a varied experience, though important and not to be scoffed at, is not the sole factor of personal development; this is not the motivating force. A person's self-revelation – arrived at by himself or with the help of his superior – of his strong and suitable traits, is the asset pushing him to succeed and flourish. But in this very unique, sensitive and exciting scene – while one is about to hear all the naked, and at times unpleasant, truth about himself – it must be internalized (as ironic and painful as it may sound...) that in some cases common sense is the least common of all senses to be used...

In addition to all the above, the art of "tough love" bestows on the superior the mental energies required to face his subordinate and point out his defects – while still letting the poor guy feel that all is being done for his own good – that's what turns senior clerks into exceptional and outstanding managers and leaders: the ability to give advice openheartedly and in the most penetrating manner – even sacking when necessary – and still retain a great friendship.

Organizational Excellence – the General Good is Much More Important than Personal Gain

Back in 1776, the Scottish philosopher and political economist, Adam Smith, wrote in his book *The Wealth of Nations* that each individual in the organization strives only for his self-interest; his own benefit and security. Thereby he is led by a "hidden hand" to promote, actually, a goal which he never meant to. By chasing after his private welfare he, nearly always, acts for the good of the company in which he functions, in a much better and more efficient manner than what he would have intended truly to do in the first place. For the moral attributes guiding Man's free actions give birth necessarily to the most proficient means to advance humanity as a whole. In other words: egoism gives birth to altruism. And perhaps one may share the view argued by John Hubble, father of the titanic astronomer Edwin Hubble, in 1900: "The best definition we have found for civilization is that a civilized man does what is best for all, while the savage does what is best for himself. Civilization is but a huge mutual insurance company against human selfishness…".

This should be the leading motto of a manager preaching to his subordinates about the need for "organizational excellence". He may as well express it differently, even if not uttering explicitly the motives described in the clause above; however, there is no doubt that such a presentation is far superior to the popular, hollow, worn clichés and empty echoing slogans normally fed to employees when discussing this sort of subject, squeezing out of them a grimace of contempt. And when they finally inculcate that the framework's success betters their own situation, it becomes much easier to explain why all should stand as a unified body attacking the common targets of the system and strive constantly and indefatigably to a permanent improvement of its output; thus it is simple to infuse them with the notion that excellence is not only a matter of hard training, but actually a way of life which must become a habit. It makes a lot of sense to educate that uniting the fronts does not mean the creation of two separate "companies" within the same establishment, a management group and a labor squad; for if one of these flourishes and the other does not, reality shall be cruel: the entire business would explode and collapse into pieces and everybody would lose.

And in certain cases – in corporate entities with a very special nature – it is necessary to plant within the workers a culture which supports the notion that **the "individual" takes part in a general and**

encompassing operation of the "togetherness" – thus the "us" is usually more important than the "I"; the success of the "collective" overcomes the ambition of the "private"; everybody here is as one on this "ride" and should take the same sharp and dangerous turns together, noting all traffic signs and limitations, in order to make it jointly to the common purpose; and he who misses the bus may eventually be run over by it. And if this sound a little bit extremist, reminding one perhaps of the slogans of dark regimes from the past, suffice it to paraphrase the famous saying of the 35th American president John F. Kennedy: *My fellow employees, ask not what your company can do for you, ask what you can do for your company...*

And borrowing out of the enlightened world and from the strength of progressive humane government systems, it must be understood that democracy has not only a right but an obligation to take all measures in order to protect itself against those using it for its destruction. It should not commit suicide by protecting people exploiting its spirit to devastate it. This is a kind of a natural, correct, clear and legitimate self-defense action; hence no special legislation is needed for it...

Consequently, it is important to invest everyone in the firm with the feeling that he is inseparable from it, having the required capacity to contribute to its success and flourishing; otherwise he'd better not be in it. As John C. Maxwell says: "You should never hire a person who has no potential to become a partner in the organization...". And when individuals in the firm become a group, understanding that the ambitions of the whole pay, ultimately, much more than the successes of one person here or there – then as a team they become the most effective executive arm of the system, instead of each man on his own. That is to say that the level of interpersonal communication and the ability to operate in harmony should be among the central criteria of being recruited to the post and turning into an integral part of the framework. And these traits are supposed to give every worker separately and all of them together an ever-growing segment of the general esteem and praise given by the employers, while following that – monetary compensation, of course. And in all this business of uniting the people and inserting the organizational excellence as a motto, **the tempo of the manager is that which dictates the manner and rhythm of his subordinates' performance.**

However, concerning personal distinction, one thing is very important to remember: in a culture mostly dominated by "mediocre", where the "average" is nearly the majority, it is totally forbidden to use plain numerical standards as the only benchmark to measure the real champions. Such a test wrongs the choicest in the bunch and is an explicit transgression of reality. In spite of what is expected from the prima, that their yield and its quality would constantly remain on the right-hand side of the "Gauss Curve", it is unfair, even impossible to quantify their product against their past results only, instead of weighting their contribution – as against all the others busy at present within the same domain in the organization; and when occasionally the superlative are doing less than what the system is used to receiving from them, the unit superiors find it difficult to accept and accusingly look at these individuals. And those who normally put in, through their activities, more than the rest in the company are suddenly seen as failures simply due to the fact that they abruptly and uniquely pale in their performance when related to their former outcomes; but this can actually be as a result of factors out of their control. It is required, for this reason, to find a way to continue assessing their achievements by a long-term analogous averaging, compared to their competitors and according to the general relevant conditions during the current time of the examination. Sometimes it must be understood that the mere keeping of yesterday's results is a considerable attainment in itself. For it is famously said that **however difficult it is to become first in the league, it is sevenfold harder to stay there.**

One Must Always Invest in Good People

Talented people all around a cumulative creative entity must have the power to initiate. Responsibility must be given to those influenced by it. Pushing job-holders to extend their commitment does not result from hierarchic structure, but mainly from **organizational wisdom**. Brilliant and ambitious employees are in fact the fuel of the future, which set the entire factory in motion; for they always try to do more than anticipated from them – just like the industrious bees, addicted to their toil in such a manner as to derive from it now and then "sickly pleasure". As Moshe Dayan – the (fourth) Israeli Chief of Staff during the Suez War in 1956 and the Defense Minister during the Six-Day War in 1967 – used to state: "It's better to slow down galloping horses than to spur lazy mules...".

Hence, most of the time must be dedicated to this sector in the company, for talent is a multiplier of output; the more one invests in these people, the higher the yield. When such employees improve, and their creativity develops, they must have a free hand in running their own affairs. In the firm and in reality, there is a tendency to turn extra attention upon the losers, out of an intuitive assumption that they are in a need of additional help. This is a grave mistake! It is the "stars" in the organization who may change their behavior patterns due to their disappointment and despair at the small amount of personal notice which they get from the boss, in relation to their high value and contribution to the system, compared to the other mediocre workers existing within it. Investing in the good is the most lucrative use of time by the manager and the system he heads: firstly, because this is the right and decent thing to do; secondly, it is the most effective way for him to study; and thirdly, because this is the only path to **continue fostering organizational excellence.**

A Manager Who Does Everything on His Own Defies the Mission

One cannot do everything by himself; thus **it is imperative to delegate**. Even if the manager – by his huge talents – can perform as well as a couple of workers, he still is unable to be "two people" at the same time. And though his actions and efficiency might be totally identical to the produce of the above-said pair, if he does their job it will certainly influence and reduce his dedication to the leadership of the factory or the unit he runs as a whole. And a system leaning on one person only is analogous to a machine lacking spare parts, a basically defective mechanism. As long as it functions properly everybody will be satisfied; but the very moment a small problem emerges, it is completely disturbed and stopped. For that reason it is so important to bestow autonomy – in a proper manner, of course – to assistants and people beneath; so that the entire thing is not dependent on the head personality, whose absence absolutely halts the entity utterly. The following dictums may best express the limits of Man's ability to absorb knowledge, digest and internalize – while striving to do all on his own: "One studies all his life – to finally die stupid..." Or as most humbly claimed once by an old Romanian Sage: "I can surely write a book with what I know – but certainly support a library with what I don't...".

Furthermore, in order to broaden and upgrade his span of control, the supervisor must enlarge and ameliorate the **"managerial capacity"** of the organization he is in charge of. To wit, he has to inspire his aids and subordinates to act independently – however, in total accordance with the spirits of his intentions – and educate them to do the same with the teams below their command. Such an attitude is very efficient and pragmatic – all the more so in the contemporary age of globalization, because with a worldwide running of companies the man at the top has no time to deal with any small detail in each and every framework he guides and oversees. And as the organization grows bigger, dominating many people, processes and sub-units, there is a urgent need to develop a wider and more sophisticated delegation mechanism (and on the other hand, of course – a tracking and monitoring array over the operational domain as a whole to ensure its effectiveness and proficiency…).

Nevertheless, such a decentralized management system requires a very specific fabric of relationships, leading to an outstanding synthesis between the senior and his juniors in the hierarchy; a web in which authority distribution to middle-rank directors and administrators flows from a total confidence in them and a sense of security that the company's policy in all its domains and levels will be executed and sustained as written. And when the business functions in such an atmosphere it keeps on getting better and progressing all the time. Moreover; **initiative and self-commitment "flourish" in an openly encouraging environment** to such a degree, that now and then it is recommended to let the subordinates struggle with any problems (even those concerning them directly…) lying at the superiors' doors; and they would, definitely, reach the best solutions on their own, putting them on the bosses' table "half-digested and ready almost to swallow" – and by so doing would make it much easier for the organization causing the work to continue moving fluently without breaks.

And when adopting the leadership style described above, four important principles must be internalized:

The first: such an approach has its own price tag, of course; one cannot make an omelet without breaking a few eggs. But a smart managing and guiding routine means taking into account such costs and be ready to pay some learning penalties while doing the utmost to continuously minimize them.

The second: delegating authority should be a very meticulous and careful process. Under no conditions should power be given to a single employee, making him the supreme "dominator" regardless of his status, job, talents, intelligence or loyalty. Such supremacy is a corrupting factor of the first degree, which may result in haughtiness and aggressiveness; this is a fundamentally unfit work style, according to which everything depends on one person's will. In principle, accepting rights and sanctions is a very positive process as well as inevitable in the global business world, but when out of control it may demolish the whole organization.

The third: it is always forbidden to trust he who tends to rely on and hand over responsibility to any everybody (without even checking each one's merits...).

The fourth: not everything is delegable, since in addition to leading squads operating under their jurisdiction, managers must guide and conduct themselves as well; sometimes they simply ought to be personally involved and trust their own skills and abilities to run things as they truly intend to.

And one last word in favor of the above commended way of handling things.

The man at the top of the pyramid has to understand deeply and internalize what delegating actually means to those who are actually getting the authority; how much it contributes to the strengthening of their professional confidence and the growing of their satisfaction from the job they are fulfilling. And the main issue – what great rewards and advantages the corporation eventually gains from this kind of firm running and supervision approach...

Behind Every Employee Lurks the Person in Him

The employee must be respected. This is one of the manager's most important imperatives, for behaving tactfully is one of the less common habits in the modern business universe.

Firstly, the superior should emphasize gestures of magnanimity towards his juniors for good work and successful operations – that is to say: simply to show true happiness and authentic enthusiasm in their personal achievements, be generous in congratulating them, adding explicit compliments for every attainment.

Secondly, the man in charge must lay down the proper communication means with his subordinates. Every contact with them – even while remarking or admonishing – should be conducted in the most polite manner; for it is forbidden to forget, even for a second, that these are human beings standing there. And when worse comes to worst he has to behave, at least, in a politically correct style. For example: to "hit" an employee when he is in a good mood, but never aggravate his condition too much when he is in a bad one. Praise should be public – even in writing and wide circulation – but rebuke, on the other hand, ought to be conducted in private. And in this matter the following practical-humane rules are strongly suggested:

✓ One should never "roar" if he cannot be afterwards a "lion"…

✓ There is no need to rush and pull out a "red card" in the heat of the moment. It's better to use clarifying logic – commenting in good taste, but determinedly. One may even be a bit stricter, pulling a "yellow card"; but never doom anybody impulsively – taking tough decisions that are difficult to reverse later…

✓ It is forbidden to ignore people and step on their heads while walking the way up to the top, because one might meet the same individuals on the road down…

Thirdly, the person in control has to create for his subordinates a human work environment, top to bottom; something fitting mankind, proving that the organization respects its employees regarding their physical conditions. All of this is in order to form a place, to which they would be glad to arrive every day anew, contributing to the best of their abilities.

Dignifying any member of staff means respecting him in monetary terms as well. His salary should always be paid on time and as agreed (in order to enable him, first of all, to maintain his life's routine without being humiliated...). In addition, as a sign of esteem to his contribution and work, an appropriate bonus would do no harm only if the company is profitable, of course. Because, if he is expected to invest his body and soul in the firm, he should be also a partner to its success. Otherwise, as the American street saying goes: "If you pay peanuts, you get monkeys...". And the very moment any betterment is bestowed on an employee, especially a financial one, this is the right time to broaden his responsibilities.

And in general, the management should generate a compensation mechanism for the worker that seems worthwhile, is directly connected to his performance, having objective, clear and above-the-board criteria for their estimation. There is no doubt that money is the best motivator for increasing productivity; however, it should be remembered that there are some other energizers – for a short while after a payment raise, the exaltation evaporates and the grayness of routine takes over again. There are different ways to push the people beneath to be more effective, including: ambitiousness, a public recognition of their activities to the unit, the joy of doing and the interest in it, getting further responsibility, promotion within the hierarchy etc. These prodding factors are not easily forgotten, having, mostly, a mental value much higher than mere financial benefits.

And to sum up all that was said in the above paragraphs of the present article, one thing should be remembered: essentially, there are no bad employees, there are only workers who feel bad...

Common sense dictates **also listening to everything the subordinates wish to say, concerning them directly or otherwise** – including things not pleasing to the ear – even just for the sake of maintaining the fertilizing dialogue among all partners to the activities of the organization: tolerance – recognizing the existence of different opinions and the unlimited right to express them – is the name of the game. As was said by somebody: "An institute should be founded where folks are taught to listen – such as schools for oratory…". Most people are not aware of the fact that real communication is two-way.

Unfortunately, the habitual talking culture nowadays is of the kind in which each person has three opinions on any subject – and nobody knows how to pay attention or receive feedback. The strongest norm that man usually has is to teach the others especially what he should learn himself. Even the Greek philosopher Zeno of Citium postulated, as early as approximately 300 BC, that God created human beings with a pair of ears and one mouth so that they would listen twice as much as talk. So, after all a good boss really needs to attend to his people – at least as much as he demands to be heard.

On the other hand, it is forbidden to forget that eventually the system is hierarchical: just one is supposed (and has the right…) to make the decisions since he is the sole person to take all responsibility. Consequently it is recommended that the manager should thusly heed his subordinates: hear all of them while adding his own opinion, all the arguments that the others are not always exposed to, the influence of his interfaces with the higher echelon and the owners (frictions having, by the way, so many colors, states, formal and informal contacts et cetera…) and only then conclude. But in any case, letting the present attendees feel that their points of view are important and that the organization's conduct is being outlined and carried out only after taking into account all the relevant factors.

One of the most "delicate" stages in an organization's life, during which it is compulsory to attend very carefully to the entire workforce and be acutely aware of the feeling of all partners in the activity while being all (extremely sharp...) ears (until being able to even hear the rustle of the morning star Venus crawling slowly and silently up to the sky at dawn...) – is when deciding on **structural changes**; such as are typically meant to improve everything for the qualitative workers (one of the first and most common examples for this is the shortening of bureaucratic processes...). But due to the sensitivity of the subject, directly influencing employees' lives, they must be considered too in the decision-making procedure, so to understand that they are an inseparable part of the system that determines their faith (even though, frequently, it is a pressed, inconvenient meeting between the "burdened" side and the "compelled" one...).

Regularly, changes that are executed in the administrative structure deal with reducing manpower or focusing on the essential competencies of the communal creative entity, which fit its unique nature. And there is a considerable difference between those two types of variations: when a company lays off workers, jobs are disappearing; but when it outsources tasks in order to save money, functions are only shifting in its organogram and are changing for the better. Then again, it is prohibited to forget that these movements also allow for a flexible reassignment of manpower. This process prepares the leadership for the difficult challenges at peak and low periods of business life.

Moreover, a "conflict-resolution body" should be established. Processes within the corporation giving rise to arguments and disagreements between the management and workers are very legitimate, as long as no side deviates in its reactions from the normal proportions, procedurally and physically. However, in order to gain the confidence of the inferior side it is obligatory to stretch out a clear and transparent agenda, guaranteeing everybody that each divergence is taken care of in the utmost fairness. It has to start with an immediate and suitable treatment of any complaint – official or otherwise – continue by mediation and arbitration issues and guidelines as set by the law, and end with the fulfillment of all orders given by any legal authority.

From an Ordinary Laborer – to an Enlightened Worker

One of the cardinal drastic turnovers occurring nowadays in the piloting and controlling character of nearly all neo-classical companies in the world is the institution of effective and well-oiled information mechanisms for their operational systems. But it should be obvious to all that such instruments are not intended solely to reduce manpower but to integrate a wiser team of knowledgeable professionals running whole processes in deep thought, not just as simple task-performers. This is definitely a tool turning a regular laborer into an enlightened employee; and the more people within the factory – juniors as well as seniors – thoroughly learn its administrative, research, development, production, marketing and sales networks – them more wisely and relatively easily can they lead it to success and prosperity. This is to say: the data running and supervision array – including its instruction and distribution – is not meant to replace the human being but to make him more efficient. Therefore, it should be treated as an investment in the "intellectual property" of the company; something like **boosting the total IQ** of the organization as a whole, leading to an upgrading of its collective thinking. And in certain firms, the above-said "communal intelligence assets" is all the harvest they have to sell, and by this alone is it possible to appraise their value and reap their yields.

Nevertheless, it becomes apparent that there is a component not less important that the total degree of communal intellect of a productive establishment, and that is the amount of global collective **emotional intelligence** within it. This is the key to **a foremost talent of group thinking and judgment, born out of the social harmony of its teams**. Improving that mode by which people work together is the best tool to give a lift to the mental capital of the company. Corporations wishing to prosper and even to survive must better nurture and promote their systematic emotional intelligence in addition and far beyond their scientific superiority.

The difference between the mediocrity of a firm and its world greatness lies in its **team spirit** alone. In most cases the total of the technological wisdom of the framework equals exactly the sum of all separate specific capabilities of all individuals within it. It may be that a partnership such as this is much "stupider" than true potential concealed in it, if these people do not share one with the others on a regular basis their professional expertise. Moreover, usually the main reason preventing talented workers from advancing in the system is their inability to work with their colleagues. Thus it is possible that **a dose of common suffering is necessary from time to time to motivate lone human beings to cooperate**, because dark skies turn very bright after a storm...

For that explicit reason, **the general intellectual property, the combining emotional intelligence and the uniting inter-personal fabric of an organization add up to its human assets (or capital...) – its I^3**, depending which side of the "spiritual balance sheet" is examined. Because it has been known for long that human resources are part of the company's assets, and do not appear anymore just under the expenses rubric.

So it involves, therefore, the three major **I's,** set in an easy-to-remember formula:

The Human Asset = I³ = Intellectual (Property) x **Intelligence** (Rational & Emotional) x **Interpersonal** (Structure)

This subject should be studied very painstakingly day and night, since neither it nor any of its elements are born out of thin air.

And the current attitude these days is that material assets and liabilities, having a real financial worth within the company's financial reports, relate to about sixty (60!) percent alone of its total market value – a fiscal component that keeps on shrinking. In fact, the abstract contributors emphasized above – the spiritual – are not quantitatively measurable in a scientific acceptable way and not designated by an accurate numerical assessment in the appropriate economic-monetary presentations; those ones which are growing in their importance to the appraisal of the organization's firmness, especially that of their robustness to exist and survive for a long period of time.

The Hierarchy's Pyramid – the Proper Steepness

The hierarchical structure of any organization should be "flat" enough to allow for a flow of information and straight-nonstop connection between the directing echelon and the workforce layer, and vice-versa. From the other side, it must resemble a pyramid, high enough and owning a bright and unambiguous ladder of differentiation – so that the seniors will oversee and administer and the juniors will execute that which is ordered by their superiors. For leaders should outline strategy and courses of action. And as was earlier said, a single person or even a group cannot specialize, by hook or by crook, in all matters and fine points of the company – definitely not to deal with each and every one of them. Moreover, in order to obtain quality general managers, they are forbidden in principle to exaggerate their concentration in a sole subject to an extreme.

Yet, the measure of the "organizational steepness" is influenced by the size of the cumulative body, the technology it is involved with, the mass of information it is required to process, the products or services it manufactures or renders, the objective conditions under which it functions and most importantly – by the owners' nature, ambitions and explicit as well as hidden wishes and whims. Because these characteristics setting the breadth of authority delegated by the executives to their subordinates – and especially the width of the monitoring over what is happening – are in direct relation to the degree of mastery forced upon these men in charge by their immediate supervisors, the frequency of the reports they are asked to pass up, the number of details associated with this afore-said data sheets and meetings and the urgency with which they are expected to present actual results to the big boss. And those factors are subjective, of course, to the common conduct culture of the company, the managing-administrative tradition evolving with it over time, the personnel and professional mixture of its participants and by the climate of the relevant business domain it occupies and its surroundings.

In summation: the scale of seniority outlined in the corporate's organogram constitutes the skeleton by which it designates the hierarchy and all of its functional fineness; and it should be flexible enough to fit any controlling option possible which may develop over time while stepping ahead.

The Opening Speech – Love (or Hate...) at First Sight

The first meeting between the manager and his upcoming underling staff is of crucial importance. In most cases when people meet, the primary impression each has immediately at the introductory creates usually the basic "mutual typical signature" betwixt them. Even if sometimes there is no connection whatsoever associated with this initial feeling and the real characters of those participating in the gathering, it may yet decide in its wake the color of the elementary relationships amongst them. Hence, there is an extreme significance in the opening speech at the initial encounter of management and the crews supposed to work under his authority.

Such a meeting is a necessity and unavoidable, as the employees wish to know the new boss firsthand – and he, on the other end, wants to declare his positon openly and in front of all; thus there is no use in delaying that event. The right timing for this happening is the minute the appointment is actuated, since from that moment onward he is formally responsible for the running of the organization. And because someone had already said with irony mixed with truth that "the fear of an audience is one less degree than the fear of death…", this conversation should be navigated with an utmost wisdom, caution and sensitivity, as it is tense anyway and very influential for the future.

There are two rules, nearly axioms, to leading such an "opening speech":

The one: it's better to carry it out after having been somewhat acquainted with the place and spending an overlapping period for handing over the job with the previous holder of the post (if possible before receiving the formal mandate to start steering the business…).

The other: it is desirable to say the minimum of what is necessary in that setting, since an over-spouting whale may be eventually harpooned…

The following are some additional bits of advice on the conduct of such a gathering and what should be voiced in it:

- **It is desirable to start with a short professional personal background presentation.**

    In most cases this kind of information is already known to everybody, for there will always be some "generous souls" who investigated the new boss's past in detail and spread the findings even if not wholly accurate. Therefore it is appropriate to emphasize, shortly, just the experience and qualities relevant for the assignment while avoiding bragging about a surplus of other skills. Accuracy and some particular points are very important, so as not to create an impression of hiding something or dissembling.

- **It is appropriate to voice a kind of a general "creed".**

    Everybody awaits the message; hence it must be transmitted anyway very carefully. It should be on a level of generalities, setting global targets only, not getting too much into details, in order not stumble into nonsense due to insufficient knowledge of the organization. In any case one ought to keep away from being interpreted as over-determinist in the show while committing to things "engraved in stone," so to say. The last thing needed for the staff is a "prophet" promising the impossible, as well as hinting at a managerial impotence prior to his arrival.

- **It is a must to avoid slandering the predecessors.**

    Defaming antecedents and stressing their activities as substandard and unsatisfactory may hurt also the actual partners to the current communal path (it is as if one indirectly blames the people sitting opposite him, those with whom he is supposed to start working, telling them to their faces that they too share in the responsibility for the present horrible situation...). It is strongly recommended not to show contempt for what has been done (even if things look really bad...) and it is much better to exhibit restraint and not to express things arrogantly concerning the future. This is condescension, crying out loud: "My predecessor is an idiot and whoever is going to be my successor must be a moron..."; or in a more theatrical-political manner: "People of the former generation were born old and decrepit, and those of the next generation shall die young and inexperienced..." – a useless statement, arousing on the contrary not a small amount of antagonism, which may turn this assembly already into a sort of minor confrontation right from its commencement.

The favored tactic in this case is totally different: it is even advantageous to find the proper words in order to praise the "handing over of the post" period, and the organization's status as found in general; and if this is truly so difficult, then it is appropriate to really try this approach without specifying too much, using words to honor the event and the speaker.

- **It is preferable to shun immediate changes.**

On the contrary, it is actually best to declare at the very beginning that whatever was is still valid, until explicitly reformed, only if truly necessary. Even if it seems that revolutions should be instituted right at the start, it is possible to move cautiously, without extravagant declarations, unless the organization's existence or the employees' lives are in real danger!

Since nobody likes changes – especially the kind lacking a solid base – such a message will be welcomed because it allows people to continue their daily routines, not fearing mistakes and saves questions regarding the preferences of the new manager. Moreover, immediate variations are perceived as lack of appreciation (to say the least...) of what was so far done within the company. There is and will be enough time to generate serious modifications and adjustments after a thorough and deep study of the place. However, there will always be those divulging past habits, showing interest in favorite alternatives, voicing their opinions, of course, on the way these should take place – done to flatter in order to be the first to gain the boss's confidence; hoping that perhaps a dependency upon them will be founded, promising them an indefinite status in the organization.

In this kind of cases there is one useful rule, such as goes the banal American saying: "If it ain't broke, don't fix it...". To wit, one should not swoop down on the first opportunity to bring about instantaneous revolutions, if they aren't really vital but only to demonstrate the arrival of a new chief. The essential should be done in the right measure and time, only if it is justly required – not to show off or for public relations purposes.

- **It is imperative to create a mood of unity and conformity.**

    There is a need to implant the feeling that not all wisdom "sits" at one side of the table, insinuating that there is still a lot to learn – and it should be done together; to focus on the "us," and not on the "me." An obligation to convince that materializing and creation would be an outcome of incorporating all in the business and of their trust in one communal target: the success of the organization. This encounter is meant to embroider together this purpose on the corporation's flag – not to expose "wise guys" or "dickheads", leaders or saboteurs, investors or parasites, reckless publicity seekers or modest and conscientious workers, manipulators or loyal employees, small-minded politicians or charismatic leaders. For as far as the disclosure of all these, time shall do its own.

- **It is important to induce an atmosphere of relaxation, calmness – and honesty above all.**

    Talking quietly in a pleasant way and avoiding vehement or pathetic utterances is the correct manner. The feeling of a new era for all, without prejudices, must be bestowed. A sense that everything said in the room is devoid of selfish motives and intrigue based on political considerations, and that things are meant only for the benefit of the organization and its employees should be conveyed. A slight hint clarifying to all that a collective success means personal gains as well, and is attributed to each and every partner contributing to the toil is strongly recommended. And the most essential factor is to back up the entire speech by the right tone of expression – convincing that it is really coming out from the bottom of the heart – because the note is what makes the music...

And it must be inculcated: contrary to what some say, that there are no second chances to make a first impression – even if the opening shot misfires, it is not the end of the world. Really good people always get future opportunities to correct whatever needs fixing; as the old Spanish sporting saying goes: "It's not how you start that's important, but how you finish...".

However, settling the accounts then requires a much larger effort.

From this moment on, it is desirable to hold such interpersonal encounters on a regular basis (weekly meetings, monthly sessions and so on...) because they are irreplaceable in creating the correct climate of management and conduct. An ongoing dialogue permits the voicing of directions, tendencies and goals from above – and listening to feedback, opinions and objections from below.

Most People "Tend" to be Dragged – rather than Chart their own Course.

In general – and as much as it sounds strange – **most people choose willingly to be led**. They prefer others to tell them what to do in their daily routine, since it makes life easier – without the effort of having to plan each day anew; and usually it includes even the super-talented employees in the organization. Therefore the one in charge should not be "ashamed" to guide and monitor also these exceptional skillful workers (when he senses that it is actually required...) and supervise their missions – tactfully and intelligently of course – because they need it just as the rest do. For the majority of them, and sometimes all, are "ready" – even "love" – having feedback delivered about their doings; they interpret it as a personal attitude of the boss – especially as alongside the remarks it includes compliments too, and in particular it paints a clear picture of their status in the framework and the value of their performance (for after all everybody likes praise-, somewhat caressing one's ego...). And as was already said previously, he who is satisfied with himself delivers, usually, the whole package. What's more, nearly all people are potential winners, meaning that they favor being always on the victorious side. Even lacking the energy to continually invest of themselves for the above-mentioned purpose, they have a little dream: to flourish in order to enjoy life, and if possible with a minimum of fuss. Thus it is clear to them that wise and methodical leadership and tutoring, spiced with the huge experience of other gifted individuals born for greatness – would turn them into successful "heroes". And even if they did not intend to be such from the beginning, why not jump on the available wagon of quality anyway?

In other words: by reading deeply the history of human evolution, one may find out that like all animals, birds and fish – man exhibits probably an impulse for gregariousness.

However, concerning the majority's tendency, previously described here, two important topics must be kept in mind continually:
One: the preference to be led does not mean the creation of a totally passive group of people, responding automatically to any whim of the man at the top. It is evident that such singles or bands have an important function in the firm's dynamic, never to be underestimated. They are best operating with a leadership approach compatible with inner inclination: autocratic, democratic or libertarian. To wit a charismatic totalitarian headship style – or one based on knowledge, professionalism and analytic skills which transmits confidence, tranquility and sanity; an inspiring and sweeping guidance methodology – or a sophisticated management, that maneuvers everybody to industrial quietude for the utmost productivity. A lack

of harmony among the directors and their underlings is in most cases the core reason for a company's failure, despite its basic potential.

Two: good managers know how to locate the natural "principal figures" amongst the workforce of the framework over whom they are appointed, those after which all the others are "dragged", obeying their orders. Their identification is a very effective weapon in running the organization: the use of positive "middlemen" – if one knows how to win their cooperation – will sweep everybody towards the desired direction. And the price of this is rather low, usually. They should be treated respectfully. The fragility of their status must be recognized; consulting with them occasionally as they are coming from the field is highly recommended. Allowing them to win some minor "struggles" so that they can prove beyond any doubt that they care for their followers is a very smart move. It is even permitted to consider compensation, open or private, in order to station them on the right side of the barricade. Trying to undermine their position in the group is unwise, but it is necessary to know how and when to effectively and determinedly put them in their places, so that their special circumstances will not cause them to "lose their heads", pushing them to aspire for power and domination over and afar the good of the company.

And regarding the afore-depicted conception, one rule is always correct: **he who can be "well-led" will, most likely, when someday given the authority, prove himself to be a "good leader"...**

Relationship with Subordinates – Axioms worth Adopting

In building a relationship between the executive echelon and its underlings there are some extremely important fundamental rules, which gives a much deeper validity to this way of mutuality compared to what is customarily conducted by the common managers. These are not preconceived formulae, but sage words and understandings opening a skylight to the secrets of **the real attachment between the leader and his crews underneath; a symbiosis based on a correct human balance between his wishes on the one hand, and their satisfaction on the other**; a partnership in which each side extracts the wanted benefits from the other.

The following are all the insights – those exemplary patterns of behavior – to which the management is obliged (taught, by the way, to contemporary youngsters in every "leadership workshop" held in any neighborhood boys' scout meeting…):

- ✓ Never to relegate a senior executive's responsibility to others – all the more so to juniors.
- ✓ To promise a little but stand by every word.
- ✓ To relate to each individual exclusively not as another within a large community.
- ✓ To make peace with the fact that people are hardly prone to change – but it is possible to ease their way by overemphasizing their unique advantages.
- ✓ To let everyone feel good with himself as he wishes while helping him to better his inner frame of mind and be more.
- ✓ To try and be a genuine friend of any subordinate, letting him sense and believe that this proximity is truly personal, by showing an honest interest in his real condition.

And all of the above do not contradict the **legitimate demand** from the workers to have a serious and adequate attitude for the job, appropriate performance discipline and exemplary good respectable customer service.

And the "school of life" teaches three imperative lessons, which reputable leadership must internalize regarding its conduct with its human capital:

The first – each person is different than his fellow mate, and every one is a world of his own. Therefore people do not change easily – if at all. Thus, it is appropriate to do all which is possible to extract the **remains of the real good left in them,** using their help and will of course, reaching a sort of agreement with them: not to waste superfluous resources and endless efforts trying to "push and add to their character" what is perceived as "mistakenly left out". The task of utilizing any individual is already quite heavy enough, as hard as parting the Red Sea.

The second – everyone has his own "partition", and there is no need to peek beyond it; moreover, it is unnecessary to foul the river with clay, if its crossing is not compelled by the fixed path to the target. Furthermore, the virtue of those who by the power of leadership and guidance are used to reading between the lines and hearing what was unvoiced, should be enhanced by the ability to avert the gaze when it is really required and to understand that aside from directives, there are also common habits. This holds true as long as the general functioning of the system to reach the goal is intact, and all in all the personal balance of the worker is positive and he is definitely delivering the "merchandise". And the best possible example of this is a line attributed to the 16th US president Abraham Lincoln, concerning the intemperance of General Ulysses S. Grant (considered responsible for the turning the tide of the Civil War because of his wisdom, professionalism and manly courage, leading the Union from one victory to the next, until the final surrender of the Confederates…) – who drank too much and even got tipsy here and there: "I wish some of you would tell me the brand of whiskey that Grant drinks. I would like to send a barrel of it to any of my other generals…".

The third: each crisis starts and goes on in three dimensions:

personal, ideological and political. It is simply a must to learn how to cleverly, sensitively and quickly neutralize the "bad blood" which might arise from each of them.

The relationships between the senior executive and his underlings are best described by the 19th-century German philosopher, Arthur Schopenhauer, in his "porcupine parable": in the winter the porcupines are cold. Therefore they draw near each other to warm up; but when they are too close they hurt each other with their quills.

Too far – dying of cold; too close – bleeding to death.

So in order to extract the best from the situation, they must find the exact distance – cozy enough while not getting injured.

He Who Seeks Loyalty Should First be Faithful Himself

In order to run a healthy, open-minded and fearless organization – while maintaining mutual loyalty between leadership and its personnel beneath – one must inspire within it an atmosphere of full sincerity, whose cardinal keys are:

- **Making the workers feel that they are trusted.**

    It is totally forbidden that a local failure, here and there, or a sin of a single person, entails a collective punishment on the entire workforce and an end of trust in all; even worse is that the thing be transmitted downwards explicitly in such a manner. In a managerial, professional and socially robust organization, one ought to face occasionally a local disappointment, as bitter as it can be, because someone committed a mistake which should not have happened; and it must be known how to overcome the obstacle if people support each other, believing in the group's ability, being ready to hold hands together and harnessed to correct the damage. And there is no doubt that in the long run this attitude pays itself off, for eventually it is the one to build authentic and true inner vigor and attachment amongst supervisors and their employees.

- **Backing up subordinates.**

  In principle the man who leads should stand firmly behind the people below him and support them, especially if they trip and fall – as long as their conduct and actions are in full loyalty to the organization, compatible with the dictated policy and procedures, carefully judged (according to the information known to them at the point of time while making those decisions…) – and no negligence may be found in their doings. On the contrary! The superior should even compensate an "appropriate failure" – a mishap as a result of trial and error subjected to the rules above – in the same way that he would invigorate certainly a "successful experiment". But here, one should be very careful not to categorize automatically all missteps under the seemingly "forgiving" title of "human error". These type of errs have occurred, are happening currently - and will continue to appear in the future due to totally objective reasons. However if it is found in a very painstaking debriefing of the matter that some of them might have definitely been prevented by an appropriate handling in advance, then sometimes this label attached to any mistake is intended to cover up something much deeper regarding the employee's behavior or the inner system. This actually indicates methods of action that must be thoroughly examined.

And when workers in the corporation feel confident as to the **trust in them** and **with the backing they get** from their superiors – a certain "almost-blind-faith" starts to be built up gradually towards that particular management ("almost" – keeping in mind the quotes of Buddha and Einstein concerning the seventh key axiom at the end of the first treatise…). Thus in fact a covenant is signed between the man in charge and his underlings, expressing actually **two-way unlimited loyalty**; as was once said by a certain sage: "If you wish your people to worship you for the rest of your life – be their slave first of all...". And the head must develop inside himself proper tools to locate and recognize immediately the initial cracks opening in that pact the very minute they show up – a breach clearly indicating the beginning of the collapse vis-à-vis the "memorandum of understanding" between them. What's more important: he ought to find the technique to react appropriately and prepare to continue the business's activities with the minimal harm.

On the other hand, it is highly recommended to remember **one imperative reservation** concerning all the above-said: it would not be right to try analogizing for the way the manager must act for his superior – whenever his loyalty is required – and expect his subordinates to behave always in the same manner, every time their fidelity to him is needed. Such a mode of acting should always be put to the test when it is supposed to happen – in order to avoid deep disappointment...

At the core of the company's intelligence, the leader must make his people believe that in spite of all, the **entire framework** headed by him is a very **encouraging and supportive** one which will not desert them in their hour of need, especially at their retirement. As Prof. Lester Thurow argues: "The biggest unknown for the individual within the knowledge-based economy is how to have a career in a system where there are no more careers...".

There are no Teams of Stars – Only Stars within Teams

Beyond everything said so far in this chapter about the secret of choosing the right folks, he who cannot **work with all sorts of**

mankind – should not bother managing others ever. Human traits are normally distributed in the shape of the Gaussian Bell Curve, meaning that most people are of average capabilities and an undistinguished character; and if these compose the largest part of the population, then in daily reality they are also the ones occupying most jobs. Therefore there is hardly – and usually would not be – any entity based solely on "geniuses", "diligent", or "extremely efficient" individuals. Launching work teams consisting of just gifted, intelligent, capable workers is a luxury, occurring only rarely during the career of whoever is chosen to head any system. This is for two reasons:

Firstly, when a new director joins an existing framework he would certainly find some veteran employees, so he cannot force a substantial change of personnel – at least not immediately when he starts his job. And most of the public there would probably be composed of mediocrities of all hues, for this is the way of the world, as explained above.

Secondly, it is impossible, as well as unwise, to set up systems merely of stars; in which every huge talent will influence the framework in such a dominant, strong and sweeping manner as to nullify its functionality. Such an array cannot focus because all the contrasting superpowers would tear it apart, wasting most of its efficiency. Would Brazil's national soccer team have produced its "football concerts" in Mexico 1970 if all eleven players had been as talented as Pele? Would the Chicago Bulls have reached their exceptional achievements in the NBA during the 1990s if all their players had been Michael Jordans? Certainly not! For true generals – even giants of their generation – need some "common soldiers" to execute their brilliant ideas; just like an alpha male in a band of wolves needs others in the herd to carry out its hunting stratagem. It is a must to be able to recognize these special ones – if they exist indeed within the group – and build around them the operational tactic as a whole. (This in contrast to one of the famous maxims of American sporting life, "There's no

I in team..." – in whose context the same Michael Jordan stated contrarily and wittily: "There's not, but there's an 'I' in win and two in championship!"...).

Collaterally, and not less important, is Winston Churchill's dictum: "The greatest lesson in life is to know that even fools are right sometimes...". Since even a broken clock shows the correct hour twice a day.

Exactly for that reason the practical wisdom – as noted in the beginning lines of this present strategy – is the know-how to **lead to success with an aggregate of what is currently on hand** – not counting on random specific personal achievement from within the existing group. For at the end of the day, the company is measured by its communal product. Therefore the man in charge is examined, inter alia, on his ability to **create partnerships of nearly always "lone singles"** (which are, by the way, anomalies that may subconsciously shake once in a while quite strongly the entire collective...), trying to draw out the very best from them as a gathering. This since they are absolutely different one from the other, and in most cases are not considered good even when they are alone. And their composition is built on the finest outcome each individual can yield (although sometimes barely able of getting it out of himself...) – but only when he is positioned where he can wield the greatest influence: places enabling to form links based on gluing separate "I"s into a communal "we". These are combinations founded on the unification of people in which it is necessary to accept their weaknesses on the one hand but to do everything possible to intensify their positive points and advantages on the other; a merger trying to bring forth a situation in which the whole is generally greater than the sum of its parts.

Facing such an existing crowd of personalities (which is, by the way, a common routine...) the leader should – in addition to sighting the stars in the system if there are any – sound the cool voice of common sense, crossing the swamp of mediocrity and the morass of adjuncts. He must listen to the genuine "sirens' song" among the insipid roars and din, without letting anyone feel that what he says is utter nonsense – even if at the top of stupidity.

Moreover, it is very important to understand and internalize that it is impossible to create a framework in which everybody is always happy with any decision of the manger, liking at all times his way of conduct and mostly satisfied with the whole of his activity. But it is better to infuse an atmosphere of consensus, in which all resolutions are taken in a harmonious feeling – even if not in total accord – and an ambiance "tasting" of reciprocity. It should be thus "woven" as to allow all generators of resistance – strong as they may be – to release steam without leaving burns, even the slightest ones, on those surrounding them, a sort of mechanism which at the least would minimize damages until their total disappearance.

And finally it ought to be remembered that if the "somewhat coerced" system fails in producing the expected fruits, God forbid – no one would put the blame on the underlings but on the Chief Executive Officer (CEO) alone. For it is well-known that the coach of a futile team is the first to lose his job (instead of changing its body of players…) – even if he is the most talented trainer in the world. And the reason for that is because he is seen in the exact light his men on the pitch (as he built, raised and shaped them…) make him appear, not one iota above it…

And this is, in fact, **one of the greatest difficulties in actually leading and guiding organizations, other than all theories which are the yield of all kinds of schools. It is far from being a perfect space, while the chosen manager should do his utmost to make the best of all possible worlds.**

In summation

Employers, superiors and equals – especially colleagues and subordinates – should always be treated as **human beings equal in the eyes of God** with all it entails; **for at the end of the day everyone must know exactly where he comes from, what is his destination – and who will judge him finally.** As John Updike wrote in 1960: "The music was human; the static was natural…".

January 2000

Financial Strategy

or **"What"** are the Rewards versus the Costs

Preface

The neo-classical theories evolving since the great world's depression of 1929, discussing microeconomics – to wit the principles, processes, behaviors and considerations of small and single market units and commercial mechanisms – assume economic activities in conditions of "perfect competition". That is to say business frameworks functioning in an absolutely clear, workable environment, for accurately defined products and in preordained scenarios of dynamic financial systems. In other words, a somewhat utopian organizations "rolling" inconsiderate of problems which may arise due to their physical size, dilemmas emerging because of their hierarchic structure, difficulties tending to surface as a result of the dissatisfaction of the people involved in the their operations – or trade arrangements disregarding the fact that each non-economic goal entails a significant pecuniary fee. Therefore these outlooks present unambiguously the target of such entities as one only: **amassing monetary gains as much as possible** (like the CEO of a well-known major company who once said: "I'm not in the business to build houses, ships or sophisticated high-tech products, but for one thing only; making money – and a lot…"). This means simply to find the right way to sell something for a higher price than what its overall cost was; and in a more professional motto: how to augment continuously the incoming cash flow compared to what must be spent in order to go on surviving.

In addition to being based on a "perfect economical state", the above model is established on the hypothesis of a closed market, insulated from the global business world beyond geographical boundaries. This is a sample that stands on analysis of the facts and conglomeration of mathematical coincidences, nearly absolute, deriving totally analytic solutions independent of social-political-normative conceptions; a kind of a banal array, functioning in ideal, extreme situations which exist only in fables and fairy tales. It is a paradigm tailored to a condition of a stable fiscal equilibrium in the market being for a very specific representative product from within it – normally responding to the following assumptions, reflecting the typical conduct in such an economy:

- ✓ The units involved in the above-depicted market's commercial activities – the buying as well as the selling ones – are very small in comparison with its huge dimensions. Thus, being petite and sole entities, they have no influence on the prices of the products.

- ✓ The behavior of the individuals in it remains divided and separated, with no involvement of any government body here, and producers' or consumers' assemblies there. In other words: there is never an outside agitation regarding the supply of the merchandise; deliberate imposition of tendentious taxes or restrictions; production rights or selling to single bodies (monopolies…); secret agreements among companies to minimize competition (cartels…); private clients, buyers or customers rebellions, acting in conjunction (monopsonies…).

- ✓ The performance level of the business organizations in its limitations and their commerce mechanisms are predetermined and totally free, while all the data concerning them is open to the public. To wit, any type of market operation is possible, its setting is known beforehand, specifically detailed and all information related to it is apparent, available, and identical at every point of time and freely for all.

- ✓ There is an optimal and defined situation for the merchandise within it, meaning that each product is homogenous and supply equals demand.

However the perception described in the previous clause is rather "limited" as far as real economic scenarios meant to be encountered daily, so its data and approach may be used in certain cases only. It can be expressed, for example, in the initial-rough appraisal of someone starting a business, when trying to understand in the first phases where is he, more or less, in what direction he is supposed to proceed and what are his chances of future success; especially when there is no better current information around. And things are particularly true when specific branches in developing countries are examined while they are just beginning to grow, in small retail systems or in little economic units like households.

Anyway the actual industry, trade and fiscal picture is not that sterile and unreal. Sometimes it is the total inverse, since there are more heavyweight considerable contributors, which have a very serious influence over the whole economy; incredibly significant factors limiting sometimes on the one hand indeed, but surely not always negative on the other. This is because there are so many additional important things that are happening aside from the above-described theoretical, clean, unique and private market. The following are some typical examples of such generators:

- **State Factors**
  - Governments which are supposed to outline a fiscal policy and foresee the real ingredients of the country's economy such as: priorities of national investments and inner or outer debts (monetary deficits of the treasury…); different taxes, growth per capita, unemployment percentage, local transfer payments (like social security allowances, income support, compensation

for jobless individuals...); international disbursements (as grants from states, institutions or organizations...); various subsidies to all kind of bodies and the like.

- Central state banks that have to take care of the monetary elements whose essences are: interest-rate setting (the price of money...); dictating the credit volume (financial liquidity within the economy that can be used by businesses...); regulating inflation (the wear of purchasing power...); supervising the banking conglomerates (capital adequacy ratio for financial stability and commission rates...) and so on.

- Principal ruling authorities which ought to provide "public products" such as: security (exterior and interior...) education, health, infrastructure, essential services, et cetera; otherwise no one would take care of these in order to establish and then run a normal lifestyle for all citizens; outcomes that someone has to pay for.

▶ **Additional Causes**

- In reality the economy functions as a totally open market – importing merchandise from abroad, as well as – and this is the most important thing – exporting local products outside the country to the wide world.

- Monopolies, cartels and even monopsonies, which by their very definition and character are incompatible with a "perfect economic competition" state.

- No organization functions in total isolation, taking into consideration only those who take part in its activities de facto – meaning employees and management. Any business-cooperative entity is strongly tied by its umbilical cord to governmental institutions and local municipal authorities, complying with their rules and regulations, paying their levies and duties – while functioning interactively with them. It has also binding reciprocal and work relations with commercial banks, subcontractors, suppliers, service providers and clientele.

- There are some basic necessities of life ignored by most people such as: clean air, environmental aesthetics and local mores, which are not always prone to pricing. Consequently, the problem of their enforcement must be solved by unique legislation, pertinent applications and money-collecting mechanisms (ingredients about which the "invisible hand" of Adam Smith is not only irrelevant as far as their usages are concerned, but may even lead to considerable socioeconomic mishaps; for a situation might definitely occur when each person does his best to privately exploit these factors – but the general result would still be the worst from a collective point of view…).

In other words: in order for all various parts of the administration to function harmoniously, intending to do so (and not always successfully, by the way…) without violating the natural-economic equilibrium within it, some Western countries created an array of differentiated authorities as above-portrayed. Their combined activities are supposed to be based on a system of checks & balances – genuine contributing regulations as against hindrance and deferring speculations – in addition to the totality of inherent financial structural forces and all other objective factors detailed in this article; a kind of an optimal point between a free market and the real national interest (and not one that is driven by "twisted political dealers"…) – where each one of them has a considerable influence over the economy.

For that reason it is clear that there is occasionally an essential difference between the operational intra-organizational goals, directed at the company's personnel and all those who function within it, and its formal targets presented outwardly; so that the final outcome cannot always be the maximization of the incoming wealth. And the meaning of the term "profit" expands because the framework is currently very complex and ramified, branching no doubt into internal and external coalitions seeking subjective utilitarianism and toiling to obtain compensation, sometimes contradicting the tenor of the firm dictated by the owners or executives; the very one that intends to benefit the communal system alone. **And the monetary gain becomes suddenly a compulsion – though it would, surely, remain forever the main aim to assure the continuation of the organization, but certainly not as its one and only purpose.** So, the hands of the manager are overflowing with work and filled with the eternal tasks related to the ultimate interest, concerning all actually: the **financial engineering** of the system under his domination.

Therefore, from now on the upcoming text endeavors to address all aspects influencing the financial conduct of any cumulative productive entity, in separate essays (and mini-essays…) so to speak – but uniting into one full rational composition, whose ideas are woven together within it after serious and thorough deliberation and study. And the above-said is not meant in any way to replace the well-known specific instructional economic books and journals, but to gather a succession of remarks, observations and solutions to common problems, which are supposed to occupy the manager only – senior as well as junior – in an all-encompassing vision trough his own private spectacles .

Financial Intelligence as the Central Contributor to Economic Success

In principle the economy's dogma and philosophy focus on **financial intelligence,** which means recognizing the existence of possibilities which find expression in creative and irregular fiscal, industry and trade innovations and solutions – as far as the human mind can go. This intellect consists of several helpful qualifications which can be acquired, internalized and practiced; and of quite a few essential pragmatic recommendations worth being adopted and turned into a way of life.

Here are some of them:

- ✓ Interest and autodidactic abilities of all concerned with commercial, financial and cost-effective subjects and scenarios, while continuously endeavoring to be updated in and familiar with the latest data and novelties on a daily basis.

- ✓ Specializing in monetary investment strategies – in which money is multiplied by itself – and in their most intelligent application.

- ✓ A meticulous study and good understanding of the market's policies and rules – the main keys of demand and offer processes (where "demand" is the leading factor…) – and an optimal exploitation of the chasm between them.

- ✓ Expertness in all decrees and debates of that specific field: a high awareness of accounting dictates and the regulations of the operating area, and their most effective and precise "stretching" up to the limits of the law and ethics.

To all of these should be added a few assisting "practical commands" (despite emphasizing the private life actually…):

- ✓ One should never work for the money but make it work for him (or his organization…).

- ✓ There is a need to control the power of wealth and not be afraid of it.

- ✓ It is essential to distinguish between profitable assets putting money into the pocket to an obligation which takes cash out of it (that sometimes erroneously is considered property…).

- ✓ There is a necessity to make a living of the occupation and main specialization (the workplace for private individuals...) – but correspondingly to take care also of additional (personal...) profitable business (purchasing assets, for example...), the kind which do not require the constant presence of the owners, since they run nearly by themselves and keep on growing as time goes by (otherwise it becomes a full-fledged job...).

- ✓ And finally (additionally to the above-said, but not separately...) it is highly recommended to choose a "scalable occupation," as suggested thoughtfully by Nassim Nicholas Taleb in his book *The Black Swan*: namely, a job capable of fitting itself immediately and easily to any scope of work: a non-hourly vocation – not subjected to the amount of tasks performed; an activity simply permitting an income with many zeros, but not requiring much further energy when faced with a sudden need to put in a considerably larger effort (such as: payment for revolutionary ideas which may bring a lot of revenue or mediation rewarded by a certain percentage of the deal's value regardless of the sweat and time it takes to execute it, or a brokerage requiring the same endeavor exactly when purchasing a million securities as when buying only a hundred of them, when this speculative gamble may end in some "great luck" and so on...).

And all of the above-delineated is **financial engineering** at its best – a proper reading of the **business-system economic map**; a kind of "cost-effective high-tech thing" in the full meaning of the word; a mechanism which can lead – strange as it may sound – to a **creative destruction** if its perversions are not fully controlled. On the other hand dealing inappropriately with this particular issue will tow those involved in the field to the slippery slope, sending them towards mediocrity; since being "lukewarm" and "average" demands much less time and effort – but most people are unable to discern this devastating fact until it's too late. And that is precisely why deep orientation, profound understanding and uncompromising dexterity are so important for this subject, the general instincts, which are the results of high professionalism and rich experience.

Organizations as Convoluted "Webs" of Economic Elements

Following the above prologue, in order to be a bit more pragmatic, corporations should be observed in a manner somewhat different than the one described in the tractates and chapters so far. The right way to study them from a financial-strategy point of view is to look at those frameworks as outlines of economic parameters per-se, upon which are based on and are derived from, actually, the following central organizational and managerial terms:

- **The structure** – being the totality of all fixed and changing variants of the establishment's skeletal patterns concerned with its main physical characteristics: equity, external capital, location and size, number of central units, sum of functionaries and personnel, amounts of tools and production means, character and scope of the product or service, cost of published data, etc.

- **The behavior** – meaning the dictated policy regarding the overall running of the communal endeavor in all its domains and dimensions: daily administrative conduct, work methods and processes, the high echelon's wishes, including their personal preferences and such.

- **The performance level** – that is to say the bottom line of the company's activity outcomes: financial results and data, degree of resource exploitation, quality of yield, number of markets and customers and so on.

One may picture the above idioms as three balls filled with the specific material as detailed hereinafter. Their orbits intersect, repeatedly moving in a business space, while each circle spins around its own axis, and all together rotate over an imaginary pivot of the whole system, so that their relative position, the mixture of their contents and the combination of their contributions are constantly changing. Therefore any conjunction or essential blending is possible. Each affects the others as well as being influenced by them. Thus the starting point of this overall outlook must be as follows: there is no situation in which the economy is monolithic, consolidated and ideal; so a huge virgin deserted environment becomes the ground for indispensable research and nearly unlimited possibilities. And as the uncertainty gets deeper and the information harder to obtain, more room for spotting and identifying unique conditions is revealed – while bringing to bear most of the senses and intelligences in order to initiate and fully exploit occasional business opportunities, even short-lived ones. And what makes a mediocre manager much better than his counterparts is the push of his timing to act at the accurate minute; the basic instinct moving him to swoop down at the exact suitable moment, without missing any of what it offers.

It is possible to describe the above-presented perception from a slightly different angle; from within a combination of scenarios, modes of behavior and initiatives on behalf of the firm and its advancement as well as its benefit. This is, indeed, a different perspective, which also strengthens the standpoint that in most cases organizations are built and operated based on a web of basic economic considerations precisely serving as the backbone of all that is characterized by them:

- ✓ The businesslike vision, operating policy, the company's structure, its conduct and level of its operations **are set**, usually, by **the managerial executives** out of common positions and normal wishes such as: wealth, financial control, hegemony in the branch, taxes or any other compensation. Only in certain cases do the owners and managers consider matters like ideology, social issues, normative aspects, ordinary or irregular operative doctrinal subjects and so on.

- ✓ The main purpose of private companies is almost always **monetary gain**. Only seldom is it not the one and sole purpose in the eyes of those senior executives posted in all kinds of corporations – public establishments or voluntary fellowships, for example. Therefore, **the organizational targets and their conduct** are usually aimed to augment their material income.

- ✓ **The structure of the branch** which the corporate is involved with and the scope of the firm's fiscal activity, **can be defined** by appropriate planning and brilliant political and economic maneuvers executed at the right moment – allowing it to control quite massively its work environment. And the domain of occupation cannot and should not be merely an exogenous factor, not prone to change. Aggressive publicity and marketing, "sympathetic" legislation, setting attractive stylish and social trends, convenient pricing, reducing supply while augmenting demand so as to raise the merchandise's value, merging products and companies to increase efficiency and break through to new commerce arenas – are simply some examples of economic methods easily implemented with sophistication, in order to acquire dominance over markets up to an almost exclusive control of them; each ingredient and its influence due to its timing and might.

And if the realistic scenario above, accompanied by its special circumstances, is mixed with the previous real-pragmatic perception, then the perfect recipe is obtained – by which one may build and shape the most all-encompassing financial guiding principles of the communal productive entity and hit the road.

Building a Budget as the First Realization of the Policy

The sole way of translating a business strategy into fiscal terms is by laying out a budget plan accordingly. Consequently, it is imperative to do this before any other commercial activity. The meaning of such a process is then to present in simple numeric-financial language a detailed forecast, as close to reality as possible, of the way economic affairs and everything related will proceed: preliminary researches, sources of funds, operation modes, market penetration methods, development routes, advertising, marketing, sales and final goals. All of that is in order to estimate whether there is a reasonable possibility for money-making fulfillment by the afore-mentioned prognosis – to be followed later on by making the right decision.

And in more pragmatic words: a budget is needed for the following reasons:

- ✓ To define the necessary resources required to execute the dictated policy.
- ✓ To draw a map of the cash flow to and from the coffer.
- ✓ To demonstrate how to put in money to support the totality of the intended activities, so as to ultimately make much more profit out of it.
- ✓ To present envisioned revenue compared to assumed costs.
- ✓ To supply an infrastructure for follow-up and control tools to analyze "performance" as against "planning".

It is strongly recommended to build a long-term budget, one that gives an economic outlook for at least five years. Additionally, it is needed to use only relevant data when spreading this plan out, taking into account as much as possible, of course – merely current details explicitly contributing to the decision-making process in the present. Concurrently it is important to include also in the "forecast equation" just those elements directly influencing each proposed alternative for action – those financially based, strictly taken from the most updated cash flow reports available. On the other hand it is really preferable to extract from the accumulated history – if there is any regarding to the topic under discussion – those ingredients which would "assist" straightforwardly in shaping and refining these "expectations".

Putting on paper and editing such a document requires meticulous preparation. The course begins with the dictation of "guidelines" for all concerned with its creation – which are, as a matter of fact, the monetary principles presented by the policy-makers in charge. These are mainly the central "financial ratios" to be depicted further in this chapter, corresponding to the declared strategy of the company's management from which, immediately upon presentation, the economic state of the organization can be learnt at every following given moment. As a second step, all those responsible for the different key units and all executioners of special assignments are required to prepare detailed preliminary functional prognoses, well-explained and suited the essential nature of each job, task or duty. Subsequent to a close analysis of all that information, it is consolidated into a single file from which a general forecast is prepared. After being ratified, this document becomes the "financial work plan" of the firm to be distributed to all participants in its operations – each exposed exactly to the part relevant to him as to a very clear, delineated hierarchy.
In any case such a "statement" has to take into account the following issues:

- ✓ The cardinal essence of the business plan – actually a translation of the corporate's goals in terms of:
    - ↳ Return on investment.

- Profit on active capital.
- Pace of income growth.

✓ Financing sources.

✓ Preferred capital structure.

✓ Overhead – all costs nor directly ascribed to specific activities, but supporting and encompassing the totality of production and sales operations:
  - Management.
  - Administrative personnel.
  - Office equipment.
  - Service conditions.
  - Social allocations.
  - Public relations.
  - Legal services.
  - Insurance.
  - Research and development.

✓ Operating costs – all expenses financing the real, income-creating work:
  - Direct employees.
  - Purchase of materials, parts, tools or any other equipment required to extract output.
  - Manufacturing.
  - Advertising.
  - Marketing.
  - Distribution.
  - Sales.

- ✓ Cash capital expenses: money regularly flowing from the business to assure its normal operations.

- ✓ Financing costs: interest on bank and other loans.

- ✓ Various payments: taxes, dividends etc.

- ✓ Additional receipts: income from supplementary investments outside the organization and capital gains.

- ✓ Risk analysis: pointing out the probability of missing the bottom line of the forecasts.

- ✓ Miscellaneous: all subjects not directly or definitely relating to one of the above domains.

On the other hand, it is very important to understand that a budget is not a sacred document. It is a paper to be updated on a daily basis with the emergence of any new data, changing one factor or some of them, referring to this or that forecast. Even though while first setting up the above-said statement, it is imperative to make a maximum effort to include any surprises that come into mind, and to reevaluate in great detail any possible prospective financial activity whatsoever; presenting the most realistic potential, pictured in the context of any vicissitudes. A mistake in the present estimation certainly may lead to operational failure or complete future paralysis.

In addition, it is highly recommended to impose on all **the above-detailed expenses** a "sensitivity test"; to wit, adding 5 to 10 percent to the bottom line of the cost column (depending on one's tendencies, whether an optimist or a pessimist…) so as to cover all unanticipated expenses. In other words: it is better to hold in store a "security cushion," able to minimize shocks of all kinds. Moreover, it is imperative to keep in the background the following two "compromise keys" so as to remain with both feet on the ground. For at the end of the day, this budget is nothing but a plan, which might be based on some flawed data resulting from existing knowledge gaps.

- **Flexible budgeting** – taking reality into account and presenting minimum and maximum potential ranges of activity levels and sales volume.

- **Standard budgeting** – allowing for efficient examination of all parts in the entire firm, by comparing theoretical costs according to common standards with what they actually are.

The Power behind Management Strength – Absolute Domination of the Financial Details

An imperative, basic rule of business says: "**know your numbers**…". This is possibly the strongest financial-engineering decree that ought to be dictated to the manager. Moreover, perhaps it should also be suggested to any human being wherever he is – whatever his métier may be; since economic knowledge is never considered to be solid unless quantified and expressed in numbers, for there is no an alternative to a complete control of sizes and percentages derived from fiscal, - industry and trade processes – to their minutest details – and the ability to work with and maneuver them fast and easily. And the key personnel of any organization must be able to thoroughly extract their huge mastery of such data, and to immediately realize in any business scenario the advantage they enjoy by such acquaintance. And whoever finds himself in a continuous day-and-night competition involving a fickle market is obliged to have the capacity to run and roll in his mind, according to the information he possesses, all combinations and permutations in any potential direction – in order to exploit any opportunity presented along the way.

Metaphorically, even in the evening, when everybody routinely dealing with the operational aspects is resting from daily toil – the executives, economically oriented, ought to continue delving into the latest financial report, in order to sum up and decide how to proceed and improve. And this can truly be achieved only by an absolute, meticulously unshakable proficiency in the organization's cost-effective scales and monetary values.

And in contrast to the past – when the main motive for gathering numerical info was a rather limited and one-directional examination of "revenue versus expenses" – today's goal must be much broader. The rationale behind it is to create a type of sophisticated intelligence tool, capable of presenting the smallest detail and bestowing the aptitude to painstakingly and comprehensively digest and analyze the totality of financial parameters and outcomes of global economic occurrences; an instrument supplying any spark of required information, especially concerning markets and the demand for the company's specific product or service. Therefore the "data management system" (to be honored with a future chapter in particular…) is there to gather, sift, sort and process the various feedback and criteria constantly flowing from the field itself. To be exact, it is imperative to create inner numerical standardization storage – not for its own purpose in any case, but to serve as an aid for the supervising leadership – becoming indispensable for:

- **Economic Control:** the way to appraise the extent of the corporate's proximity to its target or final achievement, and the measure of its success regarding this particular angle in its competition with rivals.

- **Financial Stimulus:** the factor goading the various units within the system to do what is financially best from the organizational as well as the personal aspects, concerning its business profits.

And this idea is best expressed using the mantra uttered by the Greek philosopher-mathematician, Pythagoras of Samos (6th c. BC) apropos the best tool for analysis and understanding: "Everything is in the numbers...".

Credit by an External Source – or Equity

A second basic, extra-important rule deals with how to organize monetary sources in support of the firm's activities. The type and origins of financing demand a decision, first of all, about the capital structure desired in the company according to its business character – and especially that of its key shareholders and managers. Only then is it possible to fix on a fund-raising strategy and where it will come from – in order to finance the present specific operations of the organization and all other subjects such as: its future cardinal purchasing, performance, growth and cost of manufacturing in the medium and long terms. In other words: what is the preferred ratio of wealth coming from external entities (banks, the stock exchange and so on...) as against cash flowing from the owners' pockets – and the total amount of interest-carrying loans in comparison to the entire equity outlay.

The ratio among these components in a company is known as its **financial leverage**. This proportional size – directly related to the external sources equated to the internal corporation's volume of properties – is a very controversial issue. On the one hand, it displays the owners' level of trust in the business they establish, run and develop by the sum of private money they are ready to invest, coming from their pockets; on the other hand, it signifies the risk which other partners and stockholders are willing to take, due to their estimation of the enterprise's chances to succeed.

Preferring large leverage is justified when:

- ✓ The costs of credit (forced by banks or otherwise…) are considerably lower than the potential profits that might be incoming from the use of equity if wisely utilized.
- ✓ The percentage of the capital raised from securities' public offering related to the company's fiscal property hold in aggregate does not risk at all the owners' dominance of their firm.

The advantages derived from this are:

- ✓ A rise in the organization's monetary value due to the growth of its financial assets – which will lead, of course, to a jump in its stock value compared to its capital-raising expenses.
- ✓ Indirect savings because of the interest payments on loans, which are considered a tax-deductible expenditure.

And the disadvantages of it are:

- ✓ Risking the shareholders and partners in situations when interest costs are higher than the profits; this may result in financial crises leading to the company's dissolution. And during liquidation, "loan providers" enjoy a priority over all types of securities owners, while distributed assets are used as reimbursements for the various claimants.
- ✓ Appearing as if there is a deficit in the firm's own pecuniary hold, in case it happens to fall into operational troubles; especially when a need to try and mobilize credit from other external resources becomes crucial.

It is therefore clear that any entity enjoying the smallest influence over the corporation will try pushing in the direction most profitable to itself – even if it is for a short term only.

Regardless of all the afore-mentioned, in most cases it is preferable to start doing business with external capital – not with one's own money – even involving an investment in financing costs, rather high actually, compared to using the cash already in the organization's coffers. The idea behind this is that if one starts a communal framework such as this, whose growth income cannot cover, at the end of the day, the return on loans and other expenses due to them and still leave a reasonable margin for finer profits, enabling not only its continued existence but its development as well – then there is no economic sense in thinking of establishing such a commercial body and running it in the first place, as private funds should be safeguarded for other purposes and different times...

And in order to secure themselves monetarily, many firms set a guideline for the range of the financial leverage they are willing to take upon themselves. The convention is for the equity to be fivefold the size of the interest expenses they are ready to incur. In addition, the more optimistic and confident managers direct the business activities of the mechanism they are heading so that it covers three or four times their financing expenses. In other words, the profit before interest should exceed the interest costs by three or four times; otherwise, in their view, the enterprise's performance is not paying for itself money-wise and not robust enough commercially.

But, in addition to all the above-depicted, it is imperative to internalize two auxiliary rules, derived from the prevalent financial engineering and from what was said so far:

The first: in times of particularly high interest rates, it is cheaper to buy a company than to launch one; since when money is "expensive", it is very dangerous to venture into the kind of processes the entry to which is clear enough but the future exit from it is in great doubt. This matter tends to be involved with adventures – even partially familiar from the past – such as: instituting new entities, virtual business alliances, investment in research and development, etc. Even if the deal is assisted by bank funding including a "generous" credit line, for the most part, it is more profitable to purchase at a fixed and known price something already existing -- especially when it is very difficult to foresee the height to which tomorrow's financial costs may climb in the current interest situation, as a result of the state's monetary policy. This is mainly because in **borrowing money** one ethical decree must remain forever foursquare and has to be carried out in the good old customary way: **paying back exactly – to the last cent and in a timely manner – everything taken.**

The second: it is always forbidden to enter a business which is essentially capital-intensive but rather dull technologically, compared to the sums invested in it – commencing by bringing in a lot of cash while its cardinal operation is only "rolling" it. Since finally it will be "transferred" to the ownership of the banks or to those other lenders who assist financially in setting it up. Beyond preferring to raise funds from a serious body, amenable to ongoing, fertile and friendly partnership, it should be, in addition, a strategic investor that contributes an added value to the continuation of the organization's **professional-unique** performance – and not one chasing only after its fiscal gains at the end of the day. And if someone like this is found, intent on filling his pockets effortlessly with easy profits, he is a "parasite" who deserves to be immediately "exterminated".

And much the more so, making money out of money is a counterproductive and totally useless occupation, not producing – and not meant to do so – even one real workplace.

However one old cliché should be remembered, ringing so true: **when money "talks" ideology "walks" (away...).** And silence in cases like this is actually equivalent to consent...

In summation, the afore-described teaches the reader that consolidating the capital of a company and formatting its structure is a thoroughly scientific process, and should be done with deep consideration and based on personal as well as socioeconomic aspects. And when standing before the decision of the manner by which to raise the funds needed for the organization's operations, the following factors which will influence the firm's future life must be taken into account:

- ✓ Readiness to accept some external intervention in running things.
- ✓ The duration of the period for which the money is required.
- ✓ Willingness to be tied up in long-term commitments.
- ✓ The appropriate financial leverage.
- ✓ The extent of financing expenses management is prepared to take upon itself.
- ✓ Tax benefits and other available bonuses.
- ✓ Fund mobilization costs.
- ✓ Enhancing or damaging reputation.

How to Make a Profit – Welcome Priorities and a Practical Choice

There are two proven ways to make money: to sell more product, or to gradually cut the general expenses – relative, of course, to the scope of the profits. However, it is better to try and do both simultaneously – which might create synergy – as long as the entire "commerce weight" is being thrown on the first while the best brainpower, talent and energy are invested in it. For this path points towards an assured future success, promising real yields in the short term, and definitely in the long one. And the rationale behind that mode of thinking is:

Firstly, it is in no way possible to become richer just by cutting expenses and avoiding waste – even if carried along all the way.

Secondly, low-priced stuff is not necessarily profitable, given that at a certain stage of its existence the cost of its frequent faults may become extremely high (or as the banal saying of the old Eastern

European merchants in the early years of the 20th century went: "That which does not cost money is apparently not worth money; as in the end one gets exactly what he paid for..."). So it is absolutely feasible that eventually, this seemingly expensive "merchandise", so to say, becomes actually the cheapest – depending, most likely, on the true value of what has been received in return.

Thirdly, it is impossible to keep shrinking and cutting costs indefinitely without a logical end, and in particular beyond an acceptable optimum – as there is a real danger that over-economizing may mistakenly turn off even the light at the end of the tunnel...

And if a decision must be taken to execute some drastic measures to reduce, as much as possible, the expenditure (the less recommended course of the previous pair – but necessary here and there hoping foolishly that this act will be the one to keep the business alive...) – two very important things ought to always be remembered:

The one – even when it is compulsory to slice into the "body" itself, it should be planned to be done only to the fat – not in the living flesh where every injury may, ultimately, hurt now and in the future; the basic necessities and capabilities of those on whose behalf the organization was established in the first place. And there will always be corners containing redundancies accumulated over time to be cut.

The other – since the first to desert any drowning ship are the rats living in it, why wait for it to sink to the bottom of the sea? It is better – and highly recommended, in fact – to start by throwing them overboard, getting rid of extra weight, while trying to avoid the worst of all: going down the drain. In other words: when it is necessary to reduce outlays, it is appropriate to start with those whose daily contributions to the flourishing of the company are null – these who in times of trouble, when the situation is not as cheerful, would be the first to cross the lines to the company next door; and who in business has not felt the pain of such experiences...

And one more precious thing to remember concerning this subject: although the number one rule warmly adopted by most businessmen is: "never lose money…" – it ought to be understood that it's impossible to constantly only be on the gaining side. There will always be less successful enterprises; and as **the occupation fields are genuinely broadened, the chances to falter in some of them grow**. But it is really prohibited to become too depressed in spite the fact of losing sometimes. (However, it is very legitimate to feel bad for a while, but in the end it is necessary to get out of this sad mode and continue pushing forwards…). The trick is to know how to ensure that the total economic value of the successes is larger than the financial scope of the failures, minimizing the price of malfunctions and missteps while augmenting the worth of achievements.

The following are two trivial examples how to accomplish the above:

First – when one big business is profiting nicely, it is appropriate to try and develop some sidelines, relevant commercial subjects. Even if they are missed, the financial damage caused by them would be rather easily absorbed in the margins of the main branch earnings.

The second – taking offensive action based on maximum "exploitation of success", – that is to say: riding on the "chariots" of other business activities borne around the main flourishing operation planned ahead. Their fiscal attainment was not foreseen because they were not in the mainstream of the performance path; however when discovered to be profitable and contributing to the major economic-operative targets, it is a must to cling to them exhaustively and extract the most out of their realization.

Moreover, one rule is always practically helpful in such cases: when down in the dumps and seriously feeling that the positive wave is about to crash, it is worth to exchange the aggressive-active strategy for a somewhat careful-defensive policy; for the story of life – naturally, by the way – is almost constantly a map of high and low tide. And one needs simply to learn how to keep from drowning when at the bottom of the rollers – in order to produce the best of their energy when surfing on the top...

The Price – Fixing Without Erring

Normally the **"value" of the organization's product (or service...)** is set by an interaction between the forces of its demand and the ability to supply it related to the current market – all subjected to the local laws and rules. In other words: how much are the customers willing to pay for a specific purchase after due negotiations, and which regulations (mainly economically and commercially...) are valid as a dictation of the federal and municipal authorities.

Theoretically, this is the highest sum of money which the company would strive to get for its products. Such a sale would be profitable only if the reward is larger than all expenses in aggregate, formed in the organization as the outcome of running the entire **"value activities"** due to the extraction of the said merchandise: operations being the variety of very basic toils, by which the business is managed from A to Z. Those are the totality of carrying out all technological as well as economic-administrative rolling tasks – dissimilar, by the way, one from the other. Some involve the physical activation of designated people and special means in the manufacturing routines itself, while others are supporting missions concerning human beings and tools (functions that are performed daily though, but not always in a direct connection to the execution proceedings per se...). This applies to every single one of the different infrastructures in use and the whole mixture of services, being utilized currently all year long – whether fabrication work is made or not – assigned directly and indirectly to enable mainly (but not only...) the perfection of the mission for which the communal creative entity was established in the first place.

And actually, in order for a **real profit** to materialize, the quoted price of the produce intended to be distributed and sold in the markets must equal numerically the "**most total cost**" of all its research, planning, design, manufacturing, promotion, advertising, distribution processes and activities (including the full administrative expenditure encompassing these...) – from birth to its final delivery – with an added **markup;** a system known as "cost-plus pricing".

With reference to all of the above, the totality of the money spent on the entire production operations should be calculated very carefully, since the omission of various seemingly irrelevant expenses and payments may cause losses eventually. Consequently, from the simplest financial viewpoint, without being a certified accountant, it must be understood that the term has to be established upon a very thorough evaluating procedure containing in an **extremely strict manner** the following:

- **The amount of the fixed outlays**: those completely unrelated to fabrication part (called also the overhead expenditure...), encumbering the organization even if it stops manufacturing absolutely; along with

- **The variable costs in aggregate**: the ones directly associated with the pace of the extraction phase, growing when it is broadening and diminishing with its reduction.

Or in more financial, practical and detailed language, it can be described as equal to the sum of:

- **The total investment in stock** needed straightforwardly for the making of the designated merchandise, for its purchasing de-facto and schlepping to the factory's yard; plus

- **All direct operating costs**, physically linked to the whole produce creation processes from beginning to end; in addition to

- ▶ **The totality of the adjunct ongoing expenses** of the company for its daily conduct; the money required to come in and go out, and the all-around fabrication routines.

To wit: this is the portion of the global outlays, accumulated from the procurement of raw materials until its appearance as a buyable commodity on the shelf, calculated per **one sale unit**, which is actually the **very bottom price**.

On the other hand, its **ceiling charge** is fixed by many policy considerations of the corporation's top echelons, as described hereby.

Setting the markup limit is a proper strategic decision done by management only, but it has to lean on – beyond gut feeling – the **science of Cost Accounting**, that professional field setting out the stated arithmetical measures, intending to determine the price of the product or service in conjunction with:

- ✓ Its real cost.
- ✓ Competitors' activities.
- ✓ Its market age.
- ✓ The marked profit goals.
- ✓ Its presented value and perceived one.

The above resolution is meant, therefore, to accommodate a fair monetary compensation for the firm's investment at such a rate that would give it, first and foremost, a comfortable (to what degree…) living space, and will afterwards permit the continuation of its intensive operation (at what level…) in all the various plateaus and domains: for its technological development, business expansion and financial growth. But while deciding on the proportion of the relative "price overloading" against the "most total costs" – it is strictly forbidden to ignore the considerations raised by the following questions:

- ✓ Were all **efficient organizational processes** truly exhausted, so that the bottom worth of the fabricated item is really the lowest possible?

- ✓ What is the **price level** demanded by competitors in the field for similar merchandise?

- ✓ Whether the estimation of the current **life cycle** stage of the manufactured good necessitates using a "penetration price" in order to permeate potential clients' minds?

- ✓ Is the **company's policy** directed to break others' monopoly in order to survive or to grab a larger market share for business expansion?

- ✓ Were **sales-promoting psychological means** used sophisticatedly enough, e.g.: raising price points to a more valuable standard, fake reducing costs (deliberately elevating and then lowering them as an artificial attraction method...), real seasonal discounts (temporarily, so as to prove they are genuine...), or any other "trick" intended to increase the trading volume?

- ✓ Does the **existing market status** barely enable a financial "rolling" – or is it sufficiently wide and robust enough to allow real "skimming" by introducing a new, innovative product?

Thus, before the final decision is made, it is very much recommended to conduct a painstaking comparison of actual tariffs and "acute price lists" relating to the domain, those "going around". Correspondingly it is a must to acquire the right feeling for the business atmosphere encompassing the product; how is the company's might and prestige positioned in the eyes of the public in general; and what is the highest feasible price for the marketed crop in the present commercial ambiance.

And due to the cardinality of both above subjects to the organization's economic vitality, the manager ought to be personally and meticulously involved in the judgment and execution of the sentence. In such important special conclusions, it is highly suggested to be assisted by choice financial, technical and administrative people, in order to strengthen and verify the final verdicts. Since, in the end – as goes the somewhat funny saying heard somewhere, but enjoying a lot of business reality – the definite difference between a correct and a wrong resolution depends on the unimportant digits – the zeroes: how many of them pass the comma…

For that reason it is extremely vital that the most senior of all executives would be very well connected to these very sensitive financial processes.

Yet, for an immediate general economic status examination regarding the organization prior to entering any managerial function – or a quick study of the company's level of efficiency after reforms and offsets have been executed – or a brisk analysis of any decision concerning the beginning of a project which may entail fiscal outcomes on the communal productive entity – the following approximate principle of calculation, designated from now on as the **Instant Status Audit Formula (ISAF)**, can be of assistance:

$$\frac{\text{Fixed Expenses}}{1 - \dfrac{1}{\text{Designated Markup}}}$$

(Where the value of the "designated markup" should be presented by a decimal number above 1…)

This expression, presenting the ratio of the total "fixed outlays" to the "profit margin" decided as wished, yields the **minimal required "sales turnover" bringing the company precisely to a break-even point** – in other words: a reality in which the firm consumes exactly all the revenues from its main occupation.

Any additional income results, therefore, in profit (and tax payment, of course…).

The Competitive Advantage as a Winning Cause

Actual profitability would hence proceed from posing a considerable competitive edge vis-à-vis opponents; from coupling the organization's strong points and emphasizing its virtues as against its rivals' drawbacks and deficiencies. Such superiority should result by factual minimizing of the production expenses as described above, in comparison to all the others; or by bestowing a combined quality ambiance encompassing the merchandise itself and its presentation, and perhaps as an outcome of both. This kind of priority would direct the company to a substantial uniqueness in contrast to the additional different entities in the same field, placing itself ahead of them – leaving that way a nice margin for a respectable monetary gain from the sales of its products; or marching to a situation where allowing themselves to demand a higher price for these goods would seem natural and totally justifiable – a sure step to cause the flourishing of its growth generators.

Taking those seemingly common measures – cost falling on the one hand and price rising on the other – becomes possible in fact only by increasing efficiency and improving the general firm's conduct and behavior habits on a daily basis – all together and continuously. This tendency – including all the dimensions and spheres of the organization – is known as the phenomenon of **operative effectiveness augmentation**; a trend that causes a clear gap relative to competitors in the market – an upper hand lead to be guarded above all else.

Such an advantage is achievable by observing the term **"product value"** from the previous paragraph in a commercial manner, a bit different and deeper than usual; applying surveillance through a prism of improved production – but with a marginal fiscal surplus, interwoven with attendant supply and service processes, significantly more qualitative (and therefore, understandably, pricier than similar products…). Alternatively, this may be accomplished by exacting standards regarding its technical merits and virtues as before (and much cheaper than what the opponents offer due to lower manufacturing costs compared to the past…). But the best method is apparently a mixture of these two giving rise to synergy. In other words, an amplification of the **operative efficiency**; meaning actually pushing the productivity limits (defined as the total of all management techniques, operational skills and the best acquired technologies and inputs existing at any given time within the organization…) higher and again untiringly – by doing analogous things better than rivals, but with the same rate of expenses approximately.

Howbeit, it must be internalized very well that the steps taken to ameliorate operational effectiveness are not enough by themselves, and surely cannot serve on their own as a substitute for strategy. First of all, because modern management techniques and innovative contemporary work technologies can be easily copied; better customer deals and upgraded client service can be simply imitated too. Secondly, all companies' benchmarks are nearly identical; consequently if the start level and the basic operational character of the organizations are becoming more and more similar, then firms by themselves turn out to be nearly equal. As everybody is outsourcing most of their marketing and sales tasks in order to achieve better economic efficiency and the progress they effect in quality, in production and delivery cycles, in creating partnerships with suppliers all over and in their execution policy – they are already one and the same. Thus everything appears to be generic.

This is, somewhat, akin to an athletic competition in which all runners are struggling towards getting to and tearing the finish ribbon in parallel lanes with nearly equal talent. The same is true in the business world: everybody is doing his best striving to the desired top. Thus an exhausting race is run, whose winner is far from pre-ordained – but the gap between him and the losers is certainly going to be minute. But if in the Olympic Games, athletes fight for whatever increment, be it the smallest possible, sometimes in a photo finish (a verdict which bestows on one eternal glory whereas the others are nearly forgotten after the medal ceremony…) – then the usual and monotonic economic struggle involves a kind of long and tedious war of attrition, proving in the end not to be worth the effort to cross the target line first; a fight definitely leading nowhere. This is because the point of reference is on the same scale for everyone, and all adversaries are equally capable, more or less. That is why their relative places ultimately do not change much, and the differences between their profits are more and more marginalized.

To wit: in the fiscal, industry and trade spheres – if one desires to position himself ahead of all his opponents – being OK is really not OK; it is absolutely not enough…

It becomes clear then that **improving operational efficiency** and technical excellence are the most important factors in truly attaining the **competitive advantage** over rivals in the field – but only so long as they are an inseparable part of a dictated and fully understandable policy, which is thoroughly backed by **deep and well-positioned strategic standpoints**, that are very hard to duplicate and fake. The whole difference is reflected, if so, in the management's worldview, in its tactical operational aspects and mainly in its human tendencies. And this is expressed in a proper and effective utilization of the corporation's collective emotional intelligence elements (as a basis for efficient organizational operations…) developed over time and being, in fact, the glue cementing the activities of all individuals, groups and the persons in charge; the unifying material that combines nicely their technological assignments – turning them into one crystallized, massive body, functioning with superior harmony, symbiosis and productivity.

And these specific capabilities and dexterities – which merge and ultimately unite people from different classes behind an unfailing, continuous communal target – are nearly impossible to imitate.

Economic Success – Achievement out of an Unconventional Orientation

Since the competitive advantage is based on enhancing productivity, namely, enlarging the gap as much as possible between "output" and "input" – it is imperative to do the very best in order to keep working on **widening that space**; a project which should never stop. Yet it is necessary to begin by understanding in details the meaning of the term and its preconditions. From a general cost-effective perception, a firm's productiveness can be described as the maximal capacity of the produce flow for a given cost. Its size will be influenced by the microeconomic factors within the organization as well as by the interaction with the external macroeconomic forces.

Within the tiny economic niche, productivity depends – as previously explicitly defined – on the most efficient management of the employees' skills and proficiency, on scientific implementation and on the best input applicable at the company's service; that is to say, the finest operation of the intellectual assets, material resources and existing infrastructure in the communal body for a maximal extraction of its manufactured goods. And as these activities approaches optimal capacity, so does the throughput.

Conversely, relating to the external commercial aspect at the corporation's borders, it is obvious that productivity depends upon an extensive range of factors which are not directly controlled by the firm and its workers, such as:

- ✓ The weight of exterior objective limitations and conditions on the manufacturing assets.

- ✓ The intensity of demand in local and international markets.
- ✓ The size of domestic and world-wide competitors.
- ✓ The influence rate of similar or supportive branches.

Actually, recognizing the fact that an authentic competitive edge over the adversaries is very hard to achieve, is meant to serve as a mental impetus for exploring all kinds of economic processes, and to be the source of unconventional business development in the organization's portfolio – micro as well as macro – based on simulations in the market dogma. These were born for giving birth to unusual and very interesting links of location and global networks for that one entity. Such an outlook points towards very certain preferences and virtues due to new occupations areas from one side, and integration of cosmopolitan work teams and varied technological discoveries from the other. And this is accomplished by distributing the operations to many and various sites – even beyond normal geographical borders – for the purposes of exploiting cheap input, reaching foreign markets, bypassing intentional limiting regulators and concurrently developing "revolutionary" products which were unviable until now. All of it in order just to be always one step ahead of the rest in this intellectual arms race...

Moreover, monetary, industry and trade success usually occurs when the organization's microeconomic considerations are derived from the macroeconomic view of the entire commercial arena and integrated within them. But a **genuine financial sweeping breakthrough** may crop up in the company only if a wise path can be found where its inner motives will lead to meaningful accomplishments – even when these are incompatible with the global policy evaluations around, sometimes contradicting them too – as long as these antitheses stem, of course, from real-pure business arguments (but never out of psychology – ignited by panic, euphoria or "herd phenomenon"

– causing crises, imaginary sometimes, in the financial markets, which may spread compellingly into the factual markets "realizing themselves"...).

Given, that one must swim in the river in order not be devoured; however the best way to do it is by not being passively swept by the current on the one hand, while also not to swim exactly against it on the other.

This is to say: unconventional paths alone lead to above-the-average success. Knowing that the market's conditions are not fixed and actually can be changed, pushes in fact towards the thought that instead of winning competitions already taking place in it, perhaps it is better to elevate the concrete contentious conditions one stage higher, hence presenting a totally original response to the commercial needs of the clientele. To wit, confronting the corporate's advantages directly with the other side's shortcomings may not be enough – as was demonstrated in the "offhand" winning dogma presented in one of the previous articles dealing with strategy. That's why it is also obligatory to turn the competitors' clear superiority into their largest inferiority. (And one of the best examples supporting the afore-said notion, not to be mentioned in the same breath, is the trick played by Col. Thomas Edward Lawrence – known as "Lawrence of Arabia" – during the Arab revolt against the Ottoman Empire in the years 1916 – 1918, as described in his book *The Seven Pillars of Wisdom*. Since the Turkish army ruled the Arab tribes utilizing an iron fist and incontestably, with a chain of fortresses being its major strength, Lawrence blew up any train he could reach, as well as large segments of the Hejaz Railway, which was the main artery connecting these strongholds. And at the same time when the Ottomans were preoccupied with safeguarding their supply lines, confined thus to their forts, especially in the El-Medina region – he left them to their own devices, bypassing them safely on the way to his destination...).

It is possible, therefore, definitely to achieve a considerable advantage over rivals by positioning novel stages and fresh, inventive competitive benchmarks. They should be done **with the flow of the market**, and only when running into a **very unique opportuninty** also, **against it**.

However, it is imperative to keep away from the "financial bubble" syndrome characterizing the Western market systems in the last two decades. Phenomena like blowing up the value of certain companies out of all reasonable proportion in the high-tech domain during the nineties of the previous century, or the "economic balloon" in the real estate field during the first eight years of the third millennium; scenarios which lead to far-reaching fiscal failures stemming mainly from negligence in risk rating, inattention to control processes, ignorance of very clear warnings, faulty monetary overseeing and unsuitable commercial research. These were tragedies occurring due to intentional misrepresentation of things selfishly motivated, far from being cost-effective – driven by crooked methods built ad-hoc to satisfy the lawless wishes of their inventors to make money out of thin air in the easiest and fastest manner.

And to sum up, business creativity is a much recommended issue. Conversely, it must be always remembered that when doing things successfully there would always be someone else to enjoy the glory – but upon failing, the price is usually paid by one alone. So, in order not to turn imaginative and inventive thinking into a predetermined chronic failure, it is truly preferred for all strong, determined and original thinkers to doubt their notion now and then, checking these and themselves each time anew.

The Business Development Division – "the Right Intelligence Lobe" of the Manager's Virtues Graph

The "business development" unit should be established exactly according to the view which supports the unconventionality expressed in the former paragraph. Essentially it combines a team of financial, technical and administrative people designated to assist the manager in initiating new, unusual and groundbreaking businesses – local and universal too – bringing these to the company while widening its organizational commercial span. And this "wisdom tooth" of the firm – as accustomed to think related to human beings – while growing and "positioning" itself reaches fresh maturity from one side, but suffers also painful adulthood from the other. Therefore it is absolutely required to allow this body the most diverse boundary conditions and widest rules of the game, supplying it with all the optimal means and maximum time necessary, to think in the best profit-making interest leading to the upmost prosperity and flourishing.

Conversely, this division is supposed, as an independent entity, to surround itself with an ever-flowing interactive circle bubbling and boiling 24/7 – sending the thinnest of tendrils toward any interesting business domain so as to be connected and up-to-date. All this is with the intention of pure, real and weighty content of assumptions and estimations in the center of the management's consideration system, in line to make the right decisions regarding everything concerning the economic-technical development of the organization, to sow the seeds of its growth engines.

The Wisdom of Specialization – being Engaged only in what is Best Understood

As was pointed out earlier, a corporation wisely operated is meant to concentrate its activities in its unique area of expertise, things in which it is most proficient; subjects comprising its professional-technological core competency. And all other concrete assignments not befitting its special skills and specific character ought to be outsourced. Taking such a step produces four very clear financial advantages:

- ✓ Diminishing significantly the fixed and variable expenses by saving "tuition fees": costs that would have accumulated when acquiring dexterities, capabilities and experimental technical means each time a new job is introduced; missions straying from the firm's main professionally specialized line of action.

- ✓ Fixed pricing projects, while promising to deliver in the required quality and the allotted time span (avoiding delay penalties…); a course allowing for accurate economical and operational planning from its inception.

- ✓ Best exploitation of the company's personnel, infrastructure, facilities and tools, due to dealing with known activities only within its main operational path.

- ✓ Shortening the overall duration of different work done under one roof, by performing similar assignments on identical components concerning different projects, all at the same time.

So in sum, it is truly advised to adhere consistently to the ancient Chinese proverb: "When in very deep doubt as to what to be occupied with, it is better to keep on doing what is best known…".

The Art of Business – Integration or Seclusion

The **optimal business art** is seeking and identifying opportunities for exceptionally attractive commercial applications outside the organization in order to nurture unconventional strategic cooperation. All this is intended to take responsibility over them to complete the manufacturing lines of a private product, or incredibly specific service processes assisted by other companies', or entities' technologies and goods; these are actually a practical expression of the term **business integration at its best**. This observation ostensibly contradicts the one described in the previous paragraph – but such activities, in fact, do not mean to highlight weaknesses, but to point out the clear advantages of each one separately with its own expertise. These attributes make it possible to extract compositions that only a few people may distinguish and classify regarding the genius synergic potential that would result from their construction and professional unity. Mergers can encourage technical attachments and administration arrays beautifully combined and supremely sophisticated, sure to win major economic achievements in the future; bodies that sometimes turn out to be totally different in managerial and scientific terms. However, by setting one collective goal for the entire entity and by drawing an operative interaction that fits well the new mutual framework – never before seen or conceived – it becomes possible to skyrocket, reaching summits of success much beyond the local business swamp where competitors wallow.

And this is, perhaps, the place to emphasize that the "Niche Companies," those who specialize in one specific domain – which raised a lot of interest among investors at the end of the 20th century, especially in the hi-tech fields – are over for good. These firms were much too technologically oriented and far less commercial. Moreover, it slowly became obvious that at the end of the day the winner would not necessarily be the one merely presenting the scientific ultimate development – but the one that would certainly bring the technical super-global solution, as well as the most economical one. Only he who would point to the highest added value bestowed on the customer compared to all others in the field, with the ability to solve complicated, varied and difficult problems – not just local, specific and limited issues – could flourish and prosper far above his competitors, even if they were huge conglomerates. And qualitative advance of this sort comes, normally, due to combining efforts and linking hands, amalgamating when possible some separate applications of different enterprises into one universal product, creating a business octopus. And processes like these indeed demand an "open mind" and a sober reading of the situation, as in sports: he who cannot win the championship with his current team alone buys the most outstanding talented available in the market.

Yet, on the other hand, it is forbidden to stop looking for special niches in the wider totality of the corporate's business maneuvering. Every now and then this can definitely be the right step, bringing finally the sought-for competitive edge. But it must never be the sole occupation of the whole establishment, just the cherry on top of the sundae of its diversified and varied operational portfolio.

And the most significant upheaval concerning business mergers of the type discussed here is internalizing that partnerships among entities are no longer, as in the past, the domain of creators alone. Today it is also the name of the game for strategic tycoon investors. Those who used to contend in struggles to the death prefer in the present to walk together, supporting as a team the companies chosen by them – not out of love for each other, but mainly to diminish the risk taken by every one of them individually.

The Business Vision – the Essence and Way of Persuasion

The business vision of a company is meant to demonstrate the future benefits to its owners, partners and employees: the advantage or profit (monetary or else…) to be created at the end of the day from what it regularly is engaged with; a compensation intended to persuade decision makers on the **need to invest in establishing an organization** (not yet existing…) **or in the economic utility of its continued operation and development**. The first case deals with enterprises "on paper", the second serves to present a commercial body whose management plans to enlarge, or one that for some reason does not yield its projected incomes. These two above processes are designated to raise money for implementation of construction and progress of ideas – or to materialize notions of how to pull the communal creating entity out of its unpleasant fiscal state.

To achieve this, it is good to be assisted by a general concept, meant to detail all strategic and tactical aspects of the present or considered money-making frame – in short, a **Business Plan**. This should resemble an all-encompassing and concise "complementary card" regarding the offer, brought before the top selected group's leadership or external investors, hoping for their assistance in financing, credit, partnership, purchasing and so on – and not to consign it, God forbid, to the garbage heap of History.

The role of such a model is to unfurl an up-to-date exhaustive map outlining the entire actual pattern – from the birth of the idea to the final balance sheets of the company at the finish line. Thus, it makes sense to attract attention to the character and quality of such a program, requiring (depending on of course which of the two cases above is discussed…) among other stuff, to be:

✓ Brief and easily readable; not overburdened by "tiring" details and "overblown" alarmist terms.

- ✓ Absorbable and simple to understand; straightforward and quick to scrutinize, annotate and conceptualize.
- ✓ Reliable and realistic; convincing beyond any shadow of doubt.
- ✓ Mirroring a clear and perceptible situation, based on an obvious and short summarizing analysis including:
  - The essence of the business, its history and that of its owners.
  - The offered product (qualities and functionality...) and the genuine need for such a thing.
  - The market ingredients (branch background, business climate, target clientele, possible competition, social milieu, commercial potential and the like ...).
  - Main milestones of the executing strategy.
  - Human resources plan (optional organogram, personnel, professional development, et cetera...).
  - Production methods (R&D, technological approaches and means, costs, timetable, outcome versus projection control, quality assurance and so on...).
  - Current financial state of affairs (current situation, required investment, equity sources, external fund-raising resources, estimated cash flow, and such...).
  - Marketing policy (advertising, sales outlines, techniques of penetration and distribution, forecasted demands and so forth...).
  - Risk evaluation.
  - The latent financial potential of the proposed program.
  - Practical profit outlook.
  - Policy and tactics for future growth.

In case the plan is displayed as a video-audio **presentation,** a written copy should be sent in advance to all future participants to serve them as preparatory background. Then it is recommended that in addition to the above-said, two more things should be added in its preparations:

1. A lead that should precede the encompassing document described so far: it is the **Executive Summary** which includes in a concise, most clear and simple numeric terms – and especially very convincingly – the following key issues:

    a. What is the demonstration talking about.

    b. Who is standing behind the proposition.

    c. The expected reward and its timing.

    d. Principle resolutions to be taken.

For most of those responsible, powerful, influential figures bother to read only this extracted synopsis.

2. On the other hand, it is essential to ensure that this short preview sent to potential attendees will include a full **back-up information outline** in a form of **very detailed and reliable appendixes and clarifications**. This in the event that someone among those decision-makers would like anyhow to delve more thoroughly into the proposal's logic and verify the written data before taking a real stand.

While executing the demo, it is strongly suggested to adopt some common rules for such a stand, as follows:

✓ It is necessary to evoke throughout the whole meeting a personal-touch atmosphere accompanied by a mood of intimacy between the presenter and his audience.

✓ In no case should a situation arise in which the conference would turn into a confrontation; a "brainstorming" sentiment must be bestowed upon all attendees in the room with the intention to weave a partnership amongst the entire crew, and actually welcome points offered by the listeners.

- ✓ It must be focused on solutions – not on the methodology which serves the groundwork of the research.
- ✓ It ought to expose practical ways as potential answers to all problems brought up; no unresolved topics should be left out. It is even appropriate to discuss conflicts in order to draw on the so-called opinions and experience of the participants, granting an obvious sense of openness to ideas and initiatives of any kind.
- ✓ It is very desirable to use attractive and easily understandable visual aids, since a picture is worth a thousand words.
- ✓ It is required to shorten the formal part.
- ✓ It is imperative to allow time for a wide dialogue, meaning the informal phase.
- ✓ It is recommended that professionals of all relevant fields concerned with the above data demonstrated be present at the show, in case some of the attendees wish to go into technical details in addition or for specific supplements.
- ✓ It has to be remembered: what works very well for those making decisions are the following cardinal issues, expressed in mere numerical values:
  - ⁕ The essence of the business strategy: how to turn a theoretical idea into real money.
  - ⁕ A commercial outline or recovery plan whose ingredients are: selling dearly, payments' collecting in advance and getting suppliers' credit.
  - ⁕ What should be the basic investment in fact.

- The financial potential of the offered opportunity.

- A practical demonstration of the daily routine expenditure regarding the funds to put in (use of pounds in a more accountancy language…).

- How fast will they recoup their initial capital.

- A "realistic" profit outlook for the next five years.

- Is the proposal the right thing to apply in order to "stay healthy" in the long term or is it just a passing episode.

And the most important concern: such a presentation should be methodically prepared in an extremely deep manner: superior knowledge and expertise related to the overall picture and the general goals, as well as familiarity in the very smallest details when required, must be exhibited all throughout this performance, since the way of this introduction might doom its whole destiny. It is forbidden to allow an hour of bad appearance – while deteriorating, for any reason, into "garbage talk at money time" – to ruin the hard work and tremendous effort already invested, causing those who can truly decide to rule and pass a verdict only by personal tendencies and a faulty momentary impression. Because this is analogous to **marketing the most vital brand of the entire organization**: the actual agreement on its establishment – or approval of its continuous existence in fact.

Therefore it is highly recommended that the people originating the ideas for the above-said demonstration certainly be those writing and correctly phrasing it; they are definitely allowed to seek help of external experts to identify defects if there are any but should be the ones to put the things on paper by themselves. This is because editing such an important document requires an unshakable proficiency in the material, one-hundred-percent commitment to its content (creativity at its best…) and – full involvement in everything occurring around the ideology – in order to have the ability to "tackle" any unexpected question raised by the audience. It is like angling with one's limbs as bait; unless he is alert, they will become fish food in no time...

Considerations of Organizational Financial Engineering – Things to Internalize and Adopt

Here are some extra subjects concerning organizational financial engineering, which may form and stabilize the totality of this strategy. These are issues derived from daily conduct and routine business activities, included here in writing because of their substantial influence on management considerations, while dictating the global policy regarding economic viability. And the sooner they are thought of and taken into account in due course, the better will be the company's financial outcome. Collaterally, the life of the man at the top will be much easier than if he is surprised by them later downstream.

Headquarters Staff – Thrifty or Wasteful

A manager needs a team of assistants – as long as its size is **not exaggerated**. Many organizations employ specialists in various fields as a squad of scholars – but not always because of professional concerns. Sometimes it's done to announce an image of sophistication and innovation in order to impress those being exposed to the firm he is in charge of. And occasionally – in the worst case – due to the obligation stemming from nepotism for all kind of relatives, cronies and lobbyists' factotums.

On the other hand, it must be understood that a good staff of aides, uniting above-the-average people of all activity domains within the corporate itself, fully engaged with its daily life and routine needs

– is actually the "council of sages" who may help the leading figure in all concerning the implementation of the operating policy in the present, stamping future strategies and serving him in bringing new businesses into the company. In most cases they are his private "junta" and absolutely loyal "secret members", forming the executive of the cumulative productive entity – in addition to their initial defined function, without any extra cost.

However, in a less expansive institute, there are other options. With an efficient and well-directed data management system, small to medium size enterprises can develop and operate like really huge ones, without erecting a fixed, bloated and expensive mechanism of headquarter personnel and offices.

If and when a decision is taken to establish such a supporting and assisting entity, it must be assured that the functionaries manning it are fully aware of **the five to eight central operational subjects**, standing at the top of the organization's priority list in accordance with the long-term work plans; those which are derived from the principal targets pointed out by the owners and management. Such a team needs to understand not only the precedence in these matters and agree with them, but also to know the areas where the firm would have to compromise with other domains and projects In order to materialize the business chosen to be first in line. And this exactly they must inculcate wisely and sensitively among their underlings and in the corporation as a whole – in order to assist the man in charge in fulfilling his task appropriately.

And here is probably the right place to abolish the wrong perception which has taken root among most salary payers with reference to the importance of good administrators in the headquarters. Even if it seems to them that jobholders not in direct and full contact with the extraction of the product or service, in its marketing and selling, are only costing money – not bringing in anything to the system –

experience teaches all that it is totally the opposite: these are the real operatives of the company, and they are the workhorses that take care of (among other things...):

- ✓ Coordinate all other operational bodies in the organization.
- ✓ Certify everything moving due to commercial reasons, in order to avoid unnecessary motion.
- ✓ Supervise purchasing processes and procedures.
- ✓ Maintain all aspects of the management and personnel service terms.
- ✓ Manage flying, driving, lodging of the firm's people and its guests.
- ✓ A thousand more seemingly trivial things, which no one wants to bother with – as they become their responsibility simply due to not knowing whom to address when it turns out to be essential to deal with them...

Thus it is clear that an administrator must be first and foremost a very professional individual, and only secondly a jack of all trades. And when he functions diligently and efficiently he prevents additionally much duplication, waste and expenditure; meaning, keeps from pointless cash spending. And **saving money is exactly as gaining capital**. For that reason, such people are very imperative for the system.

Stock – as a Financial Cause

Too much stock is a grave sin in the "thin management" dogma; in a way it is a lack of control and fluent data mechanism in the organization. From the economic standpoint it is a **redundant investment** and a **horrible waste**, since it is capital nailed to the factory's floor, unserviceable for any other target. In addition there is quite a risk in keeping it for too long: a sharp drop in the merchandise's market price from one side, or a regression of its worth due to amortization from the other – may cause retroactive loses (jobs to be performed at an original high cost, sold cheaper due to a reduction in their real value over time…). So it is obvious that there is a need for an actualization of the existing facts and figures in the system; allowing a diminution of raw-materials set aside in the stores – those not immediately required in high frequency for daily assignments. Then it becomes possible to define an estimate advising the exact rate of the reserves within the total current assets of the company, suitable for its character and nature of its activities; a lower limit warning sounding whenever a refreshment of the quantity is due.

That is to say: it points towards a transformation of high-cost material assets into comparatively cheap electronic and human communication channels, to wit: considerable savings in fixed expenses. However in order to avoid a real financial waste, a data system must be established required to always be reliable, constantly available, free-flowing and updated in real time; this demands a continuous monetary, technical and managerial Investment.

Then, this content becomes a precious resource at the service of the decision-makers.

By this approach it is possible to manage stock utilizing the "Just on Time" method, for example: ordering accurately what is instantly needed. This is one of the excellent means, for instance, to cut costs. However, such an attitude calls for superlative, responsible and most of all well-organized proficient warehouse-managers on the one hand – and reliable, dependable suppliers on the other; otherwise the loss will overcome the gain…

Finally, it must be remembered: when dealing with stock, besides looking at it as a fiscal burden on the books, it will appear also as a monetary asset. This is how to report it and that is the way it should be presented in the balance sheets. It is equivalent to "current coin" property, for it frequently becomes, in fact, circulating cash.

Treatments' Planning Ahead as a Profit Multiplier

Continuous **preventive maintenance** is economically a kind of "profit multiplier" for the organization. It keeps infrastructure, facilities, machines, instruments, apparatuses, devices and tools – hardware as well as software – always ready to ensure optimal services for the firm itself and the clientele too. Furthermore, such a treatment policy enables normal life permanently in the company – encompassing its entire operations. Without this kind of regularity, costs in all activity domains would be bloated. By the very fact that all types of work can be performed at the factory's premises and immediately, a double efficiency of non-waste is achieved: first – by avoiding the need to look for external alternatives in times of pressure to execute urgent assignments (and then the demanded prices for these substitutes skyrocket, somehow...); second – in saving precious time (equivalent to money...). Thus the gap between expenses and turnover may remain fixed, perhaps even widen. Daily care assuring full fitness of all means on the corporate's grounds is definitely tomorrow's price-earnings ratio.

But since it is unfeasible to promptly perceive the savings brought by maintenance activities to the firm's coffers – it seems clearly, on the contrary, a process costing money only. Hence this expenditure will always be among the first in line to be eliminated from the previously planned budget. This is a domain too often disdained (monetarily as well...) and in some cases passed over, not fulfilled as required and totally forgotten. That's because when everything runs properly it is unappreciated, until something breaks down seriously at the most inconvenient moment (how else, according to our acquaintance Murphy...) – totally stopping work and threatening binding schedules. Therefore it is the highest obligation of the manager to be strict about allocating all the financial resources intended for preventive maintenance (and its performance as dictated, of course...) **even in**

dire times when every penny counts. Or as the old British adage goes: "Prevention is ten times better than cure…"; much cheaper and definitely less pressing…

And to illustrate this, let us consider the following metaphor, told once by a father to his son convincing him of the importance of safeguarding bodily health, in order to avoid as much as possible unnecessary and sudden illnesses which may be mentally detrimental and very expensive. A person arrives at the dentist's office, suffering like hell, crying as someone who lost a beloved family member – tormented so that he is afraid of losing his mind. After putting him in the chair and thoroughly checking his mouth, the doctor immediately noticed that the man has been disgracefully neglecting his oral hygiene, so much that there remained no choice but pulling out the infected tooth. On feeling better, regaining his normal color, the patient asked about the fee. The dentist replied: "Give me just a quarter of what you were ready to pay when you walked into my clinic in the first place…".

Purchasing Power – Life with Inflation, Deflation and Stagflation

The cost of living is one of the engines accelerating the **devaluation of the currency**, causing exorbitant uncontrolled market prices; it is in fact one of the reasons for the creation of a very severe social problem (loosing the trust in business's processes between people…). Consequently, any present and future fiscal plans of the organization must take into account the subject of **financial escalation**.

And just as operating in an **inflationary commercial environment** (long-term cost increases…) must be known and internalized – it is obligatory, on the other hand, to learn and be well-prepared to subsist in **deflationary terms** (supply surplus of products or a lack of demand for them, causing a continuous deepening slowdown of growth…). And moreover: to absorb and inculcate the peculiar way of going on surviving during the worse possible case – dangerous, even fatal – when the above two are hybridized into **stagflation** (an "industry and trade recession" accompanied by inflation…). This is a much more awfully significant economical phenomenon than its well-known and really common afore-mentioned sisters are. An extreme serious pecuniary condition that disturbs to a great extent the regular operation of the market and its monetary system.

Online Training – Efficiency Improving and Employee Control Means

Employees' training should be included as a part of the infrastructure costs, since it is an explicit investment in building the dexterities of the accredited and expert might of the organization as one unit – and not only the instruction of the individuals within it. Conversely it is possible to cut these expenses rather substantially by online coaching. This unique and sophisticated teaching, tutoring and exercise method is more than worthwhile, because it allows a large number of people to participate together in classes intended to raise their professional level without leaving, for a single moment, their working seats. The gain is manifold: firstly, it is quite a considerable saving of cash and time (which is money too…). Secondly, it is possible to control, throughout the process, students' activities and learning effectiveness. What's more, this technique is especially a very useful one for global organizations spread all over the world – as it can be also applied to install doctrinal updates and detailed procedures immediately and currently for any member of staff anywhere, even in the remotest place on earth.

And if the topic is training and developing advanced expertise, in most cases those issues are equivalent to monetary bonuses and even beyond it. For instead of people being educated in managing their conduct and guided in performing their assignments – it is more profitable for them to acquire the knowledge of how to do it on their own; and so it is for the corporation...

Financial Accounting: a Standard Presentation of the Company's Performance (Trusted Measure of Management Quality ...)

There is a unified language – a kind of code shared by many accountants and economists, but not just by them: an array of symbols and indicators meant to create an equal pattern agreed by all to serve as a communication mean. This is a professional terminology, expressed at presenting the activities of all firms within the commercial world in numeric-monetary terms (depending, of course, on their character...) to their owners and managers, to the authorities and in quite a lot of cases also to the general public – through which it is possible to gather a rather concise concept of the quality of their conduct. This data is extracted in a homogeneous outline of periodic statements designated as **financial reports**, from whose analysis it is possible to elicit yardsticks known as **fiscal criteria**. That information attends, first of all, as a basis for calculating the change in the added value – the addition to worth – of any productive organization (assuming it functions principally as a limited company...) within a specific frame of time. Additionally this written economic breakdown helps spread, in a flash, the business performance of the communal establishment and its results offering a clear enough status description of its current pecuniary position.

Summaries of these examinations are made and distributed, normally, once every calendar year; however they can also be circulated as **interim tests** at a higher frequency when demanded (each quarter, for example...) as **trial balances**, introducing intermediate outcomes to obtain an existent situation intended for feedback and impression during the flow of operation. This is in order to take immediate corrective actions, whenever deviations are spotted which may prevent arriving at the targets marked in the beginning.

Moreover, this informative array well serves the superintendents of the collective framework – especially all owners of capital and stock standing behind it – protecting them from unsavory financial surprises. And these statements are written in a vocabulary meant to be understood also by a manager who is not too well-versed in economics, so there is no fear in delving into them until a full orientation is achieved. And to paraphrase Einstein's saying about research of the universe and its phenomena and effects, one may argue: "The most difficult thing to understand in accounting, is that it is actually rather easy to apprehend after getting used to apply it...".

Accounting to Monitor Activities as the Basis for General Information

The first step in permitting a correct and reliable preparation of the financial report is building a detailed and accurate database, a solid and credible infrastructure for all described therein. The main purpose of the following lines is to present a **financial recording technique**, designed for the man in charge too whose goal is one: to display before the top echelons of the organization succinctly and precisely all the essential information – and that which can be learnt from it – so that they will have a totality of the most important tools required to make operational decisions.

This is, actually, a sort of a managing-supportive bookkeeping procedures, based on a batch of relatively simple methods, aiming to collect, measure, record and classify – according to an agreed-upon standard (directed and approved by the local authorities…) – all data related to the income and expenditure moves due to the different activities in the company expressed in financial terms, in order to follow them:

- ✓ So that they can be examined, adapted and analyzed.
- ✓ To make it possible to fix a price suitable to the worth of the final product.
- ✓ To provide income from the sales thereof sufficient to allocate the right resources for the entire job.
- ✓ So its dynamic operation can continue without any problem.

And all this must exist while maintaining close and fluid control, assuring that what has been planned is indeed exactly that which is being carried out.

These monetary-managerial records are supposed, consequently, to enlighten **instantly** the executives' eyes with all the important parameters regarding the organization's commercial behavior. As mentioned already above, this information is meant to show the essence of these givens – especially what may be learnt and concluded from them – for the purpose of guiding the decision-makers as to the delineation of the firm's strategy: its current operating policy and future development paths. This is for one clear goal: **reducing costs and enlarging revenues** to achieve a **constant growth in profitability**. This procedure, designed in fact to continually compare yields to inputs in the communal productive entity, must certainly be reliable and available at all times.

In order to extract the most from processing the financial terms henceforth presented, two central leading motives should be adopted:

▸ **The Equation Principle**: comparing that which was actually achieved to what could theoretically have been attained. That is to say: examining the actions done while trying to identify possibly better alternatives in terms of a more frugal cost / benefit ratio – or a higher income for the same investment.

- **The Relevancy Principle**: using actual economic data having a direct influence time-wise on decision-making in the present and the way those rulings are made; matching these parameters, only the ones capable of contributing to each alternative considered to be performed in the future, to the authentic period of their execution (to wit: actuarially…), cancelling any other financial factor having no effect on the choice of options (whereas accumulated history in this case helps shaping forecasts – but definitely not designating them…).

The above-depicted fiscal documentation encompasses a very large quantitative and analytical variety of research methods and study techniques. Understanding the financial reports and the ways to utilize the wealth of information derived from them, places the manager in an excellent knowledge position, simply by putting at his service the right tools to identify and recognize today's situation of his organization and tomorrow's direction, due to the examination and analysis of the following:

✓ Financial controlling.

✓ Profitability exploring and measuring.

✓ Cost-cutting designing.

✓ Performance upgrading.

✓ Correct and realistic pricing.

✓ Choosing between purchasing or self-manufacturing.

✓ Product development.

✓ Fabrication capacity directing.

✓ Determining the market portfolio.

- ✓ Deciding on the sales and distribution patterns.
- ✓ Budget monitoring.
- ✓ Long-term activity planning.
- ✓ Estimating and outlining capital investment.

The domains, keys and cardinal parameters dealing with the pecuniary info gathering, documentation and tracking processes so far described – all for the purpose of laying on the table in front of the executive echelon the economic aspects as an accurate and up-to-date database – are as follows:

- ▸ **Accounting by capturing of:**
  - **Costs**: recording all different outlays of the organization, classifying them according to commercial behaviors following accepted rules: fixed, variable and gradated (those whose values move up and down only with considerable variations in the activity levels…).
  - **Overhead expenses**: pointing out all of those costs incurred in the previous paragraph not related to any specific assignments, but derived from the execution of the totality of the company's operation array; separating them from the rest of the expenditure to treat these independently and differently.
  - **Profit and loss centers**: presenting income and expenses by the diverse units within the system for the purpose of: identifying bottlenecks, ranking operations quality according to those responsible for them, defining authority and marking expectation from these at their top – and correct estimations of bonuses due.
- ▸ **Analysis born of:**
  - **Costs**: distinguishing between the characteristics of various

expenses by product or location (standard, marginal, differential, alternative and such...) for: quantifying, investigating and evaluating their weight on the entire framework's operation course so as to minimize the cost / benefit ratio in the process concerning the merchandise or output extraction.

- **Profit / turnover ratio**: computing net income rate of the total sales for the sake of:
  - Identifying junctions and parameters requiring increasing efficiency.
  - Forecasting financial results in cases of shake-ups and changes forced on some sales ingredients.
  - Realistic product pricing.
  - Quality management control so far and future direction.
- **Break-even point**: defining a business activity level in which all income equals the total outlay (as suggested in the present chapter's essay "The price – fixing without erring"...) in order to determine exactly the manufacturing stage when finally a profit will be realized.
- **Sales mixture**: setting the influence measure of a change in the variety and character of the produce on trade scope, in order to ascertain the optimal marketing output mix.
- **Diversity**: finding all detailed reasons for the difference between what actually happens and that which was budgeted in planning regarding costs, overhead, revenues and profits; plotting the correcting paths needed for execution.
- **Risk evaluation**: calculating the business success probability by estimating the chances of the basic ingredients being the foundation of the initial forecasts, to suddenly change unexpectedly (for example range of demand, computed inflation, rising or falling markets, unknown competitors, cash

flow, unpredicted costs, etc....) – and the size of the resulting losses due to those factors. All this is in monetary terms, but related to the same time framework.

- **Pricing trough the method of**:
  - **Absorption**: ascribing all costs – fixed or variable – from the start, via the totality of overhead, comprising all production itself and the administrative investments related to it, down to the sum of sales expenditures, advertising and transportation.

    To wit: re-evaluating the costs incurred per manufacture of one product unit, taking into account the worth of the raw-material stock purchased, the price of hauling it to the factory, the rate of real physical work invested in the fabrication line, "historical and present" payments surrounding the extraction process indirectly, and the total monetary charge of marketing and distribution until the merchandise reaches the consumer's hands.

  - **Marginal costs**: determining all expenses varying in direct relation to the scope of production: those caused by processes explicitly touching on product or service creation per se. This approach enables a thorough understanding of the factors actually influencing the desired outcome mix of goods, the question of whether "to purchase or do alone", realistic pricing, sales volume and finally, of course, profit level.

  - **The standard**: defining costs for the manufactured merchandize by a known standard at the outset. In such a manner it is possible to measure the system's efficiency by comparing genuine to theoretical designated expenditures – and not only to past performance, which might have been not at its best.

- **Budgeting:**
  - **Financial**: A planned allocation scheme of the organization's

resources in solely fiscal terms, intended to support one-by-one all of its predicted activities – assuming the future commercial operation perimeter to be at a more-or-less unchanging level.

- **Flexible**: as in the previous item, however taking into consideration the spectrum of maximal and minimal ranges that can emerge due to many different economical or else causes.

- **Zero based funding**: focusing on utilizing specific envisioned costs only – and not as a continuation of an average historical outflow allocation, or of the last expenses allowance.

- **Capital**: pointing at rates and locations of the investments, based on the corporate's revenues from its routine action and yields obtainable incomes dependent on the character of outlays.

▸ **Control:**

- **Budgetary**: comparing real to originally well-thought-out expenses.

- **Operative**: checking the correlation of actual to predicted performance in monetary terms.

Reporting Principles as a Basis of Language Comprehension

In order to obtain the best from the afore-mentioned financial reports and the data within them, each executive in the system must be familiar with at least the basic rules used as guidelines in preparing and building up these statements. The cardinal fiscal principles steering this economic analysis – and the process of making business decisions – are as follows:

✓ All facts concerning the organization's performance (expenses vs.

revenues...) assets, investors' demand to that property and profits and losses accrued due to their use, are weighed and expressed in pecuniary terms only. No numerical worth, whatsoever, is given to subjects such as personnel's quality, team spirit, originality of ideas and conceptual innovation (so called "Human Capital"...) which are hard to be measured by money alone.

- ✓ The company's equity (or owner's claims on the capital, in professional terminology...) equals its assets as a whole minus all its obligations.
- ✓ The firm's resources are represented in the afore-said reports in their actual costs; meaning their concrete purchasing charge at the time they were bought – not in their current price if offered today on the market. Therefore, in order to endow these detailed data with full authenticity, they must be shown at their present estimate. This can be done by:
  - Inflation-correlated accounting so as to match exhibited numeric evaluation according to their worth at the moment of delivering this economic statement, using capitalization and actuarial techniques.
  - Appling reasonable depreciation figures (as prescribed in the local legislation where the corporate's action takes place...) – articulating the stand that the financial value of assets is diminishing with time. This is because first of all, they are getting old – and secondly, those parts of them that are being utilized for carrying out the jobs are also worn out. In other words: the above devaluation of certain fixed means used for the system's activities, is intended to display the scattering mechanism of slices off the original purchase costs per dictated calendar periods – so that the company's capital does not decline and remains apparently whole (while these components, by the way, are exploited downstream as

well for getting benefits and gathering earnings due to their involvement in the production phase...). And on the other end it shouldn't be forgotten that from an economic point of view, procurement (or building...) of property is considered an expenditure – whereas its operation is concurrently in fact defined an outlay too.

- ✓ The organization is examined as a totally independent financial entity, living and existing businesswise and functioning correctly in the technical aspect; and this test is carried along a specified period. The meaning of such a reality is exposed by:
  - ❧ The idea that its assets are calculated on a par supposed to produce merchandise and introduce money – not in their worth if they were currently up for sale.
  - ❧ The fact that the monetary projecting events within it are accounted for in real time; to wit, when the services are supplied or used and create income – not when actual payments take place. In other words: adopting the perception that revenue is recognized as it is generated and costs are ascribed to the time of their causation – not when money actually changes hands. This means specifically that:
    - It is necessary to write down prepaid payments as well – even if they cover activities relate to a point beyond the submission of the final reports.
    - It is requisite to indicate expenses for services supplied within the present recording phase (even revenues from their utility, if such are expected...) despite the fact that actual charges for those costs (and the yields...) will be done for the next statement.
    - It is required to provide for financial expenditures in the informed accounts for the examined period even if these are outlays yet unpaid and no merchandise has been derived from them.

- ✓ There is a very high importance to stick to two more rules imperative for everybody, considering the manner in which to edit and serve the things above to their addressees:
  - ↳ The data gathering, arranging, classifying, writing and presenting should be unified and consistent throughout.
  - ↳ Those fiscal encompassing data sheets must be formulated with a strict severity tendency, namely: to include within them income and profits only when these actually occur; but on the other hand to ensure putting aside money in advance for any monetary obligation in the future.

Financial Reports – Analysis of Management Quality and Monitoring it

The manager should be acquainted with the main accounts' statements: their definitions, essence and the principal conclusions to be drawn from their analysis; the "balance sheet" and the "profit and loss description" are the major ones, the most important and instructive for of the organization's conduct and the eminence of its leadership.

- ▶ **Balance sheet**: a financial declaration of the corporation for a certain date, presenting its total assets on the one hand and its capital and obligation on the other. It is an objective status pictured in pecuniary terms suitable for a particular point in time only, based on an equation of the three cardinal ingredients mentioned above: **the value of all the company's assets always equals the sum of its total obligations plus equity** (sometimes denominated also as "owner capital"…); where the last one may be negative – meaning: in deficit.

    In the **assets** column are listed all cash and bank surplus, all money owed to the firm and not yet collected, raw materials and merchandise in its possession, ongoing work (the **currents** or **variable** components altering according to the business activities...) – as well as all movable properties installed permanently on the communal productive entity's premises (the **constants** or the **fixed** ones necessary to its continued operation...), all arrayed by their liquidity: from the immediate to the most deferred.

Conversely, in the **obligations** column appear all **up-to-date debts** due for payment by the company in the next twelve months, all its debtors (creditors, taxes, bank obligations, dividends etc...) plus **long term liabilities** which the business will settle after the period mentioned above (part of a long-standing loan to be paid in the next year, compensation reserves and so on...) listed by their maturity day, from near to far future.

Equity is actually the owners' net private investment in the corporate – the real money they bring from their personal sources (at its founding stage...) in addition to the sum of all financial assets within the establishment accumulated as reserves up to the reporting date (such as remaining profits, unpaid stock capital, premiums not paid, unshared dividends, reserved funds, surplus and the like...) and including long-term loans (taken for the initial construction and development...). The equity worth will increase with growing profits and decreases (or altogether disappears...) due to losses only. And if all the above gains are distributed as dividends to the shareholders, it will remain unchanged. Legally, this is the part of the balance value possessed actually by the investors, expressing in fact their ownership claim on the firm's assets.

There are two main criteria to be learnt instantly by analyzing the balance statement:

- **The organization's liquidity**: the amount of cash (or readily realized belongings...) in the company's custody to fulfill its short-term obligations; otherwise it might lose control over its properties.

- **The capital structure of the corporation**: the general sources and means by which the enterprise may fund its activities, equity vs. commitments to stockholders and external debtors; namely, the actual size of the **financial leverage**.

Further detailed explanations of the terms mentioned here are to be found in various paragraphs of the current chapter.

▶ **Profit and loss statement**: offering the status of revenue vs. expenditures; meaning the growth or decline of net assets (or an increase in the owners' claims, as cited sometimes in the professional jargon...). Practically, it is a tracking of the "current" deals in aggregate held by the concern in a defined timeframe. To wit: all the sums received for services performed and products sales (already terminated...) due to which the firm charged its customers; or any other income registered – compared with charges "on paper" – received by the organization for all of its outlays and costs, bound to the totality of its commercial operation in the afore-mentioned period. In other words, a detailing of all invoices (lawfully...) issued by the cumulative body to all its debtors on the one hand as against those received for its obligations on the other; not necessarily speaking of cash flow properly. Talking definitely about valuables, they add up to its net gains or losses for the said schedule.

Four types of earnings are distinguished in this report:

- Gross Profit: income from sales minus the total costs of goods sold.

- Operating profit: gross profit minus administrative expenses (directors' and managers' payroll, outside consultants and supervisors, office staff, depreciation, uncollectible account provisions and so on...), advertising, marketing, distribution of the produce (including wages for these involved in the last three activities...) and R&D.

- Profit before tax: operational profit plus yield on monetary investments (capital gains...) minus the cost of financing.
- Net profit: profit before tax minus taxes.

The present report allowing for a flash financial analysis is used, for this reason, as an indication of four key criteria in the cumulative productive association:

- Net efficiency.
- Financial stability.
- Economic sustainability enabling to go on dealing in the same field.
- Rate of expected capital allowing for future renewal and growth.

Consequently, this is the best review tool in any competitive business supplying the most authentic data, permitting decision-making concerning the improvement of the corporation's commercial performance.

▶ **Appropriation statement (or changes in equity)**: a notice expressing the management's intention relating to earnings made by the company on the one hand, and possible changes in the equity's structure on the other. By this declaration investors are checking the yield of their stocks compared with the financial value of alternative assets owned by the firm, similar at least in risk level, for a certain timeframe. In other words: examining the profit's size allocated to depositors – dividends – proportionally to the extent of the owner's reward from their equity and its using purposes; and this rate is simply shown by the account balance at the stage of the previous final report, plus – or minus – the net income or expenditure for the up to date coverage period. All of this – when a dissatisfaction among members of the public partners with these decisions – if appears so to happen – may cause sharp reactions such as shareholding sales, decline in their value, and finally loses to the business which will drive away other securities' buyers as well.

- **Cash flow statement**: mostly included in the previous report types. However, sometimes in special circumstances it is required separately (to expose future cash fluidity or to get an idea of fiscal liquidity dimensions and its periodicity, etcetera...). This is a current status picture from the coffer's resisted point of view of all revenue intakes and outgoing payments of the organization, given and settled really during a defined period – and the difference between them.

  To wit: genuine cash streams that entered in fact the firm's "pocket" or truly left it.

Normally, but not always, the financial information depicted up to now is accompanied by two additional sorts of reports, intended to somewhat assure its quality and correctness:

The first is the **board of directors' report**. Edited and submitted separately by the top executives, reviewing correspondingly and in addition to what was already put forward, all changes occurring in the commercial doings of the corporate and in its monetary results during the covered period. Such a money-wise description may very well shed light on significant aspects of the communal entity's business umbrella assisting in their understanding.

The second, the **auditor's report**, is being prepared by an external accountant and serves to reflect propriety of the information spread-out within the financial statements above-described, relating to the fiscal condition of the company, the results of its operation and trade movements, the changes in equity and its cash flow during the afore-said timetable (including a sample inquiry of evidence supporting the facts and numbers as written; in their content together with a general examination of the meaningful estimates derived from them by the directors and crown leading directors of the firm...). That is to say: demonstrating a reasonable degree of trust that those reports are not essentially misleading and are in conformity with accepted accounting rules and customary review standards.

Notwithstanding this, and importantly as well, very penetrating scrutiny should be dedicated to the clarification appendixes – the footnotes – of those statements; for the core and open bookkeeping part of these affidavits are sometimes rather secretive. Thus the elucidations at the end of the economic analyses detailed above greatly enhance the text – remembering, of course, that everything must be disclosed and fully committed to due diligence.

Conversely, however, it must never be forgotten that exposing all the information of the type described here is casting an immense light on the organization; fact-finding as a whole is brought before the general public, including the most "intimate" data and details of the business entity that should not always be out in the open and advertised for no reason to anyone.

So it is imperative to think solemnly and very deeply about what is going to be included in this kind of sensitive data, **when its contents are read and researched**, certainly before **making it known to all** (if and when a decision is taken to become a public concern, for example…) because these reports leave the communal productive body stark naked…

Initial Financial Criteria for Instant Economic Analysis

It is definitely possible to instantly elicit from the records appearing in those statements some metrics, yardsticks and fiscal ratios, permitting initial study and evaluation – accurate enough – regarding the organization's monetary position. The necessary technique for that is based on simple arithmetic: identifying pecuniary parameters which represent various operational domains and factors in the company, prone to exact quantification, in order to compare and find relations among them – as long as they are placed in the right column of the registered pages; and by such an analysis to expose, actually, tendencies influencing the firm's performance, changeable by taking some practical action to improve its final business outcome. However, these assessments do not replace a meticulous and exacting examination of essence, content and economic process, down to a single digit level in the collective institute's books when necessary by the **most dexterity and professional people in existence.**

These central criteria – some of which discuss the qualitative skill of the organization, while others point to the efficiency of its use – are calculated to yield only numeric information per se in conjunction with all of its major measurable action domains as listed hereunder (but not the sensory ones or those related to its intellectual property…):

- ✓ The company's net value.
- ✓ The owners' trust in their own business.
- ✓ The willingness of external entities (and the public…) to invest and risk their money in the firm.
- ✓ Cost.
- ✓ Performance.
- ✓ Breakeven point.
- ✓ Profitability.
- ✓ Liquidity.
- ✓ Equity structure.
- ✓ Productivity.

- ✓ Efficiency of stock deployment.
- ✓ Credit spectrum vs. collection frequency.

Financial Values – the Organization's "Identity Card"

The following idioms promptly expose the organization's character:

▸ **Company equity**: a figure which describes the corporate's worth at any given moment. This is a pure accounting term – a kind of superficial number actually, as defined in the equation depicted previously regarding the balance sheet: the difference between all assets and the entire obligations, but not to owners (namely to stock and debentures holders or any other entity in the world – provided it does not have any kind of proprietorship on the body's business…).

That is to say: in order to invest in the joint industrious enterprise or buy it, the equity would be computed as the total sum of all liquid and fixed assets in addition to the rest of its properties plus **reputation** – minus all short and long-term debts and obligations. Conversely, if the firm is about to be closed down – this is the aggregate remaining for the owners following the sale of its possessions according to their "last balance statement" (i.e.: realized rate…) and the disposal of all its liabilities.

As for reputation, it can be calculated, therefore, as the **company's value** minus its **assets' worth** at the date of its auction (or closure…); where the company's value is the "net profit" multiplied by its **price-to-earnings ratio**; while its net profit may relate either to the last twelve months or to an average of the most recent three years (if it is a more-or-less stable business; in case of a volatile one, a five-year sample must be employed and sometimes even more…).

And the price-to-earnings ratio (or sometimes called **price-to-**

book-value ratio...) is an accounting size, actually indicating the number of years needed to recoup the "initial investment": the amount paid to purchase it, for example, divided by the net profit as defined above (if it remains at the same level during the coming years...). It is possible in fact to "change" the price-earnings assessment by setting the clear gains to be drawn from the communal production body.

From the other side, there are those who view it as a typical fixed criterion common to each branch and field separately: a parameter expressing, due to experience, how many years of "economic vigor" are allotted to every business in a certain domain prior to a reduction in its profits – which can guide "beginners" when the estimates and data needed for the acquisition deal are not lucid enough.

And one more thing: for a public company listed on the stock exchange, the price-to-book-value ratio is computed by dividing its present worth by last year's net profits (or its current share price divided by the gains of that same stock during the indicated period...).

And in any case, when delving into the subject is necessary, it is strongly recommended to hire the most dedicated professionals for that topic.

▸ **The relation between the company's obligations of all types and the size of the owner's equity (invested in the first place...):** a simple quotient understood by its definition, being an imperative gauge which reveals in fact the owners' trust in their business – as well as the real risk and total responsibility they are willing to assume in the event of a commercial failure. The lower this decisive factor is, the more it shows the real financial coverage of the corporate, to wit; the actual fiscal backup that exists at hand. As it grows, it expresses the genuine readiness of investors – and it certainly matters who they are – to endanger some or all of their capital in times of bankruptcy and / or a forced sale of all its assets. In addition, it is highly recommended to examine the risk ratio, as below.

Financial Ratios – The "Report Card" of the Organization

The following parameters allows a quick, but rather encompassing, indication of the company's organization and the technical grade of the quality related to management conduct and leadership: the talent to motivate people, operational dexterities and genuine performance skills.

▶ **Cost ratios**: values presenting the size of all company's expenses in comparison with its total selling deals; the principal ones are:

- **Overhead-to-sales ratio**: the entire expenditure, not pertaining to a specific activity in the production process, divided by the totality of income from all trade transactions.
- **Functional cost ratios**: the aggregate of fabrication cost divided by the total accumulated sales revenue.

To exhibit the above second quotient in more details, it is necessary to replace the numerator with the following figures:
- Materials costs.
- Distribution and marketing costs.
- Administration costs.
- Wages costs.

And the like.

- **Cost per output unit**: the aggregate production outlays divided by the number of units manufactured.

From these rates one can learn in principle the percentage of the company's revenue in a whole which expenses represent – a key to determining its productivity.

Despite the lack of suggested concrete numerical worth for the last two criteria, it is recommended to try minimizing them as much as possible without compromising the **product's quality**: by reducing the amount of the raw materials from which it is extracted, the duration of fabrication processes and client supply services outlay. And concerning the first indicator in the above list, any case when the overhead share is less than twenty percent (20%) of the entire sales, is considered to be good (depending, of course, on the business's type and location and operation environment…).

- **Operational ratios**: values presenting the company's earnings compared to its selling deals; the most important are:
  - **Yield-to-sales ratio**: aggregate operational profit divided by income from produce outflow.
  - **Turnover-to-assets ratio**: total trade transactions' proceeds divided by all possessions.

  In order to detail the second, it is necessary to take into account the following components:
  - **Fixed assets** (or separately: real estate, construction, machinery, vehicles etc…).
  - **Current** (or **Variable**…) **assets** (or individually: stock, running projects, debtors and such…).

  These criteria demonstrate actually the economic viability of the product extraction; the flourishing rate of sales and in what measure they succeed in sticking to their level due to the demand boosted among consumers, by a correct marketing process and the fact of its continued perception as qualitative.

  As for the sizes suggested for these two indicators it is desirable to push them as high as possible depending on the business domain (this again, without reducing the quality of goods…). An eighty percent (80%) operational profit would be considered adequate in conventional technology industries, while in hi-tech toil and among artistic professions, "the sky is the limit".

- **Productivity ratios**: determining the output levels in the corporation and the added value entering its coffers compared to the employee numbers; and the central are:
  - **Added value per person ratio** (sometimes described also as **gross profit per person ratio**...): total income from selling deals minus their accumulated costs, divided by the total employees' numeral.
  - **Profit per worker ratio**: the sum of operational profit divided by the aggregate number of workers.

  And in the same manner it is doable to display the **sales or production ratio per employee**. From these rates, it is easy to learn the basic efficiency of personnel exploitation in the firm. These measures tend to lack recommended concrete numbers too. The wish is normally to augment them as much as possible, depending on the field and country discussed – but without "enslaving" the labor force individuals above their salaries or infringing on their social human rights, regressing to pre-Industrial Revolution times of mid-18th century England.

- **Profitability ratios**: values exhibiting the company's yields in relation to capital investment; the chief ones are:
  - **Yield to active capital ratio**: the whole operational profit divided by fixed plus variable assets, minus current obligations (sometimes professionally called **net assets**...).
  - **Yield to capital ratio**: the total revenues minus interest payments and dividends, before taxation, divided by owners' stock equity plus retained earnings and reserves in the treasury.

  These fractions can teach technically the measure by which the titleholders' or proprietors' and partners' investment is protected.

There are no explicit numbers in this case pointing to a huge success, for here – more than regarding any other criteria – the desirable standards depend on the field of occupation and the specific country in which it functions.

Additional Indicators – as a Complementary Gauge of Financial Management Efficiency

The parameters hereinafter display right away the efficiency measures of fiscal management within the organization: the commercial talent together with the control, collection and pecuniary mastery system's effectiveness – as well as the exploitation of economic resources to the extraction of monetary advantages.

- **Capital structure ratios**: values presenting the sum of loans taken by the company compared to the equity brought by its landlords:
  - **External capital to equity ratio** (or **financial leverage**): all cash borrowings and money drafted by securities, divided by the full wealth coming from the owners' pocket since the establishment of the firm.
  - **Debt to asset ratio**: total short and long-term fiscal liabilities divided by the quantity of fixed and current possessions.

As noted at the beginning of this sub-chapter, it is possible to instantly evaluate from these rates the weight of the proprietors' trust in their business on the one hand, and the credit given to it by the banks, external investors and the general public on the other; additionally, they also show the expected yield of initial deposit. For as financial leverage increases, questions arise concerning not only the communal productive entity's own monetary stability, but additional quandaries, as already described in detail in the previous pages of this section:

- First – concerning the proper management of the cash flow

due to expenses caused by financing costs (since interest must be paid and it never gets smaller...).
- Second – with regard to securing control of the firm; for in times of crisis, debtors outrank stockholders in the creditor hierarchy.

However, it must be understood – as brought up earlier – that a business not earning enough to cover its own expenses and support its owners "honorably" and continue developing in the future, is worthless.

▸ **Liquidity ratios**: revealing in aggregate the company's resources easily convertible into currency, compared to all its current obligations. The key ones are:

- **Current ratio** (or **working capital**): all present assets (in cash and readily realized...) divided by the total worth of existing obligations.

- **Acid-test ratio**: the sum of the current properties minus the stock component on hand divided by all up-to-date debts.

These fractions mainly point to the commercial entity's financial firmness, as far as its "available money in the coffers" to immediately fulfill its liabilities in order to survive.

Liquidity is therefore in most cases the first factor the lack of which may defeat corporations; for in the business world **cash is "king"**: hard to come by, to be jealously safeguarded when obtainable. Or as our petty shopkeeper ancestors in Eastern Europe used to say with biting irony – though involving quite a lot of consistent truth: "Without a coin nothing goes on; since only air and seawater are free commodities...".

In general these indices should not be under one (1) because it means that the organization is unable to pay its debts, in the short term and in the future. On the other hand a situation when they are above two (2) means a higher level of money or stock than needed – pointing likely to poor capital management. To wit, optimally they should be between one (1) and two (2); preferably closer to the upper limit.

- **Cash-flow planning ratios**: indicators representing the summation of customers owing to the company, or bad debts due to it not to be reimbursed anymore – compared to all sales. The main of which are:

  - **Debt-to-sales ratio**: the total of the outstanding balance due by customers divided by the turnover.

  - **Bad-debt-to-sales ratio**: the amount of all money owed by clients not to be collected divided by selling deals' revenue as a whole.

These rates let one elicit in fact two cardinal criteria, one being the company's average routine collection time of arrears, compared to its proclaimed credit. The other points to all clientele debts for merchandise or services supplied which for various reasons will never be paid.

And for the common quotients of the afore-depicted indices, they had better be as low as possible. However, regarding the first's size, in order to create a positive flow, it is desired that the corporate's remunerating terms be longer than the median period of gathering its outstanding debts. So much the more so, the greater the tenure it gets to forfeit its subcontractors, it means that this activity is being financed by third party's goods without remunerating any interest. Though, it must be remembered that a policy used to delay supplier compensation may become quite a high obstacle in time – for after a while no more merchants will be ready to deal with the firm, after finding out the regular credit levels and the payment conditions it seeks.

- **Stock relations**: values showing the amounts of raw material within the company in relation to its total sales, costs and current assets. The chief ones are:

- **Stock rotation ratio**: the sum of sales divided by the entire worth of goods and raw materials available for sale or use in the store.

- **Stock-current assets ratio**: the totality of the above-defined merchandise and provisions price divided by all current assets.

Based on these rates, it is easy to discover basically what part of the company's wealth is invested in its warehouses' contents on the one hand, and on the other what the **stock cycle** is: the time the corporation takes to refresh (or to "roll" as It is sometimes pronounced…) its entire store's variable inventory in a specified period (in most cases during one year…).

Like in some earlier connected subjects, there are no recommended numbers for those ratios to try and get to, because these criteria divulge information on a few indices contradicting each other quite a lot.

As for renewing the stock, the more frequent it is the better (depending, of course, on the specific field of occupation…). From the other side, a rapid exchange will be more costly for the business (double transportation, redundant shipment and such; expenditures which can be saved by diminishing the regularity of supplies…). A four (4) times per year occurrence is definitely a good indicator when dealing with conventional technology industries. Regarding the right raw material reserve size which the communal productive entity must be in possession of (recommending **stock levels** as a percentage out of all the company's current assets…) – a precise criterion is very difficult to determine. This, because as was already said, extraneous store's contents is a waste of money, risking loss – for a not-inconsiderate share of the firm's cash is "locked in" actually by this crude substance, jobs in progress and finished merchandise. On the other hand, a lower inventory than needed may cause delays in provision due to production impediments.

However, this index – combined with similar data from previous years gives a historical average, enhanced by current information and present updated forecasts (such as crop quantities and supply dates…) – is intended to fix **optimal quotas** (so to ensure a very precise holding of what is needed for production processes and a little more for unexpected cases…) from one side, and **minimum portions** (levels under which it is totally forbidden to fall, since they were calculated as an interim exact answer, enabling the continuity of work until the arrival of new raw materials of the same type…), from the other side. On reaching these "**red lines**" someone must immediately top off those delineated amounts of spare parts in order to prevent any disturbances to the ongoing flow of the merchandise extraction; all this is in order to provide the clientele the promised products on the exact days scheduled.

- **Financial risk ratios**: values indicating the company's total revenues compared to interest it has to pay to its debtors on the one hand, and dividends due to its shareholders on the other. The central ones are:
  - **Interest coverage ratio**: the entire earnings prior to capital gains and tax payments, divided by the rates of gross charge for borrowed money to be defrayed.
  - **Dividend coverage ratio**: all profits optional to be assigned for stockholders' bonus, divided by the actually sum decided to be paid.

In principle, these numbers show the probability of non-payment-obligations to external investors, as well as the financial benefit to the owners: the risk of a situation in which revenues fail to cope with bank loans first of all, preventing later dividend allocation to shareholders.

The recommended optimal values are:
- For interest coverage ratio, two (2) is satisfactory for a

business whose running conditions are usually stable. In a company characterized by highly fluctuating profits (due to seasonal reasons, changing fashion, developing product, unsteady demands and such…) the number may grow to three (3) or even four (4).

- As for securing owner dividends, an index of three (3) is considered healthy. In other words: an interval allowing for a situation in which the profits intended for distribution may diminish by a factor of three (3) – still permitting the allocation of payments into the shareholders' pockets – is a good enough safety factor.

In addition, using the **Instant Status Audit Formula (ISAF)** stated earlier in this chapter – which is considered as an acid test recipe signifying the **business's balance point** (where the activity level dictates a situation in which all revenues equal exactly all expenses, namely there are neither gain nor pain…) – provides a global picture of the firm's monetary standing: all-encompassing, detailed and correctly reflecting the reality in which it operates.

However, in all concerning the financial indices and criteria described so far, it is highly recommended never to forget that the ways of accounting are mysterious. One general declaration of the organization about so-called positive future intention is enough to "beautify" the numbers. Playing with numerical values allows for the moderation of influence, even the concealment, allegedly, of unwelcome results when introducing the corporate's performance to the main involved-absorbed parties. For example: one may offset losses with tax revenues and to erase profits with levies payments, as necessity calls for.

Still, it should not, Heaven forbid, be interpreted as license to change statements' results or bypass the accounting rules as a consequence!

Moreover, it must not be forgotten that the above estimates are meaningless unless equated to:

- ✓ Declared tomorrow's economic targets.
- ✓ Historical accumulated ratios at the same commercial body.
- ✓ Other businesses with an identical or similar occupation.
- ✓ Norms or standards built up over time in that specific field of operation.

And when on the brink of taking very serious decisions with reference to future activities of the communal establishment, it should be done very carefully while taking into account restrictions which may arise from the subsequent causes:

- ✓ That the above quotients are based on data from reports that are influenced by local policies (differing from one country to another…) and contain here and there some theoretical subjects, e.g.: depreciation appraisal, stock calculation etc.
- ✓ That financial accounts represent quantifiable fiscal parameters only but not teaching at all about other non-measurable ingredients such as: human capital, team morale, accustomed working ambiance and so on.
- ✓ That a ratio is a comparison of two givens; a numerator and a denominator. Therefore, first, it is not always possible to know the changing of which would result in a real improvement; second – and more dangerously – due to the desire to show a constant positive advance managers would do all in their powers to correct the numerical proportion so it would look better – instead of dealing with the essential issue in order to really ameliorate the situation.
- ✓ That among all values, criteria and pecuniary relations there is a reciprocity; none of them stands alone since they depend on each other. Thus all limitations – described up to now ought to

be internalized, and ever yone of these must be used as a starting point for a corrective action in its domain, for the purpose of bettering the total performance of the firm – especially its profits.

Consequently, in addition to the monetary information brought to the manager's attention, he should also adopt the following paraphrase of Galileo's dictum about the link between the bible and heaven's kingdom: "The language, the reports, the indices, the principles, the ratios, the indicators and the midterm economic study above are meant only to show the person exploring them the road to the final fiscal analysis – not how to do it...".

And this conclusive systemic breakdown should be derived from a very objective examination of the keys and facts above – laid out before whoever is required to make the ultimate decisions concerning the operation of the organization – but based only on his intelligence, skills, dexterities and feelings.

Proper Cash Management as a Cardinal Goal

One of the main objectives regarding **comprehension of the reports** so far described and all that implies for them – besides displaying a real and penetrating picture of the corporation's leadership quality – is to provide the man at the top with a solid foundation for a full economic analysis, so he can guide the body he runs in all which concerns its **cash management**. Actually, there is not always a link between the company's earnings and the amount of money it owns; it is perfectly possible for a firm to be very profitable while its coffers are empty (e.g.: due to past debt defrayments or advance payments to suppliers...). Such situations not only indicate, as already noted, the stability of the concern derived from the available capital in its possession or the ways it takes to route correctly its monetary liquidity – often they influence preponderantly the chances of its continuous existence.

Thus, each of the four reports above-elaborated and every ratio mentioned up to now has, in fact, to be investigated separately – while the conclusions regarding the financial situation of the examined company must be deduced from a synthesis of all these aspects together. And the very basic target of the vocation, denominated "cash management", is then to ensure that the capital flowing into the business will always be larger than the money leaving it. In other words, to see to it that the funds needed for the firm's proper running and its expansion – and the profits from its operation will always be available for the decision-makers' utilization:

- ✓ Without having to enslave too many own independent sources – such that can yield larger gains from alternative investments (on the one hand…).
- ✓ While Avoiding overreliance on external loans (on the other…).

This minimizes meaningfully the dangers emanating from:

- ✓ Reaching an "over-commerce" situation – a process resulting from growing too fast and making huge profits on paper – which still does not translate into a positive cash flow, so the coffers remain empty.
- ✓ Losing control of the company in hard times, when a financial liquidity crisis occurs and the banks not only refuse to give more credit, but forcefully demand their due (while receiving priority in debt payment, as the capital suppliers, over all other shareholders…).

Indeed, even the largest conglomerates would be wise to emulate small shopkeepers and many household heads are doing, since time immemorial: **saving for hard times**. Be "somewhat stingy", in so many words – in the good sense; or as goes the old saying whose origin is somewhat obscure: "It is desirable to put aside some white (or dry…) money for dark (or rainy…) days…". In years of plenty, it is worthy to think and prepare for a drought, if and when it may come. In professional terms, one must always establish and stabilize the stores in equity as a solid base for business activity in the future. For showery days, it seems, are much more common than the majority thinks…

Therefore it is clear beyond any doubt that this subject should be given the maximum particular attention, and quite an effort ought to be dedicated, alongside deep thinking and utmost care, to laying out the steps leading to the right current money movement's management within the organization. It must start with building up a suitable operational budget: a pecuniary layout which takes into account costs and capital gains, an accurate drawing of hard currency paths to the corporation and from it, tax payments, dividend distribution, chain of installments to external credit suppliers, various expenses for purchasing what is needed to run the firm – and all that derives from local legislation wherever its operation takes place; all of these as against a very realistic – deliberately rather a hard line estimation – stream of revenues. And here comes the exposition of the cash-flow report; studying it reveals the company's essence and its business character, an examination which allows deriving from its financial history an efficient capital-funneling plan in the future, while having a clear sight and a profound understanding of the general administration cardinal keys as offered hereby:

- ✓ Forecasting accurately money transactions within the system.
- ✓ Planning a correct and balanced cash flow in and out of the corporate.

- ✓ Following up on debts and those who are responsible for them.
- ✓ Controlling strictly credit ranges and overdraft durations.
- ✓ Minimizing funding costs as much as possible.
- ✓ Choosing the most promising investments.
- ✓ Identifying potential monetary risks as "over-commerce" and / or "stock surplus."
- ✓ Introducing flexibility in the operational scheme to fit into the current capital resources.

Thus, it is necessary to weave a supper-systematized, scheduled and very "well-oiled" mechanism, encompassing a great number of methodical processes, aiming to diminish constantly and in the best way ever all liquidity problems, to ensure tools for a very professional management – economically loyal and financially efficient – of all internal organizational capital activities inside and out.

Because the name of the game is usually "**cash**" – not always "profit" precisely; for the business has no better friend than Mr. "Ready Money"…

In summation

All in all there are basically two simple philosophies of the business world's daily "pecuniary engineering", which a priori make sense to guide crafting a complete strategy. The one: "revenues first, expenses later…"; and the other is its opposite: "in order to make money there is a need, before anything else in principal, to invest money…". These two only seemingly contradict, for their views do not refer at all to the same juncture of the organization's evolution. If the primary deals with the most initial steps of establishing the business, then the second applies to the stages when its feasibility has been already proven and it has started, as a result, rolling along by itself in practice. So the leader has to accurately estimate which point of development the body he is in charge of occupies; subsequently, it seems that **the combination of both – not misunderstanding and confusing them**, while giving an operational priority to the first notion, is probably the cautious, safe recipe, for success; especially when just starting out on the bumpy road.

At the end of the day, the only thing that really matters is **profits**, meaning in the private sector – a lot of **small change**, and in the public one – **benefit**: authority, advantage or some kind of compensation. In other words, the three "**Cs**": **Control** (as power…), **Credit** (as respect…) and **Cash** (whereas the last one, it must be remembered, is like saltwater: quenching thirst instantly with the first sip but immediately awakening a huge desire to drink more and more…).

November 1998

Marketing Strategy
or **"How"** to be the Best Seller

Preface

The first to express the thesis in which the central factor of the extracted harvest's scope in any market is the **demand** – and producers are those that adjust themselves to the consumers – was John Maynard Keynes, a British economist in the late 1930s. This scholar apparently understood already then what is clear today to any intelligent person involved in sales – that even the rarest and most revolutionarily manufactured merchandise will never reach shop shelves, without being requested. However, it took the standard-bearers of the free Western economy some more decades before this cardinal idiom was burnt into their cognition and adopted by them as the principal motto. Until then, and even for a long duration afterwards, the provision component was before all other elements; sowing the seeds; growing and harvesting came first – and only later clients were sought to do business with.

And from the time when Keynes' idea took root amongst all the international economists, **the world of advertising, promotion and publicizing has been constantly occupied in finding ways to maximize the quality of relationships between the business and its markets**. In practice this field is supposed to deal especially with the main following factors:

- ✓ Past, present and future clientele.
- ✓ Domestic and international suppliers.
- ✓ Competitors today and in the fullness of time.

- ✓ Opportunities and chances vs. risks.
- ✓ Methods of sales and distribution.
- ✓ Publicity of all kinds.
- ✓ The policies and regulations of the central regimes and local authorities.
- ✓ Planning, executing, following up, controlling and collecting feedback.

The front line of this occupation – perhaps more than any other sphere mentioned so far – **starts with management**. Because in its essence marketing emphasizes, in fact, the deep and real virtue standing behind the entire action of the organization, while diligently providing proof justifying its existence; that which emanates from the company's top directly – straight from its supreme leadership – whose involvement with it must be total.

And it is amazing how much schmoozing with the Chief Executive Officer (CEO) in this domain affects the customers.

The practical aspect of the marketing process is the **identification of a specific demand that "floats" in the air – trying to satisfy it, persuading clients that the answer exists in the offered product**. Its influence on the corporation's final target – attaining incessant profitability to go on growing – is very significant. This development of ideas builds the group's collective activity and effort chain: starting with spreading the notion, continuing by mediating the deal and transferring the merchandise, and concluding with sales as such – putting money at the end of the day in the firm's coffers.

That is why the art of advertising, promotion and publicizing is the name of the game.

The term *marketing* – this is not synonymous to salesmanship, which only complements the entire scenario in some cases – includes some very dominant characteristics of selling traits, for it is in essence a dream-vending dynamic. And a good promotion person's wisdom is to build a set of logical arguments while exhibiting his goods, that alongside his representative prowess and rhetorical skills, will convince the consumer via his personal logical channels (apparently…), his state of mind and on his own (so to speak…) – that there is something very useful in what he is about to buy. And the closer one gets to the last stage of the distribution chain, it is necessary for him to wear covers upon layers of elephant hide; never to be offended, even after some rejection, or become ashamed to return over and again. One must not avoid scheming – within common ethics of course – and aggressiveness with lots of tact, in order to achieve the desired goal: purchase of the product by the shopper.

The optimal "temptation" state of affairs is, therefore, the one that creates a situation where the client finally desires exactly that which the **company leads him to want** – and not what he thought initially he was longing for; this is the marketing process at its peak. And if it does not work, the following "persuasion" scenario is to be enhanced by so-called "business schizophrenia": fighting the inner feeling (as a salesman…) concerning something he himself really loves personally, trying to sense at the same time what "works" best for the potential buyer, while strengthening within him with plenty of words the belief that his choice (even if a hundred and eighty degrees different from what the vendor prefers…) is the most correct. And then if the customer is more satisfied with his purchase than what the promoter promised in praising the merchandise, the latter has done an outstanding job. The theoretical value of the product became something tangible and totally real, and its advantages are presented and advanced above and beyond what can be objectively proved. It is like selling the sizzle along with the steak…

The uniqueness of weaving this present strategy – unlike its predecessors – is embedded in two cardinal aspects:

The first: building up such a policy appropriately **minimizes meaningfully the risk factors** latent in an ever-changing and swaying market; because this doctrine as the last in the organizational planning umbrella necessitates especially – and perhaps more than everything described up to now – a thorough study of the operation field's status in particular and the entire market in general. This analysis is supposed to contain all diagnoses continually performed according to the other three strategies portrayed so far, in addition to the present one itself in order to position the competitive, challenging stand leading finally to an adoption of the company's business vision. And an error in the links of this chain, closing the circle of the commercial process, might give birth to a sad and disappointing conclusion of all the corporate's efforts to fulfill its tasks, bringing a loss instead of profit. But when the vital information is properly studied, regularly, understandably, fluently and freely in the firm's arteries and is cultivated for every occurrence concretely in real time – the economic uncertainty component shrinks to a minimum and decision-making becomes easier and more accurate.

And the second: experience teaches that an entity with **a successful marketing orientation widens the gap of the competitive advantage**, vis-à-vis its race in the arena of occupation; a stake that will grow with the amplification of superiority given to the quality of the advertising, promotion, distribution and sales scenarios, expressed in the two following central functioning perceptions:

- High sensitivity to the business climate; immediate internalization of the customer's tendencies; a realistic estimation of the adversaries' achievements in the domain and a weighted and concrete evaluation of the economical-social-political-technological variations in the operational environment.

- Adopting flexible, fast and unique ways of thought and reaction, permitting daily confrontations, rather simple and relatively cheap, with upheavals – even drastic ones – in the specific sphere of action.

The topics appearing until the end of this chapter contain the basic ingredients of the whole marketing policy. Thought they emerge as solitary written texts, like single pieces of information, separate ideas and segregated notions – this is only superficial. These are the central pillars around which the current strategy – the distinct subjects of the following articles (and short compositions…) – that may materialize and be consolidated into one comprehensive puzzle; and all of that after these essays have been researched, studied and understood as they deserve. Moreover, the reader must consider them not just as a advertising, promotion and publicizing expert – but from the point of view of the establishment's senior executive individual; the person in charge of its conduct and entire performance.

The Marketing Mix as the Central Being

As explained above, a marketing strategy is the totality of tools, instruments and means pointing out the company's public commitment to its active partners – employees, customers, sub-contractors, financial supporters and other service suppliers as one – concerning its future intentions in all fields of its operation. The gist is composed of the central components – the four "**Ps**": **Product**, **Price**, **Place**, **Promotion** – and their dictation to all those mentioned here, contributors also known by the term the *marketing mix*:

- **The product**: its shape and qualities (the material character…), the choice of the "father invention" on the fabrication line and the variety of alternative versions regarding manufactured-goods of the same type.

- **The price**: fixing the value for the client by cost-plus pricing, while conducting an accurate business relevant examination of how much the competitors ask similar merchandise.

And these two practical elements has already been widely discussed in the previous chapters dealing with the technological and financial strategies, but in addition to that a response is also required for the following pair of operative elements:

- **Distribution**: choosing the channels through which the produce would reach the consumers. In such an activity, a couple of totally different basic situations should be observed:

The one – in which all yield is sent to the markets via the usual manner and means, to be purchased there by occasional buyers of all types and strata.

The other – when some preferred goods are supplied personally to a very specific public targeted ahead of time, according to the best planning, using unique provision paths, by exclusive delivery methods and unusual schedules.

As may be understood, the difference between these two is embedded in the essence and power of the ties binding together the producer, the middleman and the customer, and obliging them one to the rest. And it is clear-cut that the originality and quality of the second element above described are exactly those that assure a competitive edge over all the adversaries. Thus there is no doubt of the great weight attributed by the various attitudes and ways chosen to spread the commodities, in comparison to all other components of the marketing mix. That is why in any process – whatever it may be – the subsequent factors must be seriously considered:

- The company – operation area, resources, technological skills.
- Product characteristics – perishable goods, seasonal and complex.

- Merchandise destination – domestic souks or abroad businesses.
- Target audience locality – geography and concentration.
- Present and future distribution paths – middlemen, wholesalers and retailers.
- Competitors' dynamics – identical points of sale, parallel routes and alternative means.

▶ **Sales promotion**: circulating information concerning the existence of the merchandise and ways to convince people to buy it. In other words: leading potential clientele on a path starting from complete ignorance of the encouraged object, taking no notice of it and transporting them in a considerate and well-planned manner through the following steps: getting to know the product, accepting, understanding, internalizing, having faith in it – and finally purchasing it. And the evolution must progress along the route as hereby:

- **Pinpointing the target audience**: locating and identifying by any means and method future potential consumers, who are established, able and willing to change their attitude to the offered commodity in particular and the company and its competitors in general.
- **Drafting the exposure message**: creating a "signal" made of a variety of words, images, sounds and musical notes – normally unique signifiers as well – all of which are destined to bring about one idea or more, until the product penetrates and burns itself into the consciousness of latent or hidden buyers and they are finally caught in the net. And such dispatches belong to two important categories:
    - The natural – tending to disseminate knowledge concerning the goal by a very systematic survey; one that treats and clarifies all desired points in a most organized and logical sequence.

- The convincing – that which uses the "notion" of planting attitude related to the purchase of the boosted item by the following acceptable steps: **Attention, Interest, Desire, Action (AIDA)**.

And it is definitely possible to combine both of them in order to achieve synergy...

- **Examining ways of connecting to the public**: using electronic or written media (national and local...), direct mailing of brochures and flyers, phone solicitation or personally selling from door to door – to wit: creating a massive advertising array of the product or service, meaning aggressive marketing in the positive sense of the word; exposing the saleable article to the awareness of as many potential clients and implicit communities of shoppers as possible (especially the target audience...) by all doable techniques and continuously – but tactfully – in order to generate a situation where more and more customers, passive so far, start exhibiting a tendency to buy it.

- **Result evaluation and planning due steps**: checking the effectiveness of the merchandise advertising and advancement upon people's consciousness, by thorough market research before and after displaying it and its qualities; observing the portion of change in the public's opinion relating to this particular product and the ensuing interest in its purchase as a consequence of the aforesaid; drawing conclusions from the analysis above to decide on the future activity pattern. Still, it must be remembered that it is rather difficult to find – certainly within a very short period – a direct and immediate link between the initial reputation imparted on the product and its actual scope of sales. So it is highly recommended that such a grand trade promotion deal will be a permanent campaign – not a single, one-act, commodity profile-raising.

Market Study: Basis of Advertising and Promotion Technique

The most important thing in business is being the frontrunner in the field of occupation. Assuming a total conviction in the quality of the manufactured goods or service offered by the company – then in order to be in front of the pack it is imperative to lead, first of all, in marketing technology. To achieve that, not only is falling asleep at one's post forbidden, but in addition the firm and all its partners involved in its performance must be kept constantly on their tiptoes. And management ought to adopt a combination of a long-term industry, trade and financial outlook on the one hand and the ability to make immediate commercial decisions quickly and with no hesitation when necessary, on the other. Consequently, the road starts with well thought-out strategic thinking, without rushed "drawings", for irresponsible haste may perpetuate the rule of natural chaos: unorganized, non-directional and unjustified. So it is just right to start with a meticulous and fundamental examination – market investigation – of all those main issues which comprise the advertising, promotion and publicizing policy, heel to toe.

The analysis depicted in the paragraph above depends on two basic ingredients around which the whole doctrine is built: **the product and its target audience**. Those cardinal components are normally the first step to start examining the totality of feasible ideas concerning the whole business, leading later on to a pair of elementary commercial keys: studying the field's de-facto data and deeply understanding it, and thoroughly exploring the forces coming into being due to these fixed and variable findings, including looking for and identifying as many "black swans" as possible.

The following are the chief facts and the relevant influencing rudiments related to any domain of vocation, having the power to dictate the present chapter's strategy:

- ✓ The suitability of the product to the sales environment vis-à-vis alternatives.

- ✓ Designated potential areas for possible deals and target audience – as against the local clientele's bargaining behavior.

- ✓ Prospective depth of the commercial arena – compared to the daring of new participants in the field and their financial robustness.

- ✓ Competitiveness – regarding the rivalry that may bubble from within.

- ✓ The efforts and means required to penetrate different market segments – compared to the negotiation abilities of suppliers and middlemen.

- ✓ Stages of the directed and arranged operating plan in respect to time – with reference to the sporadic necessity of alternative selling activities promotion processes and the ad-hoc demand for innovation and originality in the distribution channels.

This is therefore an ongoing testing of the business environment (sort of a "pest control"...) meant to exhibit the advantages against weaknesses in the right ratio, and to yield very realistic outlooks of opportunities versus risks. This requires tools and data-collecting methods in a systematic and organized-manner processing, recording and preparing for when they become necessary. It is a course of action that begins with fact-finding, continues with qualitative-analysis techniques and operations research, and ends with presenting totally "digested" information to be examined by the decision-makers before setting the marketing doctrine. This serves to minimize, as much as possible, the scope of the unknowns and uncertainties of operation, derived from an attitude advocating fast reaction to constantly fluctuating commercial moneymaking surroundings in order to be at their top instead of being dragged by its vicissitudes. Since **he who leads sets the pace** (that is why it is very easy to understand the difficulty in "breaking" the serves of a high-quality tennis rival...).

The vectors emanating from the above-said atmosphere reality are thus the main elements which may contribute to profitability, or alternatively cause losses. And the first organization to find their most efficient use – while flowing with them to diminish the effects of continuous performance variations – will gain, as a matter of course, a meaningful competitive advantage over the other players in the field – and present, no doubt, financial achievements far above the average of all sundry opponents struggling in the domain. Because a firm must not **take its place in the market for granted**; it should **constantly examine, analyze and estimate its situation** in a consistent and incessant routine – acting accordingly; for standing water gets quickly filled with algae…

However it is imperative to remember the existence of preferred professional methodologies to conduct the afore-mentioned research. Since the data to be unearthed from such seeking and study is of extreme importance to the corporation concerning the decision process for its global strategy; and it is highly recommended to use in general very skilled and dexterous teams of experts in that territory, so that they can perform their work fully, efficiently and ceaselessly.

The Organization in Relation to its Operating Environment – a Coordinated Segmented Strategy

Now, when the working zone is somehow familiar, the rules of the game are quite clear and the characteristics of the opponents facing the company are sufficiently known – it is imperative to learn to accurately coordinate its real abilities and perform to the best of its capacity in this area. This in order to determine the intermediate goals and the final targets of the corporation. Such a ritual of business identification and concrete potential examination of what is latent in the firm in comparison to the global conditions surrounding it must be repeated with fixed regularity; for woe to he who falls asleep behind the wheel on a traffic-congested road...

For that reason, the one at the top must uphold an intra-organizational dialogue and keep asking himself day and night the four basic questions below, in line to find the real-optimal balance above-described. Simultaneously, he orders a painstaking market research before making any operational verdicts, as he must explicitly dictate the survey types and observation mode, regarding the professionalism of the technical and administrative behavior of the communal body he has to guide, for the purpose of truthfully answering the following queries:

- ✓ Where is the communal productive body currently standing?
- ✓ What is its destination?
- ✓ How is it going to get there?
- ✓ And who ascertains that it has attained its ends?

Replying truthfully to these four central questions requires soundly analyzing that which many economists call the "three **Cs**": acute, relevant and specific aspects of significant importance in fixing the marketing achievements required as a part of the organization's general strategy: each **Company** ought to reexamine itself every morning anew most objectively, regarding its pros and cons, inferred in accordance with the variety of daily possibilities and unique opportunities presented to it by the **Customers** – compared to the abilities of its **Competitors** in the arena to succeed in positioning their goods as adequate response to the innovative products and services it is capable of delivering.

This is a sort of a triangle whose sides are all dynamic vectors and therefore its angles, as well as its area, are constantly changing, transformations occurring due to trial and error processes intended to find the exclusive combination defining those chosen segments from among the variety of commercial events in the field of activity fully compatible with the corporation's strengths while neutralizing its weaknesses. And when the aforesaid market slices become evident it is necessary to focus – rigorously and patiently preparing a puzzle – all establishment's resources and collective attention in these directions that reveal the best chances for business success (just like a carpenter's joint, where the projection of one part supremely integrates with the recess of the other and vice versa...).

There is no doubt that a marketing strategy built up to give a particularly direct answer to these unique fronts, fitting completely the specific outcome – driven by an optimal combination of the organization's product essence facing the demand conditions for the yield and its absorption by the clientele – is preferable to a decision pushing towards a sweeping multi-channel operation, spreading over many disciplines in the arena of occupation, outside the definite professional specialization domain of the company. Such a setting guarantees a high level of success. Only a coherent policy, well-matched to the sectors in which the firm enjoys a high probability to excel in comparison with others in the field, will result at the end of the day in a competitive advantage.

The Customer as the Pivot around which Everything Rotates

The customer is the central pin for and around whom the present strategy is woven. Therefore it is imperative to concentrate all of the corporate's employees on **solving his problems** – not those "interesting" or acute as far as they are concerned; because the real standard of the demands is set by the consumer – not the supplier. That is why the **clientele's satisfaction** is any business's first priority. And the target which must be shared by all workers in the organization is to maximize the number of returning shoppers; to reach as many potential buyers as possible, joining them to the circle of permanent frequent re-visiting audience. And the most significant accomplishment is that people, on getting to know the product or service of the firm, become its "external advocates" – **"aggressively" loyal followers and supporters**. Not only they do not purchase anywhere else, but they warmly praise the company and become its **most effective sales force**. And they are finally the real "fertilizer" with which – perhaps more than any other factor – the system grows continually.

In order to win such zealous allies it is essential to fulfill all their expectations for special treatment; handling they consider themselves deserving as fiercely faithful customers. Simultaneously, two very basic conditions must be met:

- **Accuracy**: absolute diligence in gratifying their demands at any time, whatever they feel entitled to.
- **Availability**: allowing them quick and direct accessibility for services.

The above are the minimal stipulations to avoid clientele's displeasure, but definitely not enough. And since they are common – for any business tries to treat its devoted regulars in this manner – they do not contain the ingredients promising the growth of a clear competitive edge. However, any commercial entity that fails to satisfy even those would soon wither and totally disappear.

Nevertheless, for the purpose of turning random buyers into fanatical-constant consumers it is necessary, in addition to the two previous attributes, to conquer their hearts by planting in them the taste of:

- **Partnership**: full attention at all times to their relevant wishes, giving the impression of being on the same side of the barricade, bestowing a feeling that they, in fact, are part of the system's performance.
- **Consultation**: teaching them to carry out some of the firm's activities and being ready to offer help whenever they encounter problems.

These are the upper layers of the reciprocal relationships with the clientele, and their constant implementation would signify the completion of the journey's final leg to turn vacillating purchasers into committed patrons, becoming "keen campaigners" above and beyond.

And let it be said here and now: all along this current article the term *client* refers to any consumer with whom the company has a long period of business relationship, as well as any random buyer. For there is no doubt that from what is written from now on, it is always possible to deduce from one customer type to another and find those points, or some of them, which match this kind or that sort at all times.

Despite the above it should be remembered that **decent treatment of the patient is not a substitute for the right diagnosis.** Unawareness and faulty analysis of the client's character, needs, intentions and real wishes – notwithstanding honest and pleasant service – may push him to cross eventually the lines to the competitors on the other side of the street, as soon as he is perceived to be getting there even a little bit more. So the essential wisdom is to find the way of **"touching" the customer in real time, frequently,** and using intensive care especially tailored **for his personality**.

The views and commands appearing below sum up in the best manner, perhaps, the central outlook concerning everything in conjunction with establishing a relationship with the clientele. Since the marketing process does not end with selling the product – which is in fact a kind of "contract-signing" phase with the consumer for the longest duration possible – but actually starts with it. The true quality of this tie, examined daily, starting with initial service through the fulfillment of the entire sale agreement's details (something like an unwritten, so to speak, "supplier-customer covenant"…) and finishes with the provision of the final merchandise, finds expression in the trade continuity measurement between both sides – in short: does the buyer come back? And in order to bestow a practical-realistic shade to the thing discussed here, it is necessary to take into account that in the **magnets' business "playing field", the relevant information dealing with commercial profitability and proficiency is passed, nearly always, by word of mouth.** For that reason the real important patron community is formed as in a social club: a pal brings a buddy…

This is exactly the reason why the following issues referring to the **client** must be internalized:

- ✓ That he is the most important visitor to the company's premises, and should be given full attention, assigned the best service at every meeting and offered the respect as if he is the one and only individual whom the firm's success depends on.

- ✓ That it is forbidden to let him feel as if he is a stranger who has no links to the business. On the contrary, he should be treated as an inseparable part of it.

- ✓ That a strong sentiment ought to be implanted within him in order to lead to the sense he is associated with and being consulted during the entire planning, development and fabricating processes concerning the goods being manufactured for his use. This is the way to inspire an atmosphere of openness and unity giving birth to a positive involvement from him, namely: a totally clear inclination toward his real wishes, a full attachment to the product-creation procedures and fertile, honest feedback regarding the final item.

- ✓ That it is better to share with him all problems arising while advancing with the extraction course of the subject intended for his use (or existing already in the given outcome...) in the most overt and real manner – and not create a situation where he may expose things that somebody is trying, prima facie, to hide from him.

- ✓ That it is recommended to protect fanatically all desires he has with regard to what is being done for him – even if they contradict the corporate's interests related to this issue – since the meaning of such a tendency is replacing intra-organizational contentment, and perhaps some achievements for the business in the short term, with a grain of tranquility derived from the results concerning the merchandise's characteristics for the rest of its life cycle (just because its fabrication path perfectly fits the customer's requirements, who normally knows best what his requirements are...).

- ✓ That it is strongly suggested to support his arguments whenever disputes arise between him and the company's sub-contractors as to the manufactured goods meant for him, since the firm itself is actually considered as his hired solicitor in such a case.

- ✓ That his technical and economic wishes must become the targets directing all those taking part in the work for him.

- ✓ That it is more than right to make him proud of the end result – in the same high spirits as a patron, deeming himself among those who invented, gave birth to and built it from scratch.

And the most important thing is to generate an atmosphere of total faith between the client and the provider, while transmitting it loudly and explicitly; that is to say: impregnable reliability of the producer, keeping the vendor's integrity. Since in the first credibility crisis which may erupt, the lie (or something sounding like one…) can travel half the world before the truth can put its pants on. And if one consumer loses his confidence in the salesman he is dealing with, it becomes the perfect recipe for doubts and fears amongst many other of his colleagues who might follow in his footsteps.

The nature of the marketer's work resembles a hunter in the forest who is shooting at any moving object, until finally one of his bullets hits randomly some juicy game which falls directly at his feet. Even if the image sounds unflattering (especially since the buyer is presented as a victim of some sort…) and aggressive, it contains a lot of pure business truth in it. For finally proper, wholehearted advertising, promotion and sales personnel are expected to be allegorically ready to attack "like a shark that senses blood in the water" every fragmentary chance of profit – if by the end of the day his belly may be swollen by "devouring" a few more customers. And contrary to the opinions of the most extreme bleeding-heart liberals, considering themselves to be the world's conscience (even believing that their shit too smells like perfume…) "In war – behave like in war." Undoubtedly, survival combat in the commercial universe may be compared to the bitterest struggles of "to be or not to be" (with one sharp reservation: these at least are conducted by the jungle rules: preying only to stay alive – unlike the codes guiding some organized criminal gangs according to which life has no value – and enacting the virtue of personal cleanliness, as obliged by the most common inner morality and public hygiene ruling the activity districts, and what's more important: not even a single genuine physical casualty...). Thus it is totally forbidden to give up any meeting opportunity with a new shopper of any type that pops up on the road – even if he seems small and the poorest of all paupers; because it is never known which one of them may become in the fullness of time the goose that lays the golden egg from the fairy tales...

Yet, the next two phenomena should be prevented at all costs:

The first and the more common is the reflection of veteran and loyal clients in favor of recruiting new regulars (and it does not matter whether they be chain or boutique-owners, agents or regular random people; even if middlemen market the product, the business name will always be emblazoned and looked upon as responsible for anything which happens to it...). In the beginning huge mental, physical and financial efforts are invested in any consumer, hoping to win so much as the smallest deal; and after he develops a positive attitude towards the company, becoming a captive of its goods and services to the point of "aggressive loyalty", and his relations with the firm turn to be somewhat "intimate", he feels suddenly deserted in spite. All of this is because the organization starts casting all its burden on chasing new shoppers (exactly like an apparent and loyal suitor being dumped...). Then he merely rises and leaves, being lost forever. And no special plans, stimuli or benefits can bring him back, for it is much more difficult to restore a disappointed customer's confidence than gaining the heart of one whose acquaintance has just been made. And the real danger is that all new sharp-eyed buyers will understand the matter very fast, signaling to them their future fate when regarded as obvious. And from this it is imperative to beware as of fire that quickly spreads all over the forest...

The second and less conventional case is the reality of one "huge" client (or some purchasers joining forces together...) allowing him (or this afore-said group...) full control of the firm's prices: a monopsony, meaning a situation when the company depends on a small number of large patrons – instead of building itself on a wide and diverse spectrum of many medium and small-size consumers. This is a kind of a "shoppers' semi-monopoly" which may cause a constellation where a "desertion" of one of them can considerably influence the organization's revenues, a very dangerous economic scenario for nearly all of the communal productive entities.

And in summation it must be understood: no corporation has the "right" over the customer's money, while he in return is precisely the one to determine if the business will survive. Moreover, from any competition among suppliers the buyer expects only to win commercially. Therefore it is obligatory to do everything possible – above and beyond – to win each and every consumer. And even if the most common cliché among the majority of the sellers around the world – "the client is always right..." – is far from being absolutely true as a matter of fact (for often he is annoying and sometimes irritating as well...) it is necessary to be sophisticated enough to let him sense at all times that he is actually right: only for the purpose of making him feel relaxed, satisfied and respected enough so that the deal will materialize just in the way the firm plans to.

The Art of Marketing: Building Emotional and Brand Identity

Accumulating wealth in a system based on private property and **free enterprise** in a capitalist regime is the best industry and trade method the world has ever seen (or perhaps the least bad...). This, because it is established (theoretically...) with an unconstrained business environment, such that the answers for its fundamental social-financial problems are presented by the demand and offer forces only (that is why it is also called the "free-market economy"...); or by that which Adam Smith called metaphorically "the hidden hand": a mechanism powered, in fact, by the enlightened self-interest of the human being, resisting an external involvement or interference of the government in the prices and commercial agenda (also known in French by the term "Laissez-Faire" – meaning: Let [people] Do [as they choose]...).

The outstanding advantage of this materialistic behavior is encouraging working as hard as possible, since everyone is compensated corresponding to the effort he invests: the really industrious receive their due, and their offices and factories turns from being conventional and boring into an invigorating and challenging post of the highest degree. Following this modus operandi (or maybe modus vivendi...) the system above generates the most important thing: the genuine locomotives pushing towards huge business growth; because facing "fresh" targets positioned each time anew becomes, as a psychological key, the main engine of the consuming economy which moves and spins the modern world's wealth and prosperity existence (while in the meantime creating more jobs and diminishing unemployment...).

This above-depicted provident approach is so common among all Western states that communal criteria were set for it to examine and classify the freedom index of industrial, trade and monetary processes and happenings within them, published internationally from time to time. But it should be remembered that the real value of this system must be inspected meticulously in light of two central subjects in every financial framework:

The first: the aforementioned kind of creative concept should not contradict the actualization of the welfare-state policies toward those in need. And this as Bill Gates, former Microsoft CEO, said: "I still believe that capitalism is the best economic regime; however, I am certainly disappointed by the fact that advances in technology, health programs and education serve the rich, bypassing the poor...".

In other words, the material outcomes from this way of operating / living are not properly channeled and mainly used privately, since the number of inhabitants on the gobble occupying the lowest level of income is much higher than those at the top – and the gap keeps on growing. Conversely, it is more than clear that this is the only format to seek the appropriate solution for this deepening chasm: spreading solid safety nets under the disadvantaged strata at the right place and time on the one hand, while on the other allowing the entire market powers to be fully expressed without any influence by factors having nothing to do with proper commercial and fiscal incentives. Thus, it is necessary to find the best way to live with those two, applying them not only without a real conflict, but within a fertile combination which may even lead to synergy. Meaning, to behave according to new thinking, another type of capitalism and its implementation, reformed and much more democratic ("by the people and for the people…"); one displaying a none-too-small grain of socialism (oxymoronic as it might sound…) and a rather strong cooperative motif, a mode that does not presuppose the superiority of free commercial zones of operation and their power as the sole monetary worldview while being less sure of itself and its endless profitability…

And the second: it should always be remembered that the line between an "open" and a "wild" market might be very thin, if the government does not stabilize the economy when really needed. Therefore the most important contribution of the central authorities to the industry-trade-fiscal way of rolling (in addition to what was said in the introduction to the chapter dealing with financial strategy…) is perhaps in utilizing a correct and wise business practice: by preventing pecuniary doctrine anarchy and monetary lawlessness due to an obsessive, brutal, unrestrained, destructive, corrosive, irresponsible chase after possessions, lacking any acceptable commercial humanity – at time verging on the criminal – in which the only important thing shoving money into one's pockets; in curbing peddlers' huckstering frenzy and cuffing Smith's hidden hand by nationalizing industries, sometimes with regulations wisely operating, when they are clean of irrelevant political considerations and executive intrigue manipulating the "corporate bazaar" (averting cartels, monopolies, monopsonies, financial bubbles and so on...); by spotting those who may cause a fiscal holocaust for the entire community, treating them mercilessly and making sure the ones who have already sinned against the public pay back at least a part of what they stole from it. All this must be out of the full understanding that the market is sometimes unable to solve by itself all crises it actually creates – and that it is forbidden to believe blindly in the unique capabilities of its powers to balance themselves. In short: it is impossible to run a pure economy unless assisted by a controlling, supervising, ordering and supporting political system, able to punish the outlaws trying to misuse and abuse it.

However, if it is still desired to maintain the business challenge and interest as "growth generators" alongside reasonable freedom and decency in market habits and conduct. Moreover, to enable commercial-fiscal genuine flourishing and minimizing artificial boundaries, it should also be recognized that such an involvement of the central authorities – even when mobilized to save the burning house – must be limited for a period of time and restricted in the ability to take control of private conglomerates and communal entities. This is because, at the end of the day, it must be internalized that governments are meant to lead the market and in no case be its owner. They would better find ways to fix the broken parts in a free-property and enterprise economic regime (including a powerful set of quality public services and their assimilation, which help a lot and incontestably benefit in widening the base of the aforementioned booming engines...) instead of changing the whole system. In other words: it is preferable that they push, in fact, towards the formation of a much more enlightened, shrewd and mainly sober sort of capitalism...

One of the powers mentioned above is driven by the real competition over the client's heart – especially his pocket (to be more specific…). For it is worth recalling that despite the classical Keynesian theory, the **Offer** motif has also a more-than-negligible influence over the fluctuations of the economic equilibrium points in the commercial operating arena. Consequently, the most important challenge facing any company is the creation of a **brand identity** for its goods. And this is actually the foundation of the organization's **marketing art**, a significant saying intended to reflect its business strategy while transmitting to all its partners and customers a promised value. If the firm's yield is not a trademark, it would be considered a commodity and its success would depend on the price collectable for it; and in this case, the cheaper one wins uncompromisingly.

The departure point from which to build up the brand identity is first of all a presentation of a concise and reliable image of all the product's characteristics; something simple of necessity that can be easily integrated into the listeners' comfort zone, even if he is one unversed in the common technical branches. These depicted features must be emotionless relevant values, so-called objective, understandable and measurable without any difficulty. And it is recommended not to load the client with overly detailed redundant data, to stick to reality in describing the merchandise's merits, to estimate realistically the timetable for its fabrication and to avoid exaggerating anything. The worst damage in marketing is false promises, presenting the marketer as someone talking much but doing little.

And in order to make the manufactured goods an icon of quality – not just an ordinary commodity – it is imperative to find the best way of explaining to potential consumers in all aspects why is it also in their favor to buy it; a step meant to raise their interest in what they see, causing them, perhaps, in the end to take the exhibited item. Because the term *benefit* enters now the picture – the advantage or profit expected by the customer from procuring the product or service; the answer to the main questions bothering him no doubt: "why is this good for me? What do I get from it?" So anyone trying to promote only the dry technical qualities of the article, without selling in addition the real compensation for purchasing it, fails totally. This is true since anyone **entering into any deal (or obtaining arrangement…) is interested, in fact, in gaining some kind of a reward**; something to convince himself (in most cases his relatives as well…) of the correctness of his actions; to feel (and present whenever necessary…) the total bonus attained by him for what he paid.

The above-said is an essential condition, but not a sufficient one. Because in order to truly achieve a considerable advantage among customers over the rivals in the occupation field, there is a need to make something really meaningful for the clients; a move that will draw them in differently than all other competitors, in addition to the feeling of being economically beneficial; to send them a **marketing massage touching their sentimental pleasure chords**; a process of talking forcefully to the buyer's emotions – above and beyond his cold, calculating mind – while about to decide whether to acquire the marketed goods. And the individual who succeeds in investing the fruit of his toils with value, exciting to the onlooker, giving him a sensational experience, creates a sign of uniqueness and excellence. For the heart's inclinations play a very important role in the purchasing course of a product or service – even if its character is purely technological.

And here, in fact, it is compulsory to use all rhetorical-representative skills to trick – in the most positive meaning of the term – the client's mind and eye. This with the ability to sell a good merchandise package as a quality dream enhanced – on top of its material worth – with elements "penetrating under the customer's skin" touching inner sensitive points. For example: equipping the buyer with ammunition that enables him to bestow a feeling among his relatives and friends of a real upgraded personal status, only due to holding something which belongs, in so many words, to an elitist society solely – that fitting in is simply impossible without this purchase.

And nothing is better to demonstrate the afore-said than the two following illustrative stories:

The first is the study (a bit amusing...) conducted by four neurologists – Antonio Rangel (an associate professor of economics at Caltech...) and his colleagues (H Plassmann, J O'Doherty and B Shiv) which was published in the monthly magazine *American Academy of Science*. The scholars aimed to prove that "emotional marketing" may deceive the neuro-stimuli of even very experienced consumers, bending their conclusions concerning a very well-known item they are dealing with; the possibility of influencing, in fact, potential buyers' subconscious by conveying to them deliberated data, so that their feelings toward the product would change for the better due to this misdirection, not the real value of the commodity to be bought.

All this academic exercise was based on the ability to identify different reactions of the brain to the environment, by a functional Magnetic Resonance Imaging (fMRI) machine attached to the skull. It became evident that this scanner can spot and categorize – with some considerable limitations, though – pleasure and pain sensations by the type of the waves it receives.

For that particular test, twenty volunteers (ostensibly very experienced and competent at their jobs...) were asked to try and taste five liquor samples. The only information given to them was the different retail prices of the liquid in the glasses to be tested: $5, $10, $35, $45, $90 per bottle. While the subjects evaluated the beverages, their heads were scanned using the above-mentioned fMRI. The results definitely showed that they had the highest enjoyment when drinking the spirit from the $90 bottle in comparison to all others (a certain region of the brain called the medial orbitofrontal cortex, exposed much more activity when drinking the wine they said was more pleasurable...) and consistently reported so.

Furthermore, the researchers "tricked" the examinees in two ways: first – they took that same liquor and presented it to the "guinea pigs" twice: once as the most expensive wine and then as the cheapest; secondly – the high-priced beverages were marked low-cost and vice-versa for the cheap ones.

However, nothing could "mislead" these unique "delicate palates": the so-called "intoxicating liquid" introduced to them as expensive was perceived as the best liquor and those which were exhibited as cheap were stuck in their mind as the bad and tasteless – regardless of the content: the type of grapes, the place they were cultivated and the year of vintage. The illusion of having an exclusive beverage worth price was the fact that determined their degree of pleasure in drinking it. To wit: the quality of the inspected fluid was determined in accordance with its supposedly exclusive financial worth – not due to its genuine aroma...

The other (less funny but more authentic...) deals with a few examples described hereinto of the reality common to many domains: every morning anew different advertisements invite the public to buy houses in close proximity to celebrities; as well as teenagers to volunteer for a challenging, exciting and very useful military or civil service (as pilots, naval officers, commando fighters, diplomats etc...) or to enroll for studies of the most difficult disciplines available to outstanding individuals only (offered, of course, by famous universities, fashionable colleges or other unique institutions and so on...). The same goes with complicated entrance examinations for those wishing to live in certain communities. And the only intention behind this is the marketing: associating with an elitist group of the population, living among the well-known, succeeding where only a few do and the like – just for the purpose of doubling and tripling the value of the business. Mark Twain, the American author and humorist, portrayed it in *Tom Sawyer* (1876): "He had discovered a great law of human action without knowing it – namely, that in order to make a man or a boy covet a thing, it is only necessary to make the thing difficult to attain…".

There is no doubt about the afore-said, but what really attracts people is the magnification of their ego; the idea that the product they buy or the society they join will invest them with a superior status, a sentiment elevating the rate of the acquisition or action far above its mere monetary cost. And daily life excels in presenting numerous examples of some defined merchandise selling economically beyond its real price, just due to the region they are sold in and the population putting its hand on it, and definitely not for "the material's" real worth.

In order to endow the sold object or service with a special brand, adorned with a unique commercial symbol technically and emotionally identified, it is necessary to recruit the relevant professionals, such as the best advertisers, copywriters and designers available in the market. The manager's job, on the other hand, is to provide these creative people with the proper scientific-factual data based on the experience accumulated so far concerning the merchandise and to make sure that they use it correctly in order to turn the specific output into a **power brand – a sentimental business icon**; something presented, finally, as a consumer-directed production line fixed within the buyer as a part of his existence, to which he attributes a nearly human identity. This is **a product that the client finds it very hard to live without**; becoming in fact a tool releasing him paradoxically from the horrible struggle of tormented choice by considerably minimizing – to his relief actually – the selection alternatives into one known preferred object to him and to which he is sensitively attached…

And for the purpose of succeeding in such a "persuasion assignment", it is imperative to choose from among all those toiling at the above task these who, aside from being representative and blessed with fine speaking skills, are also able to understand very well technically, commercially and psychologically the material which they are advertising and promoting. Because, as was said by the afore-mentioned Mark Twain: "Get your facts first, and then you can distort them as much as you please…".

And all of this is precisely what turns a mediocre marketer into an exceptional one!

Characteristics of Competitive Positioning: Four Customary Observations

For the reason of keeping a leading status in the occupation's domain for a long time, the organization must adopt an outlook of daily, consistent and uncompromising struggle. Only internalizing the fact that all partners in the creation and activities of the company must be bestowed with the motto of a **competitive positioning as a way of life**, can keep it at the top of the field it is in continuously as much as possible. However, it is unfeasible to point at specific-homogenous generic traits suitable for all firms as one, whose implementation would really cause the foundation of a strong permanent concurrent pose as a sustaining path de-facto, for each communal productive entity has its own unique performance standards. But it is certainly realistic to find, based on past experience, similar and general commercial concepts within many corporations being the backbone of their policies – and that is why they grew so much – while their competitors, ignoring these business attitudes, see a considerable waning of their routine operation's perimeters. And these are:

- **Avoiding the local exclusiveness – abstaining from becoming a monopoly**; an enterprise structure which is the definite recipe for failure in the long run (contrary to the common perception about singularity in the field, where everybody seeks to be lord of the county…). Uniqueness is like narcotics, for all wishes, mostly the inner, are frequently directed at fighting to preserve the existing pie and its distribution among various interested personal parties, while explicitly neglecting the product's quality and its enveloping service. Such a situation is due to the overconfidence prevailing in the company, as a result of the estimation that there are no worthy adversaries in the commercial sector it is dealing enable to endanger its status. But while it is asleep, caressing within a dream its paunch in great pleasure, dynamic challengers sneak about in the shadows (and in the present era there are plenty of those in all domains, growing daily like mushrooms after the first rain…) penetrating silently but deeply into the "playing arena", laying the foundation for their standing modestly vis-à-vis the current clientele. And one morning some functionless in the organization wake up – too late of course – to a new reality where the last train car disappears beyond the horizon. Or as once claimed by Ronald Coase, an economics professor at the University of Chicago: "In a market of durable products each monopoly contests actually against its future 'identity and nature' by creating a competition with itself in fact – instead of nurturing a healthy confrontation with its potential real foes in the business field it is in…".

On the other hand, when encountering and rivalry are encouraged, the specific occupation is elevated all of a sudden – especially the success and profits of the really good performers – because now everybody is obliged to enhance and foster commercial efficiency; at its center lies the search for ways to give consumers a much greater benefit for an identical price – or to credit them with the same worth of merchandise for less money due to total operational improvement; and all this stands in comparison to other "players" in the field. And what can be better than an atmosphere of such tendency which pushes towards optimal growth and prosperity?! So even coming by chance into exclusiveness it is imperative to inculcate all the above, to remember that no one is infallible forever and to act as if the market is flooded with a lot of enterprising opponents.

- **Innovation and creativity in providing value to customers** – namely a constant advance of original and modern products and services, with a low inner-organizational cost-effective ratio, enabling buyers to attain things hitherto impossible, promising them the opportunity to enjoy a better, more resourceful and extra comfortable life. As said previously, the key to commercial and financial expansion is an unceasing struggle on behalf of the client's interests and his wealth in particular.

- **Globalization** – the meaning of which is the identification of universal business activity spheres for focus and specialization while performing professionally in them, requiring an attempt to form a leading status beyond regional and national boundaries of local markets (which sometimes are nothing but hucksters' home swamps…).

- **Mergers and acquisitions of companies and technologies** independent of their geographic location on earth, these being the only vital ingredient of progress and world-wide growth.

Such a strategic attitude – especially as presented for the two last items – should embrace original-innovative thinking, yielding unconventional operative outlines intended to offer the consumer a superior unique mixture of the company's peculiar significance. Discovering and identifying special situations and opportunities unknown to others in the field – even briefly occurring – where their optimal exploitation are the spearhead of entrepreneurship in the full sense of the word. And these are the openings which generate a modern, stable and attractive business mesh, tempting and attracting new clientele to the obtainable market or drawing them from established positions, their previous daily lot to the counter side of the barricade.

Globalization and Mergers: Creating Next-Generation Business

There is no doubt that technological-managerial integration beyond local activities, as advised above, is among the main factors creating a monumental added value for any firm. This is a new business outlook, somewhat daring, that would bring the beginning of the competitive edge; a commercial quantum leap which considerably expands the production and trade span, urges growth, increases momentum and thrusts towards a real breakthrough. This is because it rescues those going with it from their existing "narrow-mindedness", opening a wide vista while crediting all concerned with exceptional opportunities to employ comparative advantages of people, venues, cultures, customs, currencies – which are different and unusual – in addition to very interesting possibilities to extract utility from regulations and universal rules unknown heretofore. These are the plateaus of confrontation unequivocally augmenting the personal and organizational dexterities of the company's executives and thus its total managerial capacity. Or as was best defined by the Indian hi-tech giant Nandan Nilekani obstinately claiming that: "With globalization geographic, language and cultural obstacles have disappeared...", inventing the revolutionary punchline "the world is flat..." (in contrast to Aristotle's dictum from the 4th century BC, exceptional for its time, regarding the earth's curvature...); a saying adopted by Thomas Friedman from *The New York Times*, concurring and using the afore-said sentence as the title of his book dealing with the subject (selling over one million copies in the US...). Such an attitude would certainly cause the identification of that very specific performance niche, giving birth to a situation precisely difficult for others at the same spot where it becomes much easier for those who already performed the merging – a position where the adversaries are weakening, starting to lag behind, whilst the unifiers keep digging forward, only getting much stronger.

Moreover, it seems that the real gain in struggling to be ahead in the practical field of action, would be driven by the very fact of not being attracted to common evolving market tendencies (in the attempt to do something similar, only better than others...) – but taking steps to assume a leading status beyond the borders of the technological-geographic routine. This is for two reasons:

The first, being dragged by a regular widespread commercial fashion gives birth to evidently senseless prices for any object "starring" in it, sought for purchase in that particular period; going for such subjects is financially incorrect.

The second, because once choosing to join the ordinary business trend a reality is accepted wherein global economic fluctuations, specifically characterizing it, are those dictating, more or less, the rate of success or failure for one and all – not the unique peculiar capabilities of any organization itself. When the weather turn for the worse it becomes bad for everybody in the same measure; and then no company enjoys, in fact, any superiority over the others. Consequently it is forbidden to judge the money-making value of commercial channels by what is common in the local market, and that which everybody is running after is not necessarily the right thing to do. The real wisdom lies in being able to foresee the direction of the future's irregular wind, generating fresh processes and building updated bridges, guiding the firm to penetrate the unique domain fitting it and settle there, far before this enterprise fashion grows and swells, conquering the financial highway.

And all of this while nourishing a brave business tradition, distinguished by openness, flexibility, innovativeness and improvisation up to impudence on the one hand – and on the other exhibiting obstinacy, reservation and even constant dubiousness (explicitly if needed...) about regulative authorities and what seems obvious and accepted by the monitoring environmental policy, so to speak, dictated by the powers that be.

Then, as the ancient hunters used to say: "Let the finest prey go to the best shot...".

For this reason, it is extremely important to understand in detail how to execute a process similar to the state actuality described here. And when one delves deeper into the issue of merging bodies (or acquiring them...) it turns to be more than obvious that a scenario like this should receive the utmost attention. This because the entire process comes into being while bringing about a real, profound change in the business's behavior and existence, laying actually the infrastructure for the next generation of its professional life, a development definitely reminiscent of marriage. Here are some of the basic rules for a consolidation of any kind:

1. **Information gathering**: the result of this phase must be very credible. This sort of parameters' collection should be built on cardinal, thorough and all-encompassing market research. One must not be incited or overexcited due to a lone opportunity or partial data, but see the general and overall picture and only then decide accordingly. On the other hand, it is prohibited to wait too long lest the merger may slip from between the fingers. And in any case it is appropriate:

    - To speak the same accounting language when examining each other's fiscal status. Since each region or country has rules of its own (particularly these coming from the Far East and those which belong to the developing economies or third-world states...). Different jargon may lead to absolutely wrong conclusions: so much that sometimes certain unique professional terms may even be interpreted one hundred and eighty degrees backwards.

- To prepare normal financial reports including a realistic projection for the coming years – especially a concise analysis of present and future profits and losses – in order to avoid any unexpected surprises in "the coming days".

2. **Planning and strategy**: now it is essential to observe, identify and define exactly the added value due to both sides joining the pact and check its viability for each of the parties separately. And it is possible to categorize four business targets, every one of which may augment (besides of enlarging the coffers' contents, of course…) the specific worth of this current partnership, in order to lead for sure to the expected competitive advantage:

- Increasing operational and administrative efficiency.
- Broadening and enriching the product basket.
- Invading new markets.
- Strengthening the Research and Development (R&D) section.

Since the likelihood to reach all of these goals together is very slim – and it is actually totally forbidden to strive for that – it is imperative to choose among the above-said the explicit gaining attribute which will bestow on the "young couple" an preference over its rivals in the contest arena, setting up and outlining the appropriate strategy for that aim.

In other words: the merger (or acquisition…) formula should be very simple: buying and improving in order to raise revenues (or at least start and sell with profit…). And this principle contains the secret of upgrading capabilities: arguments over evolving ways may occur; however it is vital for them to be ethical and clean ones, target-oriented for proper betterment only, without ego or concealed agendas tainted by impure interests to make illegal and dirty proceeds, which might lead to dealing with the peripheral instead of the essential.

3. **Identifying and choosing the right associate**: as aforesaid, the unification process is similar to starting up a family; theory becomes suddenly praxis. Realistically it is crucial to consider not only the future spouse, but perhaps one's ex as well and how to get divorced properly and calmly when there is a need for it. Thus it is prohibited to view the above depicted association procedure like a scenario of winning a jewel and nothing else – because some important central aspects have to be very carefully examined, before deciding "whom to jump into bed with":

- What is the preferred partner's size – equal in dimensions and perimeter, smaller or bigger (for sometimes huge, menacing conglomerates from the one end merge with little energetic and volatile firms from the other...).

- Whether to remain homogenous or to become heterogeneous (since a joint venture may be the most expected multi-blessed exit – selling the ownership to others – after waiting for such a long time...).

- How much autonomy will be left to each partner after the unification (because it is known that mostly the conqueror is the more active and efficient of the two...).

- What is the way to perform the consolidation (acquire all of the new spouse's stocks versus purchasing its activity or assets only; for at times it is wished to change sides in the globalization game, to endow instead of always being the one empowered...). This is a process which may occur, inter alia, through one of the following known methods:
    - Buyout – utilizing means of credit.
    - Private equity – through a personal investment fund.

- Mezzanine – by giving a "bridging loan" to a stumbling entity in trouble in exchange for an option of a partnership and involvement in its management.

Generally it is highly recommended to inspect companies' responsiveness, among other things, to the following basic criteria:

- Technologically mature enough (a product that has already passed the feasibility stage of assessment, for example …).
- Having a predictable sales expectancy (in a reasonable plateau, enabling existence …).
- Being able to create an export span (good enough to be a significant factor in the market…).
- Possessing potential growth engines (realistic as much as possible…).
- Encompassing a price-earnings ratio which fits the operative domain (the "elders of the tribe" advise it to be not larger than six [6] in the hi-tech field and not smaller than ten [10] in other conventional occupational areas…).

And one rule is always correct: it is better to merge with a fantastic company (or buy it…) for a reasonable price than unite with a reasonable firm (or procure it…) for a fantastic price.

And just like seeking a partner for romance, here too it is prohibited to compel. When it does not work, one ought to continue searching until the right person is finally found – made, seemingly, of the same "fabric": allegedly related to an equal "assembly line"; creating, so to speak, a match like that of Fred Astaire and Ginger Rodgers, the famous dancing couple from cheerful 1930s Hollywood…

Therefore, it is appropriate to test only the most select candidates.

4. **Life with the partner and the way to treat him**: after deciding with whom to wake in the morning after spending the whole night "indulging in love" – it is essential to settle on clear guidelines

as to how to spend the rest of the day with each other before returning to bed. Thus it is strongly advised:

- To discover proper leadership (personality wise…) in the parallel company in order to create managerial flexibility.
- To build a sensible and simply-defined organizational model, so as to create good communication among all individuals in the new organogram.
- To insist on an open and fair intra-framework data system to ensure a full and healthy transparency among the parties.

And above all, it is necessary to constantly remember:

- In really large mergers, there are no secrets actually. The "prenuptial negotiations" are totally transparent. Everybody knows everything about everyone: the same numbers, estimates and analysis of either system and the full knowledge of what surrounds them. So it is totally forbidden to even think about trying to hide something, starting the "marriage" on the wrong foot.
- In any partnership, both sides must gain some achievements (a win-win situation…); and it should desirably be in fact a sort of synergy. Otherwise the whole experiment would be worthless and the consolidation would soon dissolve (exemplified by the actor and director Woody Allen's sarcastic saying: "The most expensive sex is free sex…"). Moreover: each of the associates must earn a real private added value as a result of this challenging composition, something to justify the aforementioned amalgamation. The whole combination is based on a two-way wish, as one is weak, his fellow is strong and vice-versa; and every factor may express itself where he is at his best. It is also imperative to internalize that the size of the ownership any party gives up while joining together is unimportant; what is significant is the identity of the

entity who is supposed to gain from it in turn. This is in order to complement and to balance both of them simultaneously so as to enrich their common business life or the bottom line, the mutual coffers.

- Of all the visible opportunities, it is always preferable to choose the merger – even if it seems quaint at a whole in the beginning – to guide the new organization to making the most out of this journey, leading it to a very specific success, being impossible in any other way.

- The whole move should be done with the intention to carry out the joint venture for the long term – not a one-night stand or occasional fling.

And the best recipe for protractedly living together – beyond the initial term of charm and (sexy…) attraction – is embedded in the following four contributors: sharing **Responsibility**, reciprocal **Trust**, **Space** allowance and mutual **Respect**: **RTSR**. That is to say: all must honor each other while expressing reciprocal reliance, allowing anyone of them to have enough room to do what he does best and is necessary for the mutual purpose, sharing fairly the liability for the existence of the partnership and the duties it entails.

However, when calculating the advisability of such consolidation processes, it is crucial to understand that in a unification of two unequal entities the minor would, in principle, gain the most, for the herein reasons:

The one: the bigger partner retains its large dimensions; on the other hand, the smaller one climbs now upwards, starting to "play in the major leagues".

The other: the minor party has now the opportunity to act very differently than the average in his class – while the major side cannot behave otherwise related to his routine, for he is actually the average of his echelon.

Taking this kind of a momentous step requires lessons and conclusions of the utmost importance for both senior managements, orders meant to smoothen the road for merging entities totally foreign to each other.

First and foremost it is strongly recommended in principle to enter into new ventures and crucial investments as only in those well-understood fields.

Second, there is a need to authorize the business development personnel to prepare this sort of procedures properly from the conception of the idea. It is imperative to let them have maximum freedom of action and provide these functionaries with the best economic-analysis tools in existence, because their success leads, de facto, to a real breakthrough for the entire company.

Third, leaders initiating geographic-universal moves of the above type must be of a special level that internalizes within its ranks and stamps individuals with extraordinary perceptive guidance and a conduct codex. A fantastic synthesis is required between people running the aforesaid widening conglomerates, and a full and diverse delegation to underlings stemming for a complete trust in them. The executives on top have no ability or time to spend much on any section, unit or department of the parent-organization, which in the best case are stretched over two continents at least. As huge concerns – multinational corporations developing and becoming commercial octopuses in the fullest sense – are ever-expanding the danger of inner atrophy grows. Therefore effective, really superb control becomes compulsory: ultimate hegemony, disseminated through subordinates in the system's hierarchy, based on mental symbiosis, coordinated marketability and profit-making orientation, rooted professional ethics, invigorated public health and correlated managerial sophistication; beyond all on understanding the CEO's Weltanschauung in detail, even in absentia, derived from a deep familiarity with and esteem for the normative business-culture state of mind and imprint, inspired by him with uncompromising consistency all over his surroundings.

Fourth, and perhaps the most important one: it should never be forgotten, even for a slight moment, the risks and disadvantages of becoming an integral part of a great – at times gigantic indeed – economic puzzle; of buying a seat in a global cooperative settlement. The "Law of Communicating Vessels" operates in such unifying processes from now on, **making everything Omni-Connected**; the cost-effective ramifications are multidirectional and temporal: the small farmer in the East influences the big consumer of the West; the collapse of a financial establishment in the South would alert the Northern banks of a possible crisis; money extracted somewhere from the bowels of the earth can buy the entire sky anywhere else; and an industry and trade slowdown on one tiny front may drag the entire fiscal array into an ever deepening recession…

The reason that this multifaceted and complicated subject appears in such a very detailed manner in the present chapter (to distinguish from a few short notes woven into some of the previous articles…) is because any long voyage towards a merger, large as it may be, starts naturally with small advertising, promotion and publicizing steps. And it is due to the need to show all a high self-value and superior virtues first and foremost, selling those to the other side in order to become as tempting and attractive as possible – the marketing technique at its best.

Timing is occasionally a Matter of Luck – but Grasping and Exploiting the Opportunities it presents is Totally Different

The essence of life's events (including business episodes...) is timing, normally (despite what everyone says...) is derived from simple **luck**; and strange it is how sometimes the most important things on earth take place with total casualness – even if the full implication of their occurrences is at times unnoticed and not absorbed. However, it is forbidden to just accept the vicissitudes of the existence; instead, one must do everything possible – even above and beyond – in order to influence the unpredictable twists and turns of fate's decrees (nothing but the somewhat frightening concept behind which hides the apparently infelicitous terms "happenchance" or "happenstance" – a combination of circumstances, so to say...).

The wise and experienced vehemently consider luck to be a necessity, and it is truly desirable to leave a small corner of the heart for the belief that miracles happen (as was already mentioned earlier in this current tractate...). This means that even if the timing of events is not always governable, it is definitely vital to be the masters of the moment and to counter and cope properly when they finally appear. In other words: in a situation when planning and initiative are out of control, it is required to know how to develop the unique capabilities of instant reaction to gain a market advantage, or at least to avoid losing it. Then the **business reflexes** of the corporation are measured by the immediacy and tempo of its responses to emergencies. Its fitness to easily tackle unexpected occurrences is, probably, the most basic criterion of competitiveness. Apropos, it was once seriously claimed: "Maybe there is no perfect life, no perfect family, not even a perfect friend, but there is for sure a perfect moment to act and execute...".

And human history is capable of telling all about those who succeeded "big time" not by foreseeing crises or prophesizing unusual phenomena (for they are very difficult to anticipate…), but by recognizing before anyone else the opportunities created due to these incidences and the practical intelligence to totally exploit them; by realizing ahead of others that no wave of hardship or low tide should be simply wasted. However each one must act according to his resources, his might and especially his daring. As was once argued by Winston Churchill: "Men stumble over the truth from time to time, but most pick themselves up and hurry off as if nothing happened…".

Therefore, when already certain of something which must be done, it is positively advised to move as fast as possible; to "play" it in a staccato and come to a great and powerful crescendo, if needed. For there is a chance definitely that if not forced to run now and then, even walking becomes inconceivable. As dictated by Sun Tzu, the Chinese general and military expert, in the sixth century BC: "Such is war – where its most important consideration is speed…"; quickness, but not recklessness.

Moreover: if the firm cannot comply with the client's demand rapidly and without harming the class and value of its products, **its competitors will**. This is the consumers' double pressure phenomenon: to improve the quality while cutting production and distribution time. However, when prices enter the picture it is desirable to tactfully (and with some humor…) hint to the customer: "You are given the options of **Fast, Good, and Cheap**, and told to pick any two to be applied simultaneously…" – notwithstanding the fact he should feel as if he is receiving all three…

But sometimes the most significant contribution to the "speed" factor **is not technical, but cultural or mental**, a change in the collective organization's perception. The survival of the whole company depends occasionally on the measure of urgency and the flow of operative reaction coming from each and every one of its employees. Besides, **a deal not reaching closure in a short while** – reasonable in view of its size – **will probably never be completed**. That is because investors (or clients…) are impatient and cannot hold and keep money aimed at one lone commercial goal for too long a period (especially when everything seems "burning" with attraction and success appears to surely lie waiting behind any corner to be swept up…). Therefore they will look for other sporadic opportunities emerging on their way, which can be realized rather easily and give the impression of quick profits.

Hence, in a case as above described, when insisting on achieving a matter thoroughly discussed and crystallized, **he who does not respond, proceeds and set out when required will ultimately be annihilated and disappear** (an idea so true that here and there it is necessary to actually inch forward in order to simply stay at the same place…). And this is the exact opposite of the preachers' cliché: "Haste is from the devil…". It is required to clearly distinguish between the two, for even a fast movement should be taken with redoubled conceptual care, in spite of the difficulty to educate the human mechanism to get used to such an oxymoron; for it is very desirable that the brain's gears perform far ahead of the body's shifting motion; so, in addition to the impetus, according to which it is not always clever to wait for the ripened apple to fall from the tree before plucking it, when it is merely hanging around there to be picked, it is heartily recommended to take the advice of the same Churchill aforementioned : "Festina lente…", namely "Make haste slowly…"; meaning "When you are in a hurry – act gradually…".

Some Other Considerations of Marketing Methodology

As portrayed above, the marketing theory is based on many layers, covering quite a large number of fronts. Concurrently it comprises the central skeleton upon which forms the strategy discussed in the present chapter; and among other things, it sums up the global operational policy of the organization in this domain. Consequently, we find that beyond the cardinal content compilation woven into this dogma, some other subjects enjoying quite an influence are attached to it. The following is a representative, selected file of such adjoining chosen matters assimilated in daily conduct, deserving very serious attention while integrating the overall advertising, promotion and publicizing doctrine.

The Product Between the Marketer and the Client

The product is the thing on whose behalf the business is established and its *raison d'être (cause of existence...)*. This is the object that is supposed to financially maintain all those who commit quality and time to it; the purpose around which the entire organization lives and acts. So there is no issue more important in the marketing process than exhibiting the fruits of the company's toil in the best way. And that is why during the presentation, inserting the commodity above into the consciousness of the targeted audience, it is so fundamental to emphasize the differences between its **characteristics** and **advantages**. While the first are the unique givens, its merits and virtues, which are worthwhile trying to accommodate to the clientele's demands and wishes – the last are parameters pointing to the gap in comparison to the competition's output and the preference over it. On the other hand it should be remembered that projecting the distinction between one term and the other should, of course, depend on the ears towards which such introductory exposure is directed.

In other words: **the marketer mission** consists not only of convincing the customers that their specific needs will be fulfilled when purchasing the proposed merchandise package, but also pointing out all its benefits, proving it is the one and only response to their desires. Thus it is imperative to be very meticulous in choosing the right person responsible for this task, for two reasons:

The one – because those accountable to accomplish this assignment should not only be proficient in advertising and promotion, but also very knowledgeable in the **technical facet** of the product or service which they introduce to their consumers: in its way of fabrication, nature and class. As well they must be familiar with the history, professionalism and unique qualities of the institute they stand for and in whose name they operate. Furthermore, it is forbidden for salespersons to be surprised by the questions posed to them by their listeners, and even worse to be unable to answer those queries **instantly and convincingly**.

And the other – since each type and scope of the aimed demonstration requires the most suitable functionary from the point of view related to his status in the professional-managerial hierarchy of the corporation. For marketing the whole firm is definitely unlike distributing and selling a sole item from its extraction system; as it is clear to all that these two are not the same, neither in the rank or content of the things needing detailing and explanation, nor in the figure supposed to enlighten and clear up the technical-administrative aspects, certainly not concerning the people in front of which they stand. And in order to bestow on the whole matter the most wanted weight of persuasion and impression, it is necessary to allocate to each "campaign show" the personality and resources most representative and intellectually proper for that scene.

And another practical principle: among the product variety offered to the public at large, there must be something for each social stratum – not only those put forward to everybody. The majority of the population is not well-off. Thus, it is better to go for the premium segment of the targeted audience – than for the general mass of the whole market. For even in times of depression the rich become wealthier. Hence there should always be in "stock" some "small delicacies" and "interesting toys" for them too.

"Practical" Modesty – a Virtue that Surely doesn't Harm

As an advisable-pragmatic rule it is desirable to do first and talk later. In principle it is a very correct worldview intended to guide also all human beings in things concerning their overall doings. Regarding the marketing policy in particular, the practical connotation of this perception is expressed in the ability to distinguish between the time in which it is crucial to use publicity as the main means preceding distributing and selling the merchandise (in the sense of describing the **value of performance** that brought it to its present status…) – and the chosen moment of building it already a magnificent reputation (akin to **praising it and voicing** out the great its worth…); being the second stage of its assimilation in the entire and target audience while enlarging the circumference of its buying. For, as was said previously in the present tractate, the product's excellence would vouch for itself better than a thousand designated promoters and salesmen all together. To wit, it is essential to prove that the manufactured goods really have the qualities imputed to it before starting to glorify its name and merits.

In other words, it is definitely legitimate to expose the advertised object, giving it a very aggressive and loud profile-raising, so consumers start grabbing it off the shelves; but on the other hand it is imperative to present **hard evidence** from the field about its peculiarities, before waving promises as a part of a **"PR" creative journey** – in order to craft for it a mark of an exceptional emotional-commercial icon. The recommended way to implement the aforesaid is by creating an amplifier to convey up-to-date and easy-to-remember web of messages, enhancing the product's image in the eyes of the common; employing any random publicity tool at any possible time to demonstrate the commodity's virtues and to promote its selling quantities – only if it is by now beyond finishing successfully its initial consolidation in the market, proving its real value to all and sundry.

All of this serves to avoid repeating many cases in which the technological-business history portrays, with a somewhat sarcastic irony, wasted efforts invested in launching new products by an unconvincing and inadequate propaganda alone; a process that fits absolutely the worn clichéd "much ado about nothing…". (Such as the abortive introduction of the fresh Windows 98 program package at its premiere, done with a great deal of haughtiness and over-complacency – just like the biblical story of Jephthah from Gilead – by the software giant Microsoft in the presence of its legendary chairman Bill Gates and facing the whole wide world at the Comdex convention, in Las Vegas, April 1998. This was after every hi-tech magazine's wildly shouting for several months, announcing the coming appearance of the afore-depicted multifaceted enterprise before even proving that it can solidly and credibly replace the previous version of Windows 95. Some true practical humbleness would have served well the unsuccessful event…). Or as it was humorously described: "It looked and sounded like collecting sun-rays in plastic bags…".

Suppliers and Brokers – More about the Middlemen

Suppliers need not compare themselves to their best competitors, but to the finest **service companies** – for the matter is not dealing only with transporting the product and bringing it to its destination; it is actually in comprehensively being engaged with all touch points, and in nurturing all their daily contacts related to their consuming audience.

And brokers must **add a real value to their giving occupation package**, for otherwise what use are these intermediaries? Everybody feels that they make money without doing nearly anything. In any case there is a sense that those people are nothing but profiteers "joining the train one station before the last", so as to reach the desired goal and collect a commission; the Rosie Ruizes of the marketing and salesmanship process (Rosie Ruiz Vivas was a Cuban-American declared the winner – and world-record setter – in the female category of the Boston Marathon in 1980 without really sweating too much. Anyhow, her title was stripped after the judges discovered that she had not run the entire course, doing most of it in the underground, only "sliding" into the race merely for the last three kilometers ahead of the finish line...).

Otherwise – in the era of internet mastery, a situation might be created win which all these advertising and promotion middlemen soon find themselves jobless. In principle, everybody wishes to try trading in a kind of a "free-of-human-friction market" in order to save, of course. However this notion is totally wrong because there still is – and always will be – a superior sine-qua-non importance to the direct attachment of people coming in a concrete business relationship (unlike buying a simple commodity...). For there are things – especially in the more discreet layers – enhanced with an intimate-personal touch, impossible to execute for the moment through computer screens only – **if knowing, without any doubt, how to interlace them in the most proper personal manner**; talking mainly of the client's private feelings and his pleasure of sensing that he is more than just an email address in an endless ocean of "electronic post" sites.

So, **instead of skirting** the above professionals, it is better to know how to combine them into the service lines given to the consumer in a sophisticated and efficient manner, so as to extract the maximum from their activities (particularly, since anybody enjoys the right of an honorable living – as long as he is working honestly, fairly, loyally and devotedly for that purpose…).

In Summation

In order to keep improving and upgrading the marketing policy as a crucial part of the general business strategy, it is imperative to create feedback loops flowing from whatever is going on in the field, regarding the following:

- ✓ Client's product assessment and recommendations to solve acute problems.
- ✓ Challenges and difficulties in the salesmanship and distribution channels.
- ✓ Domains and places requiring more attention – especially where the competitors become stronger.
- ✓ Developing further merchandise versions and advanced services popping up due to customer demands.
- ✓ Penetrating new developing commercial arenas – by delineating and drawing an "opportunity map".

Because sometimes the outmost amazing technological idea is expressed only by its **brilliant marketing route**.

February 1999

Entrepreneurship

or The Bud of Business Development

Preface

In its most concise definition *entrepreneurship* is the unquenchable thirst of people to **establish-invent a business from scratch** – meanwhile **discovering and "creating" themselves each day anew**; it flows from insatiable curiosity, fantastic imagination, sharp observation and remorseless logic; being the mixing, weaving and binding of crazy stuff, hallucinations, flashes, pieces of information and well-thought-out ideas into one apparently rational outline; an outcome of the ability to join totally different extremes – seemingly existing in absolutely different places and belonging, so to speak, to completely dissimilar domains – with the childlike skill of assembling a puzzle into one global picture, even in the absence of any "instruction manual" on the back of the box. The resulting amalgamation is meant to yield a new ingenuity – an operative-practical innovation – stimulating the mind whereas awakening intuitive inferences in an immediate and unusual manner.

There are some unique prominent traits – for good or bad – which a fine entrepreneur must always exhibit:

- ✓ A very remarkable vision and an unusually fruitful mind.
- ✓ Untiring diligence – uncompromising stubbornness (perhaps even fastidiousness…).
- ✓ Chutzpah (the nerve to go on trying continuously…) – unashamed daring.
- ✓ An "elephant skin" – superior powers of restraint.

- ✓ The talent to read at a glance, appreciating quickly and correctly the map of events concerning the occupation domain.
- ✓ An intelligence to weave relationships among subjects that have no obvious affinity and whose common denominator is far from trivial.
- ✓ An upper than average sensitivity to changes the moment they occur.
- ✓ The ability to identify rare opportunities – which others miss, in particular.
- ✓ A capacity to perceive, better than others, potentially original commercial ways to generate a tangible gap between themselves and competitors.
- ✓ The flair to excite and inspire – especially in surrealistic presentations.
- ✓ A very prominent ego – a strong belief in the "self."

And all in all, some luck maybe wouldn't hurt...

In addition, it is required to treat the craving for that storming business spryness; impossible-to-confine enthusiasm, pushing to conquer new heights; that untiring investment of spiritual and material resources – a DNA slice, not a virus. This is a positive Weltanschauung, strongly expressing the **soundness of initiation** – not the sickness of closure. However, it is apparently still a "secret genetic unit" not yet discovered in the recently human genome research: something like a chronic itch which one must scratch...

Nevertheless, it should be emphasized already here and now, despite the fact that dealing with the present exclusive domain and the character required to really flourish in it is extremely interesting, presenting a very challenging world – the following is meant to show the contribution of this dimension on the one hand, facing the havoc it may wreak on proper supervising and administrating on the other. Though the descriptions from now on may seem a deviation from the key subject and touching areas having no direct connection to the company's driving issue, it is only apparent. This is because they are here orientated to overstress the supreme importance of the continuous effort to find the right amount of entrepreneurship within the total management cake; the optimal allocation allowing for unusual sparks of forward thinking endlessly without detracting from the best possible running of the organization.

The Manager as Entrepreneur

Since the business environment requires constantly rowing forward, it is crucial that the **entrepreneurship bug reside** within any executive in charge, to one extent or another. For as in all other parts of life, stagnation means retreat; and as necessity gives birth to invention – the gift (or "disease…") of free-will enterprise and creation is embedded in the identification of a need to respond to some existing distress and skirt an acute problem; to handle innovatively in an as-yet unknown manner an obstacle founding a predictable impasse. At this moment of recognizing constraint it is vital to take all measures to alleviate it; while it must be done patiently and determinedly following these suggested steps:

- ✓ Burrowing for ideas and methods to materialize the recognized requirement.

- ✓ Searching and discovering already obtainable similar technologies as an answer to the afore-said, or deciding to build up such from scratch.

- ✓ Examining very meticulously the feasibility of the above and then the implementation options.

The ability to push the limits of business further and beyond by formulating each time again new original and unique operative schemes and techniques is what distinguishes among three types of managers, junior or senior, from the lowest to the highest quality:

The first – being mainly a performer: taking some firm and harnessing himself totally to leading it as defined for him from above or by the book, improving and really moving the unit forward.

The second – his commercial visualization is confined: even after succeeding in shaking things up and promoting in an exceptional manner the communal body under his command – he keeps on "swimming" in the local activity "pool" only.

And the third – endowed with a global perception: in addition to the required driving action, like the two fellows above, he is the winner among them; with routine management and guiding skills as demanded by the entity under his responsibility – he enjoys the intelligence, foresight and courage to break through the thinking and geographical barriers of the corporate's basic function, flying and elevating it to unforeseen heights (as the future of the modern business world lies in entrepreneurship applying globalization...).

However, it must be remembered that the present article deals in general with **leading an organization** – not the beginning of the ideational process of its establishment or accompanying its first steps entering the commercial arena; **for the world of management is totally different from the universe of entrepreneurship**. Seeking fresh development directions is indeed the elixir required for the continuity of the company's existence, but it is not, in any way, the sole activity for running it de facto on a daily basis and constantly later in the future. Though it is essential to exploit with maximum efficiency any innovative bit which may be of a use to accelerate the firm's advancement – inventions alone do not give birth to any business scenario. Revolutionary thoughts and outlooks are merely a primary spark, eventually moving the entire machine; but for the motion to be in the right direction, balanced, safe and free of collisions, one must wrap and build around the "engine" all the other layers and organs constituting the entire vehicle. And this is exactly the task of the strategies' texture so far portrayed, leading to the operational policy of the organization; it is analogous to the chassis of the car, enveloping the engine's core, enhancing and protecting the discoveries above as a full creative work in order to turn them into practical and durable products.

And that is precisely the aim of this entire book!

Moreover; it is totally forbidden to fall victim to the charms of self-ideas and become 100% devoted to them with all bonds of the soul (while deserting all the other leadership and controlling aspects...) – even if they seem initially the most brilliant notions. This is out of apprehension of slipping into pits, dug inadvertently by their thinkers or of being captured by soap bubbles blown, unintentionally, from their mouths. Falling in love with steps born in someone's sick mind, without heeding other sounds, may push to a fixated; to numb petrification. The trouble with "local patriot" entrepreneurs is that in most cases they are hostile to inventions not originated by them (because they regard their own opinion as something like a precious property, very difficult to part from – so when they express-issue a kind of an assumption-outlook, there is nothing in the world that can make them change their judgment...). And then the mental freezing in weaving intellectual analogies (those which would have arisen from listening to other people, by the way...) can bring the whole system to a halt thanks to the neglect of the additional routine activities required to administer the organization.

Entrepreneurship – a Blessing or a Curse (When Needed to Manage the Daily Routine, of Course…)

Since this is a very extensive and worldwide subject – much beyond management per se – it is worthwhile to describe here a few very unique facts and situations, seemingly sounding rather "overblown", regarding all those in this specific "playground". These are actually the basis of their entire Weltanschauung, especially in light of the internal conflict which might trouble every executive in any system: concerning the question of how much of his total energy he ought to invest in entrepreneurship proper at the expense of the correct running of the company under his charge, and vice-versa; a dilemma (whose problematic essence and principal pains-exertions were discussed at length earlier in this book…) presenting the organization's man at the top two sets of considerations contradicting each other in fact:

On the one hand there is no practical or valuable substitute – mainly in the moral-concrete sense – for entrepreneurship. Without the "freaks" and their drive to make new discoveries and run after modern solutions, not even one idea would have been born to the betterment of the comfort, welfare and conduct of daily life; total stagnation. Because those addicted to inventions are actually the life and soul of the developmental totality of any human society wherever they exist medically, scientifically, technologically and economically. This is according to the somewhat seemingly patronizing motto "I believe since it isn't understood…" (paraphrasing the dictum attributed to Augustine of Hippo – the neo-platonic philosopher and Christian theologian of the 4th century – regarding God's powers and actions…).

On the other hand, it is crucial to be very cautious about this contagion which may spread – even epidemically – with no ability to stop or at least confine it. Outside business, entrepreneurship is analogous to that troublesome bug continuously buzzing about the head; one which generates those possessed by it into a crazy race to the top; arousing a kind of a hidden, but uncompromising, "basic instinct" to reach the zenith of scientific ameliorations of all types. The extremists, those really "sick" ones, truly insist that it fizzes from the inside with a taste of hype, meaning: intentional warming to a special occasion, a stimulus touching the very edge of one's capacity, a strong, utterly irresistible sensation. And in the worst cases, it becomes a mental preparation for a great futuristic event assisted by alcohol or now and then doing drugs.

In short: a hard involuntary enslavement, usually uncontrollable.

Furthermore it is a fanatical impulse, the grounds for an incessant quarrel of the individual with himself: a nearly "neurotic" constant struggle between his brain and spirit; an impulse resulting in internal restlessness, continuous and constant, stemming from a wild chase from one invention to the next. People of this type ultimately become super competitive, chronically aggressive contenders. Paradoxically, they always hope that each event, progressing as planned and taking them to the yearned success which they expect, would indeed pass and be done with; it stops being interesting, in fact, due to the uncontrollable urge, teasing and pushing them to start dealing already with "the upcoming case awaiting treatment". And from a current passionate race to the other, and without any early warning, their lives end before they have an opportunity to delight in their achievements – instead of slowing down, staying with every pleasant moment as much as possible and enjoying every given minute as a gift. Someone once told jokingly about a former friend of his who was always "dying" to move on to the next stage of life. First he was "dying" to finish elementary school and start junior-high; then he was "dying" to pass his matriculation exams and join the military;

afterwards he was "dying" to finish the army and start his own business; subsequently he was "dying" to get married, raise a family and retire from work; **until he finally died one day and suddenly discovered that he forgot to live...**

This stands in opposition, in fact, to what was preached at the beginning of the first tractate: learning to take pleasure in what lies finally at hand.

Moreover, entrepreneurs honestly believ they can act and behave **contrary to the laws of nature.** Some bizarre individuals have a unique and nearly indecipherable personal code, sure they are able to exist in a physical-mathematical-economic anarchic universe; a very special environment created by them for their own comfort; something like figures out of Walt Disney's movies, creatures walking in an empty space or moving in the air without any problem – totally ignoring the laws of Isaac Newton and Albert Einstein.

A well-known hi-tech entrepreneur once depicted - this dreamweaving and the hallucinatory wish to make a physical reality out of those: "It's like being amidst a thought process of crossing an imaginary river on a fictional bridge, made of separate boards lying side by side, in a straight line over the waterway, except having no connection between them. And he who walks on the above sheets steps, but barely touches one time only each wooden plank, because he must desert it at the very moment he feels it sinking under his overwhelming weight. However, at the same moment, his other foot lands on the next floating piece, which then starts submerging immediately. So the traveler must leap again and again, further down the row, so on and so forth as fast as possible. And he runs jumping over the lighter supports, hardly tapping these, from one state of imbalance to the other. And for a lineman standing not far away, it looks like someone is running on the water – a phenomenon out of the *X-Files*, appearing in the dim twilight zone between abstract logic and fantasy – until he crosses the stream reaching, **if he does not fall and drown on his way**, the opposite bank...".

Thus, they incessantly try to breach hermetic walls while always fantasizing about the impossible...

And precisely because of their prominent irregularity as afore-described, they keep on "drawing fire". This springs from having often (not always justified, though...) the common feelings about them due to the following reasons:

- ✓ They refuse to grow up from their "wondrous" world of ideas, symbolically representing the Peter Pans of invention, maintaining all the time a portion of huge childish interest in any subject, without considering that life outside is much more complicated.
- ✓ Their unrealistic concepts and estrangement from authenticity are now and again at such extreme levels, as to think that the regular most favorite "lucky numbers" ironically embraced by them, are the irrational ones like: **Pi** (π – the ratio of a circle's circumference to its diameter...) which equals 3.1415926535..., or **Phi** (φ – a figure considered the "Golden Ratio" or the "Divine Proportion"...) whose known value is about 1.6180339887...
- ✓ The evidence of their discoveries are not exactly the proof of Fermat's Last Theorem presented and resolved by the mathematician Andrew Wiles in 1995.
- ✓ They carry a very strong belief in having a kind of volcanic-intellectual melding with "Mother Nature".
- ✓ Most of their initial ideas sound like the beginning of fables or fairy tales.
- ✓ Their distinctness and strangeness are so irritating as to seem provocative in the eyes of those surrounding them, even expecting to be attacked; as the old Japanese saying goes: "Any nail protruding upwards would be hit by a hammer...".

- ✓ In their so called "revolutionary innovation" they every so often become a "one man spammer" – spreading "nonsense" such as the ability to light a whole city with one lamp.

- ✓ Their efforts to translate the practice into hypothetical notions are insatiable – especially when the business world is craving for the opposite process! They fail to understand that speculative-academic assumptions and conjectures are indeed the basis for everything – but can be also wrong; and only real-pragmatic life alone make it possible to distinguish a good hypothesis from an abstract bad dogma. Because theory (as suppositious thinking…) resembles Western governments (or medicines…): often useless, necessary sometimes, always self-serving and occasionally deadly; therefore it should be used with care, moderation, under close adult supervision – and always kept away from children…

  Or as argued by Alfred North Whitehead (a British philosopher, physicist and mathematician…) in 1925: "Ideas won't keep; something must be done about them…".

- ✓ Their optimism is shrouded in infinite, somewhat eccentric naiveté, now and then bordering on truly annoying stupidity; making those individuals ignore warning signals transmitted by reality – even when in plain sight – which might also push these characters to move with false self-confidence from one failure to the next, thinking they are still walking on the path of success.

And the last and most enervating:

- ✓ What motivates those people – continuously it seems – is a sense of a mission from Heaven, and their main tendency is to leave some fingerprints on the coming generations; a kind of an indelible stamp in the entrepreneurship quagmire. Besides, these characters have a somewhat arrogant conviction that they own the specific aptitude to deal with subjects above the dimension of time – and in such a manner to defeat human race's transience;

so their yield counts a hundredfold more than its creators. This is because glory, even evanescent, is embraced by the universe; while anonymity, in contrast, is eternal. And money for them is, in most cases, just a marginal product...

Additionally, such individuals simply do not recognize that by their constant crazy quest for novelties and inventions, they merely corroborate a famous law of nature (working, by the way, contrary to the interests of the organization these people exert themselves so much for...): the second law of thermodynamics – a rule expressing, figuratively of course, that the entropy – the utilized energy in the system within actually they act – would just keep up growing over and again. And with this, when the obsessive push to rake in discoveries almost every minute, is lacking logical control, those guys really "harass" continuously the framework to which they belong, shifting it from its main goals without pointing, actually, at any other practical target: a rise in investment and expenses – in spite of the disappointment, no solutions or results being visible on the horizon.

Not to mention the confidence these unique individuals have in their exceptional-human-supernatural capacities as described above, and the belief that all type of grandiose plans can be implemented due to their future predictions (which in fact were never adequately checked...). Ideas seeming like a sure trip to the stars – but may lead to disastrous "business-hubris". And this might pull – because of big eyes and an "insatiable hunger" for wealth – to throwing money on the "gambling table" driven by a feeling of the proper choice and a "sure hope" in prosperity; a decision which eventually results in **empty pockets**. So exactly this subconscious "enslaved" routine of thinking, surrendering to a weakness as to addictive desires – whether from classical (canine...) instinctive-Pavlovian tendency or out of Skinnerian-operative (rat- or dove-like...) conditioning – should be categorically avoided. After all, the final outcome possibly will push towards a scorched earth.

And those characters refusing to admit that **hyper-entrepreneurship** is a kind of illness – especially when losing control of bad desires and impulses – convince themselves in a variety of ways, trying to show it isn't so. They claim, for instance, when a large enterprise fails, it is sometimes analogous to "blessed fires"; a kind of an oxymoron expressing a graceful tragedy. Something like the horrible conflagrations destroying occasionally in a frenzy the thick vegetation of the rain forests, situated in the hearts of South American states neighboring the Amazonas River. And this is considered sacred since after totally wiping out the treetops and large parts of the trunks, a quiet ensues, a new growth of green leaves and branches begins close to the earth; these become fodder for these unable to reach the very high part of the flora in order to eat and survive.

Meaning: a downfall and lapse here offers opportunities to others there. Very true – or a false comfort probably flowing simply from cognitive dissonance?

However it is very important to internalize a central point already mentioned in the preface to the present chapter: in spite of the fact that the **cardinal essence of the book is management and not entrepreneurship**, all alleged and cited in the above paragraphs from the title up to now, has been intentionally selected – expanded, perhaps ad-nauseam, and with special highlighting, but with a clear view in mind for the following reasons:

- ✓ To demonstrate the amorphousness of the domain being described in this latest collection of articles.
- ✓ To show in what way the occupation with this topic may be attractive, up to absolute addiction.
- ✓ To emphasize how utterly absorbing the said subject may become.
- ✓ To prove the great diversion from any other essential activity which the depicted theme might cause.

✓ To warn of the danger inherent in becoming enslaved to that assignment, when management liability is literally the main task.

Moreover and tremendously substantial: there is no tendency to present the "enterprising guidance" dimension as something negative, God forbid. On the contrary; despite their very special character – and possibly because of it – these people are so vital to development in all fields of life. So the renovation and improvement fronts is not only significant, but imperative to all existence levels in general and particularly for business. But as a consequence of all written here, one very momentous principle must be strongly inculcated: **management should be left to managers – and entrepreneurship to entrepreneurs**.

And the main insights to be extracted from what has been explained here at great length are two:

The first: since the entrepreneur must always look for the next thing – seeing in each reed a flute, playing it himself before throwing it out and moving to the next instrument – he actually ignores what is happening around him routinely. Thus it is crucial to beware of appointing such candidates for managing positions; for these individuals – who are too much of pure inventors in their nature – simply do not fit, clearly, this kind of position and cannot run a company on a daily basis for a long time.

The second: even the most energetic CEO – the ultimate hyperactive initiator – must learn to separate and draw the exact border between the two spheres: to set a dosage of the enterprising anxiousness mode suiting him personally as part of the governmental, instruction and monitoring work he performs – without hurting in the smallest manner his core task's objective: guiding in general a framework expertly and with forethought to dictate and lead most practical and concrete assignments.

Entrepreneurship with Control – Setting Limits for Managers

There is no single well-tailored solution guiding the executive in charge where to place precisely the line between his current job – running the corporation and its employment – and the temptation to aspire and innovate while performing in order to better promote what he is doing. As aforesaid it definitely depends on his nature and inner tendencies. But he must keep one "sanctified rule" regarding this matter: over-entrepreneurship must not stand in the way of the ordinary, daily and future administration and supervision mission carried out by the man at the top – otherwise the whole system may be hurt and suffer!

In other words: there is no intention to sterilize the manager's above groundbreaking traits, on which so much has been said so far, nor to prohibit him from generating some vital and blessed fresh enterprising and impresario activity on the side (when the matter appears to be necessary and does not harm the current planned routine…). But – and this is a very big one – he must deeply understand that there is a stage in the development of any project or organization, when all in aggregate which has been imagined, thought of and foreseen fit to do in the past – should be carried out hour after hour and point by point. What's more, he ought to stop his restless urge from trying to invent repeatedly new things already designated in order to continue changing; in that way the work will never be accomplished (just like withholding the nesting bacterium from annihilating its host's body…). So, it is strongly forbidden to cross the lines.

Here are a few recommendations which may help the director to set the aforesaid border:

✓ Calculated risks are permitted, but abstaining from getting entangled in bizarre-stupid daredevilry must be always seriously considered. It is preferred to be a sober adventurer – mainly a pragmatist realist – knowing when to kick off something new, however only after completing what is required to be already done; conservative enough not to endanger what was achieved by now and is satisfying.

- ✓ A smart suggestion is to think far ahead – while still go on taking care that the present is safe; as was once said by a politician when asked about his plans a year after establishing a new party: "It's good to think about the roof – but first one should deal deeply and with thorough attention regarding the foundation of the entire building…". Because he who does not survive the day has no chance, whatsoever, of seeing tomorrow.

- ✓ Before deciding to execute the whole strategy it is desired to prepare the tactics to be taken, and to ensure all details are clear to all performers.

- ✓ It is proposed to separate between the functions of the individual who originated the business and the one supposed to be nominated for running it in the future. There is quite a difference, and sometimes a bit of a contradiction, between theory and practice; a difficulty in the efforts needed to finally turn those academic hypotheses into real deeds. And the likelihood of an idea popping up in a person's mind – the same who knows also that he would be the one obligated to apply it later on – to be stored away or shelved, is very high; because nobody wants to get mixed up in uncertain activities if required to deliver results at the end of the day.

   Not to mention the fact when now and again it's better for an enterprise vision (and not only…) to materialize far from the figure who gave it birth; for such obsessive zeal may definitely disturb its realization…

✓ There is a need to adopt a materialistic Weltanschauung of a "spherical bastard" (to use the 20th Century Swiss cosmologist Fritz Zwicky's pejorative mantra...): just as a ball looks the same from every direction – a manager should be perceived as business-sophisticated on all aspects, promoting any commercially profitable issue while not blocking it due to inconvenience.

And in general: since there is **great daring in entrepreneurship**, it is better not to stick at one initiative praying to the Good Lord in Heaven for success. It is wise, as aforementioned, to think beyond the visible horizon, to hold the reins intelligently and forcefully while nurturing ideas in different courses. Only a sound and well-planned risk distribution process, as well as adapting the best technique to control them, would be the solid basis allowing continuous freedom to invest in the future. And all the old clichés about eggs and baskets – including Mark Twain's differing philosophical perception already presented in the chapter dealing with technological strategy in this tractate – are correct.

A supplementary attitude to avoid later unpleasant surprises requires wariness of immediately accepting any business offer seemingly economically viable, without checking it with seven eyes to the innermost sanctum sanctorum. A clever executive administrator is not tempted easily by any apparently moneymaking adventure coming his way, because in a torturously commercialized world, in which dreams are sold as original ideas, even top leaders bump sometimes into bodies or people offering them quite alluring proposals – something like an invitation to a "trade and industry" partnership.

As a result of the above the CEO is advised to walk in a very, very controlled and sober step, before being swept along by all kinds of innovative business inventions, which may give him the feeling he is entering on a major scale the field of entrepreneurship. To wit, it is highly suggested to evade trying embrace the entire world (somewhat virtual…) with a sole pair of arms while missing what is offered by the principles of pragmatic management regarding the walks of life generally and piloting organizations in particular. It is therefore suitable to adopt unhesitatingly the following logical commands:

- ✓ One should never bite off more than he can chew.

- ✓ Occasionally it is good to slow down and even stop altogether, in order to enjoy the yield (such as selling a winning stock or taking a dividend after a successful period and so on…). As Prof. Jacob Frenkel (head of the Bank of Israel, 1991-2000) used to preach against financial greediness following a temporal success: "Trees do not grow to the sky…".

- ✓ Retiring at the top is the right thing to do (like the Swedish tennis champion Bjorn Borg after his fifth consecutive win at Wimbledon…). Namely, after totally exhausting one successfully undertaken enterprise front and making a good profit out of it, there is no sense in trying to continue and drag out this activity forever; thus the chances to keep exploiting it on and on shrink to nothing.

In summation

In the management world, entrepreneurship – important as it is – should be treated as a process which ignites the whole deal; like the journey of a thousand miles which begins with one step (paraphrasing the famous saying of Mao Tse-tung, leader of the People's Republic of China and chairman of its Communist Party for forty-something years…).

And one important thing must be remembered: **business development is the lion's share** of the obsessive mania described in this chapter. It is really the vital phase of global action meant to bring in the end a profitable quantum leap for the organization as a whole; without it, entrepreneurship is worthless.

July 2001

Knowledge Management (KM)

or The Road to Constant Improvement

Preface

Knowledge management (**KM**), in the most broadend definition, means: the process of capturing, developing, sharing and effectively utilizing the organizational formal or systematic familiarity, awareness or understanding of theoretical or practical – implicit or explicit – facts, information, descriptions, skills and expertise (which are acquired through experience or education by perceiving, discovering, learning and so forth…); and this refers to the widest multi-disciplined epistemology approach of achieving the institutional objectives by making the best ever use of it.

Furthermore, it is an undoubtedly fact that **an interlinked world is ruled by knowledge.** This is a highly vital strategy – (yes, probably the fifth one…) to ensure the proper existence of any communal productive entity; a tool whose importance is irrevocable means, first and foremost, to present the real establishment's condition to the decision-makers who run it in order to assess its business status at any point in time. Such an evaluation is used to draw lessons to be learnt from its performance so far in comparison to what could have been supposedly achieved from its total activity, and among others it examines its professional abilities and dexterities, its occupational environment and its competitive advantage as against the adversaries in the field. Additionally, the said info analysis facilitates the deducing of functional conclusions served to continuous improve management and conduct arrays, operative policy and extraction processes prevailing in the firm. Consequently, the data assisting the top corporation's echelon must be reliable in the highest degree, updated constantly, always available and given to all partners sharing the enterprise – each one according to what is required by his type of task, rank in the framework and the exact nature of his doings.

Therefore it is required to create and launch a **crisscrossing inner communication format, sophisticated and adapted to the unique needs of the company** – a mechanism enabling a current flow of relevant ideas, statistics, facts, arguments, figures and opinions to all central junctions within it for its action and the intake of feedback messages for follow-up and control; a kind of "data blood circulation", to nourish the system with all the acute-actual parameters, so as to encourage internal knowledge sharing and endowing it with its collective intellectual vitality.

The right dissemination of information occurs in four main transmission-reception directions, derived from the common organizational structure:

- **Vertical**: from bottom to top – and vice-versa.
- **Horizontal**: crisscross – a two-way current dialogue along with parallel or identical layers in the framework.
- **Diagonal**: among staff members and mixed – from all ranks and different sectors in the system – to its frontline personnel (operators, producers, marketers et cetera…) – and conversely.
- **External**: from company representatives to the various peripheral functionaries (those who are partners in the totality of its operations situated around its activities, but beyond its physical borders…) – back and forth.

The above-depicted movement of data must stream continuously with full openness and reciprocity while being compartmentalized and sorted in accordance with the hierarchical levels of seniority and restrictions delineated by the corporate.

And this is in practice the optimal implementation of contact and monitoring science; **cybernetics**: the dogma **of control, communication and feedback,** developed by the mathematician Norbert Winner from MIT, back in 1948. It is an active mechanism that serves to be the solid base for the approach of standing for strategy creation and its derived target positioning, passing them as bright messages to all those toiling and partners in the overall work – in gathering information related to comments and reactions from the field: sorting, classifying, investigating, assimilating, internalizing and analyzing all of those. This comes from a clear intention to closely follow up, test and check the policy fixed and dictated on the one hand – and on the other to build up a continuous healthy, steady, protected, balanced and **consistent improvement process** too.

Information Management (IM) – What is it?

Information management is a broad term for a basically simple idea: putting together and systematizing – counting, cataloguing, editing and recording – fixed and variable parameters and givens received in writing or verbally, and supervising them. In other words, it is the collection method of materials from the most sensitive to the open ones concerning the whole of the technological, human, financial, commercial and administrative operations in the company: the arrangement of its inspection and the manner of its use in the most intelligent way, in order to come up with the best solution to problems arising in the present and to lay down optimal future plans; an assisting instrument intended to produce the best from working with different data areas, existing inside or outside the organization. Because the concentration and study of the evolutionary history of the communal productive entity including all aspects and characteristics so far detailed in the book and the configuration control of its extraction and designated crop give it the ability not only to overcome daily obstacles, but also to continue its development in various fronts of its overall functioning, without having to "reinvent the wheel" in any of the domains each time anew.

However, it must be remembered: this is a means – not an end.

Accurate and well-ordered registration, arrangement and storage – subjects such as decisions, operative assignments, ideas which need to be developed, patents, work methods et cetera – are actually the ingredients for the entire relevant information aggregation of the firm, especially when that kind of documentation assists, among others, to attack common stumbling blocks like: disorderly overlap in exchanging posts, skipping important points or junctions due to mindlessness or shortage of time, unprofessional work resulting from lack of written procedures, intentionally hiding imperative details for the purpose of willing to dominate, knowledge dissolution via forgetfulness, the inability to control and understand processes because of the retention of past trial and error lists or precise technical specifications – and so on. And the route itself is very easy to implement if one is punctiliously and automatically methodical.

Knowledge management is, therefore inter alia, a scenario which feeds data into a neutral, totally inhuman stowage, having no impure interests, lacking any intrigue due to personal wishes – in the variety of events and occurring within all of the framework's layers; a mechanism lending itself to siphoning whenever necessary, in any wanted intersection and desired visual format, exactly in the way and the shape it is required to be presented concerning the company. And with its help in particular, a possibility to draw very objective lessons in relation to yesterday and reach very proper conclusions for tomorrow continuation becomes highly practical.

The zealots of the IM sphere conceive of a massive and exhaustive investment regarding this front; the best use of technology for the purpose of removing partitions, in fact, among different interested groups in the corporation. They proclaim it to be one of the central paths to building **bridges of insight and collective dialogue**, unifying and integrating all belonging to the organization and creating a meaningful context within as well as outside of it, with all partners surrounding it.

Data Work – Building Up and Using an Informative Array

In order to allow data work it is imperative to put together, first and foremost, an effective and fertile information management scheme; an apparatus necessitating, primarily, a definition of the diverse fields and specific parameters to be included in it. This requires a very accurate delineation in the following sequence:

1. All subjects obligated to be examined and inquired.
2. Representative factors, their character and degree of particularizing.
3. Data elaboration structure and its influence on the outcome.
4. Mechanisms to sift out any extra information which is harmful and disturbing "white noise".
5. Presentation manner of the analyzed results.
6. The method of using the finds discovered.
7. The chosen technology to operate this instrument.

When starting to establish the procedural configuration described here, it is desirable, in principle, to gather constants, variables and attributes givens and figures of all kinds, relating to the general activity of the organization. Only after thoroughly learning the technological abilities of the network to absorb and digest the information and deciding what really needs to be extracted from it, it becomes possible to clearly and precisely direct the type of details needed to be collected and stored in order to utilize it in the most effective way.

First of all, a reliable well-connected data array – even if not promising immediate answers to all questions – allows at least to display right away and in real time all the facts and a variety of parameters somehow connected to the current problem, helping find the best solution for it.

Second, **anything measured** – with no exception or foreknowledge of its future use – **only gets better with time**.

However one very important golden quality must be internalized here and now: to filter with great efficiency unnecessary information, for the reason that in most cases it becomes a harmful database. And the meaning of the command "know thy numbers…" stressed earlier in the present tractate is to dictate the study of these sizes – not only touching and contributing to analysis, leading to better applications and higher achievements of the organization – but particularly to those influencing the above-mentioned investigations and examinations. Generally superfluous aspects and too many fine points give birth to horribly destructive factors, because they may engender precipitous reactions to any change in the system's input – including irrelevant noise having no link at all to what is measured; for even statistically it is known that the more a certain phenomenon is sampled, the higher the variation within it is observed – not the gist of its essence. And then, as the old worn cliché goes – "one cannot see the forest for the trees…" – action is taken emotionally, without too much thinking, due to following wrong parameters, and serious mistakes are made.

And the best example is, perhaps, the quantity of media outlets to which ordinary people are daily exposed, in order to really understand where and how they should live…

This information ought to be, therefore, accurate, authentic, genuine and accessible to immediate and successive use, and **the employees dealing with data management must be given the quintessential means needed to accomplish their mission** – for these are the people whose productivity is expressed with the highest value: the wisdom, talent and collective skills of the firm. On the other hand, when that essential system malfunctions, it is, in fact, a horrible obstacle; this is, actually, the bottleneck of everything. And the main goal of such an efficient tool is the development of the **overall organizational intelligence**, improving the total **IQ** of the framework as a unified unit; that is to say, enhancing and designing its **global intellectual property**. Such a treasured asset – as long as it is shared communally – influences the technical-professional and managerial-operative life perception, more than any other contributing factor in the establishment's daily activity.

A correct operation of a quality informative array and its competent running means: **data streams exactly at the desired pace** (while clearing all the superfluous injurious noises described before, of course…); quick enough to always precede the "ears" of the competitors in the market from one side – but not too dense so to be able to digest the maximal amount without leaving unclear "leftovers", still allowing for a correct response from the other. And assuming that news and messages relevant in the field reach everybody's attention in the modern age, then only an effective use of the most important and suitable for the company's main occupation and their full exploitation – will lead to success. Consequently, it is required to pass and process only those facts and attributes **which are merely vital and strictly required for business opportunity developments** – especially to move the discussions upwards to the strategic level of the senior managerial rank, in order to make the most appropriate decisions. And from now on, the advantage bestowed upon the firm in comparison to all its opponents should be imbedded in the joint associated wisdom – its collective **IQ** – to match its essential abilities due to the supplied shared knowledge, and to bring the totality of its unique dexterities to a better expression than the adversaries, for the benefit of its clientele.

The usage mechanism of such a mighty aid and application of the flow of information pouring from it ought to be easy and convenient to utilize; the method and procedure of its operation have to fit the consumer and his comfort, just like the "soft-boiled-egg rule": elementary, easy and quick as its cooking, so as not to antagonize and repel those in need of its services. Since quite often in these cases if it isn't simple – then it simply won't be...

Conversely, a unique phenomenon should be seriously noted, common to most large frameworks. **Organizational IQ**, gathering proficiency for important factors and details, processing talent, conclusion-drawing wisdom and the clever link between the group intelligence which analyzes the outcomes and translates them via the most effective technology – are the most vital ingredients of the company's administration, supervision, development, progress and creation of advantage versus its potential challengers. So how come most businesses – even the huge conglomerates – lack a jobholder of the first rank in charge of running their data management systems? Whereas any communal entity of a medium size and above has an assistant general manager (or vice president...) for operations, engineering, human resources, finance and marketing – why isn't there one for IM? It is very appropriate to think about it and appoint an extremely skillful and energetic person for this assignment. A knowledge-based entrepreneurial free economy cannot, in fact, exist without a structure clearly defining the senior director of corporate intellectual capital – the collective brainpower at its disposal – and who is entitled to use and exploit it.

Information Technology (IT) and Competitive Advantage

IT, in this article, is the totality of scientific applications (utilizing sophisticated telecommunications equipment...) to manipulate the cerebral potential and the group's knowledge existing in the firm; an effect founded on the most efficient implementation of the organizational IQ, expressed in its contribution to the feature named the *value chain* of the company. And this one is a term enveloping the mass and breadth of the activities, mutually related in all technical-economic-administrative layers of the communal body itself, due to those it keeps moving and rolling. That is the combination of all active providers to the global operation of the joint commercial entity itself, reliant on each other and inter-linked (as a metaphor...) whose sum presents actually the **amount of the total work energies invested in them to extract finally the product**; a factor pointing out in aggregate the **price proportionate to the business's merchandise quality** in comparison to its competitors in the field. And the estimate described here is only the root for weighing a much broader entirety of occupations and parameters, the same exact attitude of the *value system*; an idiom including and taking account of, in addition to the above-said, the worth of endowments by suppliers, sub-contractors and all other partners outside the corporate, based on their input (which is in fact their private value chain, of course...) to and for everything.

The value chain (like the value system...) would be considered higher with the growth of the manufactured goods quality to extraction cost ratio. Thus it is imperative to properly and methodically "oil" all gears of the aforementioned – for optimal accord and partnership of all components. **And there is no other way to maintain a "well-lubricated" mechanism of such an extraordinary caliber except by an ultimate usage of data technology, involving top information,**

arrays, techniques and applications. And in order for the last to support the steps taken to achieve the desired competitive advantage, it is crucial to be meticulous in its performance, in every iota, to wit: supreme competence in operating all different organizational internal and external layers due to the finest coordination, cooperation and flexibility of the links between all managerial, operational and administrative rings. Only then can the company grow.

Consequently it is apparent that it influences absolutely the fields of the firm's occupation characteristics and structure.

However, one cardinal thing must be understood here: the real danger lurking due to the commonality of the contemporary generation's information engineering, is that too many establishments implement it identically. The result might be a homogeneity of the ingredients destined to compete for the customer's heart and pocket, because they would all do the same; a process making it very difficult for the client to choose to such an extent, that a commercially tasteless contest for all sides will develop without yielding any genuine economic achievement, while being destructive businesswise. And this leads to the conclusion that the best usage of such a scientific application would be expressed only if utilized in a totally different and much more sophisticated manner than employed by all other rivals.

Knowledge Treasures – the Way to Safeguard Them

Each company must set **very clear borders** concerning **everything that deals with the access routes to its knowledge sources**:

First of all – limiting all external elements: friendly, false and others in between. This requires the formation of the maximum efficient defense array capable of changing its operational techniques quite often – so nobody will be able to track its routine secret codes and study them. For that special purpose it is advised to hire the best professional people in the market, to install the latest modern and most effective tools, to use all possible ruses – and finally to even go back to the old methods such as: hiding in the safe a piece of paper containing certain highly private facts, parameters and details in completely black-and-white personal handwriting; and separating computers for different uses: one for intra-organizational use of confidential material and the other for external communication sharing less classified data (taking into consideration that it may ultimately leak…). And here truly the ends justify the means; since if some very sensitive knowledge would fall into the wrong hands, then all of the huge effort invested to achieve competitive advantage would be for nothing.

Secondly – and not less important – internally: related to anyone who has a touch, even the slightest one, upon the company's business activity. To wit, delineating a ranking map in accordance with the functional seniority ladder in the corporation's structure, defining a very lucid selective partnership in everything concerning the computerized and electronics networks in particular, and all info systems of any kind in general for, the sake of the overall compartmentalization. And this according to a hard and uncompromising hierarchy, meaning that each and every one of the entire personnel would see exactly – and nothing beyond – what he needs to know in order to execute his designated assignments.

Furthermore, every firm has to **protect its intellectual properties** from the adversaries – in the same manner that it should be responsive for all local rules regarding, inter alia, these topics:

- ✓ Submitting a written ownership claim to the authentic authority for any discovery or invention whatsoever pertaining to the company's main and side activities, arising or springing up by any of the staff or external workers employed by it under an official contract, namely: mooring the entire subject under **patent registry**. It is essential to ensure that the content and form of such records will be written and edited in the most secret way making it impregnable to underhanded means.

- ✓ Insisting that every one of the personnel or outside bodies coming into business contact with it **sign a Confidentiality / Non-Disclosure Agreement – CA / NDA**, and a declaration of non-use of its inner knowhow and professional specifications for any purpose other than the benefit of the organization itself, saved with explicit executive approval.

- ✓ **Correct confidential treatment** (following all proper regulations...) **of corporate documents** such as: memoranda, protocols, association codes and registration papers with the authorities, trademarks, chosen names and so on.

In any case it is desirable and highly recommended to hire for the above-said tasks the most proficient individuals specializing in that sort of work, for the purpose of avoiding problems and complications – trivial as they may be – in the future.

And there is one more extremely essential thing related to these collecting, processing and monitoring systems: it is crucial to **back up, permanently and in every possible way, any bit of treasured** information – since the storage apparatus of vital data is sometimes surprising in their unreliability and awfully low resistance...

Constant Improvement – Utopia or Practice

Continuous feedback from the field – reliable, sincere and methodical – allows the organization to internalize the changes required by actual and acute managerial-technological-economic alterations occurring daily in the market; and simultaneously to adjust accordingly, in real time, quickly and incessantly, aiming to create a **steady process of raising standards**.

Here, perhaps, is the place to explain the definition of the idiom *aspiring for constant improvement*, appearing throughout the entire book. Apparently it is fair to admit that the idea sounds somewhat utopian and unrealistic. However, it expresses, in fact, a very simple intention: the consistent desire to ameliorate each time a different link discovered to be the present weak one in the entire framework's chain; and at the end of its betterment to continue looking for the next junction, the coming obstacle and to prepare for it.

That is to say: **the process is constant**. It doesn't mean an ongoing success in immediately observing the advanced status, but the whole of the action is directed towards ceaselessly trying to; and probably in a more poetic phrase – "better the best…".

Illustratively, it is possible to consider an analogy known to everybody: the year-end report card. It is obvious that A is the highest grade one can get, but if the pupil receives the maximal score in plane geometry, for example, he should take care of the other mathematical branches. And when he is outstandingly appraised in all these, he must turn his efforts to raising his other marks on the sheet to the upper limit. And after his overall average will finally be 100%, he ought to embark on a quest to ameliorate all of his additional school conduct – and then to uplift his entire non-quantitative social activities outside the institution, over and again.

The morale of the former allegory resembles an infinite circle composed of nearly every type of domain related to human existence; and a person striving continuously for constant improvement moves on its perimeter looking inside towards its center and takes care each time of a different faulty segment. And even while it seems that the cure is finished and everything is in good health – it is obligatory to start checking anew, as there will always be a point whose quality has deteriorated to an insufficient level, and so on and so forth. This is the way to continue upgrading all the time, with an uncompromising determination, the entire benchmark of subsistence. Because naturally most people keep on seeking the path to better their lives…

Yet, when discussing processes for consistently perfecting and continuously raising the standards, two very imperative rules must be inculcated:

The first – it should never be forgotten that the enriched efficiency as against the viability of investment in it have to be examined frequently.

The second – it is prohibited to mix the idea behind the intention of "the will for constant improvement" with the demand wrapped in the idiom *zero flaws*. The latter is a perception not allowing for any mistakes and vainly putting under pressure anybody who has to withstand it. Originally it was initiated as an attitude meant to encourage reducing defects in control and quality assurance processes to achieve a negligible rate (even absolute nil…) of disqualified products. Afterwards the term was adopted by all kinds of "over-ambitious" managers wishing to project their authority upon the system they lead and its resulting effectiveness. However, with time it became clear that the above expression turned into a banner only serving public relations – failing to win the test of reality. Probably it was a ruse to cover up "spoilage" in their organization such as: bad engineering, deficient production or mere inferior supervising and administration. Instead of being a positive motivator for performance betterment, an array of false reports were born out of fear of punishment and a class of "never mistaken" people was brought suddenly into existence; something certainly not obtainable in the world of pragmatism. Moreover, such a concept harms all by blocking, actually, the ability to learn from mistakes; for if there are no errors, then how is it possible to learn from them? Where would such experience be acquired? And let it not be understood that the present declaration encourages slip-ups (justifying the banal excuse of novice cooks: "What can be done? The first pancake always burns..."); on the contrary: it ought to be clear that it is always necessary to strive to avoid disruptions and misapprehensions instantly from the opening moment, but if those happen, everything should be done to avoid repeating them and to ameliorate matters (even if dealing with culinary matters!...) in the future.

In Summation

KM is perhaps the **fifth dimension** among strategies this book had presented so far; an executive administration factor of great importance having two purposes – but also a bidirectional aim:

The one – giving insight capabilities to follow and oversee organizational processes towards intermediate goals and final targets – in order to extract lessons to be learnt from them, draw conclusions, internalize, assimilate, practice and improve the outcomes with the intention of setting higher, more ambitious benchmarks endlessly. For inquiry, study, monitoring and training are the secret of perfection...

The other – positioning a protective tactic for the company's knowledge treasures, all its personal and communal intellectual possessions and the standards of planning and operations cultivated in the past and refined in the present. Safeguarding their exclusiveness over time allows a competitive edge to such a great extent, as to enable finally the selling of products in the markets – that might be, otherwise, obtained by them for nothing...

And it is worthwhile to remember: knowledge is undoubtedly a very powerful instrument; therefore it is very dangerous if it falls in the wrong hands. For any tool may become a weapon if held properly...

March 2000

Deming in a Contemporary Cloak
Epitome of the Executive

Dr. William Edwards Deming, who began his professional career as a statistician, claimed already in the 1940s that "quality does not cost money – it only saves money…". He proved his outlook as a matter a fact in postwar Japan, where he was sent by the United States Government to help rehabilitate the defeated Empire's economy from the deep crisis it was in, and became one of those laying the foundations for its industry over the next thirty years. His approach relied on arithmetically collecting, analyzing and interpretation of quantitative commercial parameters, various behavioral data and a number of tools to measure work scenarios in productive entities. Since then he has been considered the father of the **"Quality Message"** within the functioning principles of organizations: associative management, focusing on processes with an aspiration for constant improvement.

However, only in 1984, when the research and development center of the US Navy began looking for effective combination ideas to apply the concept of overall valuable performance and its encompassing atmosphere, and their contribution to piloting any kind of communal or private creative body (and some proclaim that the definite victory of the Japanese car manufacture over its American opponent at that time was, in fact, the main motivation spurring businessmen of the latter to recruit the man and his systematical philosophy…) – did the period of testing the different mixtures of attitudes about running organizations really start. The chief conducting perceptions among them were: Statistical Process Control (**SPC**), already introduced in the most of the naval institutes; Ishikawa's Total Quality Control (**TQC**); and the principles of **"Quality Management"** according to

Phil Crosby and Joseph Juran. The result of the project was a new guidance school, well-adapted to Deming's old philosophy of Total Quality Management (**TQM**) – from which was rather easily derived the notion of Total Quality Leadership (**TQL**).

This Weltanschauung has been chosen to close and sum up this collection of articles dealing with the various topics in the book so far, not because it contains revolutionary ideas never before discussed (except, perhaps, some here and there…) but for the following reasons:

- ✓ This philosophy concludes all basic classical approaches of the greatest pioneers concerning quality management throughout history, reflecting as well the universal recognition of famous entities in this doctrine; even though these perceptions were first expressed over sixty years ago, they are still relevant and powerful due to the rationales herein:

  - Deming's teachings roots are based on the behavioral theories of organizations' running dogma, originated by Elton Mayo, Abraham Maslow, McGregor and Herzberg, who consistently argue that **the source of a communal productive entity's prowess is its human component**. According to them, large differences are apparent in an employee's output depending on his inner motivation; and this drive is in conjunction with the executive's directing, administration, supervision and controlling policy: when defective, it depresses the worker's incentive, making him what is usually called "narrow-minded". On the other hand, the correct, associative and encouragement leadership of senior corporate's officials may definitely develop personal potential, urging on the masses toiling towards continuously innovative quests.

  - The essence of the afore-depicted perception is dealing with an ever-flowing loop. Therefore the action model he proposed then (adopted, by the way, from his mentor Walter Shewhart...) to inherently improve management and production procedures was simple: Plan, Do, Check, and Act (**PDCA**) – changed over time to **PDLA** (when 'Check' was replaced by 'Learn'...).

- The Deming Prize Committee representing the Japanese Union of Scientists and Engineers (JUSE), defined the **TQM** (out of appreciation to the approach's success ...) as hereinto more or less: this is the continuous process of reducing or eliminating errors in manufacturing, streamlining supply chain management, improving the customer experience and ensuring that employees are up-to-speed with their training. It aims to hold all parties involved in the fabrication process as accountable for the overall quality of the final product or service.

  The current-mentioned method consists of four main stages:
  - **Kaizen** – concentrating in an incessant course of improvement, by making any technical-managerial procedures in the organization transparent, measurable and reversible.
  - **Atrima Inshitzu** – focusing on non-tangible influences on proceedings in the company, and the techniques permitting to minimize such interferences for the benefit of ameliorating the whole firm's development.
  - **Kansey** – analyzing the way in which the client uses the merchandise and how he may better it.
  - **Miryokotoki Hinshiu** – broadening the management's attention and interest beyond the daily produce.

✓ It is easily adaptable to **modern business reality** understood by all nowadays as well.

✓ This very outlook was the first to comprehend in a large measure the connection between the **two basic intelligences of man: the intellectual and the emotional.**

✓ Later on Deming formulated and published a compilation of fourteen principles: a magnum opus of the establishment's total activity, leading it to the appropriate prosperity. This is a collection of short sayings that **even today** can be of use, not only to the man at the top, but also to the whole executive as a **concise tagging list for self-tracking**; promising themselves and everybody around them, that they are stepping on the right pathway.

And this is, probably, the main reason that in spite of its great age, this guidance philosophy is still vital. Thus it is just right that its place – in addition to being in this assemblage of articles – **would be at the end; so as to close the entire anthology and serve as an immediate, up-to-date and authentic control tool.**

Furthermore, it is must be noted that all sources engaged with the above-detailed concept took care to enumerate the following principles in a serial manner, though they are equally important. The order of their presentation should not necessarily be of significance as long as all are adhered to exactly: each one, altogether and always.

1. **Creating constancy of purpose towards improvement as an inherent daily activity – replacing short-term reaction with long-term planning:**

    Embedding the wish (by making it actually a way of a life routine…) of being better and finer in all **managerial-organizational** domains, **strategic-tactical** subjects and **operational-technical** levels into all partners to the toil, while they are satisfied with their workplace (even enjoying it…) – in order to recruit **additional satisfied customers**.

{ And this principle exactly, as defined here, describes the key difference from Deming's original concept; a variation gathering more and more weight with the research and study of modern directing, administration, supervision and controlling foundations, as portrayed here parenthetically: the corporation's amelioration should be expressed not only in the technological production processes, but also and especially **in every dimension of decisions making toward crystallizing its general doctrine and particular policies; in the flexibility and adaptability to various situations created by the occupation's environment and character; and to what the adversaries are doing depending on their economic-commercial status**; a development intended to be constant and relating continuously to the general course of action and conduct guiding norms setting; to the spreading of future plans flowing from it and consequently to the strength of the exertion postures duly derived and daily taken. It means therefore the uplifting of all leadership-business-admin qualities of the company, those encompassing scenarios of finding the niches desperately sought by the market; accompanied by initiatives destined to build real implementations arrays of the type which creates a clear advantage over the competitors; additionally to these scientifically active elements that are very imperative indeed. In other words: improvement of operational effectiveness is vital, but should be done hand-in-hand with **deepening the total calculated strategy** positioning of the framework and its **upgrading**.

And all this is for the following reasons:

- As a result of adopting Deming's managerial outlook as is, the leadership of many companies "degenerated" with time into a state of generating ameliorations barely in the technical-functional field and towards trying to concoct no more than simple and direct transactions. From the outcome of the production being the sole considered commercial indicator, and of course the most alluring index, the temptation to elevate fabrication efficiency only turned to be a huge one (since the limits of extraction are clearly delineated, corresponding to quantify, and easy to directed; mostly, their results are instantly seen and garner praises and compliments...). This perception ignores in fact the real duty of the CEO, because moving a corporate entity is certainly more than plain bookkeeping; since **the brain behind correct firm's guidance is strategy behavioral.**

- If the executives in any business are under endlessly increasing pressures from the owners or board of directors to show real achievements in substance extraction only (presenting improvement measurable just in material-financial results...) without being required to integrate a total working advancement policy or derive long-term planning from it, to learn lessons and draw conclusions from the unique devices to follow up and control its ingredients (to lay in practice the basis for the future...) – then they'd become, in fact, **successful operational supervisors instead of victorious CEOs as expected.**

- The competitive edge can merely be achieved by knowing how to anoint the practical, routine and gray work with the oil of wisdom, vision and creativity; integrating the commercial outlook and building with them overall management and conduct doctrines in an unusual and original style. Namely: the ability not only to invest separately and in a sharp and clear manner in quality production and extraction processes – but also coming up constantly with innovative ideas related to the global operational tactics – makes the difference between a mediocre and an exceptional organization. For while the first means simply **a better technical execution of the same activities for the clients** than the competitors (who would eventually reach the same level, any way one may look at it...) – the second signifies **unique sophistication in finding upgraded-original paths to satisfy customers**, performing **assignments identical** to those of the adversaries by choosing the most specific shape to **take care of these consumers with much higher standards and superior methods**. In short: emphasizing the strong virtues of the firm as against and in accord with the weak points of the rivals for an opening move; and later on, in the next calculated phase, constantly identifying and disclosing their other advantages and turning them into their largest shortcomings.

To borrow from the world of soccer, an amazing player's dribble is certainly a brilliant performance (and there are quite a few like this...) in the full sense of the word. However, when also blessed with the ability to move into "dead" areas and "attack" unpredictably, accompanied by the astonishing timing of accurate assists to unexpected targets directly into the opponent's soft belly (breathtaking moves which win games in the end...) – it becomes indeed his forecast of the desired outcome much before the rest of the participants on the pitch – which turns out to be actually his most extraordinary strategy and tactics: the talent to identify the other side's specialties, on which its hopes are pinned (closely pressuring the rival's teammates and preventing them from getting too involved in what is occurring on the field, for example...), is enough to shift the game's center of gravity and surprise in an unforeseen direction (delivering to an associate coming suddenly from behind when nobody takes it into account, for instance...). And that's what makes him unique and one hell of a giant star very hard to compete with – compared to any other gifted dribbler who has only marvelous control of the ball...

Here are some arguments, unquestionably speaking much in favor of this managerial business approach:

- Perfecting the organization's operational plateau concerns mainly the technical and procedural standpoints of the industrious execution processes, for the purpose of extracting the best-manufactured goods technologically. Betterment is necessary to keep improving productivity and, in the meantime of course, income.

  Yet, this accomplishment can be changed from a temporal financial reward to a continuous economic success only if these proceedings are backed up by a strong enough strategy, able to practically support the fabrication progress to the extent of achieving the most profitable business yield over time. This is a contribution expressed by enhancing the inner harmony among all real action layers in the company, by positioning work stations of coordination, combination and integration of individuals and groups in the framework into a unique operative path; by focusing all workers on defeating the main "enemies": distraction from the goal and acceptance of mediocrity.

  More so, it should never be forgotten that failing to attain high performance standards, undoubtedly, injures even firms enjoying the best and most correct chosen doctrine…

- Due to its very concentration on technical ameliorations only, increasing efficiency from the execution and implementation aspects – as good as it can be – becomes quite easy to imitate; to wit, killing all competition through the heart and the pocket of the client because of uniformity in merchandise quality and that of the services around it. As a result, prices necessarily come down to fabrication cost in order to survive businesswise. The organization's viability is injured at the end of the day along with the will to keep investing in it.

  Conversely, strategies are not, normally, given to full

replication, since it is very difficult to duplicate ways of thinking behind policy building. Copying experiments may be done, but the reproduction would never be entirely similar to the real source. These corporation's conduct doctrines – when especially original and highly robust – allow for preceding the others and being first in those economy niches just awakening and unknown yet in the market, long before any of these become trends or the rest in the field understand the rules of the game. And while everybody is still busy finding a place in line, the pioneers are already moving forward to the next commercial slot.

- Many managers try to stay clear of getting involved with "heavyweight" operative schemes, complicated tactics programs and unstraightforward execution recipes. It is the surest technique to keep away from slandering criticism and being blamed for failure; since this fields requires the most unpopular decision-making, sometimes dealing with critical issues, unsympathetic and with negative connotations, such as: reasons for a lack of advance, domains to be avoided dealing with and so on. For often the true "enemy" is the inside itself. What's more, these kinds of choices concern ideas whose fruition demands a lot of awfully high efforts (if they will come to a fulfillment at all...), their cooking time is long and tiresome and the reaping is beyond the horizon. So it is far from certain that any of those partners and supporters pushing the afore-mentioned thoughts and notions would be around to enjoy the credit due to their successful realization...

In cases like these, the men at the top prefer popular rulings, choosing easy means which exhibit fast growth of quick profits. This attitude includes, inter alia, trading tricks and methods such as: adding new products to the manufacturing line, emphasizing attractive features to existing goods, promoting nearly free-of-charge extra services, allegedly popular hits – or going for reckless mergers without due diligence, turning to worthless markets having nothing to enhance the company's uniqueness and so forth. In short: a foolish and desperate attempt to improve one's image with a so-called "macho" tint, broadcasting an expansion of the business span, because avoiding the picking of casual opportunities conveys weakness. And the longer this tendency is adhered to, the more it becomes an ideology requiring justification; a notional trend fixated more and more in the consciousness of those giving in to it, since it looks like bringing extra immediate prosperity; thus without understanding that these are momentary chimeras, negligible and doing no good for the real occupational breakthrough. And not only abandoning the ordered search for those specific openings bringing a future maximal added value to the firm, but even making managers go on quests chasing any new "half-baked" scientific application without conducting a serious feasibility-viability test, for the sake of technology per se and to satisfy a personal whim to be the "stylish" leader.

Nevertheless, on the contrary! Being carried away unrestrained by the rush after temporary-seemingly progression scuttles the commercial development of the organization, while eating away at its reputation and status; a situation accelerating like an avalanche, gathering a mass of ever-growing sickness and delusion until the unavoidable crash. This is a foretold business chronicle like Chekhov's gun in the first act, which must eventually go off...

On the other hand, it is clear that in order to launch a considerate and stable system leadership, capable of prolonging the corporate's life in continuing success, a strong strategic array must lie behind it – a purpose taking upon itself the deepening of the planning-operational-technological values of the said communal entity (for correct and robust doctrines and policies intensify, thereby broadening activity volume, not the other way around...) in order to keep advancing. And this should be done by **positioning and fortifying its stances established with a different thinking: original, innovative, and sophisticated; untiring improvement of the coordination, linkage and collective intelligence inside and outside the company; and a persistent betterment of the means for the existence of all these**; while the vision, imagination, creativity, craftiness and resourcefulness of individuals and groups in the framework must be enslaved – always – to the development process above.

Moreover, executives exhibiting commitment and the courage of this philosophical-theoretical-amorphous space while making fateful decisions – even unpopular among the crowd on which they are forced – only strengthen the body under their command by defining exactly its position, destination, route, structure and hierarchy; it indicates from the beginning of the road the borders of the ideational polemic within the establishment.

Such steps not only **invigorate its status within the firm**, but no doubt form **organizational class and rank outside**. The reason for this is that its clientele, at least the serious ones, certainly take note of this supervision, administration and conduct style – and what's more important, appreciate it.

Consequently, in order to maintain the equation **ensuring a constant competitive advantage**, yielding at the end of the day increased success, it must be learnt to keep refining both activity fronts – the executional and the strategic – each one on its own, both of them together and forever. This is an uplifting which gives birth, so it seems, to a synergy. And all this occurs while adopting and adapting a daring and forceful business way of life based on an open mind, opportunities exploiting, flexibility – and a tendency for never-ending innovativeness and improvisation up to revolution per se, such as is woven with threads of stubborn combativeness, not abhorring even open criticism, when needed, of the regulative authorities, their clerks and everything common, apparently, to "government bookkeepers" presenting themselves as determining market regulation policy…

And in continuation of this Weltanschauung – here are the rest of Deming's principles expressed with a slightly different economical look and more contemporarily applicable idioms, compared to their original way of presentation several decades ago: }

2. **Adopting norms of operation promising minimum mishaps in the extraction process and the smallest defects in the product:**
   Guaranteeing best possible performance from the very first step of action under strict quality assurance (QA) policy, aspiring to avoid repairs repeatedly and aiming to stick to timetables as undertaken. Cancellation of too-wide safety margins as unnecessary "exaggerated cautiousness factors" which, definitely, incur significant extra costs.

3. **A systematic and constant ameliorated modification of the organization's production and service systems and their efficiency:**
   Establishing communication circuits to maintain a continuous flow

of feedback from the company's employees and its customers, to find and identify genuine conduct and manufacturing problems, related to production and client services. The contact means from the field and the information derived out of them must be purposeful and expedient. This data control serves to examine the explanation of the operational obstacles, to analyze their sources and find the appropriate responses to cure those obstructions – and check ultimately the urgency and reliability of the given answers, when they are not in use. The backup, investigation, processing, definition and solution mechanisms must be fully functional at all times.

4. **Quitting obsessive dependency on internal specification-meeting checks and external inspection of products that are already finished:**

    Testing at the end of the fabrication proceeding is pointless since correcting wrongs at this stage of the process is very expensive, too late from the aspect of the technical work required to fix the problem and leading to missing deadlines. The quality of goods and services should be secured therefore by:

    - Appropriately planning ahead.
    - An extraction technique as simple and manageable as possible.
    - Realistic and well-considered technical specifications.
    - And a tight control procedure throughout the entire execution.

5. **Building-up a high class team of suppliers:**

    Using a small number of well-proven providers who meet goals and ensure efficient and reliable service. These traits are tenfold more precious than the prices they demand. It is important to establish long-term relationships with them, because a low level of interim raw materials or ineffective rendering of maintenance treatments may lead to defective end products – causing finally a reduction in their value and the loss of dear consumers.

6. **Focusing on helping subordinates fulfill their assignments by:**
   - Introducing proper and suitable working conditions.
   - Taking responsibility for problems beyond their ability to control.
   - Issuing personal feedback sustained by very close and supportive guidance during the whole task.

7. **Driving away any fear within the company by inspiring an atmosphere of:**
   - Mutual trust and two-way openness.
   - Compensating true reporting and observing "worthy failures" as the outcome of trial and error.
   - Backing up even when mistakes occur – as long as they are not due to wrong judgment resulting from misinterpretation the current state of affairs, repeated carelessness or faulty discipline.

8. **Removing barriers between different units in the organization:**
   - Creating a full consciousness of information management and data work processes.
   - Inculcating that knowledge distribution – not concealment – is the real power to raise the collective IQ of the corporate.
   - Encouraging listening to everybody while quickly distinguishing between subjects of primary from secondary importance.

9. **Granting an incentive for accomplishment of combined targets:**
   Rewards for qualitative performance and/or keeping to timetables and/or production enhancement – not only for by beating one standard, the yield (an erroneous criterion pointing out quantity

alone without exhibiting first-rate attainments and adherence to binding deadlines...).

10. Fostering workers' pride:

Creating an occupation framework causing its people to be very willing to belong to it due to the most unique class regarding its general conduct, and especially on the technical-professional front; forming in parallel a practical employee compensation mechanism, both gratifying and remunerative, for achievements, initiatives, improvements, investments, knowledge-sharing, contributing to a serene ambiance, mutual help and anything which may promote each individual in the firm and its benefit as a whole.

11. Establishing personnel's on-the-job teaching, training and tutoring (OJT[3]) agenda – showing each and every individual career development and advancement horizons:

An attitude giving birth to a situation where staff turn into inherent partners, so to speak, in the communal body they are attached to – which may happen voluntarily and out of a strong feeling of commitment. And their contribution to its success will be a considerable factor pushing the entire entity forward.

12. Encouraging staff members' desire for personal and professional progress:

Assimilating values and norms of self-investment and loyalty to the organization; forming sequences of prearranged decision-making based on reliable data, valid facts and genuine advanced leadership cultures; indoctrinating the striving for excellence, mastery, dexterity and deepening of proficiency – in order to always be in line for promotion up the ladder.

13. Avoiding benchmarks and scatter "banners" which are neither pragmatic nor feasible:

Abstinence from empty unrealistic promises and declarations which produce negative states of mind, low morale and frustration.

Fulfilling goals and meetings challenges requires:

- Executives' overall reliability and absolute backup.
- Down-to-earth and detailed execution arrays.
- Setting continuously upgrading routines.
- Quantifying and simplifying goals, thus making them understandable and achievable.
- Defining clear indicators amenable to accurate assessment, with the purpose of evaluating and examining the progress of the operation path guiding to the final longed-for target.

14. Causing, casting and catalyzing (Ca^3) management commitment and dedication to all of the above principles:

An untiring thrust for personal involvement of top leaders in the organization to consolidate and fortify the course of action aforedetailed, for overall quality of all participants and every activity in all various aspects of the framework. An endless push for their complete and incessantly realization. The submission of the most senior figure in charge of the current guiding, administrating, supervising and navigating philosophy – as well as the responsibility taken upon himself in order to apply these beliefs as a whole all over and in between the subunits and layers of the institute on the move – is an authentic mirror of the weight ascribed to this leadership attitude in the corporation. Otherwise it has no chance of successful implementation.

And throughout, it is forbidden to ever forget the two following cardinal perceptions.

One: the troubles of managing a huge conglomerate and the uncompromising loyalty and adherence due to it, are precisely the same "headache" as in running a tiny plant with total esteem and devotion. So it is needed to carry out an exact cost-benefit analysis, before deciding on the size and type of the business to enter, direct and guide.

The other: it is compulsory to keep on checking with the utmost and stubborn consistency the true needs of the improvement process related to every separate subject itself that is brought up and its profitability; for each alternative proposed in any of the activity domains – whatever character it might have – must always indicate its real attached price tag...

October 1993

Epilogue

Correct Management – What is it...?

Believing that correct management is the panacea for all of life's pains is quite naïve; but it is definitely the remedy for the sickening curse of maladministration...

The Author, November 1999

From everything said so far in the book it is possible to sum-up that the general term "**Management**" lends itself to characterization and even definition – in the most concise manner – by the following ordered four mental-operative content clusters.

1. From the spiritual aspect: it means **organizing the own inside** with proper attention and a very deeply true aim on the one hand – **and in the maximally thorough and comprehensive running of all assorted external actions** throughout the daily routine, while planning for the future too, on the other.

2. From a down-to-earth perception: this is **a mixture of individual qualities – some inborn, the others amenable to acquisition and nurturing** – crystallizing within any person in a different dosage, being expressed by his conduct and activities in straight relation to his dominant tendencies; a sort of interfusions regarding key intelligences (intellectual and emotional...) and basic inherent traits, backed by solid moral strength and mental powers, intended to tackle nearly all types of crises and obstacles.

3. The right order in depositing its layers is: **self-driving, life directing and leading others**; vigorously crisscrossed, interwoven levels and tiers, learning in due course to nourish each other in a measure suitable to any human being.

4. The pragmatical eloquent is – and that is the "Law of Gravity" for management as a rule: **first of all it is a profession; but a very complicated occupation combining much science – as well as a lot of art** (where in order to sharpen the hierarchy of the above conjunction it is appropriate to adopt Schopenhauer's Weltanschauung which proclaims: "science can make do with talent – but art needs genius...").

Except the "question" concerning the theme discussed here – the one that still and probably will bother time and again those occupied with it (exactly like a chronic migraine, that is impossible to get rid of…) is:

How to know when management is being implemented in the right way?

The trivial stock-in-trade answer of almost everyone, comes from the classical descriptions prevalent in the professional literature: preaching for dogmatic proficiency leaning on ultimate extraction of natural talents, knowledge, dexterities and experience, in motivating self-processes and leading others; this – in addition to the superb effective exploitation of all human, technological, financial and marketing materials and resources, at the disposal of the individual or the organization, while maintaining a consistent and close control deriving immediately corrective action where and when it is required.

So far is the literal meaning; a basic ideational hold which may be summarized regularly by the popular saying: **the "result test" – is that which determines**; when the bottom line alone should testify to the quality and character of the management, to wit: if targets are reached as marked or dictated verbatim – and those might be materialistic, ideological, spiritual or any other type defined – eventually it can be said that the road taken to run the business is the one and only. And since any normal human being hates to lose from birth – than **nothing is more successful then success itself**; because nobody is able to proclaim against a process presenting a development at the beginning of which a dollar equals an eighth of its value – but in the end that eighth overwhelms the dollar…

Is it?

According to the managerial exegesis, even though the afore-said **"outcome check" is a first class necessity** as agreed upon amongst most of these occupied in directing companies and leading people, by itself it does not suffice; it is far from complete and should explicitly not be the sole one. Such an examination may seriously mislead the man at the top as well as those around him and become a superannuated banal cliché, meaningless indeed, if the real elements of ambition like that are not thoroughly investigated. **For it is compulsory to always study and analyze processes – may they be the most successful, apparently – for the purpose of finding out if, how and where they can be improved.**

And all of this for several reasons:

- ✓ Sometimes the desired results are local, singular or temporal, therefore ephemeral.

- ✓ Occasionally the goals may be accomplished due to reasons independent of the managing factors, just on account of totally external conditions (for example: nothing but luck…).

- ✓ In many cases targets attained are not amenable to proper numeric quantification; because an organization's produce is supposed to match the specific domain in which it is involved, so it may not always be accurately digitally measurable (for instance: the firm's integration within the environment in which it operates and what actually it is required to provide…).

Namely, there are other aspects deserving a profound inspection before adopting the conclusions drawn from a test of the above-mentioned type:

The first, whether these achievements are somewhat successive and sequential in the company – and not some local, random and unique selection.

The second, whether the blessed fruits really flow de facto from the core of the corporation's activities or are circumstantial, derived from facts independent of the operator.

However, even if the responses to the above-described are positive

– the answer to the question noted in the present chapter's title is still not settled!

Apparently there is another essential ingredient required to complete the puzzle of the right management recipe besides the dry assessment of the result merely, further than concreteness, firmness and sources; **something that generates a very unique added value enveloping and contributing to the goals beyond the fact of standing by them**; a success signature with a taste of an extremely exceptional ambition.

In other words: not only reaching the targets is imperative – but who, how and when they are attained and what is the influence of such an occurrence on the overall present and future atmosphere; the historical implications of these events and this victory.

The term *value* is defined, inter alia, in nearly all dictionaries as: worth, esteem, quantity, importance, merit, edge, excellency, grace, asset, virtue or superiority – all of which are appropriate to the topic talked about here. And this heavyweight and authoritative idiom can be expressed as buttressing goals and achievements of the communal productive entity in some ways, as follows:

- **By guarding product and service quality for a long time**: because nothing protects and nurtures better the known marks of a number-one system than the essence of its output and merchandise.

  For example: the Israeli pharmaceutical giant Teva has dominated its field for over a hundred years, becoming the world's primary manufacturer of unique generic drugs.

- **In creating a leadership array exceptional in its code of conduct**: a human infrastructure of charismatic people influencing everyone around with confidence, sweeping power, composure, bravery and target-oriented dedication; since each manager must be first and foremost a born chief.

  For Instance: Winston Churchill, British prime minister during World War II.

- **By embedding a unique organizational culture**: an operational style and behavior built on a totality of traditions, customs, legends, norms and habits of the highest degree – where all its partners are ready without any hesitation to adopt and sacrifice for.

    As a model: the Israeli Defense Force (IDF) fighting echelon up to the rank of colonels, who are always in the battle field, constantly delivering and never disappointing by winning all wars – otherwise the state wouldn't exist anymore.

- **In choosing the timing of fulfilling goals**: directing the right performance to leave the greatest impression on the pages of history; since not only predominating and mastering the domain – but choosing the moment when it happens.

    The best illustration: the triumph of Jessie Owens, the African-American sprinter – perhaps the greatest athlete ever – defying the Nazi regime and its most infamous racist leadership by winning four gold medals precisely at the Berlin Olympic Games of 1936.

- **By inventing the unique idea which yields competitive advantage**: governing the field is not enough – the key ingredient responsible for this achievement is extremely important too.

    Just as Microsoft came up with the scheme to collect a fixed sum for licenses to use its product, instead of simply a onetime compensation for selling its patents.

- **In making the organization everyone's "wet dream"**: constructing a framework allowing for exceptional challenges and interest, in addition to extraordinary good modus operandi and vivendi – so that everyone yearns to belong to it.

    As Harvard University has become over the years the mecca for any academic personality, wherever he is.

And in order to exhibit the **value** in its proper context as an additive to objective accomplishment, it is necessary to regard the attainment of the desired results as a war for daily bread, supposed to provide him with the means for his continuous existence – and the assets bestowed by the worth encompassing it as the spices intensifying the unique tastiness. So it's true that life itself precedes quality of life – yet there is certainly a critical difference between leading it with flavor versus plodding along without…

And perhaps the relation of the afore **"esteem"** term to ambition is similar to the manner in which the inner subsistence of human beings is reconciled with their material-realized performance. It is definitely possible to sustain with external success – but much better when the heart and soul receive and support it…

And not for nothing this crowning increment is a very honorable facet, lifting achievement sky-high; since if the outcomes are not enveloped by the importance of their essence, the validity of the triumph is lost.

And the above **"worth's" grace** can be felt most strongly when the partners, the clients – **and even competitors – encourage the results of victory**; then one knows the impressive meaning realized in addition to physically reaching the target.

For this exact reason two separate activity-circles are needed, varied and very extensive, robustly contributing to this common denominator – the **value: one deals with its creation and the other its marketing**.

The basic and main sphere is bound to insert with great sensitivity – but determinedly and in a most sophisticated approach – in the consciousness of those active in the organization and on its behalf, that in order to flourish and bloom it is obligatory to link performance yield with a nature of unique and superb class; since this is the singular and prominent element which can absolutely position the benchmark higher than the others, taking the corporation to the sought after summit, while all opponents are still stumbling along, possibly even completely falling.

The other loop is supposed to deal entirely with publicizing and promoting to the target audience and the masses of the general potential customers the detailed information concerning the exclusive virtues of the company. This is in order that they gather in their multitudes (perhaps even crossing the lines if they are clients of the competitors…) to sample the products, fall in love with them, become enslaved to their quality, swear allegiance to them and remain the firm's regulars forever.

And it's proper to start planting the seeds for it from day one and keep fertilizing them throughout the entire work period – so as not to be too late.

Obviously, in charge of both is the CEO; and their mutual correct execution is exactly what turns a good common administrator into an **outstanding manager**.

Beyond the supreme importance of all aspects described here, it must be remembered that for their proper examination one thing is required: **time**. Since the fact that **goals are fulfilled** in a most desirable manner (to wit:

- ✓ They become a way of life in the business.
- ✓ These are direct utilities of the organizational active core.
- ✓ Quantitatively measuring them – or at least approximately reassessing their contribution to the system's needs – is doable.
- ✓ And they bestow upon the company a degree of distinction and honor due to the value of their achievement…).

can only be really appreciated after a while, when this productive entity is already functioning fluently; at that stage of its existence when the habits of its conduct and operation are checked and found in good order, applicable and effective; at the hour when its success is proven to be a certain thing. Namely, **management quality can only be retrospectively deduced**. Because such a "prophetic device" has not yet been invented to extract lessons a priori from any process, before learning and knowing everything about it ex post facto. Or as was once wistfully said: "If I'd known beforehand what I know now – I could have saved myself a lot of sorrow and troubles in years past...". Moreover; it is very difficult to avoid mistakes while performing, not being at all sure that the elected activity pattern is really the right choice.

And history can tell a lot about so many senior executives who reached targets dictated by their bosses – or marked by them personally – but failed miserably, losing their jobs.

However, from the first day of running any system, one is required to start acting and moving – even not knowing yet the right path to walk on! Otherwise, to be convinced each time of the road's righteousness, it is necessary to get a little older; and such is true in any selection done, a routine that shortens, in fact, significantly the duration of the pleasure derived from activity in particular and from life in general...

So, how to behave in the meantime?

Everything written up until now has dealt with the answer to this penetrating and profound question: as an initial directive from the moment the man at the top enters his job, intending to lie down in front of him the basic management behavior and handling principles – for himself and the system he would be in charge of; a font of logical "imperatives" immediately permeating and plausible, nearly criticism-proof, giving him a type of fundamental guiding rules – relying on the experience and wisdom of those who undergone such processes in the past, emphasizing key sentences and crucial words integrated in them – so he may be able to plan, decide, motivate, follow up, control, extract, conclude, correct, improve and continue running the organization he is heading right from the beginning of the journey and his first tentative steps there. And the method "how" is simply spread all along the chapters preceding this epilogue – and it is highly recommended to follow every word in them to the last comma and period, since sometime the smallest details, tiniest terms and most minor points, give rise to the greatest illumination.

Though things need not automatically be applied in their order of appearance as written in the articles so far, all of them must be executed without exception. On the other hand, the chronology of their implementation must follow a very correct and sober reading regarding the real-time map in the field, according to changes in the active environment, the market, technology, customer needs, and the development tendencies generated out of those. In short: stipulated precisely by the situation and current lay of the land.

Still, it is more than essential to internalize that there are some personal traits and innate cardinal characteristics vital for the manager – so that not only what was said in the previous paragraphs and in the last one especially, always rest and rely on them – but without these the above is useless, perhaps even invalid. There are a few unique individual ingredients needed for him to permanently direct the framework he is in charge of, unrelated to its current stage or state and the road chosen to steer it along. Thus it is appropriate to present them here and now, as a sort of ending with several axioms:

- ✓ A genetic inborn competence fitting the specific occupation discussed at this point: natural talents, a deep and varied knowledge which is based on own experience and others' too.

- ✓ An ability to understand that beyond the ego it is obligatory to enlarge the management capacity personally and systematically.

- ✓ A skill to definitely distinguish between the essence and the unimportant, for the purpose of accurately directing – but in the most profitable way – towards the designated targets.

- ✓ An energy to overcome countless problems arising during execution; the potential to take care simultaneously all the time of as many subjects as needed emerging due to natural business growth.

- ✓ The courage to confront the limits of the standard, not being afraid to aspire uncompromisingly for innovation in multidimensional nonconformist thinking outside the box; however, this kind of exceptionalism causes a sort of governmental and logistic anomalies, meaning decision-making complexity and higher conduct demands.

- ✓ A talent to turn an obstacle into a springboard, a complication into a junction of promotion and a crisis into an opportunity.

All this requires knowing that halting is forbidden, even for a moment; knowledge must be acquired constantly, aspiring to improve consistently by adopting:

- ✓ Cultural education to wisely cope with a demanding competitive commercial atmosphere; successfully pursuing a struggle with intra-organizational multifarious content; and teaching also to face and handle adaptive changes derived from the professional domain in order to confront inevitable variations.

- ✓ Perceptions guiding how to draw selected, long-term and solidly grounded strategic maps – even though very often they are far from conventional, creating mighty revolutions and not merely upheavals.

- ✓ A vision pushing to discover individual weaknesses and take care of each one's painful points, so as to become better and improve inwardly, incessantly.

- ✓ An outlook championing embedding the fundamentals of excellent leadership in the next generation, and laying the infrastructure for a qualitative managerial tradition for tomorrow, with the knowledge and wisdom not to be scared of being suddenly "dispossessed" by overly ambitious successors.

Finally, in summation

Correct management is characterized by being capable and qualified to build a sort of abstract theoretical-logical gate of the AND type, uniting all the above noted foundations into a winning combination; a mixture responding to the criteria of the best **spiritual-scientific governance, oversight and control**, comprising all research and quantitative assessment methods as well as accrued emotional evaluations to establish the following delineated indicators:

1. Fulfill goals determined-dictated ahead of time.
2. Ascertain that success is due to pure and relevant execution.
3. Verify that achievement is continuous.
4. Substantiate that the above issues do not emerge only from an **"outcome check"** but a **"value test"** too.

All this while embracing and inculcating the five following conclusion mottoes or nearly axioms – inalienable truths for anyone who aspires and plans to become a manager.

Management encompasses so much that it is simply an entire world of its own; an activity sphere so complex and complicated resembling, in fact, a huge chess match that may become awfully difficult and extremely fateful. Therefore, he who is not willing to take chances is advised to close himself in a well-defended room writing "beautiful poetry" about the life he will never experience. However, the one that is consciously ready to dare and play with fire must consider that he may also be burnt quite severely...

This is a craft often requiring problem-solving with a magic spark or exceptional virtuosity, but mostly it is hard, exhausting, pitiless, gray and even Sisyphean work – despite the fact that most owners are always looking for the man with the golden Midas touch to run their business...

The secret of successfully assuming such an occupation is, probably, in the right dosage of the combination resulting from professionalism, art and science – in addition to the extent of the emotional intelligence woven into each of them...

Once one knows how to correctly manage, it does not matter anymore what is being directed, supervised and controlled – which domain of life is at issue and even how big its perimeter is...

And last but not least: he who is not endowed with the right qualities to deal with leading people and running organizations – who hesitates, even for the tiniest moment, when asked if business comes before pleasure or vice versa, without feeling deep in his very bones that business is actually his pleasure – let him find another profitable career in life aside from the work of management...

December 1999

www.ingramcontent.com/pod-product-compliance
Lightning Source LLC
Chambersburg PA
CBHW071232160426
43196CB00009B/1030